W9-ASR-601

CRITICAL
INSIGHTS
Robert Frost

CRITICAL
INSIGHTS

Robert Frost

Editor
Morris Dickstein
Graduate Center of the City University of New York

Salem Press
Pasadena, California   Hackensack, New Jersey

Cover photo: Time & Life Pictures/Getty Images

Published by Salem Press

© 2010 by EBSCO Publishing
Editor's text © 2010 by Morris Dickstein
"The *Paris Review* Perspective" © 2010 by Elizabeth Gumport for *The Paris Review*

∞ The paper used in these volumes conforms to the American National Standard for Permanence of Paper for Printed Library Materials, Z39.48-1992 (R1997).

Library of Congress Cataloging-in-Publication Data
Robert Frost / editor, Morris Dickstein.
    p. cm. -- (Critical insights)
    Includes bibliographical references and index.
    ISBN 978-1-58765-636-1 (one volume : alk. paper) 1. Frost, Robert, 1874-1963--Criticism and interpretation. I. Dickstein, Morris.
    PS3511.R94Z543 2010
    811'.52--dc22
                                                                    2009027636

PRINTED IN CANADA

Contents_____

Career, Life, and Influence_____

Critical Contexts_____

Critical Readings_____

Resources

About This Volume

Morris Dickstein

Following a brief biography of Robert Frost by James Norman O'Neill and a succinct critical comment by Elizabeth Gumport of *The Paris Review*, this volume, containing both newly commissioned pieces and reprinted essays and book chapters, brings together an unusually wide range of approaches to Frost's poetry. Though Frost has been famous and widely celebrated in the United States for nearly a century, his reputation has shifted dramatically since his first volumes appeared just before World War I. Acclaimed as a modernist by Ezra Pound when his first two books appeared in England, where he was then living, Frost became popular as a warm, accessible poet from the 1920s through the 1950s as four of his collections received the Pulitzer Prize. He was admired as homey and straightforward when modernist writing was often obscure; as a nature poet, an authentically American writer, when many modernists were cosmopolitan expatriates; and as an optimistic New England sage when his leading contemporaries produced dark, apocalyptic visions.

This image began to change decisively in the 1950s when Randall Jarrell and Lionel Trilling, two impeccably highbrow critics, rediscovered Frost as a modern writer whose outlook was not only dark but terrifying, a poet whose technical mastery matched the more experimental approach of Eliot and Pound, which until then had set the standard for poetic modernism in English. No writer in this volume goes back to the simpler Frost of the first half of the twentieth century; all take for granted the darker, more canny, more difficult writer eloquently expounded by Jarrell, then proclaimed publicly by Trilling at a dinner honoring Frost on his eighty-fifth birthday. While Janyce Marson surveys the key changes in Frost's critical reputation over the decades, both Matthew J. Bolton and Frank Lentricchia take us back to the conflicts within early modernism. Whereas Pound and Eliot wrote and promoted poetry that is complex and elusive, according to Bolton,

"Frost mastered an art that conceals art" yet also echoes both Eliot's "Prufrock" and Eliot's master, Dante, in one of his best-known poems, "Acquainted with the Night." In his landmark essay, Lentricchia discusses the issues that helped ignite early modernism, including diction, nationality, and particularly gender. In contrast with the dominant aesthetic of Victorian lyric poetry, which seemed precious and effete, Frost's early work was seen not only as unquestionably American but also as closer to prose, novelistically real and impure, and unabashedly masculine.

Lentricchia's stress on Frost as a poet who focuses on work finds parallels in other essays in this volume, including Jamey Hecht's discussion of "technology, labor, and the sacred" and Tyler B. Hoffman's examination of Frost's attitudes toward industrial labor. In the light of Frost's instinctive conservatism and anti-New Deal politics, Hoffman explores early, uncollected poems in which Frost is surprisingly sympathetic toward labor, perhaps because he himself, with very little money behind him, had already worked at so many jobs. David Sanders, exploring the background of Frost's most beloved and influential book, *North of Boston* (1914), shows how Frost's life and work were shaped by his years as a farmer in Derry, New Hampshire, in the first decade of the twentieth century, "immersing him not only in the seasonal cycles and 'country things' that would saturate his verse, but in the New England speech which he would make his poetic tongue." Moreover, those years "also made vivid and real the lives of the neighbors who would people *North of Boston* and, in wresting a living from hard climate and stony soil, would define a moral center for Frost's poetic world." Sanders shows how Frost was determined not only to reproduce features of his neighbors' speech but also to make use of it to reach a wider, more popular audience, concealing complexity in simplicity, the rigors of form in the flow of the colloquial.

This kind of poetry demands close and careful reading, as earlier, simpler versions of Frost's work did not. Though Judith Oster concentrates on Frost as a poet of nature, she puts together a revealing group of difficult work, meditations on nature that move from direct observation to subtle reverberations of meaning and feeling. Beginning with two poems that evoke the destructive element within the natural processes, "Storm Fear" and "Spring Pools," Oster threads her way insightfully through dark poems such as "Stopping by Woods on a Snowy Evening," "Desert Places," and "A Leaf-Treader." These works center on tempting invitations to oblivion but also on the speaker's resistance to that siren call—his stoicism, detachment, or determination, his assertions of ongoing life. Anastasia Vahaviolos Valassis takes a comparable path in her deeply Wordsworthian reading of Frost's poems about nature alongside key poems about death, including "The Death of the Hired Man," "Out, Out—," and "Home Burial." She touches on the "blunt economy and simplicity" of his characters' speech, the sense of fatality perhaps influenced by Thomas Hardy's poetry, and Frost's "ability to paint profound darkness with the barest strokes."

If Oster and Valassis see Frost from a natural perspective, as a poet in the Romantic tradition using nature to fathom his inmost feelings, Jeff Westover approaches him from a national perspective, since Frost had long been understood (in Trilling's words) as "nothing less than a national fact . . . virtually a symbol of America." Beginning with Frost's sympathetic attitudes toward Native Americans in little-known poems such as "Genealogical" and "The Vanishing Red," Westover examines how his sense of American history and national destiny leads toward one of his best-known works, "The Gift Outright." Robert Bernard Hass provides another context for Frost's work by exploring the poet's surprisingly complex and knowledgeable response to science. He describes Frost's fear that, in the light of the new science, the cosmos is "now more than ever capable of reducing human aspirations and achievements to an almost total insignificance," and he shows how this contributes to the vision of bleak poems such as "Desert Places." But Frost also insists that the mind's constructive power, including the autonomous ego and the Jamesian "will to believe," provides a countermovement against the nihilism of nature's entropic forces. While Frost cherished uncertainty and entangles us in mystery, he also believed in the power of metaphor to re-create the world in human terms. The result is "an art of equipoise" that helps rescue us from fear, the fear that so often beset the poet himself.

Roger Gilbert also sees Frost as an explorer but places him in a different American tradition, that of the haphazard walker, the writer who uses walking as a metaphor for enlightenment. For Frost, a devoted reader of Emerson who also called Thoreau's *Walden* his favorite poem, walking suggested the flow of discovery inherent in writing itself. The walk empowered the poet to describe what he saw, or imagined, at the same time he subtly allegorized it, as in "The Wood-Pile," "Good Hours," and "Directive," which are among Frost's most eerily effective works, descriptive yet meditative poems that stop just short of metaphysics. A nervous, avid walker himself, he turns walking into a metaphor for life's journey as well as the journey toward knowledge.

Shira Wolosky's essay takes a more formal approach to the pursuit of knowledge. Influenced by deconstructive work on irony, allegory, and figuration, Wolosky focuses on Frost's use of personification in a single poem, "The Need of Being Versed in Country Things." Whereas Frost is usually portrayed as a poet extracting human meanings from encounters with nature, she demonstrates his "sense of difference and distinction from nature." She sees two movements in the rhetoric of this poem, "a doubling of forces: one personifying, and in counterforce against it, one of depersonification." In "a move into irony characteristic of Frost," she says, "the sentimental identification of nature with human feelings, and particularly with elegiac feelings of loss, turns back on itself through self-exposure, the poem itself recognizing that it has been engaged in just such a project of projecting the human onto the non-human world." Of course, without such projection, which John Ruskin called the pathetic fallacy, no Romantic poetry would ever have been written. Yet many critics would agree, more modestly, that Frost's poems do often turn upon themselves, especially in touches of irony that may attach to their memorable aphoristic conclusions. This partly ironic turn, often a matter of voice, makes their meaning more uncertain, even indeterminate.

In the essay that concludes this volume, Denis Donoghue makes a case against Frost, or at least a case for his limitations. Donoghue's discussion is reminiscent of skeptical views that were expressed in the poet's own lifetime, such as Yvor Winters's brilliant polemic against Frost as a "spiritual drifter." Donoghue writes explicitly as a Christian and deploys the work of T. S. Eliot as Frost's main foil, comparing Eliot's interest in "ultimate values" with Frost's appeal "only to those truths or half-truths that we know by being human and extant," including creaturely needs such as "warmth, food, fighting, drink, and sex." Frost, he feels, stays connected to the earth; his poems are based on "the way things are," not more, the "middle range of experience," and hence they "rarely make new meanings," though they do "remind us of ancient meanings and place them in settings that, perhaps for the first time, do them justice." Others might see this earthbound quality as a strength, not a limitation, but to Donoghue it deprives the poetry of meditation, elevation. When Frost reaches for more he "sings falsetto." He falls into Social Darwinist slogans that Donoghue calls "a slack affair, hardly more than whimsical patter." If this seems unfair, reductive, even Frost's most sympathetic readers might agree that he is "the poet most devoted to bare human gesture." There are no consolations of faith in Frost's stark universe, no refuge to be found in dreams of transcendence.

CAREER, LIFE, AND INFLUENCE

On Robert Frost_____

Morris Dickstein

Over the course of nearly a century, Robert Frost's poetry has taken on a stature that has eluded other modern American poets, remaining unusually popular with ordinary readers, even some who rarely read poetry, while becoming warmly admired by serious critics, especially in the years since Frost's death in 1963. This broad acceptance, which meant a great deal to Frost, gives him a standing more like that of William Wordsworth, Walt Whitman, or Emily Dickinson than that of his near-contemporaries such as T. S. Eliot, Ezra Pound, and Wallace Stevens, whose works retain a more specialized appeal despite their secure niche in the canon of modern poetry.

Despite a twenty-year apprenticeship during which he published little, Frost was determined from early on to reach a general audience, not merely the select few. Unlike the best of his peers, he relied on traditional forms—such as blank verse, lyric quatrains, sonnets, and rhymed couplets and triplets—but deployed them with an uncommon freshness. Frost set his poems in rural New England at a time when the city was becoming the center of modern life. Even as he taught in universities and lectured widely, he embraced the role of a farmer-poet, lacing his poems with country speech and aphorisms that looked like timeless folk wisdom. Yet he was first discovered and published not at home but in England, and praised not by traditionalists but by Pound, an American expatriate who became the impresario of modernism in the years just before World War I. Only later did Frost's first two books come out in the United States, and they were soon followed by a third that quickly established his reputation at home.

We still think of modern poetry as difficult and obscure compared with its Romantic and Victorian forebears, but the revolution that Pound promoted in his early reviews was actually toward a new simplicity that broke with these predecessors' cherished canons of form and beauty. When he wrote that a poet like Eliot had "modernised" himself or that a prose writer like the young James Joyce had discarded circumstantial detail, he meant that they had achieved a direct economy of language and emotion without inert "literary" baggage. Pound invoked what he called the "prose tradition in verse," a poetry that abjured rhetoric for a language closer to speech, what Wordsworth described as "the real language of men in a state of vivid sensation"; his brief against Victorian poetics was exactly the same as Wordsworth's against Augustan decorum, inert metaphor, inverted word order, mythological allusion, the personification of abstractions, and "the gaudiness and inane phraseology of many modern writers." To Pound the artifice of this language had degenerated into mere poetic convention rather than (in John Keats's words) embodying "the true voice of feeling."

Frost's work was very different from Eliot's or Joyce's or D. H. Lawrence's, yet it provided an ideal vehicle for Pound's campaign. Like Wordsworth, Frost focused on rural life as a world closer to the mainspring of human speech and feeling, and on nature as a mirror of human beings' inner dramas of fear and compassion, discord and affection, vulnerability and stoic endurance. To this Frost added a vigorous current of erotic energy and a rare affinity for physical labor, from mending walls to apple picking, always slightly allegorized into larger meanings. "Before I built a wall I'd ask to know/ What I was walling in or walling out,/ And to whom I was like to give offense," he writes in "Mending Wall" (32-34). His neighbor, with his unthinking maxims of separation, seems "like an old-stone savage armed./ He moves in darkness as it seems to me" (40-41). Satiated with an almost sexual fatigue in "After Apple-Picking," feeling a great sleep coming on, he writes: "For I have had too much/ Of apple-picking: I am overtired/ Of the great harvest I myself desired" (27-29). Comparing himself to the earlier poet, he notes that "I dropped to an everyday level of diction that even Wordsworth kept above" but insists, "I have made poetry. The language is appropriate to the virtues I celebrate." He adds that Pound, in his review of Frost's first book in *Poetry*, made the mistake "of assuming that my simplicity is that of the untutored child. I am not undesigning" (*Selected Letters* 83-84).

Frost's connection to Wordsworth goes deeper than his homely diction or his anchor in rural life. Like Montaigne before him, Wordsworth, without becoming a confessional poet, gave exquisite attention to the movements of his own mind, which he often saw reflected in emblems of nature, in situations of intense solitude, or in parables of bare, unaccommodated human lives, of humanity under duress or stricken by loss. One of his most moving stories is the poem we know today as "The Ruined Cottage," which earlier generations read in the first book of a long poem, *The Excursion.* The central figure is poor Margaret, whose husband, ashamed of their poverty, takes the king's shilling to go off to war. As she clings to the forlorn hope that he might return, her life declines—we see it in glimpses, each more terrible than the last—until all that remains is the ruined cottage she left behind, a bare memorial understood only by those who can read its meaning. Like Wordsworth, Frost would return again and again, with understated emotion, to the physical remnants of such disintegrating lives, approaching them dispassionately, with a fatalistic sense of the inevitable. In "The Black Cottage," not one of his best poems, he even uses a garrulous narrator like Wordsworth's to tell just such a story. But Frost does much better with "An Old Man's Winter Night," "The Wood-Pile," and "The Need of Being Versed in Country Things," a phrase that could serve as the title of his collected poems. The first poem is about a solitary life slowly being extinguished, an old man barely holding on. The second deals with the residue of a life, the mysterious remnant of someone's hard work: a stack of firewood slowly rotting in the forest. The third poem takes the measure of a house destroyed by a fire that capriciously spared the barn, giving it an orphaned look.

Frost once wrote, "The conviction closes in on me that I was cast for gloom as the sparks fly upward" (*Selected Letters* 221), yet these are not entirely dispiriting poems. Against all odds, the old man in the first poem somehow holds on: "One aged man—one man—can't keep a house,/ A farm, a countryside, or if he can,/ It's thus he does it of a winter night" (26-28). The stack of wood left behind in the forest, though "far from a useful fireplace" (38), as the poet himself is "far from home" (9), will somehow "warm the frozen swamp as best it could/ With the slow smokeless burning of decay" (39-40). And the conflagration of the house in "The Need of Being Versed" gave "the midnight sky a sunset glow" besides providing a nesting place for birds. "For them there was really nothing sad," he says, but then, in typical fashion, takes the thought back in an ambiguous way: "But though they rejoiced in the nest they kept,/ One had to be versed in country things/ Not to believe the phoebes wept" (21-24).

Frost is typically playful in these concluding lines, in the pun on "versed" but also in alluding to poetic conventions that project human feelings on nature, yet taking a skeptical view of such projections, nailing them as little more than conventions, pretty fictions. Frost's nature expresses his stark sense of a universe fueled by endless destruction and creation, constantly upended by merciless change and Darwinian adaptation. He sees this writ large in the cycle of the seasons, with its alternations of fresh growth and decay, beauty and barren harshness. In his work the natural world, like human life itself, is constantly undermining and renewing itself. This voracious cycle is the subject of Frost's brief but perfect lyric "Spring Pools," in which the poet draws our eyes to something coldly beautiful but transient: these pools of chilly water that collect amid the bare trees, surrounded by shivering flowers, and briefly reflect the spring sky, which "like the flowers beside them soon be gone,/ And yet not out by any brook or river,/ But up by roots to bring dark foliage on" (4-6). He then turns to the trees themselves, with their threat to "darken nature" with their thick canopy:

> Let them think twice before they use their powers
> To blot out and drink up and sweep away
> These flowery waters and these watery flowers
> From snow that melted only yesterday.
>
> (9-13)

The first thing that impresses about this poem is the rhetoric: prosaic but highly condensed, with few but emphatic figures of speech ("blot out," "drink up," "sweep away"); the intricate sentence that composes each stanza; the straightforward, almost jingly rhymes that remain somehow unobtrusive; the neat parallel between two stanzas—the first about the pools, the second about the trees—which (as Jay Parini suggests [234]) mirrors the reflection evoked in the poem; the daring repetitions that turn incantatory ("like the flowers," "flowery waters," "watery flowers"); the sharply varied accentual rhythm of each line within a seemingly regular metrical pattern; the brilliant stroke of the final line, which reminds us where the pools themselves came from; but above all the mysterious stance of the speaker, which turns on a single phrase, the linchpin of the poem, "Let them think twice." This rivets our attention to what the poem is saying, and it demands a brief aside.

For three decades, well into the 1950s, Frost was largely seen as a popular poet, a crowd-pleasing country sage, somewhat in the cracker-barrel vein of Carl Sandburg, with little to offer more exacting readers, for whom the prototype of the modern poet was T. S. Eliot. It was in the 1950s that Randall Jarrell, followed by Lionel Trilling, pointed to poems such as "Design," "Directive," "Provide, Provide," and "Acquainted with the Night" to portray Frost as a terrifying poet, stark in his vision, subtle and complex in his technique—something that should have been evident all along, though it had escaped those who assembled the anthologies. This thread in Frost's work begins as far back as "Storm Fear," in his first and simplest volume, *A Boy's Will*, and is reflected obliquely in some of the best-known poems of his next book, *North of Boston*, such as "The Death of the Hired Man," with its dark ruminations on death, kinship, and personal responsibility.

In "Storm Fear" the speaker, alone with his wife and child in a house battered by a snowstorm, feeling vulnerable and undefended—yet also tempted to expose himself to the storm, to let it swallow him—wonders whether they can get through the night. The poem is not about the storm but about this tempest of emotions, at once anxious, suicidal, and defiant. Another early poem (though published later), "Bereft," delves into a similar set of emotions, with the added idea that the storm has already exposed the speaker; the roaring wind, the hissing leaves, have somehow found him out:

> Something sinister in the tone
> Told me my secret must be known:
> Word I was in the house alone
> Somehow must have gotten abroad,
> Word I was in my life alone,
> Word I had no one left but God.
>
> (11-16)

In yet another poem, "Desert Places," a landscape gradually being covered by snow, where "all animals are smothered in their lairs," evokes an even more ominous sense of loneliness as the speaker links the outer with the inner weather (6). "I am too absent-spirited to count;/ The loneliness includes me unawares" (7-8). As the snow continues to fall, he foresees an even greater void, "A blanker whiteness of benighted snow/ With no expression, nothing to express" (11-12). This vision of emptiness has rightly been compared to the blank scene of Wallace Stevens's "The Snow Man," which concludes with a vision of nothingness that is utterly without consolation. Frost, thinking of the vast "empty spaces" of the heavens above, ends the poem with a staged moment of grim bravado: "I have it in me so much nearer home/ To scare myself with my own desert places" (15-16).

"Spring Pools," though not confessional in this way, is one of the most effective of these terror poems but with a difference, an inner strength that emboldens the speaker to shake his fist at the tall trees that will drink up the pools and blot out the spring flowers, blanketing the terrain with their covering of "dark foliage." "Let them think twice," he says, not because they can think or desist but simply because he would have it so; as in "Desert Places," he needs to assert that they cannot

---

scare him. In a world of constant flux, of destruction and creation, Frost has a particular sympathy for the islands of fragile, transient beauty represented by the spring pools and flowers, which speak to him of evanescence, of life itself as a brief parenthesis between two eons of nonbeing. They are like the flowers that bloom briefly in "The Last Mowing" after the far field has been cut for the last time, running riot before the tall trees come in to extinguish them. Excited by this interim life, between the taming of men and the darkening of the trees, the poet turns to address the flowers ecstatically, as playmates or lovers:

> The meadow is done with the tame.
> The place for the moment is ours
> For you, oh tumultuous flowers,
> To go to waste and wild in,
> All shapes and colors of flowers,
> I needn't call you by name.
>
> (14-19)

This points to something different from the intimations of death and loss at the heart of Wordsworth's most celebrated poems, including "Tintern Abbey" and the Immortality Ode. Frost's intimations are at once more terrible and more hopeful, conveying the momentary ecstasy of being alive amid spasms of agony at feeling so transient, so perishable.

Frost shares these portents of doom not only with Romantic forebears such as Wordsworth, Keats, and Lord Byron but also with many other modern writers, from Eliot and Franz Kafka to Samuel Beckett. For the longest time, Frost's kinship with the bleak vision of many of his contemporaries was scarcely understood. What makes his poetry so unusual was his ability to translate his fears into language so ordinary, so familiar that it seems reassuring. It conceals the art that went into it. An important key to this powerful effect is his classical training. The conversational quality of Frost's poetry owes less to his New England neighbors than to his knowledge of Latin poets such as Catullus, Horace, and Virgil, who seemed to distill the spoken language into compacted verse with mellifluous ease. Frost's earliest biographer, Gorham Munson, portrayed him provocatively as a classical poet. Once a Latin tutor, Frost boasted late in life that he had read "probably more Latin and Greek than Pound ever did" (*Collected Poems* 877). A reader of David Ferry's strikingly contemporary translations of Horace and Virgil into English will recognize Frost's voice, as Frost's style may have influenced Ferry's translations (as Eliot's style has inflected some translations of Dante).

The key to Frost's power is not his dark vision but the voice he found to express it, the way he was able to ground it in a flow of speechlike intonations at once accessible and memorable. "Words exist in the mouth not in books," he said. "You can't fix them and you don't want to fix them" (*Selected Letters* 108). Early on, he felt his formal subtlety was not sufficiently recognized. Since those years when his technical skill went largely unnoticed, his critics have expanded on his "sentence sounds," the tension between the formal meter of his lines and the actual rhythm of his sentences. The poet, Frost wrote, "must learn to get cadences by skillfully breaking the sounds of sense with all their irregularity of accent across the regular beat of the metre" (*Selected Letters* 80). This has always been a staple of the best poetry in English. One can read through reams of verse by intricately metrical poets such as Alexander Pope, the Alfred, Lord Tennyson of *In Memoriam*, and W. H. Auden without finding a line that strictly follows the metronomic rhythm, which can nevertheless be felt as an undertow, much in the way that a vocal standard serves as a baseline for a jazz improvisation.

Frost belongs in the company of these gifted formalists not simply because of his technique but because his labile, often depressed state of mind, his anxiety and sense of solitude, demanded just such a combination of freedom and discipline, rebellion and restraint, the ease of conversation concentrated into aphorism. His belated recognition as a major modernist helped explode the narrow view of modernism construed solely as formal or experimental breakthrough. Acclaimed early by ordinary readers, he belonged to no avant-garde but remained a school of one in his ornery politics as much as in his poetics. Frost's outlook was more desperate than his early readers understood, but the constraints of poetic form provided stability and order, a way of channeling unruly emotion. This was a kind of consolation, along with the general love and fame that soon accompanied it. His old age was glorious, replete with honors, belying—or perhaps confirming—the end he himself anticipated in "Provide, Provide": "No memory of having starred/ Atones for later disregard,/ Or keeps the end from being hard" (16-18).

Works Cited

Frost, Robert. *Collected Poems, Prose, and Plays*. Ed. Richard Poirier and Mark Richardson. New York: Library of America, 1995.

_____. *Selected Letters of Robert Frost*. Ed. Lawrance Thompson. New York: Holt, Rinehart and Winston, 1964.

Parini, Jay. *Robert Frost: A Life*. New York: Henry Holt, 1999.

Biography of Robert Frost_____

James Norman O'Neill

Robert Frost's father, William Prescott Frost, was a native of New Hampshire who had bitterly rejected New England following the Civil War because of his Copperhead political sympathies. After graduating with honors from Harvard College in 1872, he had served one year (1872-1873) as headmaster of Lewistown Academy in Pennsylvania, where he had met, courted, and in 1873 married Isabelle Moodie, an immigrant Scottish schoolteacher. William Prescott Frost had taken his bride to San Francisco, where he worked as a newspaper reporter and editor from 1873 until his untimely death at the age of thirty-five, from tuberculosis, in 1885. His strongly democratic political sympathies were reflected in his decision to name his firstborn child, born March 26, 1874, for the distinguished Confederate general Robert E. Lee. Despite his aversion for New England, William Prescott Frost shortly before his death requested that he be buried in the area he still considered home.

Thus it happened that his widow took their two children (the younger child, Jeanie Florence Frost, had been born in 1876) across the continent with the casket for the interment in Lawrence, Massachusetts, where William Prescott Frost's parents then lived. Because the family could not afford the cost of a return trip to California, they settled in New England. For several years, Robert Frost's mother earned a living by teaching in various schools, starting in Salem, New Hampshire. Undoubtedly she had a profound effect on her son's development. Her Scottish loyalties, particularly her intense religious preoccupations (which caused her to relinquish her inherited Calvinistic Presbyterianism in favor of an ardent Swedenborgian belief) may account in part for the tantalizing blend of practicality and mysticism in Robert Frost's poetry.

In 1892 Robert Frost graduated from Lawrence High School as class poet and as co-valedictorian with a sensitive, brilliant girl named

Elinor Miriam White, whom he married three years later. Before his graduation from high school he had decided to dedicate himself to the life of a poet, and he found no comparable attraction in any other possible profession. His paternal grandfather was, however, eager to make a lawyer of the gifted young man and persuaded him to enter Dartmouth College in the fall of 1892. Characteristically, Frost left Dartmouth before he had completed his first semester there. During the next few years his quietly dedicated aim was concealed beneath apparent aimlessness: He earned his living in a variety of ways, intermittently teaching school, working as a bobbin boy in a Lawrence wool mill, trying his hand at newspaper reporting, and doing odd jobs. Throughout these years he wrote poems, which he continued to send to newspaper and magazine editors. When the *New York Independent* sent him his first check, for a poem titled "My Butterfly," in November, 1894, he celebrated the event by having six of his poems printed in book form under the title *Twilight* and in a limited edition of only two copies, one for his fiancé, Elinor White, and one for himself.

After his marriage, at the age of twenty-one, Frost spent two years helping his mother run a small private school in Lawrence. Then, deciding to prepare himself for more advanced teaching by concentrating on Latin literature, he entered Harvard University as a special student. After two years there (1897-1899) he again grew impatient with formal study and abandoned it with his prospects unimproved but with an unimpaired determination to become distinguished as a poet.

An important turning point occurred about this time, when a doctor warned Frost that his chronically precarious physical condition suggested the threat of tuberculosis and that country life might be beneficial. He thereupon became a farmer. His paternal grandfather, somewhat baffled but solicitous, bought him a small farm in Derry, New Hampshire, where between 1900 and 1905 Frost raised poultry and came to be known as "the egg man." Still more a poet than a farmer, he found in the New Hampshire countryside and its people an appealing kind of raw material for his lyrics and dramatic narratives. By 1905 he had written most of the poems that later constituted his first two published volumes. However, neither farming nor poetry provided adequate support for his growing family of three daughters and one son; therefore from 1906 to 1911 he taught various subjects at the Pinkerton Academy in Derry. His success as a provocative teacher brought him an invitation to join the faculty of the New Hampshire Normal School at Plymouth, and in 1911 he moved his family there.

Never wavering from his secret goal, and increasingly impatient with various diversions and hindrances, Frost taught at the New Hampshire Normal School for only one year before deciding to take one last gamble on a literary life. In the autumn of 1912 he sailed for England with his family, a venture made possible by the cash sale of his Derry farm and by a small annual income from the estate of his deceased paternal grandfather. The Frosts rented an inexpensive cottage on the edge of fields and woods in Beaconsfield, Buckinghamshire, and more or less "camped it" while the poet went seriously to work. Within three months after his arrival in England he had sorted out his previously written poems into a two-volume arrangement, submitted to a London publisher the manuscript of *A Boy's Will*, and signed a contract. The British reviews of his first book were little more than lukewarm, but the critical response to his dramatic narratives, published a year later in *North of Boston*, enthusiastically hailed a new poetic voice. Thus at the age of forty, after twenty years of patient devotion to his art, Frost won recognition in England and thereby attracted the attention of critics and editors in his native land.

Publication of his first two volumes also facilitated literary acquaintances and friendships in England, including those with such writers as Ezra Pound, Edward Thomas, F. S. Flint, T. E. Hulme, and Lascelles Abercrombie. With the encouragement of Abercrombie, the Frost family in the spring of 1914 moved from Beaconsfield to the idyllic Gloucestershire countryside near the Malvern Hills. Only the outbreak of war caused the Frosts to make plans to return to the United States. By the time they reached New York in February, 1915, both *A Boy's*

Will and *North of Boston* had been published in American editions, and the latter quickly became a best seller.

Frost returned to New Hampshire and bought a small farm in the White Mountain region, near Franconia, but his growing literary reputation brought almost immediate demands for public readings and lectures. In less than a year after his return from England, he had given readings in most of the New England states as well as in Illinois, Texas, Pennsylvania, and New York. He became one of the first American poets to make arrangements with various universities to join their faculties as a creative writer, without submitting to the treadmill of regular teaching. From 1916 to 1920 he was a professor of English at Amherst College, and from 1921 to 1923 he was poet-in-residence at the University of Michigan. After returning to Amherst for two years, he went back to spend one more year at the University of Michigan as a fellow in letters. From 1926 to 1938 he again taught at Amherst on a part-time basis, from 1939 to 1943 he was Ralph Waldo Emerson Fellow of Poetry at Harvard, from 1943 to 1949 he was Ticknor Fellow at Dartmouth, and in 1949 he was appointed Simpson Lecturer at Amherst.

Frost received many honors and awards, among them the Pulitzer Prize in poetry in 1924, 1931, 1937, and 1943; he was elected to membership in the National Institute of Arts and Letters in 1916 and to membership in the American Academy of Arts and Letters in 1930. On the occasion of his seventy-fifth birthday, the U.S. Senate adopted a resolution extending him felicitations. In 1955 Vermont named a mountain after Frost in the town of his legal residence, Ripton. More than thirty colleges and universities gave him honorary degrees, and in the spring of 1957 he returned to Great Britain to receive honorary degrees from Oxford, Cambridge, and the National University of Ireland.

Frost's seemingly simple poetic idiom is actually complicated, subtle, and elusive. At first glance many of his lyric, descriptive, and narrative poems may seem to deserve particular merit solely because they precisely observe little-noticed details of natural objects and rural characters. The poet's obvious pleasure in faithfully recording cherished images actually provides the foundation for a subtle poetic super-structure. Even in his brief lyrics Frost manages to include a strong dramatic element, primarily through a sensitive capturing of voice tones, so that the "sound of sense" adds a significant dimension of meaningfulness to all his poems. Beyond that, his imagery is developed in such a way as to endow even the most prosaically represented object with implied symbolic extensions of meaning. Finally, through the blend of matter and manner, the poems frequently transcend the immediate relationships of the individual to self, to others, to nature, and to the universe as they probe the mysteries around which religious faith is built. While the totality of Frost's separate poetic moods may explore many possible attitudes toward human experience, his poems repeatedly return to an implied attitude of devout reverence and belief, which constitutes the infallible core of his work.

From *Cyclopedia of World Authors, Fourth Revised Edition* (Pasadena, CA: Salem Press). Copyright © 2004 by Salem Press, Inc.

Bibliography

Burnshaw, Stanley. *Robert Frost Himself*. New York: George Braziller, 1986. Written by someone who had been an almost lifelong friend of Frost, this very personal biography is in part an attempt to redress the balance skewed in the definitive Lawrance Thompson work. Includes a chronology, extensive notes, an index, and a revealing collection of illustrations.

Faggen, Robert. *Robert Frost and the Challenge of Darwin*. Ann Arbor: University of Michigan Press, 1997. With copious evidence amassed for his argument, Faggen depicts Robert Frost as a poet of the first order and among the most challenging of the moderns.

Gerber, Philip L. *Robert Frost*. Rev. ed. Boston: Twayne, 1982. Begins with an objective biographical overview and follows with substantial chapters on technique, themes, theories, and accomplishments. Includes a chronology, extensive notes and references, a select bibliography, and an index.

Meyers, Jeffrey. *Robert Frost: A Biography*. Boston: Houghton Mifflin, 1996. Shapes a long life into a vivacious character study based on the conflicts that seemed to drive Frost as well as do him damage. Includes bibliographical references and index.

Parini, Jay. *Robert Frost: A Life*. New York: Henry Holt, 1999. Addresses the poet's work by examining the events of his life. Parini views Frost as someone who "struggled throughout his long life with depression, anxiety, self-doubt, and confusion" and relates Frost's personal crises to his accomplishment as a poet.

Poirier, Richard. *Robert Frost: The Work of Knowing*. New York: Oxford University Press, 1977. Substantial scholarly work refrains from partial judgments and presents a balanced view of Frost and his work. Contains a biographical chapter, but concentrates mostly on the writings, which are analyzed lucidly. Includes a chronology of Frost's writings, a limited bibliography, and an index.

Potter, James L. *The Robert Frost Handbook*. University Park: Pennsylvania State University Press, 1980. Basic and widely used resource on Frost is indispensable for both first readers and scholars. Contains chronologies of both his life and his works, guides to various approaches to the poems, discussions of the literary and cultural contexts in which the works were written, and technical analyses. Includes a thorough annotated bibliography and an index.

Pritchard, William H. *Frost: A Literary Life Reconsidered*. New York: Oxford University Press, 1984. Presents a measured, sophisticated, detailed approach to Frost's life and work. Unlike many scholarly biographies, this one is good for browsing and enjoyable for the general reader. Includes full notes and an index.

Thompson, Lawrance, and R. H. Winnick. *Robert Frost: A Biography*. Ed. Edward Connery Lathem. New York: Holt, Rinehart and Winston, 1981. One-volume, condensed version of an exhaustive, three-volume authorized biography originally published between 1966 and 1976. This meticulously researched and minutely recorded study of Frost has been judged as personally biased by many reviewers. Though solid on facts, it presents judgments of the poet that must be viewed with caution.

the PARIS
REVIEW

The *Paris Review* Perspective _____
Elizabeth Gumport for *The Paris Review*

Robert Frost is widely known as a New England poet, an austere, clear-eyed anthropologist of the region in which he spent most of his life. His poems resemble crisp, precise New England landscapes—swift, clean-lined portraits of its pastures and orchards—and often they are. "Literature begins with geography," Frost once said, and his work is rooted in the Northeast's hard soil. Compilations of his New England works are popular—one such anthology, released on DVD and touted as "a selection of Frost's poems chosen to suit a perfect New England autumn day," features gauzy shots of golden foliage—and justly so. There is the bright, bitter close of fall in "After Apple-Picking"—"Essence of winter sleep is on the night,/ The scent of apples: I am drowsing off"—and, in "Stopping by Woods on a Snowy Evening," the "easy wind and downy flake" of that cold season settling in.

But Frost's life and life's work resist this regional compartmentalization. Though he spent much of his life in New England, Frost was born in California in 1874. Only after his father's death did he move east with his mother and sister. The family briefly settled in Lawrence, Massachusetts—his father's boyhood home—before relocating to New Hampshire, where his mother worked as a teacher. Frost remained in the region until he was thirty-eight, when he moved with his family to England for several years. Though he had published a number of poems before his departure, it was not until his time in England that Frost released his first collection of poetry. Born in California and reborn as a poet in England: "There ought to be in everything you write some sign that you come from almost anywhere," he told a group of aspiring writers—and in a sense he really did.

In his interview with *The Paris Review,* Frost talked about his resistance to easy categorization; "My instinct was not to belong to any gang," he told Richard Poirier. He did not want to speak for anything or anyone other than himself. When Poirier asked, "Did you ever feel any affinity between your work and any other poet's?" Frost demurred, "I'll leave that for somebody else to tell me. I wouldn't know." We all come from somewhere, according to Frost, but in the end we are only ourselves.

This insistence on the individual bears itself out in Frost's poetry as well. In "Tree at My Window"—one of those poems so often included in the New England anthologies—Frost writes, "Tree at my window, window tree,/ My sash is lowered when night comes on;/ But let there never be a curtain drawn/ Between you and me." The window is closed, but the curtain is open: we are at once together, but we are watching each other through the glass—always and only alone.

Frost's work is thus more elegy than Georgic: the picturesque landscapes are thresholds to be crossed, gateways to dark feelings in dark seasons. In the end Frost almost always turns back to the human. In "After Apple-Picking," he writes of the falling apples—turning from "stem end and blossom end/ and every fleck of russet showing clear"— and his falling spirits. "I am overtired," he declares, "of the great harvest I myself desired." I have what I want, he says, and I no longer want it. The exhaustion of desire, to long for something and then feel yourself part from that longing: this, Frost tells us, is the sadness of our lives.

Bibliography

Frost, Robert. "The Art of Poetry No. 2." Interview with Richard Poirier. *The Paris Review* 24 (Summer/Fall 1960).

_____. *The Robert Frost Reader: Poetry and Prose.* Ed. Edward Connery Lathem and Lawrance Thompson. New York: Henry Holt, 1984.

Poirier, Richard. *Robert Frost: The Work of Knowing.* New York: Oxford UP, 1977.

CRITICAL CONTEXTS

Robert Frost, T. S. Eliot, and Modernist Poetics_____

Matthew J. Bolton

> The way to read a poem in prose or verse is in the light of all the other poems ever written. We may begin anywhere.
>
> —Robert Frost, "Poetry and School
> (*Collected Poems, Prose, and Plays* 806)

Attending a 1932 dinner party in honor of T. S. Eliot, Robert Frost found himself annoyed by the solemn adulation with which his famous contemporary was received. When the crowd prevailed upon Eliot and Frost each to read a poem, Frost tried to puncture the crowd's pretensions by playing a practical joke. He declared that whereas Eliot could recite one of his extant poems, Frost would compose a poem on the spot. Eliot proceeded to recite "The Hippopotamus." Frost followed with "My Record Stride," a poem that he had written some months prior but that he now pretended to compose extemporaneously. The joke, however, was lost on the crowd, who took Frost at face value and applauded his remarkable felicity for spontaneous rhyming (Meyers 198).

Frost's reception at the dinner party might reflect a widespread misconception of the nature of his poetry. Frost mastered an art that conceals art. Because Frost's poems can seem so simple and spontaneous, the crowd of diners was willing to accept the premise that it took him no longer to write a poem than it would take them to read it. They would not, one can assume, make the same assumption about Eliot; "The Hippopotamus," for example, begins with two quotations from the letters of the Church fathers, one in Latin and one in English. From the outset, Eliot's poem establishes a connection with written rather than oral traditions. Frost gestures in the opposite direction, toward the simplicity of colloquial speech. The immediacy of Frost's rhymes, rhythms, and images can lull a reader into thinking that Frost's verse is somehow easier to write and to apprehend than the work of a "difficult" poet such as Eliot. In the popular imagination, therefore, Frost's quality of thought and expression is constantly being flattened and simplified. The line "Good fences make good neighbors," for example, is often attributed to Frost himself rather than to an unsympathetic character in "Mending Wall" (28). Similarly, Frost's "The Road Not Taken" is misidentified in countless commencement addresses and motivational speeches as "The Road Less Traveled," a change of title that reduces Frost's meditation on the arbitrariness of experience to a simpleminded encomium for doing one's own thing. The simplicity of Frost's work can lead some readers to adopt simplistic readings of his poems. Eliot and Frost might therefore be thought of as two poles of modernism. Eliot is the poet of complexity and allusion, whose work is bound up with the whole history of literature itself; Frost is the poet of simplicity and directness, who writes of apple trees and stone walls and leaf-covered roads. This is a caricature of the two poets, to be sure, but one that serves as a useful point of departure for understanding the differences between their work. In deconstructing this caricature, one finds that Frost is, in his own way, as complex and allusive a poet as Eliot.

Frost tended to portray himself as being set apart from what he called the "Pound-Eliot-Richards-Reed school of art" (736). In the same year as the Eliot dinner party, for example, Frost complained of the modernists in a letter to his daughter:

> From Pound down to Eliot, they have striven for distinction by a show of learning, Pound in Old French [and] Eliot in forty languages. They quote and you try to see if you can place the quotation. Pound really has great though inaccurate learning. Eliot has even greater. (736)

Perhaps Frost had in mind passages such as the polyphonic conclusion of Eliot's *The Waste Land*, in which English, Italian, Latin, French, and Sanskrit vie for the upper hand:

London Bridge is falling down falling down falling down

Poi s'ascose nel foco che gli affina

Quando fiam uti chelidon—O swallow swallow

Le Prince d'Aquitaine a la tour abolie

These fragments I have shored against my ruins

Why then Ile fit you. Hieronymo's mad againe.

Datta. Dayadhvam. Damyata.

Shantih shantih shantih.

(426-32)

Toward the end of his letter, Frost reveals this to be the poem he had in mind: "Eliot has written in the throes of getting religion and fore-swearing a world gone bad with war. That seems deep. But I dont know. Waste Lands . . . I doubt if anything was laid waste by war that was not laid waste by peace before" (736). Frost knew that Eliot nettled him, writing, "I confess I have several times forgotten my dignity in speaking in public of Eliot. I mean I have shown a hostility I should like to think in my pride unworthy of my position" (734). The regret seems to be not for feeling hostility toward Eliot but for revealing it. Some thirty years later, in an interview with *The Paris Review*, Frost echoes some of these same objections about modernism's show of learning, complaining:

Pound seemed to me very like a troubadour . . . I never touched that. I don't know Old French. I don't like foreign languages that I haven't had. I don't read translations of things. I like to say dreadful, unpleasant things about Dante. (881)

Modernism, Frost argues, should not be limited to this sort of erudi-tion. Interviewer Richard Poirier suggests, "Eliot and Pound seem to many people to be writing in a tradition that is very different from yours." Frost at first agrees, but then qualifies his answer: "Yes. I sup-pose Eliot's isn't as far away as Pound's" (881). Here in the last decade of his life, Frost is in a position to look back over Eliot's career and his own and to admit, however grudgingly, that the distance between them is not as great as it may once have seemed. Perhaps in the context of an interview in which he is asked his opinion about Ginsberg's "Howl" and other works of the beat poets, Frost can see that he and Eliot were men of the same age.

It is precisely because they were of the same age that Frost harbored a degree of hostility toward Eliot and his work. This may be less an issue of what Harold Bloom calls the anxiety of influence, in which one poet feels compelled to misread the work of a powerful predecessor, than a straightforward case of professional rivalry. Frost wanted to stake his own claim. Despite the obvious contrasts between their prosody and subject matter, Frost and Eliot moved in some of the same literary and social circles, published and were reviewed in the same venues, and jockeyed for some of the same accolades and positions. In 1913, for example, Frost and Eliot were both expatriates living in or around London. Frost had already made the acquaintance of Ezra Pound, who would favorably review his first book, the 1913 *A Boy's Will*. Through Pound, he would meet the central figures of modernism, including Richard Aldington, Hilda Doolittle, Ford Madox Ford, and William Butler Yeats. Both *A Boy's Will* and his collection from the following year, *North of Boston*, would be published by English houses rather than American ones. Yet Frost worried that his association with London and with Pound would cause his work to be misinterpreted back home in America. He did not want to be too closely associated with Pound's "party of American literary refugees."

Frost returned to the United States in 1915, and so would have been back in New Hampshire when Pound's latest find, an American expatriate fifteen years Frost's junior, published "The Love Song of J. Alfred Prufrock" in Harriet Monroe's magazine *Poetry*. Over the next few years, Frost and Eliot each published several collections of poetry, and with each volume the respective poet grew in stature. By the 1920s, each was a candidate for the Pulitzer Prize: Eliot would be passed over in 1922 for *The Waste Land*, whereas Frost received the award in 1924 for *New Hampshire*. By the middle of the decade, Frost had published many of his most enduring poems, including "Mending Wall," "The Death of the Hired Man," "After Apple-Picking," "The Road Not Taken," "Birches," and "Stopping by Woods on a Snowy Evening." Eliot, for his part, had published "Prufrock," "Portrait of a Lady," "Gerontion," and, in 1922, *The Waste Land*. The poets would not meet in person until 1928, but Frost could not avoid encountering the younger poet's work. In the wake of *The Waste Land*'s radical deconstruction of form, it is easy to understand why Frost would have felt a desire to mark his own work as separate from Eliot's sphere of influence.

One way to gauge the distances and proximities between Eliot and Frost is by identifying in a Frost poem the elements that the poet, in private letters and public interviews, seemed to associate with Eliot's work. "Acquainted with the Night," a fourteen-line poem that Frost wrote in 1925 and first published in the 1928 *West-Running Brook*, is a good test case for such a comparison. It is representative enough of Frost's work that President John F. Kennedy read it as a eulogy for the poet. The poem is narrated by a solitary walker in the city:

> I have been one acquainted with the night.
> I have walked out in rain—and back in rain.
> I have outwalked the furthest city light.
>
> I have looked down the saddest city lane.
> I have passed by the watchman on his beat
> And dropped my eyes, unwilling to explain.
>
> (1-6)

There is much here that one might consider vintage Frost: the confessional aspect of the narration, the perfect rhymes, the simplicity of diction, and the strictly observed iambic pentameter. Yet the poem also ventures into Eliot country—or, more accurately, into the Eliot city. The situation and setting of the poem are reminiscent of those of "The Love Song of J. Alfred Prufrock" and the other "observations" that make up Eliot's 1917 volume, as well as of the "unreal city" of *The Waste Land*. Prufrock, too, wanders through a desolate city, down "streets that follow like a tedious argument." He is an observer rather than a participant in the meager life of this fogbound city:

> Shall I say, I have gone at dusk through narrow streets
> And watched the smoke that rises from the pipes
> Of lonely men in shirt-sleeves, leaning out of windows?
>
> (70-72)

Eliot's and Frost's narrators are entirely cut off from the people around them; they are more alone in the modern city than they would be in an empty wilderness. This city of rain and fog is the labyrinth that the narrators wander each night.

Frost, like Eliot before him, dismembers his city dwellers, wrenching feet, eyes, and voices away from their possessors. The effect is one of profound alienation, for these fragmentary people cannot speak to each other. The watchman, whose gaze the narrator avoids, is a body without a voice, and in the next stanza the narrator hears a voice without a body:

> I have stood still and stopped the sound of feet
> When far away an interrupted cry
> Came over houses from another street
>
> But not to call me back or say goodbye . . .
>
> (7-10)

Frost's narrator is divorced even from his body, for he seems to hear his own footsteps as an alien sound. The city of *Prufrock and Other Obser-*

vations is likewise one of synecdoche, in which hands, feet, and eyes stand in for what should be a whole person. In "Morning at the Window," a smile is "torn" from a passerby, while "The brown waves of fog toss up to me/ Twisted faces from the bottom of the street" (5-6). In "Preludes," a city dweller's soul is

> . . . trampled by insistent feet
> At four and five and six o'clock;
> And short square fingers stuffing pipes,
> And evening newspapers, and eyes
> Assured of certain certainties.
>
> (41-45)

In *The Waste Land*, too, a crowd of commuters flowing over London Bridge is rendered as a collection of shuffling feet and downcast gazes: "Sighs, short and infrequent, were exhaled,/ And each man fixed his eyes before his feet" (64-65). *The Waste Land* narrator is alone in the crowd, for there can be no sense of communion with these damned souls who cannot even meet one another's gaze.

Lyric poetry has a long tradition of cataloging and anatomizing the body. Shakespeare's sonnet "My Mistress's Eyes Are Nothing Like the Sun," for example, is a response to the Renaissance *blazon* tradition, in which a sonneteer would single out a series of parts of his beloved's body for praise. His attention would dwell in turn on the eyes, the lips, the hair, the hands. In Eliot's and Frost's city poems, however, the *blazon* convention serves a different purpose. The effect is not one of admiration and possession but one of alienation and disaffection. These are cities of the fragmentary, in which a walker perceives bits and pieces of another's life—a face in the crowd, a voice heard from over the rooftops—rather than a whole. This anatomization of the city's inhabitants shifts the focus of each poem from the people of the city to the city itself. While the other people the narrators encounter are elusive and unknowable, night and the city emerge as fully drawn characters.

Yet identifying in one of Frost's poems a situation, setting, and mood that are reminiscent of Eliot does not necessarily gather Frost into the "Pound-Eliot . . . school of art" that he criticized. "Acquainted with the Night" shares Eliot's vision of the modern city as a labyrinth and as a site of alienation, using synecdoche and personification to dehumanize the city dwellers and to grant human characteristics to the city itself. But Frost's objection to modernism centered on its "show of learning," and to challenge Frost's representation of the differences between Eliot and himself, one should look for allusion in this and other of his poems. At first blush, Frost seems to have avoided the allusive mode that he objected to in Eliot's work. "Acquainted with the Night" does not slip into Latin, Italian, or French, as Pound and Eliot are wont to do. Yet the poem is densely allusive, in a mode that, while strikingly different from that of *Prufrock* or *The Waste Land*, is no less caught up with the poetic tradition that precedes it. Frost's "show of learning" is not found in direct quotation; rather, it is encoded in the structure of his deceptively simple poem.

The most explicit literary allusion in "Acquainted with the Night" is found in its rhyme scheme. Though Frost would later aver that he "never touched" the foreign languages that animated Pound's work, quipping, "I like to say dreadful, unpleasant things about Dante," the terza rima rhyme scheme of "Acquainted with the Night" suggests a very different relationship to the European literary tradition (881). Terza rima is the Italian verse form that Dante Alighieri immortalized in the three parts of his *Commedia*: *The Inferno, Purgatory*, and *Paradise*. In adopting Dante's rhyme scheme, Frost puts his own poem into dialogue with the form's great master. His walker in the city becomes an avatar of Dante the pilgrim, the lost soul who begins his poem "*Nel mezzo cammin di nostra vita/ Mi ritrovai in una selva oscura/ E la via diritta era smarrita*" ("While halfway through the journey of our life/ I found myself lost in a darkened forest,/ for I had wandered off from the straight path" [1-3]). Frost's city echoes some of the allegorical resonances of Dante's dark wood.

To understand the terza rima scheme, one might label its end rhymes, producing the pattern *aba, bcb, cdc,* and so on. In the first triplet of "Acquainted with the Night," the end words are "night," "rain," and "light." The unrhymed word "rain" will become the rhyming sound of the second triplet, whose end sounds consist of "lane," "beat," and "explain." In the third triplet, "beat" becomes the rhyming sound, picked up by "feet" and "street" in the fourth. It is a graceful and supple pattern in which the unrhymed sound draws the reader forward from one triplet to the next. Dante and Frost alike know how to exploit the tension between the triplet and the quatrain, playing with the dynamics of closure that the form both raises and frustrates. Returning to a stanza cited above, notice how Frost uses the line break between his triplets to dramatic effect:

> I have stood still and stopped the sound of feet
> When far away an interrupted cry
> Came over houses from another street
>
> But not to call me back or say goodbye.
> And further still, at an unearthly height . . .
>
> (7-11)

The reader shares the narrator's momentary hope that the cry he hears is meant for him, and the line break becomes a long and suspenseful pause. The first line of the next triplet, however, makes it clear that the cry is not for the lonely narrator, and the rhyme that closes this faux quatrain—"cry" and "goodbye"—dashes the narrator's hopes. Terza rima is a challenging pattern, in that no end sounds are allowed to fall by the wayside. Each triplet is linked to the one that follows it, so the poet has less room to maneuver than he would in, say, an *abcb* pattern of alternating rhyme. This is particularly true in the English language, for the repository of rhyming end sounds in English is not as flexible as that in Italian. It is a distinct advantage to compose rhyme in a romance language, where most words end in vowels and where the number of end sounds is consequently limited. Frost's poem is a bravura performance, for the simpler he can make this difficult rhyme scheme appear, the more the poem attests to his ear as a poet.

Frost's poem therefore alludes to Dante on its most basic, structural level, and in so doing it falls into step not only with Dante the pilgrim's wanderings through hell and purgatory but also with Pound's and Eliot's wanderings through the European literary tradition. Dante is perhaps the single most important influence on Eliot's work, and his poems abound with references to the *Inferno* and *Purgatorio*. "Prufrock," for example, begins with a six-line epigraph from the latter: "*S'io credesse che mia risposta fosse/ A persona che mai tornasse al mondo/ Questa fiamma staria senza piu scosse . . .*" (1-3). A damned soul, condemned to abide in a sheet of flame, tells Dante that he only confesses himself because he knows that Dante too will never return to the living. The fires of Purgatory appear again in the fugue that closes *The Waste Land*: "*Poi s'ascose nel foco che gli affina*" ("Then he returned to the fires that refine him" [427]). Other lines from the *Commedia* are translated and echoed in English, as in the narrator's aforementioned reaction to the crowds of London commuters: ". . . so many/ I had not thought death had undone so many./ Sighs, short and infrequent, were exhaled . . ." (63-64). Eliot's modern city is an infernal or a purgatorial one, and his frequent references to Dante link its inhabitants with the damned souls of the afterlife. Much later in his career, in the magisterial *Four Quartets*, Eliot would write a Dantean passage in the second part of "Little Gidding" consisting of twenty-four triplets in an unrhymed version of terza rima. Here a walker in the city encounters a ghostly former master with whom he "trod the pavement in a dead patrol" until dawn (54). For Eliot and Frost alike, to wander the city by night is to partake of Dante's pilgrimage through the underworld. Yet the two poets allude to Dante in strikingly different ways: while Eliot quotes or appropriates lines and turns of phrase from Dante, Frost adopts his underlying poetic structure.

There is an inherent irony in both poets' allusions to the *Commedia*. Whereas Dante had the stolid Virgil to guide him through the underworld, Eliot's and Frost's narrators walk alone. Over the course of his pilgrimage, Dante recovers the faith in God that he had lost through wandering in the dark wood. After climbing from the Inferno, Dante looks up at the sky and sees a visible confirmation of this faith: "I saw the lovely things the heavens hold,/ And we came out to see once more the stars" (Canto XXXIV 138). The firmament represents an eternal and immutable order, one that contrasts sharply with the fleeting and temporal world of humankind. Frost's narrator, on the other hand, finds in the night sky only another marker of time:

> But not to call me back or say goodbye;
> And further still, at an unearthly height
> One luminary clock against the sky
>
> Proclaimed the time was neither wrong nor right.
> I have been one acquainted with the night.
>
> (10-14)

He can take no consolation in a view of the stars and can place no faith in the idea of a God. The cosmology of "Prufrock," *The Waste Land*, and "Acquainted with the Night" allows for the existence of a hell, but not a heaven.

Dante's *Commedia* is not the only canonical literary or religious text that "Acquainted with the Night" invokes. In his collection *West-Running Brook*, Frost grouped this and a series of other poems under the heading *"Fiat Nox"* ("Let there be night"). The phrase reverses God's command in Genesis, *Fiat Lux* ("Let there be light"). It is a clever inversion—a "show of learning" in another language, to use the terms by which Frost derided Eliot—that suggests that "Acquainted with the Night" should be read as explicitly involved in the Christian tradition. Augustine's *City of God*, in which the church father contrasts an earthly city with a celestial one, is certainly one referent. Frost's poem bears an even greater resemblance to Saint John of the Cross's "The Dark Night of the Soul," in which the night serves as a symbol of spiritual desolation:

> One dark night,
> fired with love's urgent longings
> —ah, the sheer grace!—
> I went out unseen,
> my house being now all stilled.
>
> (1-5)

Frost is writing in a long tradition of meditative verse, in which a pilgrim describes his journey through terrain that is freighted with allegorical significance. The "*Fiat Nox*" subtitle is a signpost for readers who might otherwise miss the religious and spiritual dimensions of the poem.

"Acquainted with the Night" therefore bears comparison to Eliot's cycle of city poems, for it explores some of the same imagery and themes as do *Prufrock and Other Observations* and *The Waste Land*. Eliot and Frost alike redeploy synecdoche and personification, long-standing poetic devices, to dehumanize the city's inhabitants and to give life and sentience to night and the city themselves. Despite Frost's stated aversion to Eliot's "show of learning," his poem is profoundly allusive, inviting comparisons with Dante and Saint John of the Cross not by directly quoting them, as might Eliot, but by adopting their rhyme schemes and patterns of imagery.

There is yet another level on which Eliot and Frost are reinventing, in their own very different modes, the poetic tradition they inherited. Much as they found new uses for the Renaissance tradition of anatomizing and cataloging the body, so do they turn to a new use of the long-standing conventions of rhyme and repetition. In Eliot's and Frost's city poems, echoing sounds become links in the spiritual chains that bind their narrators.

"Prufrock," *The Waste Land*, and many of Eliot's other poems are written in vers libre, free verse, in which the syllable counts of lines and the rhyme schemes of stanzas change in response to the changing mandates of the poem. It is a flexible pattern that widens Eliot's range of dramatic and poetic effects. Eliot's published poems often have their origins in separate, fragmentary pieces; free verse gave Eliot license to make connections between these poems and assemble them into larger wholes. "Prufrock," for example, synthesizes two poems that Eliot first conceived of independent of each other. In *The Waste Land*, Pound aided Eliot in cutting brilliant fragments from his poems to set against each other. The poem builds power and form through juxtaposition as much as through continuity. Eliot's method of composition, revision, and synthesis militated against his limiting himself to a single meter or rhyme scheme.

A poem like "Prufrock" modulates from one pattern to another, slipping into and out of rhyme. The narrator's observation of street life—one that he implies is so slight as not to register as an observation at all—is unrhymed, as is the remarkable and grotesque self-description that follows it:

> Shall I say, I have gone at dusk through narrow streets
> And watched the smoke that rises from the pipes
> Of lonely men in shirt-sleeves, leaning out of windows?
>
> I should have been a pair of ragged claws
> Scuttling across the floors of silent seas.
>
> (70-74)

The refrain that describes a cocktail party, on the other hand, takes the form of an inane and jangling couplet: "In the room the women come and go/ Talking of Michelangelo" (13-14). The banality of the rhyme reflects the banality of the conversation. Rhyme frequently seems to mock or undercut Prufrock, as in "Should I, after tea and cakes and ices/ Have the strength to force the moment to its crisis" (79-80). Prufrock *is* in crisis, but rhyming the word with "cakes and ices" deflates it. This couplet moves Prufrock out of the tragic mode and into the mock epic. The poem's unrhymed lines, many of which appear as a coda to a stanza of alternating verse or couplets, stand out in sharp contrast: "And how should I begin?" (69) or "And in short, I was afraid" (86) or "I do not think that they will sing to me" (125). It is as if Eliot is reversing the Shakespearean pattern, in which speeches and scenes in blank verse conclude with couplets. For Shakespeare, the transition to rhyme signals closure and resolution. For Eliot, in contrast, rhyme is a form of containment and repetition. Prufrock's occasional escape from self-consciousness is reflected in his occasional escape from the poem's rhyme scheme.

Repetition of lines and of phrases is yet another means by which the poem reflects Prufrock's spiritual imprisonment. The refrain "So how should I presume?," its phrasing changing slightly with each reiteration, appears three times. The lines about the cocktail party and a woman's refrain of "That is not what I meant at all./ That is not it, at all" both appear twice (97-98, 109-110). Several lines begin with "Shall I . . . ?" or "Should I . . . ?" or "Do I . . . ?" It is as if Prufrock not only cannot take action but also cannot decide whether he should consider taking action. These questions—along with the "overwhelming question" (10) that Prufrock refuses even to name—trap Prufrock in a twilight realm of the conditional and the hypothetical. The repetitiveness of Prufrock's own formulations suggests a form or spiritual paralysis, a sentence served in the prison of the self.

During their brief acquaintance in London, Pound urged Frost, too, to write in vers libre, but Frost resisted the suggestion of his "quasi friend." Later in life, he was careful to correct readers or critics who misidentified his meters and structures. He concluded a 1942 preface to "The Death of the Hired Man," for example, by writing, "By the way, it's in blank verse, not free verse" (785). "Acquainted with the Night" is typical of Frost in that it adheres to a highly regular structure:

fourteen lines of iambic pentameter following a terza rima rhyme scheme. A lesser poet working in this form might have to sacrifice sense to sound; the regularity of the meter and the interlocking nature of the rhyme scheme would be a straitjacket. Frost, however, works so deftly within the constraints he has placed on himself that one may not notice they are there at all. Part of Frost's resistance to writing in free verse may be that he was already free within the confines of a more regular meter and rhyme scheme.

Yet rhyme and repetition play a role in Frost's regular verse that is comparable to the one they play in Eliot's vers libre: they are a formal enactment of the sense of containment and repetition that haunts each poem's respective narrator. Frost exploits the closed nature of terza rima to represent the spiritual imprisonment of his narrator. Because the rhyme scheme does not allow for any extraneous end sounds, Frost must have faced a challenge in deciding how to end his poem. After all, if he followed the regular terza rima pattern, the end sound of the middle line of the last stanza would remain unrhymed. Frost addressed this by returning to the rhyming *a* sound of the first triplet. "Height" in the last stanza rhymes with "right" and "night," and the poem concludes not with a triplet but with a rhyming couplet:

> But not to call me back or say goodbye;
> And further still, at an unearthly height
> One luminary clock against the sky
> Proclaimed the time was neither wrong nor right.
> I have been one acquainted with the night.
>
> (10-14)

This is a satisfying conclusion to the poem, a variation on the repetition that Frost had used to end another tightly constructed work, "Stopping by Woods on a Snowy Evening." Yet it is a conclusion that returns the narrator and reader to the poem's title and first line. By repeating the first line of the poem, Frost creates a loop, a textual enactment of the narrator's habit of walking night after night. Poem and narrator alike make a circuit, going a long way only to find themselves back where they started.

The repetition of the phrase "I have" likewise produces a sense of containment and limitation. Fully half the poem's lines begin with "I have," and the effect is to trap the narrator in a prison of the ego. He can outwalk the city lights, but he cannot outwalk his own identity. Prufrock speculates about a hypothetical future, asking "Shall I?" Frost's narrator, on the other hand, recounts his purgatorial past. The effect is similar, in that each man is crippled by self-consciousness. But in the case of Frost's poem, the past perfect tense may offer a way out of the nightly round the narrator treads. If he *has* done all these things in the past, then perhaps he does them no more in a happier present. The grammatical distinction produces a narratorial one, suggesting that the narrator who relates the poem is no longer the one who walked the city by night and that he has, eventually, wandered from desolation into consolation.

The issue of Frost's relationship to the modernists in general, and to Eliot in particular, is a fascinating one. It would be a mistake to accept wholesale Frost's own representation of this relationship, for the poet had an interest in marking his own work off as being entirely unconnected to that of Eliot. It would also be a mistake, however, to assume the opposite, drawing easy and muddying generalizations about the two poets. Rather, by tracing out the contrasting ways in which Eliot and Frost reinterpreted the poetic tradition and redeployed the poetic conventions that they inherited, one might come to see them as two poets who brought their very different temperaments and gifts to bear on some of the same problems inherent to the modern condition.

Works Cited

Alighieri, Dante. *Dante Alighieri's Divine Comedy: Inferno*. Trans. Mark Musa. Bloomington: Indiana UP, 2004.

Eliot, T. S. *The Complete Poems and Plays: 1909-1950*. New York: Harcourt, Brace &World, 1962.

Frost, Robert. *Collected Poems, Prose, and Plays*. New York: Library of America, 1995.

Meyers, Jeffrey. *Robert Frost: A Biography*. New York: Houghton Mifflin, 1996.

Saint John of the Cross. *Dark Night of the Soul*. New York: Doubleday, 1959.

Robert Frost:
A Look at the Critical Reception _____

Janyce Marson

During the nearly one hundred years of criticism of Robert Frost, the most challenging issues have been how to locate him among other modern poets and how to differentiate him from his Romantic forebears, most notably William Wordsworth and Ralph Waldo Emerson. Unlike the poetry of many of his contemporaries, such as T. S. Eliot and Ezra Pound, which relies on heavy symbolism, esoteric allusions, and various mythological systems, Frost's poetry is written in a very simple and accessible idiom. Nevertheless, Frost's ostensibly simple mode of expression becomes far more complex as one tries to sift through an abundance of possible interpretations. This is perhaps best demonstrated by the history of Frost's critical reception, in which certain core themes were established early on and have remained constant focal points up to the present, though revised and elaborated upon over time.

During the first few decades of the twentieth century, Frost was seen as a thoroughly indigenous New England poet, devoted to the land and its inhabitants, a poet who celebrated the region's natural beauty and memorialized the country folk of New Hampshire and Vermont in his dialogue poems. Above all these considerations, however, Frost was most noteworthy for his own brand of modern poetry, and he continued to mystify his earliest readers with a style of writing that was both simple and highly enigmatic for what it resists saying, for its seeming inconclusiveness. Most characteristic of Frost's earliest reviews are the broad generalities in which the poet's themes were presented and his talents lauded. In a 1915 essay for *The Atlantic Monthly*, "A New American Poet," Edward Garnett predicted that Frost "was destined to take a permanent place in American literature." A few years later Amy Lowell, a poet and contemporary of Frost, exemplified the type of broad-spectrum criticism of the earlier commentators when she spoke of Frost's work as possessing "the very aroma of poesy floating thinly up into the air" (104). In her book *Tendencies in Modern American Poetry* Lowell focuses on the rise of a native school of post-World War I poets who write with a newly acquired "poignant sense of nationality" (v). Describing Frost as a poet of realism rooted firmly in the present moment, Lowell speaks of the way in which he appropriated his contemporary New England environment to create a uniquely modern bucolic poetry. Significantly, Lowell recognizes that Frost's pastorals no longer portray the idyllic rustic world of external beauty and ideal human relationships that the classical, conventional poems of this genre do. Rather, his pastorals have been transformed into sad occasions that depict the harsh realities of life in the New England countryside. For Frost, that pastoral world is located in the landscape of New Hampshire and Vermont and concerns the difficulties of daily life for many of its inhabitants who face harsh economic deprivations, catastrophic accidents, marital discord, and mental illness—concerns far from the carefree rural life depicted in the pastoral's classical antecedents. Frost presents a disintegrating world where people's isolated and monotonous lives—born of the decline in rural communities as younger people moved West or to cities to make their living—cause them to lose their sanity, as portrayed in "The Black Cottage" and "Home Burial." Nevertheless, for Lowell, Frost remained a passionately committed poet, dedicated to the rural countryside and its inhabitants that captured his imagination.

A longtime friend and correspondent of Robert Frost, Louis Untermeyer, whose *Modern American Poetry* (1921) extols the virtues of *North of Boston* and *Mountain Interval*, writes that *North of Boston* is a "book of people" in its dramatic presentation of country life and the natural objects that symbolize the vital aspects of country people's daily existence. He states: "*North of Boston*, like its successor, contains much of the finest poetry of our time. Rich in its actualities, richer in its spiritual values, every line moves with the double force of observation and implication" (175). The first poem Untermeyer discusses is "Mending Wall," which he praises for its powerful presentation of the "sense" of some profoundly important question regarding human relationships, transcending the competing notions expressed by two interlocutors, one of whom sees nature's abhorrence of human-made barriers and the other of whom believes that fences provide necessary limitations to human interactions. Writing in the immediate years following World War I, Untermeyer attaches a global significance to "Mending Wall," interpreting the two men's debate as the "essence of nationalism versus the internationalist; the struggle . . . between a blind responsibility and a pagan iconoclasm" (176). In a 1925 essay, Llewellyn Jones praises Frost for his ability to get close to the lives of common people in a simple, unadorned language that nevertheless produces highly original and affecting poetry. Jones discusses Frost's first volume, *A Boy's Will*, as a philosophic book from which one can glean some of Frost's attitudes toward the world, especially as each poem in the table of contents has explanatory notes appended to it. These notes "bind the lyrics loosely together as a sort of poetic interpretation of life as he mirrors it in his own individuality" (40). According to Jones, "Into My Own" is characteristic of Frost's own wish to leave the world behind, to explore uncharted territory without fear of the unknown.

Gorham Munson's book *Robert Frost: A Study in Sensibility and Good Sense*, published in 1927, is a biographical sketch of the poet based largely on letters and anecdotes from people who knew or met Frost. Though the chapter headings are based on the titles of individual poems, they do not provide any real analysis of the poems; rather, they relate details of Frost's life. The chapter titled "New Hampshire" portrays Frost's life in Derry, where his inexperience at farming gave him firsthand knowledge of the harsh realities of nature. Munson goes on to relate that when Frost was offered a teaching position at Pinkerton Academy following a very successful poetry reading at the Central Congregational Church, he immediately accepted. Based on a letter from one of Frost's students, Munson describes Frost as a popular teacher who was devoted to his students and exhibited a sensitivity that set him apart from the rest of the faculty. He also notes Frost's abiding interest in the local inhabitants. "If we took a winter walk toward Londonderry and met a logging team, . . . there would be conversation right there. Frost would have the teamster talking about logging things and horses and wood roads and such matters" (44).

In his introduction to a 1962 edition of collected essays on Frost, James M. Cox writes that during the interval between the two world wars Frost's critics were guilty of oversimplifying his work, especially when it was contrasted with the highly complex and intellectual work produced by Ezra Pound and T. S. Eliot. Cox's observation—that sharp critical thinking and detailed analyses of Frost's work were missing during the years leading up to World War II—is largely accurate. According to Cox, during those years Frost was associated with a wider and far less sophisticated audience, and his work was no longer understood as representative of modern poetry. As a result, Cox maintains, Frost received little careful attention:

> Though every one of his poems might be a new creation of himself, it was always the same self being created—the old "character" who had first appeared in "Mending Wall," the opening poem of *North of Boston*. It is not surprising that this character who emerged, but who could not develop and who seemed curiously untouched by the drift of modern poetry, should have come to seem almost quaint and old-fashioned by 1930. (4-5)

Furthermore, Cox points out that while much poetry of the 1930s participated in the period's political liberalism, Frost evinced conservative tendencies, going so far as to protest the policies of President Franklin Roosevelt and the New Deal.

All these factors notwithstanding, Frost did receive positive reviews, though they tended to speak in the same broad generalities of the earliest critics. While, as Cox observes, Frost was insulated from a larger sphere of influence by both his critical audience and his chosen subject matter, critics nonetheless noted that his poems possess a universal applicability and are always intensely felt. In a 1931 review titled "Robert Frost: American Poet," James S. Wilson praises the poet for his abiding humanity and the honesty of his portrayals of people and situations, an honesty that disguises the inherent passion of his work. Wilson declares Frost to be the most fervent of American voices, possessing an organic and inviolable relationship with his New England countryside. Furthermore, Wilson commends Frost's dramatic poems, such as "The Death of the Hired Man," calling them "short stories in verse" that re-create the true speech habits of New Englanders while at the same time allowing the characters' particular circumstances to convey universal messages.

Mark Van Doren's 1942 essay "The Permanence of Robert Frost" makes a similar appraisal in speaking of Frost's widespread appeal to both professional critics and general readers. However, Van Doren makes the point that Frost's work always has an element of the mysterious, something Van Doren argues is requisite for all new poets; this element is located in Frost's highly realistic conversational tone, which always says less than is meant and requires multiple readings to grasp its full import. Citing the lines from "The Death of the Hired Man" in which the husband and wife offer different definitions of home, whether it be a place, as the husband believes, "[w]here, when you have to go there,/ they have to take you in" (117-18) or a place or "[s]omething you somehow haven't to deserve" (120), as the wife contends, Van Doren maintains that the reader can resolve the enigma only by listening carefully to the speakers, to such ordinary words as "where," "when," and "somehow." For Van Doren, it is this very quality, the acute sense of the sound of the words demanded by his poetry, that makes Frost sui generis in comparison with those who have tried to emulate him. "His poems are said, not sung; his poems are people talking. . . . And he has been the only one to do so, despite the fact that many an American poet younger than he has tried to imitate him" (90).

In the 1937 article "Robert Frost and the Sound of Sense," Robert Newdick frames a problem that critics currently face in light of the rebirth of the dramatic poem. For Newdick, the central issue is how to transcribe works that are written in the actual speech of the present, such as those of T. S. Eliot, Maxwell Anderson, and Archibald MacLeish. Newdick maintains that this issue deserves more attention than it had previously received and argues that Frost provides the solution because he has been able to incorporate the full range of tones of "living speech" to capture a dialogue that transcends mere conversation. To support his thesis, Newdick relies on a 1915 interview Frost granted to W. S. Braithwaite in which the poet referred back to the underlying principle that there was a "sound of sense" before words existed that enabled primitive humans to communicate without formal language. Applying this fundamental premise to poetry, Frost stated that the birth of literary form was rooted in folk speech and, further, that primitive speech had, by necessity, an inherent musical quality whereby ideas and emotions were conveyed. Newdick further suggests that to gain a full appreciation of Frost's achievement one must actually hear Frost recite his poems, since even some sophisticated critics have not gotten the full import of his meaning. What is perhaps most striking in this essay is that it makes only brief mention of the actual poems, with Newdick citing only a few lines from "Birches" and "Stopping by Woods on a Snowy Evening."

In 1942, Lawrance Thompson, Frost's official biographer and close friend, wrote *Fire and Ice*, a book considered by many to be the first in-depth academic study of Frost's work. Thompson's analysis is premised on Frost's own statements that he did not adhere to any systematic theory of poetry; rather, he believed that a poem is born of an urgency to express an intensely felt experience and is rendered in a well-wrought design. Thompson frames Frost's "theory" of poetry as an organic one in which form and content are inextricably bound up as an integral whole, one in which the poet's personal feelings will be understood by his readers, a "formal fusion of distinct elements [that] shall achieve the personal idiom of the poet's expression without sacrificing that happy correspondence which must exist between his own experience and the experience of those who come after to read or hear the poem" (22).

Thompson states, however, that Frost is far different from Wordsworth, a poet who relied on "emotions recollected in tranquility" and sought a form of refuge from the troubles of the present moment by recapturing memories of bygone happiness. For Frost, in contrast, capturing and articulating the present moment in which a new perspective is discovered constitute both the impetus for writing and a fundamental component of a poem. Furthermore, Thompson points out that Frost's fresh insight precipitates a crisis that compels a vehicle for relief—namely, the poem. Inasmuch as Frost has also been compared to Ralph Waldo Emerson, Thompson sees Frost as having a closer affinity to Emerson, who likewise pursued the present moment as the way to discover and gain access to fresh insights into the design of the universe. Interestingly, in aligning Frost with Emerson, Thompson sees a connection in both poets to Puritan aesthetics to the extent that they both sought a "clarification of life" in their poetry, though, unlike their Puritan forebears, they did not seek "to redeem the individual from human depravity" (37-38). Finally, Thompson does see an inherent paradox in Frost in that the poet would search for an experience that would lead to a heightened understanding while at the same time feeling an urgency to separate himself from that experience in order to realize his newly acquired knowledge. To illustrate this point, Thompson cites the poems "Birches," in which the speaker desires to escape the world for a while only to be set down once again by the heavens, and "Stopping by Woods on a Snowy Evening," in which the narrator stops to gaze upon a scene of snow falling on a dark wood of strange beauty but is compelled to remove himself in order to continue his journey for reasons on which we can only speculate. Thompson sees this surfeit of possibilities in Frost's poem as an emotional release for the reader as well, leading to questions regarding what "promises" were made and what exactly is meant by "miles to go before I sleep"; Thompson understands that there are many possible answers to these questions.

Inasmuch as Thompson refers to the "organic" element in Frost's poetry, it is important to define what is meant by a critical term that has continued to be raised by Frost's critics. In this context, "organic" refers to a belief that a poem works only when it becomes a unified whole; this is a fundamental principle to which the Romantic poets adhered, most especially Wordsworth and, later, Emerson, with whom Frost is often compared. The definition of the organic as applied to Romantic poetry is articulated by Carl Woodring, who states that the imagination contains a unifying power that arises from the poet's quest for a viable connection with the physical universe and is realized through the vehicle of the poem: "By typical romantic argument, mind and physical nature grow as interdependent branches from one divine trunk. The imagining mind and growing nature form one organism, which the understanding would murder to dissect" (29). Woodring's thesis is that this organic unity can be achieved only in poetical works, not in prose writings, which represent the nonorganic or mechanistic. Notions of both the organic and the mechanical became relevant to some prominent Frost critics of the late 1950s and beyond, though they defined these terms in a number of different ways.

The decades following *Fire and Ice* have seen a burgeoning of full-length studies on Robert Frost as well as countless fine critical studies. Among the many topics investigated, the issue of the organic has been discussed both in some interesting reinterpretations of and in some radical departures from the Romantic understanding of the term. In a seminal 1952 essay titled "To the Laodiceans," Randall Jarrell pays tribute to Frost's unique perspective and speaks directly to the unity and profound wisdom to be found in some of the poet's finest works, even the lesser-known ones. Indeed, the very title of Jarrell's piece indicates the argument he proffers, as it is a biblical reference to the Laodicean Church, which, in the book of Revelation, is chastised for being "lukewarm" and indifferent to religion. In more general terms, this indifference can be extended to mean an apathy toward all aspects of human life, both practical and spiritual, a point of contention for some of

Frost's critics who grapple with the seemingly inherent contradictions found in many of his poems.

For Jarrell, whose work long predates the postmodern debate regarding indeterminacy in language, a careful reading of Frost does indeed offer a way out of humankind's essential predicament. Jarrell identifies the essential quandary in Frost's poems as centered on three obsessive concerns: isolation, extinction, and, most important, the inescapable fact of human beings' ultimate limitation in gaining access to the unknown. Though Frost's language is quite straightforward and shorn of rhetorical embellishments, Jarrell maintains that Frost teaches the attentive reader how to accept the limitations of human life by staying in the moment and deciding on a course of action, however flawed it may be, that has the potential to bring the individual a degree of happiness or, at least, peace with the world he or she inhabits. As discussed below, Jarrell contends that it is the structure of Frost's poems, more so than the language, that forms the crux of his argument, suggesting that structure itself becomes the predominant metaphor.

Furthermore, it is interesting to note that inasmuch as Frost has been aligned with the Romantic tradition, especially as represented by Wordsworth and Emerson, his poetry does not espouse a transcendental consolation in nature or a promise of deferred fulfillment in the divine. In Frost, human beings remain firmly rooted in the mundane world of common experience, where they stay riveted to the very same questions they are destined never to understand, as illustrated in "Neither Out Far nor In Deep." Here, as Jarrell points out, we stay fixated on the sea, on "the hypnotic monotony of the universe that is incommensurable with us—everything into which we look neither very far nor very deep, but look, look just the same," for Frost accepts the condition that we must persevere despite not knowing certain fundamental answers (540).

In another poem, "Provide, Provide," Frost acknowledges that one must accommodate oneself to certain harsh and irrefutable realities in order to find some acceptable way of living within an all-too-mortal existence. One can either die prematurely, and thereby avoid the pitfalls of precarious fame and fortune, or become defiant, determining to live as boldly as possible, albeit in a less exalted status than one might wish for. "Better to go down dignified/ With boughten friendship at your side/ Than none at all. Provide, provide!" (20-21). This last line is a simple exhortation to live as wisely as possible in the here and now. Jarrell declares the poem "an immortal masterpiece" (561).

As to the issue of structure as metaphor, the poem "Time Out" is a brilliant example of how Frost thematizes structure to emphasize the need of the individual, in the passionate quest for the truth, to be mindful of the facile and deceptive answers in "the obstinately gentle air" (12), to find joy in the freedom to remonstrate with oneself, and to take the time to discover new approaches to understanding:

> It took that pause to make him realize
> The mountain he was climbing had the slant
> As of a book held up before his eyes
> (And was a text albeit done in plant).
>
> (1-4)

Indeed, Frost is advising his readers to be actively engaged in questioning the world they inhabit, to understand that their lives and happiness are constituted by individual acts of interpretation.

For Jarrell, Frost offers us the wisdom of mortal existence, for his poems present the world as it is and for what it is, a place where one has freedom of choice despite constraints. Thus, in his own unique way, Frost gives us a prescription for happiness and celebrates the human spirit in its infinite moods; as Jarrell puts it: "To have this whole range of being treated with so much humor and sadness and composure, with such plain truth; . . . to have the parts of the world recreated, related, presented with the authority of exact realization . . . to make us forget the limitations and excesses and baseness that these days seem unforgettable" (561).

In his 1958 book *The Dimensions of Robert Frost*, Reginald L. Cook identifies Frost with the organic on three distinct levels—within his identity as a poet, within his individual poems, and within his poetic career. For Cook, the organic work of art is one that is aligned with and sympathetic toward nature, exhibits a reverence for natural forms and colors, and is opposed to the geometrical, the central characteristics of which are symbolic, unrealistic, and unnatural, as in the poetry of Eliot or Pound. Cook does state, however, that these opposing attitudes can sometimes be fused within a particular poem. For Cook, Frost demonstrates an ability to observe humankind and nature with a keen eye and to infuse his observations with beauty, thereby raising human consciousness—a talent that, according to Cook, marks Frost as an organic poet. Among the poems Cook references is "My November Guest," a very puzzling poem since one cannot be at all certain whom the speaker is addressing. The speaker may be addressing an actual person, but the poem might also be self-reflexive as the speaker tries to accommodate himself to the sorrow of autumn. Similarly, it is difficult to tell whether this person or feeling is welcomed by the speaker or seen as an intrusion.

Additionally, Cook maintains that in addition to Frost's finely honed sensibilities toward his surroundings, the poet's reserve is yet another characteristic that aligns him with the organic. That his poems leave something unspoken and submerged prompts Cook to label Frost a "synecdochist," a term referring to a figure of speech in which a part of something is made to refer to its whole. Furthermore, Cook asserts that a truth emerges when one experiences a Frost poem, as the object in the poem is natural and direct rather than representative of something other than itself. According to Cook, this "mysterious" aspect of Frost's poetry is a manifestation of an inner rapture, wherein the poet takes delight in such things as pondering unharvested apples lying on the ground, the movements of a moth in winter, an alder swamp, or autumn rain. Cook argues that this inner rapture makes Frost a classicist rather than a Romantic whose poetry, like Wordsworth's, is associated with an outpouring of emotions. Nevertheless, it is interesting to note that Cook cannot quite escape the resemblances between Frost and Wordsworth as he alludes to a line from the latter's "Tintern Abbey" when he describes Frost's ability "to look into the life of things."

With respect to the organic nature of Frost's individual poems, Cook maintains that it is created through a combination of inspired simplicity, directness, sympathetic understanding, and detachment. In "A Young Birch," form functions like nature: the tree is an object of beauty that embodies the creative impulse in both nature and humans and that unites the world of natural phenomena and the world of humankind. As a further illustration of this point, Cook argues that such works as *A Masque of Mercy* compose themselves as they unfold, infused with a dynamic life force, and that they continue to grow of their own accord with unexpected insights, ultimately becoming aware of their origins. As Keeper says in *A Masque of Mercy*:

> When a great tide of argument sweeps in
> My small fresh water spring gets drowned of course.
> But when the brine goes back as go it must
> I can count on my source to spring again
> Not even brackish from its salt experience.
> No true source can be poisoned.
>
> (542)

Once again, Cook refers back to Wordsworth in stating that Frost's creative ability is similar to the process in *The Prelude* wherein the poet "evoked the sky spirit of his heart" (77). Finally, with respect to all of Frost's poems, Cook states that they participate in the organic process in that they reflect the poet's maturation, as early themes can be seen evolving and changing throughout Frost's career. Because Frost's subject matter is not cornered into a private meaning or mythological system, his poems are accessible and the reader is thus able to judge and evaluate the poet's progress.

In *Human Values in the Poetry of Robert Frost* (1960), George W. Nitchie renders an oppositional reading of Frost in finding that his poetry lacks the integrity and wholeness that prior critics have acclaimed. Nitchie's complaint is that Frost's poems end equivocally and thereby fail to offer any clear statement of principles. Nitchie in fact takes this argument to an extreme by comparing Keats's concept of negative capability, the ability to be at ease with doubt and uncertainty, with Frost's avoidance of any precise theory of nature or how human beings should relate to the natural world, unable to accommodate himself to Keats's doctrine of inconclusiveness. Nitchie states, "Paradoxically or not, one of the cardinal errors according to Frost's scheme of values is going against nature or natural processes; at least, man does so at his peril" (7). What is most interesting in Nitchie's counterreading of the organic principle in Frost is his unique application of the term "organic." Stating that "nature" for Frost is a "protean" and therefore unstable term, Nitchie defines nature as split between organic and inorganic aspects. The organic aspects are essentially the tangible elements—such as meadows, flowers, and birches—and are subject to human control. These are distinguished from the intangible, inorganic aspects, the immortal forces in nature—such as the wind and the motion of a stream—which are "radically other" and therefore out of human reach. These immortal forces are exemplified in Frost's poem "There Are Roughly Zones," in which the foolhardy wish to grow a peach tree in the cold New England climate is pitted against the inorganic, indomitable will of nature. The speaker recognizes the human being's refusal to accept that there are forces beyond human reach, saying, "What comes over a man, is it soul or mind—/ That to no limits and bounds he can stay confined?"

There is also a further consequence of applying Nitchie's paradigm of the natural world, namely, that any moral to be garnered from Frost's poetry is highly ambiguous. However, this claim is countered in John Lynen's 1960 discussion of Frost's pastoral poems. Nitchie's reading of "The Exposed Nest," in which a man and child attempt to protect a group of young birds from the sun by building an artificial screen without knowing whether their efforts have been in vain, again illustrates his point that, for Frost, there are no ethical guidelines by which to judge one's behavior toward nature. For Nitchie, the simplicity of nature is a strategy for Frost because the phenomena of nature "do not require an elaborate philosophical apparatus for their apprehension; they are simply there, and though we are free to define our relationship with them in philosophical terms, we are not compelled to" (13). Nevertheless, Nitchie does equivocate at times in admitting of instances in which humankind defies these same inorganic powers and emerges as an equal, if not victorious, force. Nitchie's reading of "On a Tree Fallen Across the Road" is such an instance; he acknowledges that the poem points toward human beings' persistence against the intractability of nature.

In *The Pastoral Art of Robert Frost*, Lynen discusses Frost's poetry in the context of classical pastoral poetry and identifies Frost's unique application of this ancient genre. Briefly summarized, the classical genre of an ideal rustic world is based on a series of oppositions between country and city, with the former seen as an insular environment inhabited by naïve and innocent people who are self-sufficient in comparison to the sophisticated, worldly inhabitants of the urban world, whose labor is complex and often corrupt. In other words, there is always an implicit tension between the pastoral world and the city; furthermore, the contrasts that are drawn are meant to teach the reader the virtues of the pastoral world. The pastoral is thus also didactic, an element that Lynen maintains is present in Frost's lessons of humility. In other respects, however, Frost is outside the pastoral literary tradition, as his poems have none of the trappings of Arcadian myth, which envisions the rural as a utopia in which human beings and nature live in harmony with each other. Indeed, Lynen states that the pastoral poem offers Frost a structure or framework only, as the poet refrains from incorporating the traditional content of the pastoral.

At the same time, Lynen attempts to locate Frost's unique position within the modern school and finds that, although the poet has widespread appeal among both popular and professional audiences, critics have not paid sufficient attention to Frost's poems, instead preferring to concentrate on his biography and the New England personalities depicted in his work. As to Frost's diverse appeal to many audiences, Lynen believes it is precisely because his poetry is written in a clear style, employing a language that is easy and accessible, that Frost's work is so well received; it has much in common with Wordsworth's and stands in sharp contrast to the difficult and esoteric style of some contemporaries. Nevertheless, Lynen states that this simplicity is deceptive.

Finally, it should be noted that as Lynen focuses on the unity within the pastoral poem and its unique status within Frost's work, he offers yet another definition of what constitutes the organic poem. The short lyric of "The Pasture" illustrates many of Lynen's points. It is written as an invitation to look at the simple beauty of a young calf as it tries to stand on its own, and it thus operates as an invitation to the reader to become initiated into Frost's way of seeing farm life. Lyman writes, "For all its sweetness the poem is not tainted by sentimentality, because it describes the charming aspects of the pasture, it is concerned less with beauty for its own sake than with the organic wholeness which makes this beauty meaningful" (22). Additionally, Lynen reads "Stopping by Woods on a Snowy Evening" as a poem that far transcends its rural setting by presenting a conflict within the speaker as he is torn between his responsibilities and his desire to lose himself in the sensuous beauty of a wintry landscape. More important for Lynen, beyond the present conflict within the speaker, the poem speaks to the larger and more profound questions of the purpose of human existence and the ultimate destination of humankind. According to Lynen, the reader arrives at these more universal themes by returning to such details as the horse's lack of understanding as to why the man has stopped, underscoring the difference between the natural and human worlds as well as the human "love of reverie." In another poem, "Pan with Us," the Greek god of shepherds and flocks, who in classical myths freely roams and hunts in the unsullied wilderness while playing his pipes and chasing nymphs, now walks about a deserted countryside. Moreover, Pan's familiar rustic music has been replaced by "the blue jay's screech/ And the whimper of hawks beside the sun" (18-19) while the "pipes of pagan mirth" (26) have become "raveled," entangled, and confused as the idyllic pastoral countryside has likewise disintegrated.

In *The Poetry of Robert Frost: Constellations of Intention* (1963), Reuben A. Brower continues the discussion of Frost's relationship to Wordsworth and Emerson and identifies Frost as both a pastoral poet and a poet of restraint. With respect to the poet's relationship to Wordsworth and Emerson, Brower maintains that both of these predecessors had trouble admitting their doubts about nature, stating that the poet of "Tintern Abbey" had trouble clinging to a faded vision, "with gleams of half-extinguished thought," and was focused on recalling the past as a source of consolation (41). Emerson's "The Sphinx," according to Brower, exhibits "a lack of clarity as to whether the riddle of nature has surely been answered" (41). By way of contrast, Brower sees Frost as a poet of the present moment for whom nature is no longer a source of solace but, rather, something to be reckoned with. Brower sees this reckoning with the realities of nature, an acceptance of both its harsh and its benign aspects, as Frost's rejection of the Romantic vision; he cites a line from "Hyla Brook" in which Frost acknowledges that nature's laws sometimes cannot provide for all of human beings' wishes and needs: "By June our brook's run out of song" (1).

With respect to Frost's revision of the pastoral, Brower points out that Frost was greatly influenced by Virgil's eclogues, or short, bucolic dialogue poems. As the first classical poet to use the pastoral as a vehicle for social criticism and to allow elements of contemporary reality to intrude into his idyllic world, Virgil introduced important innovations that greatly affected the genre in subsequent ages. Brower finds the dramatic dialogue in "The Death of the Hired Man" to be the most authentic instance of Frost's incorporation of Virgil. Character grows out of this poem because the voices of husband and wife are kept clear and distinct. While Mary's personality is punctuated by hesitant pauses and a constant searching for the precise word, Warren's character is marked by defensiveness and selfish interests as he is much more concerned with how Silas could possibly help him than he is with the plight of the sickly old man. Warren's diction is abrupt, his reasoning self-serving and without compassion. Brower's point is that the real drama here is the dialogue between husband and wife. The tragic ending, when Warren finds Silas has died in his sleep, is not really the focal point of the poem; rather, it is Warren's seemingly gradual recognition that Silas might have more of a claim on him and his wife than on his own brother, though this claim remains only a possibility to Warren, not a certainty.

In the decades since Brower's book appeared, greater critical attention has turned to such theoretical questions as the nature of gender roles and relationships in Frost's poetry, Frost's very prominent place in American politics, and the role of science in Frost's poetry. Critics have also become more deeply engaged with the complexity beneath Frost's ostensibly simple poetic language. In response to those earlier critics who faulted Frost for being noncommittal, Richard Poirier focuses on the deceptive simplicity of Frost's poetry and argues that the poet's genius is precisely his inimitable talent for cloaking highly complex ideas in very simple language. Poirier begins his essay titled "Choices" by setting forth the many difficulties in interpreting Frost's poems, a process that requires the attentive reader to listen carefully to the poet's all-but-silent allusions to Herbert, Milton, Yeats, Emerson, and William James and his concealment of essential or jarring implications in otherwise innocent expressions. Indeed, for Poirier, the most interesting and consequential issue in Frost is the interpretive process itself, a process that requires the reader to discover a multiplicity of meanings that lie submerged beneath the most mundane signs and a recognition that this evasiveness varies from poem to poem. Poirier further points out that, for Frost, the poem is a created thing, and its truth is revealed in the course of the reader's experiencing the poem. An example is the poem "The Investment," the very title of which suggests that something of great value—whether money, time, emotion, or perhaps all three—has been expended, though the reader is left to speculate on what exactly it is. As the farmworker listens to the sound of a piano coming from an old, recently refurbished house, he can only wonder whether the music and fresh paint are the products of a newly acquired affluence, a youthful romanticism, or an old marriage determined to escape its own monotony. Indeed, Poirier's perceptive analysis of Frost's work is a further expansion of the exploration of the organic nature of his poems as highlighted by earlier critics.

In her 1998 book *Robert Frost and Feminine Literary Tradition*, Karen L. Kilcup seeks to correct what she believes has been a critical oversight in Frost criticism, namely that, until recently, the poet has been seen within the context of a very narrow masculine literary history. It is Kilcup's aim to show that Frost was indeed influenced by popular women writers, with whose work he was familiar since childhood, as well as other writers, both male and female, whose poetry is written in a more sentimental or feminine idiom. Kilcup further states that, despite the evidence of Frost's questionable statements about women in his letters, her intention is to broaden the critical scope of Frost's work by identifying the feminine perspective to be found in so many of his poems. Two such influences that Kilcup mentions are Lucy Larcom (1824-93), a Massachusetts nature poet and teacher of Frost's lifelong advocate, Susan Hayes Ward, and Henry David Thoreau, whose nature writings (*Walden*, 1854, and his posthumous *Journal*, 1906) exhibit a strong feminine idiom. While Larcom's sentimental poem "Swinging on a Birch-Tree" would appear to bear little resemblance to Frost's meditative "Birches," Kilcup notes several resemblances, including the idea that those who swing on birches require safety nets while simultaneously declaring their bold independence. Larcom and Frost demonstrate a similar talent in being able to convey an experience that is entirely accessible.

Citing "Home Burial" as a drama of emptiness and sterility, Katherine Kearns, another feminist critic, points out a familiar situation and iconography in Frost in which a woman wants to flee a depressing environment while her husband remains pathetic in his failure to understand that she is running not from him but from the loss of her child and the cruelty of gazing on the child's grave site through her window. Kearns further points out that the childlike posture the wife assumes is a gesture of sexual denial. "Her egress from the house will be a symbolic verification of her husband's impotence, and . . . the house will rot as the best birch fence will rot," Kearns concludes (193).

Inasmuch as Frost had a lifelong interest in farming and the rural life of New England, he also had a deep interest in science and nature, and indeed his work has often been compared to that of Lucretius, the Roman classical author of *De rerum natura*, or *On the Nature of Things*. Frost's engagement with scientific ideas has long been a topic of critical interest. In particular, Frost was familiar with the work of Charles Darwin, which in turn influenced his pastoral poems as well as his insights into human beings' relationships with one another as well as with the physical world. By way of introduction, Robert Bernard Hass, in his 2002 book *Going by Contraries*, points out that Frost lived in an America where science and technology were becoming predominant. At the same time, science was creating a spiritual void that challenged older, romantic notions about nature's transcendent powers. Frost understood both the consequences of this shift and the necessity of finding a new way to phrase his questions. In his discussion of "The Demiurge's Laugh," Hass takes in the utter hopelessness of the poem's speaker, who has lost complete control over the physical universe to a mocking deity. Hass maintains that, here, the speaker is in the desperate world of Dante's *Inferno*, but he also credits Frost with having risen to the occasion of the twentieth century's spiritual and aesthetic crisis as he sought to counter the claims of science by urging poets to approach their material with increased intellectual rigor. One way in which he did this was by eschewing the various poetic experiments practiced by such modernists as Pound, Eliot, William Carlos Williams, and Marianne Moore, who placed an overwhelming emphasis on images and impersonality. For Frost, the twentieth-century poet was charged with the task of elevating poetry to a rational authority that could offer its own insight into the grand design.

Finally, Richard Calhoun offers a perspective on the status of Frost criticism in "The Sonnets of Robert Frost at the Millennium" (2004). While Calhoun believes that Frost's reputation has overcome the aftermath of Lawrance Thompson's very unflattering biography, he devotes his essay to Frost's sonnets, asserting that the sonnet is a form in which the poet demonstrates considerable but as yet unrecognized craftsmanship. Citing Frost's statements in "The Figure a Poem Makes" regarding the balance of form against a vague longing for "wildness," Calhoun maintains that the very concise structure of the sonnet was the perfect vehicle through which Frost could exert control over his poem while at the same time having a chance to resist conforming to convention. Calhoun points out that Frost's sonnets are at times unbalanced, exhibiting a tension between the need for form and the desire for a freedom from structure. A case in point for Calhoun is "The Oven Bird," a poem that he interprets as Frost's acknowledgment that scientific thinking has reduced imagination to a "diminished thing." Calhoun writes, "The oven bird, a midsummer bird, comes late to song, and it sings not from the darkest, deepest woods but from midway into the woods" (229).

Works Cited

Brower, Reuben A. *The Poetry of Robert Frost: Constellations of Intention*. New York: Oxford UP, 1963.

Calhoun, Richard. "The Sonnets of Robert Frost at the Millennium." *Roads Not Taken: Rereading Robert Frost*. Ed. Earl J. Cox and Jonathan N. Barron. Columbia: U of Missouri P, 2004. 217-35.

Cook, Reginald L. *The Dimensions of Robert Frost*. New York: Rinehart, 1958.

Cox, James M., ed. *Robert Frost: A Collection of Critical Essays*. Englewood Cliffs, NJ: Prentice-Hall, 1962.

Garnett, Edward. "A New American Poet." *The Atlantic Monthly* Aug. 1915.

Hass, Robert Bernard. *Going by Contraries: Robert Frost's Conflict with Science.* Charlottesville: UP of Virginia, 2002.

Jarrell, Randall. "To the Laodiceans." *Kenyon Review* 14.4 (1952): 535-61.

Jones, Llewellyn. "Robert Frost." *First Impressions: Essays on Poetry, Criticism, and Prosody.* Freeport, NY: Books for Libraries Press, 1925.

Kearns, Katherine. "'The Place of the Asylum': Women and Nature in Robert Frost's Poetry." *American Literature* 59.2 (1987): 190-210.

Kilcup, Karen L. *Robert Frost and Feminine Literary Tradition.* Ann Arbor: U of Michigan P, 1998.

Lowell, Amy. *Tendencies in Modern American Poetry.* Boston: Houghton Mifflin, 1926.

Lynen, John F. *The Pastoral Art of Robert Frost.* New Haven, CT: Yale UP, 1960.

Munson, Gorham. *Robert Frost: A Study in Sensibility and Good Sense.* Port Washington, NY: Kennikat Press, 1927.

Newdick, Robert. "Robert Frost and the Sound of Sense." *American Literature* 9 (1937): 289-300.

Nitchie, George W. *Human Values in the Poetry of Robert Frost: A Study of Poetic Convictions.* Durham, NC: Duke UP, 1960.

Poirier, Richard. "Choices." *Robert Frost: The Work of Knowing.* New York: Oxford UP, 1977.

Thompson, Lawrance. *Fire and Ice: The Art and Thought of Robert Frost.* New York: Russell & Russell, 1942.

Untermeyer, Louis. *Modern American Poetry: A Critical Anthology.* New York: Harcourt, Brace, 1921.

Van Doren, Mark. "The Permanence of Robert Frost." *The Private Reader: Selected Articles and Reviews.* New York: Henry Holt, 1942. 87-96.

Wilson, James S. "Robert Frost: American Poet." *Virginia Quarterly Review* 7 (1931): 316-20.

Woodring, Carl. "Introduction." *Politics in English Romantic Poetry.* Cambridge, MA: Harvard UP, 1970.

Technology, Labor, and the Sacred:
The Cultural Context of Robert Frost_____

Jamey Hecht

Nineteenth-Century American Poetry

In 1844, Ralph Waldo Emerson published an essay titled "The Poet." It called for a break from European culture and advocated the development of a new American literary movement whose democratic spirit would expunge the traces of feudalism that still haunted the British mind and its "genteel" American offshoot. Emerson's call founded what today is commonly thought of as American literature, and though Emerson ended his essay on a note of yearning and doubt—"I seek in vain for the Poet I describe"—within a few years he was walking beside this very poet on Boston Common. Emerson's famous words to Walt Whitman in a letter of July 21, 1855, were "I greet you at the beginning of a great career." Whitman was not the only writer to begin a long and profitable career during this decade, however; most readers of F. O. Matthiessen's *American Renaissance: Art and Expression in the Age of Emerson and Whitman* are inclined to agree that American literature finally came into its own as Henry David Thoreau, Nathaniel Hawthorne, and Herman Melville all began writing their major works between 1850 and 1855.

While Anne Bradstreet, Edward Taylor, and other seventeenth-century poets had extended a Puritan consciousness from its origins in Britain across the Atlantic to New England, they did not fundamentally change the old, pre-Romantic European vision of what poetry was or what it could and could not do.[1] And though there were plenty of exceptions, the period between the end of the Civil War and the onset of literary modernism in the years leading up to World War I has come to be regarded as an artistic disappointment. Though the Fireside Poets—Henry Wadsworth Longfellow, William Cullen Bryant, John Greenleaf Whittier, James Russell Lowell, and Oliver Wendell Holmes—were vastly popular in their day, that day is long gone; their works are rarely read today by anyone except scholars and obscurantists. Their substantial influence on Robert Frost, who sometimes borrowed from their stock of subjects and their prosody, is among the last echoes of their once-giant presence within the American literary scene.[2]

Whitman brought to American poetry an astonishing depth of technical innovation as well as an equally deep passion for the vocation of the poet. *Leaves of Grass* (1855) enlarged the scope of poetry far beyond the often decorative, elitist, or sentimental verse of the Fireside Poets. Clearly, Whitman influenced some later writers, such as William Carlos Williams and Hart Crane, more directly than others, such as T. S. Eliot, and though Frost did not emulate Whitman's technique, he did at times assume the Whitmanian persona of the poet as working-class sage.

Like Shelley before him, Whitman was able to integrate the microcosm of the self with the macrocosm of the universe and connect both of these with the domain in between—namely, the polity, represented in the form of utopian social hope. In the prose of *Democratic Vistas* (1871) and the poetry of *Leaves of Grass*, he blended the wordless mysticism of his inner life with the worship of an amorphous and grandiose entity he called "Democracy." The expansive, almost manic spirit of his verse was expressed in a nonrhyming line much longer than the traditional iambic pentameter line could reach. By contrast, a look at the works of the Fireside Poets immediately reveals their captivity to rhyme and, more important, to a facile and almost unvarying meter that caused Emerson to refer to Edgar Allan Poe as "the jingle man." Whitman's eventual fame swept all that away. There is something to be said for the generalization that after the Whitmanian revolution in American poetics, rhyme in English-language poetry was not fully redeemed until a generation later in the work of Robert Frost.[3]

Poetic Modernism

When Frost was born in 1874, the Civil War had been over for less than a decade, Whitman and Emerson were old but very much alive, and most of the United States still lacked electricity. The nation had not yet outpaced Germany in economic activity, and the American transition toward an industrial economy was just beginning. Later in Frost's lifetime came World War I and the rise of modernist poetics. Difficult, learned, and far more admiring of pre-Enlightenment Europe than of modern America, the modernist works of poets such as Ezra Pound and T. S. Eliot did not impress Frost. Not only was this poetry inaccessible to the common reader, it was also frank in its condemnation of the culture that produced it. Pound famously referred to twentieth-century European civilization and its American offshoot as an "old bitch, gone in the teeth."

As we will see, Frost, too, was critical of the new world of industrialization, global warfare, and social regimentation; but, unlike Eliot and Pound, Frost was no nihilist. He managed his anxiety about the fate of humankind—which got harder after the destruction of World War I and harder still after World War II ended with nuclear attacks—by continually developing and rearranging his ideas about the human predicament. Frost's admirers have called this process growth, but other readers have been more critical; the once-famous literary critic Yvor Winters condemned it as "metaphysical drifting." Still, critics have argued that, compared to Frost, the modernists began and ended as doctrinaire pedants: Eliot eventually became a fervent Anglican, and Pound built a vast edifice of interlocking ideologies that he regarded as so absolutely true and obvious as to make fools of those who disagreed with him (for example, Pound explained the title of one of his own later poetry collections, *Rock-Drill* [1955], by saying that nothing else could get through other people's thick skulls).

Frost met both of these poets in England while living there with his family in 1912 and searching for the literary success he had not yet found in America.[4] Though Frost returned to his own country less than three years later, the English interval proved crucial to Frost's career: he received both popular and critical acclaim for the two books he published there, *A Boy's Will* (1913) and *North of Boston* (1914). It is fitting, if ironic, that three of the most important American poets of the period met in the very country from whose cultural womb American poetry had had to escape for its birth. From that vantage point, they were better able to appreciate the enormity and impact of World War I, and, like many expatriates, they were forced to consider and reconsider what their own national origin meant to them.

Labor and Technology

In general it was the younger poets of the period who either, like Wilfred Owen, directly addressed the subject of war or, like Eliot and Pound, lamented a general loss of meaning and purpose in Western culture, of which the war was both a symptom and a cause. References to the war in Robert Frost's poetry are generally oblique: he seems to see it as an extension of the violence inherent in the industrial economy. Frost's work poems are concrete and can be read literally, with a minimum of interpretation; yet they are also highly suggestive of deeper issues that require metaphorical reading. This is a factor in his remarkable popularity, since naïve as well as sophisticated readers (who are, of course, often the same persons at different stages of life) find them gratifying.

Frost's poems of work can be sorted into those that celebrate and even glorify preindustrial manual labor (e.g., mowing, picking apples, chopping wood, building haystacks, and hoeing) and those that confront and lament the brutal power of industrial machines, large or small (e.g., the power saw, the mill, and the newly ubiquitous telephone pole he called "a barkless specter" ["An Encounter" 14]). People came to expect this of Frost. "They like," he told interviewer Richard Poirier in 1960, "to hear me say nasty things about machines." By 1960, of course, those machines and the ethos they represented had become so pervasive and entrenched that an intelligent artistic attack on them was becoming a strange and valuable experience. The great Russian poet Joseph Brodsky, coauthor of *Homage to Robert Frost*, related in an interview how during World War II the U.S. military issued an armed-services edition of Frost's poems to American soldiers—people living and working in the heart of industrialized war—and remarked "and they liked it a hell of a lot, yes?" ("Robert Frost").

It is important to note that Frost's deep ambivalence toward modern technology and its social consequences did not constitute a thorough rejection or an uncritical nostalgia for a vanishing past. Frost was too smart and too sane to divide his world in such a stark manner. Instead, Frost's critique bears on the way new technologies and their wealthy beneficiaries had begun to intrude into what might have remained (and, to a small degree, has remained) a traditional society of self-reliance, cautious but genuine fellowship, and respect for the sublimity of nature. "Out, Out—" is the strongest and most horrifying of these poems. Taking its title from one of the most nihilistic passages in Shakespeare, Macbeth's despairing speech upon learning of his wife's death, the poem depicts an industrial accident in which a boy dies after his hand becomes entangled with a buzz saw. Although a kind of conscious agency is tentatively attributed to the machine, Frost is exceedingly deliberate in his refusal to demonize it. The saw "Leaped out at the boy's hand, or seemed to leap—/ He must have given the hand. However it was,/ Neither refused the meeting . . ." (16-18). The personal nature of the boy's death has a gravity that makes the reader reluctant to connect it to any larger issue. But then, immediately after we learn that the boy has died, the last two lines toss compassion aside: "No more to build on there. And they, since they/ Were not the one dead, turned to their affairs" (33-34).[5]

Though we may be appalled at the way "they" turn away from any mourning and back toward their own affairs, we do the same; we have to, because, like the boy's life, the poem is over. If we have the coldness to consider the phrase "No more to build on there" in a social sense rather than a strictly personal one, it seems like a verdict on the vanishing nonindustrial world and life, the semiobsolete "manus" in the word "manufacturing."

Absence and the Sacred

In a later poem, "New Hampshire," Frost writes "Nothing not built with hands of course is sacred" (394). Taken together with the finality of the hand's loss in the earlier poem, this claim would seem to force us to choose among a limited range of alternatives (an obligation that Frost, in a somewhat different context, calls "a narrow choice the age insists on" ["New Hampshire" 404]): turning away from the sacred in favor of some competing value, as Wallace Stevens did in exalting "the imagination"; retreating into traditional institutions regardless of their distance from new conditions, as T. S. Eliot did when he became a pious Anglican or Robert Lowell did during his brief conversion to Catholicism; searching for new avenues of access to the sacred that would not require the survival of old folkways, Hart Crane's program in his magnificent work *The Bridge* (1930); or genuflecting to the sacred as immanent in the strictly natural world without yearning to transcend nature, as Robinson Jeffers did. With a versatility reminiscent of Emerson, Frost experimented with each of these options, and he can hardly be identified with one alone. The famous line from "Mowing" is as clear yet enigmatic as any Zen koan: "The fact is the sweetest dream that labor knows." Here fact and dream are yoked together, baffling the intellect like the paradoxical discourse of mysticism. Dylan Thomas uses this same strategy in "Poem on His Birthday" (1952):

> Heaven that never was
> Nor will be ever is always true,
> And, in that brambled void,
> Plenty as blackberries in the woods
> The dead grow for His joy
>
> (50-54)

Frost seems as ambivalent about the power of the sacred as he is about modernity's incredibly powerful machines.

Like "Out, Out—," the longer and somewhat earlier poem "The

Self-Seeker" is a heartbreaking evocation of the way the new machines of modern industry can diminish and destroy human lives. There, too, body parts are lost—feet this time—because of an accident involving a machine to which a strange kind of agency is attributed: "the belt," says the injured man about a dangerous part of the mill, "doesn't love me much" (33). Unlike "Out, Out—," this poem contains a speaker who represents industrial capital (the corporation's lawyer, who pays off the injured man and says, "We're very sorry for you" [230]) and another who impotently defies it (the hurt man's friend, who responds, "Who's *we*?—some stockholders in Boston?" [232]). "The Self-Seeker" appeared in *North of Boston* in 1914, the first year of World War I. The horror of the war raised the stakes of Frost's urgent question—"Who's *we*?"—and generated several different answers,[6] none of which seems to have fully satisfied Frost.

Immediately following "The Self-Seeker," as if juxtaposed to it for contrast, Frost placed "The Wood-Pile," an homage to manual labor with especial love for its nonrational nature. Little could be further from the strictly regimented factory where the new assembly lines produced wealth for a few and misery and bodily harm for many. Even as Frost was writing the poems of *A Boy's Will* and *North of Boston*, Frederick Winslow Taylor's *The Principles of Scientific Management* (1911) was prescribing a new system of surveillance and discipline that would come to dominate the American workplace during this decade. Taylorism blurred the distinction between dehumanized, deskilled workers on one side and blind, amoral machines on the other. Frost, in contrast, is at times deliberately ambiguous about the degree of agency that a tool or a house or a machine can be said to have, and his thought points backward to a Romantic, and even archaic, panpsychism as well as forward to a future of total industrialization in which free human agency has been usurped by a utilitarian regime of mechanical power.

The manual labor of "The Wood-Pile," "The Tuft of Flowers," "Mowing," and "After Apple-Picking" is a principle of connection to the earth, to the past, and to the reality of other people. This is perhaps clearest in "The Tuft of Flowers," in which the poem's titular flowers nourish the spirit with beauty. Like the flowers that the amateur botanist of "The Self-Seeker" loved so much but could no longer reach, this unmowed tuft is a figure for "sheer morning gladness winking at the brim" (28). In typical Frostian fashion, however, the self is closest to the other when the other is not present: "'Men work together,' I told him from the heart,/ 'Whether they work together or apart'" (39-40). This revelatory moment arises only because the previous worker has left the scene, leaving some of the work undone, and that for aesthetic, not practical, reasons. The spared tuft of flowers can bear plenty of interpersonal human meaning without any effort or strain because it is not mere description: it is still a real object, rooted in the earth. Just so, the hidden layers of a Frost poem are not merely matters for literary criticism: the subtext is still the poem. In "New Hampshire," Frost writes: "The only decent tree had been to mill/ And educated into boards" (376-77).[7] The spared tuft of flowers can be seen as representing the almost accidental survival of that which modernity threatens to obliterate: poetry itself, manual labor, and the bits of old New England that remain wooded or hand-farmed. In the terms coined by critic Raymond Williams, these are "residual" elements of the past, which are spared by the otherwise decimating "emergent" new world of unprecedented energies at unprecedented scales.[8]

Regionalism

Though he eventually became a well-traveled, national figure and perhaps the best-loved poet in the United States, the California-born Frost turned himself into a New Englander and remained one. Unlike southerners such as John Crowe Ransom and Allen Tate, who championed a lost rural America while also licking wounds left by the Civil War, when Frost wrote about rural New England he was paying homage to a form of life, not to the history of a region per se.[9] The title poem of his fourth book, "New Hampshire" (1923), includes some apparently provincial boosterism, but a closer reading shows as much mockery as tribute, if not more. The poem makes a virtue of New Hampshire's dearth of natural resources, repeatedly using the phrase "commercial quantities" to suggest that commerce is somehow tainted: "The having anything to sell is what/ Is the disgrace in man or state or nation" (7-8). Though it might suit a ruined European aristo- crat, this is an unusual attitude for an American to espouse, and as soon as Frost articulates it his reader should detect the satirical element of the poet's intentions.

Frost's New England was like a lens through which he focused a vi- sion of the universe—and yet, apropos of this poet's Emersonian cast of mind, the converse is equally true: it was, indeed, New England through which Frost chose to focus the observations, emotions, and ideas that constituted his worldview. Though Frost reciprocated Ran- som's admiration, even accepting an invitation to visit him at Vander- bilt University and lecture there in 1922, his spontaneous accord with the Southern Agrarians ultimately had little to do with geography and nothing to do with participation in their group. While they all shared mixed feelings about the triumphant industrialism of the Northeast, Frost's alternative lay "north of Boston" and theirs south of the Mason- Dixon Line. The California-born Frost chose to affiliate himself with rural New England and chose to do so for deliberately symbolic and cosmopolitan reasons, whereas the Southern Agrarians' identity was rooted in history and not altogether freely chosen.

Robert Penn Warren, an important southern poet who was teaching in Colorado during the mid-1930s when Frost visited there to speak, described the older poet's lectures: "[They] were deeply in harmony with what the Southern Agrarians were saying, although he put every- thing in his own very personal and memorable way, usually playing concepts off one another, pairing them and switching them" (quoted in Parini 298). Everything following the telling concessive conjunction "although" shows Frost at the same Emersonian game of enlightened self-contradiction that he plays in his major poems. This is not just a peculiar manner of speech, the personal idiom of an eccentric: Frost had a deep anxiety about constraints of every kind, especially those that threatened to absorb or diminish his own individuality. In this connection, the poet-critic Randall Jarrell once archly referred to him as "The Only Genuine Robert Frost in Captivity." Movements, ideological systems, groups and clubs, and political parties and affiliations all repulsed him. In the same way, even his successful exploitation of the local culture, flora, and landscape of the region "north of Boston" was a matter for mixed feelings. The first poem in that volume, "Mending Wall," features a benighted neighbor who "moves in darkness as it seems to me,/ Not of woods only and the shade of trees" (41-42).

Further on in this book, "The Mountain" opens with a similar aversion to the dark: "The mountain held the town as in a shadow/ . . ./ I noticed that I missed stars in the west,/ Where its black body cut into the sky" (1, 3-4). The poem's speaker encounters a farmer who, despite having lived in the shadow of the mountain his whole life, has never climbed to the summit. When asked whether a person could walk around it, he replies, "You can drive round and keep in Lunenburg/ But it's as much as ever you can do/ The boundary lines keep in so close to it" (99-101). With a remarkable density, these three lines state and restate the intensity of the farmer's commitment to the land: he is so bound to it that he assumes that the speaker wants to "keep in Lunenburg." But if the speaker only wants to go around the mountain, why should he be anxious to "keep in Lunenburg" throughout the trip? One implied meaning of the phrase is hard to miss: lacking the desire ever to consider leaving his town, the farmer cannot conceive that another may wish to leave. The "boundary lines" that "keep in so close" to the mountain are like the psychic and cultural constraints that have made him not much different from the yoked "white-faced" oxen he drives: "He drew the oxen toward him with light touches/ Of his slim goad on nose and offside flank/ Gave them their marching orders and was moving" (114-16). These particular oxen are not plowing a field at the moment, and we never learn just what their errand is. But the structure suggested is a sort of climbing spiral that never reaches a summit. As the narrator puts it:

> "There ought to be a view around the world
> From such a mountain—if it isn't wooded
> Clear to the top." I saw through leafy screens
> Great granite terraces in sun and shadow,
> Shelves one could rest a knee on getting up—
> With depths behind him sheer a hundred feet. . . .[10]
>
> (58-63)

Though Frost's Lunenburgian speaks of a brook at the peak, he has never actually seen it. The undertone of supernatural mystery and danger surrounding the mountain is strengthened by its name, "Hor," which suggests Mount Horeb, the biblical mountain upon which Abraham nearly sacrificed Isaac.

What, then, is the mountain in "The Mountain"? Death, because it blocks out the western stars; because neither the farmer nor the narrator knows what is at its summit; because the fabled brook has never been seen and it seems impossible for it to be "always cold in summer, warm in winter" (52); and because of the way the narrator defers his intention of going there: "Is that the way to reach the top from here?—/ Not for this morning, but some other time:/ I must be getting back to breakfast now" (37-39). But it is also the hulking, mute fact of the physical world outside of the human mind: "The mountain stood there to be pointed at" (29). The mountain also suggests the labor of a poet's career, traditionally called the "ascent of Mount Parnassus," in the telling phrase "There is no proper path" (41).

Poetic Structures

Many poets of the modernist period, such as Pound, abandoned traditional poetic structures because, like the accumulated centuries of

European architecture, they were destroyed by World War I. As Allen Grossman and others have argued, the subsequent rise of nuclear weapons and the astonishing scale of Nazi atrocities pushed poetic structures further into irony and obsolescence. Frost often used traditional structures anyway, defending his poetic practice by famously remarking that to write free verse is to "play tennis without a net." Yet Frost's whole body of work is shot through with a dialectical interplay between discipline and freedom, security and exposure. As he writes in "Mending Wall," one wants to know what one is "walling in or walling out" (33). And as for the mysterious "something there is that doesn't love a wall" (1), within five years of that poem's publication some 240,000 French buildings had been destroyed in the bombing of World War I. The writing of "Mending Wall" came before the war, while the reading of it came almost entirely after and in a cultural context transformed by astonishing new levels of violence. As Frost is read by new generations in the twenty-first century, the possibility of apocalyptic nuclear violence is still very much a part of human life, but it has been eclipsed by new worries about resource scarcity and environmental degradation, especially global warming. Though our world, and not least the United States, is teeming with new life and new information, our question remains that of Frost's "Oven Bird," posed in our time with a new urgency: "What to make of a diminished thing" (14).

Notes

1. Over the centuries, poetry has competed with philosophy on one hand and religion on the other for the impossible job of satisfying our deepest human needs. In the case of a poet like Taylor, whose work continually extols God from within a particular religious tradition, poetry is in no position to claim sovereignty over that rival. Consider, for example, John Milton's strange mixture of hubris and self-abasement in the Hymn to Urania at the opening of Book VII of *Paradise Lost*. There he is terribly anxious to keep poetry and its spiritual ambitions utterly subordinate to Christian scripture and belief. The opposite attitude, in which poetry is exalted above religion and philosophy, is perhaps best exemplified in the work of Romantic poets such as Percy Bysshe Shelley and, in the United States, Walt Whitman.

2. See Lawrence Buell's "Frost as a New England Poet."

3. Other masters of rhyme in the early twentieth century were Wilfred Owen, whose craft rivaled that of his hero John Keats and who wrote some of the finest (anti)war poetry in the English language until his death in battle only days before the end of World War I; and W. H. Auden, whose consummate use of rhyme can be seen as a victory over the literary dogmas of Ezra Pound.

4. In a 1960 *Paris Review* interview, Frost claimed "I went over there to be poor for a while. Nothing else" (Interview 51). Typical of Frost, this absurd claim seems designed to vex highbrow literati by contradicting their assumptions about the poet and his motivations.

5. "Out, Out—" bears a strong kinship with a later poem of equal or greater fame, W. H. Auden's "Musée des Beaux Arts," which was written soon after the poet's visit to the titular institution in 1938. Each poem considers the death of a boy whose use of prosthetic tools (a power saw as an extension of the hand it destroys; a pair of wings as a hubristic supplement to the earthbound human body) goes horribly wrong. In each case the boy is destroyed and the community moves on.

6. In Russia, for example, the salient criterion for a shared identity was class, as realized in the October Revolution of 1917. In post-World War I Germany, a xenophobic "blood and soil" movement took root, and its pursuit of *Lebensraum* ("room for living"—that is, other people's depopulated lands) set the stage for bloody expansionism. In the United States, the social progress of Reconstruction had been wiped out and replaced by Jim Crow laws segregating "Negroes" from "whites"; these anticipated the "Jewish Laws" of Nazi Germany by several decades. Still, despite his focus on ordinary rural and industrial workers, Frost refused to elevate class over nation, a strategy that he thought could tear the country apart. Despite his celebrity as the quintessential American poet, however, texts like "The Self-Seeker" show class as an often-bitter division within that nation.

7. This is an ancient idea and can be found in Homer's *Iliad*, which contains the story of a green sapling that was cut, stripped of its bark, and studded with golden nails so that it could serve as the symbolic "talking-stick" for the Greeks in their assemblies. Through a process that is labor for humankind and death for nature, the tree becomes wood; the living natural object becomes the dead object of human use. Although the idea is ancient, industrialism has enlarged its scale. Homer's transformation of the meaningless but living tree into the meaningful but dead scepter is a figure for the same transformation that affects warriors in battle: when a hero is killed on the field, his natural life is destroyed and replaced by a symbolic form of life called *kleos*, or "honor." In Frost's day, however, this system of war heroism had just begun to fail. As Wilfred Owen's poetry makes agonizingly clear, military technology had reached a scale of energy and efficiency that utterly discredited the old warrior ethic, straight from the *Iliad*, that British soldiers had been taught as schoolboys. A tour of a vast modern cattle farm, or an hour watching a five-ton combine harvester vacuum up a monocrop, is enough to make the same point (though it is well also to remember the machine guns of the Somme, which killed almost twenty thousand British troops in a single day, July 1, 1916).

8. Of course, the vexing issue of how to regulate and control those energies ade-

quately was a central aspect of the Cold War. Frost was a direct participant in that global ordeal, having personally met both President John F. Kennedy and Soviet leader Nikita Khrushchev during their terms in office.

9. Recall that, from the southern point of view, the Civil War was fought over three issues, not just secession and slavery. The third and more amorphous issue, at least in nostalgic hindsight, was the preservation of the southern agrarian lifeworld against the impersonal industrial capitalism of the North. A modified form of this southern cause was taken up by influential poet-critic John Crowe Ransom in his 1930 essay collection *I'll Take My Stand*. Ransom and his fellows not only minimized the horrors of slavery, they also failed to provide an economically viable alternative to the industrialism they rightly considered dehumanizing. By 1940, Ransom had abandoned his program, calling it "a fantasy."

10. "Shelves one could rest a knee on getting up" is perhaps one of Frost's many veiled allusions to the opening of Dante's *Inferno*, in which the pilgrim in the dark wood walks the steep slope "with firm foot always lower than the other" (30). The next line may recall Horatio's words to Hamlet about the depths below the height, in act 1, scene 4:

> What if it tempt you toward the flood, my lord,
> Or to the dreadful summit of the cliff
> That beetles o'er his base into the sea,
> And there assume some other horrible form,
> Which might deprive your sovereignty of reason
> And draw you into madness? think of it:
> The very place puts toys of desperation,
> Without more motive, into every brain
> That looks so many fathoms to the sea
> And hears it roar beneath.
>
> (69-78)

Works Cited

Alighieri, Dante. *The Divine Comedy: Inferno*. Trans. Mark Musa. Bloomington: Indiana UP, 2004.

Auden, W. H. *Collected Shorter Poems of W. H. Auden, 1927-1957*. New York: Random House, 1995.

Brodsky, Joseph, Seamus Heaney, and Derek Walcott. *Homage to Robert Frost*. New York: Farrar, Straus and Giroux, 1996.

Buell, Lawrence. "Frost as a New England Poet." *The Cambridge Companion to Robert Frost*. Ed. Robert Faggen. New York: Cambridge UP, 2001. 101-22.

Frost, Robert. Interview by Richard Poirier (1960). *Poets at Work: The Paris Review Interviews*. Ed. George Plimpton. New York: Penguin, 1989.

_____. *The Poetry of Robert Frost*. Ed. Edward Connery Lathem. New York: Henry Holt, 1969.

Grossman, Allen. "On the Management of Absolute Empowerment: Nuclear Violence, the Institutions of Holiness, and the Structures of Poetry." *AGNI* 29/30 (1990).

Jarrell, Randall. "The Other Frost." *Poetry and the Age*. New York: Alfred A. Knopf, 1953.

Matthiessen, F. O. *American Renaissance: Art and Expression in the Age of Emerson and Whitman*. New York: Oxford UP, 1941.

Parini, Jay. *Robert Frost: A Life*. New York: Henry Holt, 1999.

Ransom, John Crowe, et al. *I'll Take My Stand*. New York: Harper & Brothers, 1930.

"Robert Frost." *Voices and Visions*. Writ. Jill Janows. Dir. Richard P. Rogers. Public Broadcasting Service. Videocassette. Intellimation, 1988.

Shakespeare, William. *Hamlet*. Ed. Phillip Edwards. New York: Cambridge UP, 2003.

Thomas, Dylan. *Collected Poems of Dylan Thomas, 1934-1953*. New York: New Directions, 1954.

Whitman, Walt. *Leaves of Grass: Comprehensive Reader's Edition*. Ed. Harold W. Blodgett and Scully Bradley. New York: New York UP, 1980.

The Paradoxes of Robert Frost:
A Meditation on "Discordant Elements"

Anastasia Vahaviolos Valassis

After Robert Frost sailed to England in 1912, he settled in Beaconsfield, "a little cottage in the suburbs," and was determined to devote
himself to writing. He collected pieces he had composed over a period
of twenty years, only a couple of which he had actually published. Initially, Frost worried that the volume would be too "obviously inconsis-
tent and self-contradictory" (Thompson and Winnick 159). This was
an understandable concern; the lyrics collected in *A Boy's Will* reflected tumultuous times in his young life and traced the developing
talent of a maturing poet. Frost had already endured bewildering
doubts about his relationship to his wife, Elinor, serious vacillations in
his life's scope and direction, and deep depressions that tried the unwa-
vering faith his mother attempted to pass on to her children. Later Frost
wrote to Ernest Silver that the book was "a study in a certain kind of
waywardness," further propagating his theme and embracing the volume's manifold directions (quoted in Thompson and Winnick 162).
Frost is a far cry from the American poet who declared boldly and directly in 1855, "Do I contradict myself?/ Very well then I contradict
myself" (1324-25). And yet, although Walt Whitman embraced contraries in "Song of Myself" (among other poems) to reflect an expansive poetic personality, and to level democratically all people and ideas
in his very self-fashioning, Robert Frost sees inconsistency and paradox not in any modern notion of individuality or prophetic vision of an
egalitarian America but as an eternal and natural form, modeled by the
Earth herself.

Randall Jarrell, who first acknowledged a darker poet in Robert
Frost than most critics of his time could see, notes that "the limits
which existence approaches and falls back from have seldom been
stated with such bare composure" (28). This comment testifies to the
poet's deep metaphysical concerns and almost deceptively simple lan-

guage. The "bare composure" Jarrell sees as unique to Frost is indeed remarkable. The speaker's steady voice recounts stories of aging, domestic trouble, loneliness, and death with a blunt evenness. A picture is placed quietly and almost unemotionally before a reader whose sympathies are aroused and who is left to grapple with faith or reason and possibly to mourn. Like Jarrell, Lionel Trilling was interested in Frost's unqualified delivery of difficult observations and occasionally capricious truths. He said that Frost is "not carried out by reassurance, nor by the affirmation of old virtues and pieties" (quoted in Meyers 318). For this reason he called Frost a "terrifying" and "tragic" poet. Frost himself seemed aware of how his candid view might shock an audience and made allowance for human sensitivities that would be too affected by his rawness: he refrained from reading "Out, Out—" and "Home Burial" to audiences because these poems were simply too shocking.

Diminishing Things: Seasonal Change

Frost's poetry gestures toward both a reluctance to embrace the course of nature or human events and a staunch acceptance of changing seasons and heartbreaking human destinies. Like Whitman, Frost reveals an honesty in his varied moods, and perhaps he presents a more accurate portrait of the complexity of human experience. Whitman, too, is frank by not defining himself in one way or committing himself to a single narrow ideology. Ralph Waldo Emerson, an influence on both Whitman and Frost, had written in "Self-Reliance" that "a foolish consistency is the hobgoblin of little minds" (24). In other words, great minds are pliable and capable of changing opinions in order to arrive at mature thought. However, Whitman approaches hyperbole by insisting on being everything and everyone, becoming omniscient and omnipresent—something more than human. He includes the diversity that makes him an increasingly expansive paradox. Frost, whose feelings and perceptions betray the mutability he captures in spring blooms, reflects a common man's experience rather than transcending it. The poetry parallels the cycles in human life with nature's own cadences.

Changing seasons are found everywhere in Frost's poetry. He is interested in that liminality—those fragile moments hovering between two seasonal identities and capable of betraying characteristics of each. This is particularly compelling to Frost, who pauses also to capture events that mark transitions in the lives of his characters. In "Reluctance," a poem he wrote in a dejected state, concerned that he was losing Elinor, Frost depicts a snowy winter landscape confronting the weary speaker at the conclusion of his journey. Despite all the speaker has seen when he "looked at the world," he comes home to the decay of dead leaves and withering witch hazel, and an aching directionlessness (4). The concluding stanza asks an important question:

> Ah, when to the heart of man
> Was it ever less than a treason
> To go with the drift of things,
> To yield with a grace to reason,
> And bow and accept the end
> Of a love or a season?
>   (19-24)

The poem incites humankind to fight against nature or the seeming inevitability of a barren, sterile life. "Spring Pools" likewise warns the trees before "they use their powers/ To blot out and drink up and sweep away/ These flowery waters and these watery flowers/ From snow that melted only yesterday" (9-11). Frost explodes traditional connotations of the seasons with "Spring Pools." Winter, normally the ominous scene of death, is replaced with a threatening spring, whose budding vitality erases the beautiful but temporary pools that are necessary to feed its "dark foliage," which will eventually crowd the "total sky" still visible to the pools (and presumably to people) on the ground.

Other poems present an acceptance or even a beckoning of seasonal changes. "To the Thawing Wind" is a resounding apostrophe harnessing the agency of the spring wind. Each line begins with a clear command: "Come," "Bring," "Make," "Melt," "Burst," "Scatter," "Turn." The cumulative effect of these verbs is almost an incantation; the words seem to work like a chant to conjure the magical southwester. This thawing wind can powerfully transform the landscape by discovering the "brown beneath the white" and melting all the ice (5). It takes on mystical qualities in giving "the buried flower a dream" and making life and growth possible (3). It is interesting to note that the power of this wind does not affect only the natural world; it also happily disrupts the life of the hermit-poet who speaks in the poem, scattering his work and forcing him outside. Here the change of a season is not necessarily an allegory or a parallel for some alteration in human life; it is actually the impetus for a life beyond the cloistered hermit's "stall," a life of action, vigor, and socialization made possible by warmer weather and ultimately vital to the poet's project. Frost, like Silas of "The Death of the Hired Man," hates "to see a boy the fool of books" and advocates an active physical life instead of a sedentary academic one (101).

The poem "The Oven Bird" offers one of Frost's most beautiful and haunting meditations on the pause between seasons. The bird anticipates the fall, declaring, "Midsummer is to spring as one to ten" (5). The figure of the oven bird is something like a bard itself: "He says that leaves are old" and "the early petal-fall is past" (4, 6). His is nature's wisdom; his song witnesses and records the delicate turn of a healthy summer bloom into a fading growth. The poem concludes with a distinction between this bird and others: "he knows in singing not to sing" (12). This line appears initially puzzling and contradictory, but in Frost's characteristic economy and simplicity of diction, he uses the same word, "sing," with multiple layers of meaning. Singing refers both to the actual noise of the oven bird and to celebration. The song cannot be an expression of happiness or life because its very existence undermines the cause for celebration by introducing the season of its silencing. The bird shows an intelligent awareness of change in a type of lament. Frost anthropomorphizes by figuring the bird pausing to consider the fact of this seasonal transition. Though he frames the question "in all but words," the bird—something we imagine as a creature of instinct only—wonders "what to make of a diminished thing" (13-14). A human anxiety is projected onto the animal world, which is normally free from the consciousness that brings along worry and hesitation. This line places the poem somewhere between the urgent beckoning of "To the Thawing Wind" and the wary resistance of "Reluctance" and "Spring Pools." In some ways it captures Frost's abounding interest as a poet, his concern with diminishing life, career, love, ease, choice, day, and season. It is curious that Frost's readers can hear the song of this midsummer bird in the background of his other works; its contemplation of the ephemeral becomes a permanent and abiding theme. Although Frost's theory about "the sound of sense" relates more specifically to the sound of the actual words of his poems (which he deems more significant than the meaning itself), it seems apt to consider how the metaphorical "oversound" of the work is precisely the quality of wondering, questioning, pausing, and puzzling captured in the oven bird's otherwise unintelligible effusions. And so what does Frost make of diminished things? He sings alternately and never quite conclusively about fighting against and reconciling oneself to the fact of this fading.

Human Death: Fate and Mourning

Despite Frost's preoccupation with the natural world, he is also deeply involved in studies of people. Early on he rejected the novel as a form for such studies. His debut in writing blank-verse narratives and character portraits is in *North of Boston*, published in 1914 and a huge critical success. Ezra Pound, who had a fraught relationship with Frost, remarked after his release from prison that by writing this book Frost had repaid him fully for his initial help in introducing the American poet in English literary circles and building his reputation (Meyers

315). In *North of Boston* Frost, more confident, "was not troubled by . . . inconsistencies" (Thompson and Winnick 169). He reconciled himself to moods that demanded lyrics in addition to narratives. Thompson's description of Frost's impulse for the dramatic is particularly revealing:

> It would have been difficult for him to say how far back in his own experience he had become conscious that his inner hopes and fears acquired poetic voices that talked back and forth. He had learned, particularly during the painful years of his courtship, that the opposed voices and postures of his divided consciousness were as vivid to him as any voices of actors on a stage, that out of these inner tensions the lyric voice that triumphed—no matter how briefly—might find expression in a poem he felt and heard before he could ever try to write it down. (Thompson and Winnick 169)

Therefore we see that dialogue, an integral component of the narratives, is inspired as much by Frost's careful listening to various people as by his own internal debates. Thompson's analysis shows how we might view the narratives as capturing vital paradoxes Frost contained within himself.

Two moving poems that meditate on diminishing life, of an aged worker in "The Death of the Hired Man" and a child in "Home Burial," also consider the divisions between husbands and wives in the ways they sympathize with others and console them in their grief. In "The Death of the Hired Man," Mary and Warren consider the sudden return of Silas, an aged hired man who is not much help anyway and who has exasperated Warren by his wandering. Mary works to convey the change she perceives in Silas, to offer up a picture to her husband that might soften him. Silas's frailty arouses her concern and sympathy, crowding out all other considerations. Warren appears initially unmoved, preoccupied with Silas's value to him and the responsibility of Silas's own family to provide relief and charity. Frost emphasizes the disparity between a practical view of the subject and a humane one, although Warren never appears cruel or inflexible, and the two figures engage in a delicate conversation instead of the heated argument that seems to divide irreparably the couple in "Home Burial." Typical gender roles are evident in both poems. In "The Death of the Hired Man," though it is the woman, Mary, who looks at things sentimentally, Frost does not dismiss this view and writes Mary's voice, with her careful rhetoric, as the dominant one. Her instinct, too, is correct, despite her husband's skepticism about the end of Silas's working days.

The poem concludes abruptly and typically for Frost, who does not temper the blunt finality of Warren's declaration: "'Dead,' was all he answered" (175). The poem concerns itself with the value of a life that has no utility in society. The piece, after all, is called "The Death of the Hired Man," a generalization and abstraction from what could have been "The Death of Silas ———." Frost is interested in the tragedy of a man defined by his humble work (not by his family, social ties, or accomplishments) who is no longer capable of engaging in that work. Is there not then still an inherent worth in his existence? Is there not an entitlement to kind treatment, pity, and charity? Despite the differing definitions of "home" offered by Mary and Warren, both silently accept that their farm is a type of home to the itinerant Silas and one that, although he might not deserve it, will serve him as a refuge.

Although Frost has been attacked (by biographers, for instance) for his social conservatism, here he seems to offer up a theory not unlike William Wordsworth's in "The Old Cumberland Beggar." Wordsworth depicts the beggar as a unifying force within a community that, if by nothing else, is brought together in a spirit of philanthropy. Wordsworth retained his political belief that charity should be distributed by individual village people rather than by impersonal government organizations. This older system served an important social function. Less directly than Wordsworth, Frost too warns the reader through his portrait, "deem not this man useless." In "The Old Cumberland Beggar," Wordsworth writes:

> . . . 'Tis Nature's law
> That none, the meanest of created things,
> Of forms created the most vile and brute,
> The dullest or most noxious, should exist
> Divorced from good, a spirit and pulse of good,
> A life and soul to every mode of being
> Inseparably linked.
>
> (73-79)

"Home Burial" treats a subject more pitiful than the death of an old hired man; it describes, obliquely, the death of a child who is buried within view of the parents' house. The main substance of the poem, as in "The Death of the Hired Man," is the effect this event has on surrounding lives. We are introduced to the characters as the husband attempts to gain some understanding of his wife by physically positioning himself so that he can look at the view that preoccupies her. This is a brilliant moment in Frost, in which the literal and the symbolic seem so completely interchangeable that neither faithful realism nor profound meaning is sacrificed. Interestingly, the husband perceives "'The little graveyard where [his] people are!'" (24). His ownership of the graveyard indicates some possession of grief, though his wife, Amy, feels betrayed at his composure and seeming callousness. She blames him for digging the grave, for "'Making the gravel leap and leap in air,'" as though the energy manifested in the digging is an expression of a light rather than a heavy heart (79). Amy's anger is projected irrationally onto her husband for lack of any other outlet for her riotous emotions. She cannot come to terms with the continuation of human affairs after her own world is destroyed; she later reveals this as a general observation rather than simply one of her husband's response to the tragedy:

The nearest friends can go
With anyone to death, comes so far short
They might as well not try to go at all.
No, from the time when one is sick to death,
One is alone, and he dies more alone.
Friends make pretense of following to the grave,
But before one is in it, their minds are turned
And making the best of their way back to life
And living people, and things they understand.

(97-105)

The anonymous husband works first gently and ultimately with violence to repair the chasm that alienates them from each other. We can trace the progression. He asks Amy to unburden herself to him rather than another person—this "'someone else'" who is likely also the "'someone coming down the road'" (115) later in the poem, threatening to invade the marriage and revealing the extent Amy will go to console herself. The husband shows moments of real compassion and eloquence:

Let me into your grief . . .
What was it brought you up to think it the thing
To take your mother-loss of a first child
So inconsolably—in the face of love.

(62, 66-68)

But Amy's most direct accusations are about his speech. She believes he is sneering, and that he doesn't "'know how to speak'" (49). His remarks about the rotting birch wood momentously symbolize for her his apathy about their child's death. Finally, as he encourages her to consider her own angry words as a catharsis, she becomes irate: "'*You*— oh, you think the talk is all'" (116).

What is Frost accomplishing here? He proves his ability to paint profound darkness with the barest strokes. The nearest image we have of the tragedy is the mention of "'the child's mound'" (31) and Amy's reference to "'the darkened parlor'" (100). This understatement works for the reader, who needs only to understand the emotional climate in order to reconstruct imaginatively the scene of death. That minimal suggestiveness contrasts with the deluge of words that moves around the topic. Amy is frustrated by the inadequacy of words to reflect fully and assuage her grief. Perhaps she believes that they too only "'make pretense of following to the grave'" (106). But she also misreads her husband's meanings by assuming a superficiality in his conversation. His comment about the potential for a good birch fence to rot with "'Three foggy mornings and one rainy day'" appears to her to ignore what has befallen them (96). And yet in its blunt economy and simplicity, it also touches on the very idea that human creations—whether birch fences or children—are inherently fragile and subject to conditions outside mortal control. Ultimately, everything will die and decay, although this may be cruelly accelerated. It is interesting to note that the husband's objectionable line sounds something like Frost's poetry. It is as though Frost comments on the potential indigestibility of his own method of expression, even if it carries emotional weight for the speaker. If "Home Burial" is indeed about how speech can approximate human experience and either alienate or unify people, it is also about how "plain talk" in poetry can approach metaphysical problems and reflect the shadowy depths of the human heart.

Although it is in "Home Burial" that the wife complains bitterly of the ability of people to move on with the business of daily life, the theme resurfaces in "Out, Out—" and "The Need of Being Versed in Country Things." In "Out, Out—" the snarling, rattling buzz saw provides a portentous beginning to the poem about a "big boy/ Doing a man's work," a picture that is immediately alarming (23-24). We are shown how instantaneously the tragic fate of the boy is sealed with his sister's single word. The ironic description of the accident, "Neither refused the meeting" (18), might have been influenced by Thomas

Hardy's 1912 poem "The Convergence of the Twain." Both poems consider how such "meetings" are brewing, although things are far accelerated in "Out, Out—." "The Convergence of the Twain" is about a momentous and recognizable event in history, apparently heightening the significance of the stroke of the "Immanent Will" (18). The poem begins with the *Titanic* at the bottom of the ocean, allowing us first to observe the sad mortality of this luxurious liner, this symbol of "human vanity" and "Pride of Life" (2, 3). Time goes backward. The result is clear, and the scene of opulent glass and sea worms at the beginning seems stable and nearly peaceful. The drama of the weighty creeping toward the crash does not then derive from any suspense; Hardy means for us to understand the decree of the "Spinner of the Years" (31) as both inevitable and impossible, what "No mortal eye could see" (26).

Frost, like Hardy, introduces a perspective that forces the reader to anticipate the dreadful accident. The buzz saw snarls from line 1. Even so, the poem maintains a calm evenness: the breeze is "sweet-scented" (3) and we can count "Five mountain ranges one behind the other/ Under the sunset far into Vermont" (5-6). Life appears as usual. The speaker's voice then interferes, uncharacteristically, to express regret: "Call it a day, I wish they might have said" (10). This brief sentiment from the poet/onlooker is the extent of the mourning. The poem concludes with a chilling line that smacks the involved and sympathetic reader with a cold, unsentimental view of the episode: "And they, since they/ Were not the one dead, turned to their affairs" (33-34). The speaker echoes Amy's observation in "Home Burial" without her violent objection and melancholy bewilderment.

Frost's many poems about death also illustrate his most profound paradox. Though confronting death may be humankind's deepest philosophical problem, it is also the most prosaic and the most necessary. Frost involves his readers intricately in the lives of the figures he portrays in his poems—particularly in the narratives in which the characters really take shape—and yet he ultimately expects them to understand how these people rage against or mourn inevitabilities. John

Robert Doyle, Jr., says of "Reluctance" what is also applicable here: Frost paints "the eternal clash between desire and the facts of actual existence" (60). According to Doyle, "It is man's rebelliousness that creates the drama" (60). But what else does man have aside from an ability to rebel against the course designed for him, particularly when it is a cruel one? "Tree at My Window" proves that there is a relationship between the outer and inner "weather" of our lives. The speaker will not draw the curtain so that he may observe the tossing of the tree outside and the tree may look in and sympathize with his own tumultuous sleep, presumably plagued by melancholy, fear, or anxiety. The poem does not necessarily propose that the relationship is symbiotic, however. Despite the apostrophe, the tree is unresponsive to the "inner weather" (16) of the speaker, who stares out his window and who will likely be the one affected and altered by what he observes taking place outside. In the final stanza of the poem, he remarks, "Fate had her imagination about her" when she united him with the tree (14). But the speaker's tone betrays his understanding that though they (he and the tree) may both be "tossed" and "swept," their commonality ends there. Frost's poems repeatedly show that internal tumult has no capacity to change external events and human destinies.

Frost's interest and complexity come from the way he depicts tragedy as both familiar and alien, specific and general, devastating and surmountable. "Out, Out—" reveals some of these tensions. Part of the reason the poem is so shocking is that the reader is made complicit in the tragedy. The reader can guess its outcome early and morbidly plows on for the conclusion, anticipating and beckoning the fulfillment of the course that will render the buzz saw as terrible as it initially appears. But the reader also has just enough distance from this scene affecting anonymous people to detect something odd about the poem's diction. The buzz saw is not slicing, or irrevocably cutting, but "leaping." The boy "must have given the hand" (17), according to the speaker, rather than recoiling in confusion, horror, and pain. Frost, unable to alter the sad accidents of human life, employs his rhetorical powers to override common and grotesque descriptions of such a calamitous meeting. Blood does not spill, but "life" does. The marker of death is that there is "No more to build on" (33), no foundation to support mortal machinations. So are these expressions inaccurate, oblique, or euphemistic? Do they lack the directness so prevalent in Frost's writing? Doyle notes that Frost's poems, though direct, move beyond the level of simple information and capture "image and emotion" (6, 4). He corrects Amy Lowell's comment that Frost's writing is "photographic." Though the poem concludes almost disturbingly as people get on with their lives, the very existence of the work and the freshness of the writing testifies to the slow, careful study the poet has made even of a haphazard disaster that will inevitably be pushed into the past.

Isolation and Communion in Nature

Frost, like Whitman and Wordsworth, two important predecessors, concerns himself with an inquiry into the human being as a social or an inherently isolated creature. Do human sensibilities alienate individuals from others or enable them to commune with those who also struggle to persevere in the face of painful mortality? In *The Prelude* (1850), Wordsworth famously documents how his youthful love of the forms of nature leads to a love of humankind. He says in book 8, "For I already had been taught to love/ My fellow-beings, to such habits trained/ Among the wood and mountains" (69-71). He claims that nature inspires him with goodness and grants him his first sense of contentedness. This inner satisfaction enables the young Wordsworth to embrace the "stranger in [his] path . . . a brother of this world" (78-79). While this is not the case with Frost, he does seem to prove that there is a communion among people who work in nature, as though the land itself helps to bind them, particularly when the physical remnants of their work are recognized by others.

"The Tuft of Flowers" begins with a resounding sense of isolation. The speaker detects the work of "one/ Who mowed it in the dew before the sun" (1-2). The speaker seems to chase a phantom: "I looked for him behind an isle of trees" (5). Quickly he comes to an understanding that he must be alone as the mower was. In a sagelike generalization, the speaker imagines that this is the essential human condition; it is true "'Whether [men] work together or apart'" (42). Led, however, by a butterfly to a tuft of flowers spared by the scythe, he considers this a message from "a spirit kindred to [his] own" and no longer doubts the brotherly communion of those who work the land (35). Though Frost despised Whitman's work particularly for its open sexual content, this poem, like "Crossing Brooklyn Ferry," shows how it is possible to forge connections to people across space and time. Whitman declares with his bellowing omnipotence in stanza 3, "It avails not, time nor place—distance avails not,/ I am with you, you men and women of a generation, or ever so many generations hence." Frost's idea, again, is more modest. The grass is freshly cut and so the earth still bears the mark of another's presence. The tuft is likely an accidental sparing of the flowers that provide a temporary resting place for the butterfly. But what does this "message" offer to the speaker that is inspiring enough to alter his initial dejection and isolation? Although it seems romantic to imagine that the mower purposely left the tuft as a marker of his presence and a sign of his concern for the butterfly, there is no evidence of this. The speaker is actually moved by hearing the mower's "long scythe whispering to the ground" (34). Perhaps the imperfect work betrays some humanity that was not previously evident on perfectly cut grass. Is it that small omission, or imperfection, that renders the early mower's labor recognizable?

"The Wood-Pile" begins similarly, with a wandering speaker and a mystical messenger in the form of a small bird that brings the speaker's attention to a pile of wood abandoned in the swamp. The speaker puzzles over the contradiction between the care taken in measuring and cutting the wood and the pile's obvious abandonment. The speaker can only hypothesize about its presence:

> . . . I thought that only
> Someone who lived in turning to fresh tasks
> Could so forget his handiwork on which
> He spent himself . . .
>
> (34-37)

Here there is no sense of kinship with the laborer, despite the physical remnant of his work. Its presence allows the speaker to construct a psychological portrait of the man who left his wood, illogically, "far from a useful fireplace" (38). This type of insight is absent in "The Tuft of Flowers," where the reader is left to guess at the speaker's understanding of the work before him. But "The Wood-Pile" lacks the euphoria in "Tuft" that stems from feeling oneself connected to others by virtue of engaging in a common task. This poem, instead, presents the senseless decay of the abandoned wood, leaning silently toward a disapproval of the one who would neglect his work in such a way.

The desire to turn to fresh tasks is not necessarily reprehensible; in fact it might lead to fruitful activity and production. Frost himself embodied this very spirit in his youthful life, wandering from job to job and continually abandoning his work in a short time. Frost reflected in older age that the constant moving resulting from his passion for fresh tasks actually helped to define him—and it certainly provided inspiration for his poetry. Nonetheless, it seems that the poem asks us to consider the waste of the wood in its "slow smokeless burning of decay" (40). That it is "smokeless" testifies to an invisibility, an erasure, but the paradox is that the speaker notices it, even if sadly, though it is quite possible that no one else will. And if he disapproves of the result of this man's labor, he still theorizes about and forges a psychological connection to the absent person. As he stands alone in the frozen swamp, nature offers him, if not a love of man, a possible understanding of one man.

Robert Frost's poetry applies Wordsworth's idea expressed in *The Prelude*:

The mind of man is framed even like the breath
And harmony of music. There is a dark
Invisible workmanship that reconciles
Discordant elements, and makes them move
In one society.

(1.352-55)

Works Cited

Doyle, John Robert, Jr. *The Poetry of Robert Frost: An Analysis*. New York: Hafner Press, 1962.

Emerson, Ralph Waldo. *Self-Reliance, and Other Essays*. Mineola, NY: Courier Dover, 1993.

Frost, Robert. *The Poetry of Robert Frost: The Collected Poems*. Ed. Edward Connery Lathem. New York: Henry Holt, 1969.

Hardy, Thomas. *Selected Poems*. Ed. Robert Mezey. New York: Penguin Classics, 1998.

Jarrell, Randall. "The Other Frost." *Poetry and the Age*. New York: Vintage Books, 1953.

Meyers, Jeffrey. *Robert Frost: A Biography*. New York: Houghton Mifflin, 1996.

Thompson, Lawrance, and R. H. Winnick. *Robert Frost: A Biography*. Ed. Edward Connery Lathem. New York: Holt, Rinehart and Winston, 1981.

Whitman, Walt. *Poetry and Prose*. New York: Penguin Books, 1996.

Wordsworth, William. *William Wordsworth: The Major Works*. Ed. Stephen Gill. New York: Oxford UP, 1984.

CRITICAL
READINGS

Frost's *North of Boston*, Its Language, Its People, and Its Poet_____

David Sanders

North of Boston was Robert Frost's second book of poems but the first to reveal his full dramatic power and moral awareness. It was also the first to explore the culture of rural New England in which these poetic powers had grown to maturity. Published in May 1914 in London, fifteen months after *A Boy's Will*, *North of Boston* gained a warm reception in England and by September had made its way to Henry Holt in New York. Holt, buying the American rights from Frost's English publisher, David Nutt, reissued *North of Boston* in February of 1915,[1] making it Frost's first American book and ending what had been, for him, two decades of obscurity at home. Reviewed by Amy Lowell in *The New Republic* the very week of Frost's return from England,[2] the volume announced Frost to literary New York and Boston and revealed to America the poetic voice—vigorous and vernacular, yet subtle and complex—for which he would soon be widely known.

North of Boston also established Frost as a poet of people and place. Presenting earthy characters mainly in blank-verse narrative and dialogue, it takes us into the lives of working people in Frost's early twentieth-century New England. Even the volume's first-person lyrics—"Mending Wall," "After Apple-Picking," and "The Wood-Pile"—contain strong narrative and dramatic elements. Structuring the book through their strategic placement, they sound a keynote for the volume in their use of a conversational style, their exploration of character and motive, their emphasis on traditional skills and labor in a life in which winter is always near and survival never assured.

All of the sixteen poems that comprise *North of Boston* underwent final revision in England during the summer and fall of 1913, when the Frosts occupied a rented cottage in the London suburb of Beaconsfield. Yet the creative sources for these poems and their vernacular style go back to Frost's decade (1900-1909) on a small farm in Derry, New

Hampshire. Frost, having left college a second time and suffering worrisome chest ailments, had, with money from his grandfather, turned away from the factory work and teaching that he already knew to try poultry farming, which promised to leave him time to write while supporting his family in a healthy rural environment. While the Derry years never quite made Frost either a farmer or a living, they shaped the poet he had determined to become, immersing him not only in the seasonal cycles and "country things" that would saturate his verse, but in the New England speech which he would make his poetic tongue. In doing so, the Derry years also made vivid and real the lives of the neighbors who would people *North of Boston* and, in wresting a living from hard climate and stony soil, would define a moral center for Frost's poetic world.

Considering his interest in its people, we might ask why Frost's comments on his verse in the year leading to the book's publication focus so thoroughly on matters of technique. The question is answered partly by Frost's immediate situation. The public response to *A Boy's Will* had raised doubts whether the artistry of his seemingly natural style would be understood by the audience, including the reviewers, of the volume in preparation, which Frost saw as pivotal to his career. In April 1913, for example, the *Times Literary Supplement* had described the simplicity of *A Boy's Will* as "naively engaging."[3] Ezra Pound's review in *Poetry* the following month had carried a greater sting. Although he had helped to promote Frost's name, Pound had made "the mistake," as Frost would soon complain to John Bartlett, "of assuming that my simplicity is that of the untutored child."[4] Little as he had ever trusted Pound, Frost must still have felt betrayed by so cavalier an assessment from one who styled himself Frost's champion. He may also have worried that Pound had laid a path for others to follow. But perhaps more unsettling was Frost's own realization of how well-concealed his artistry could remain, even—or perhaps especially—to a cultivated audience.[5] If such readers could miss so much in *A Boy's Will*, he feared what they would make of this next book, which took naturalness so much further, more obviously transgressing conventional boundaries between poetic language and ordinary speech.

The public response to *A Boy's Will* partly explains the vigorous discussion of poetic prosody that Frost developed over the following year with the English poets Frank Flint and T. E. Hulme and with Sidney Cox and John Bartlett back home. Frost hints at the value of this exchange when, early in July, a few days after the first of their specially arranged meetings, he thanks Flint, saying, "My ideas got just the rub they needed last week."[6] In a letter to Bartlett three days later, Frost is more expansive. There, the dimensions of Frost's boast—"To be perfectly frank with you I am one of the most notable craftsmen of my time. That will transpire presently" (*Letters*, p.79)—suggest how much is at stake for him and, thus, how important it was that he articulate the principles at work in the poems. In fact, for much of the latter half of 1913, when he was shaping *North of Boston* as a book, Frost viewed his remarks on prosody as the dry run for "an essay or two I am going to write" (*Letters*, p. 113), even suggesting that Bartlett save his letters for that purpose. One can imagine something like Wordsworth's Preface to the *Lyrical Ballads* that would assert the method and sophistication behind his poetic experiments. In the end, Frost, who disliked writing prose, did not write the essay, perhaps trusting that the principles needed to appreciate his work were well enough understood by a few of the book's likely reviewers. Or perhaps he found that, in bolstering his own confidence, the important work was already done. But Frost may also have felt that the poems, like the people in them and the language they spoke, would be diminished by any effort to explain them[7] and could only distance him from a world of values that the poems had made his own.

Even in this pivotal year, then, Frost's reasons for stressing poetic technique are hard to disentangle from the moral aims embodied in his book. I stress the connection because, unlike his two most prominent models, Wordsworth and Emerson, Frost admits to these moral corollaries only rarely and obliquely. It is true that over the longer span of the book's development, roughly 1905-1913, Frost's most definite aim was to capture the sense of living speech within a metrical frame. Granted, too, that for an unproven poet measuring himself against both traditional and modernist rivals, technical mastery had a natural priority. And so, with an extravagance noted by William Pritchard and John Walsh,[8] Frost announces himself to Bartlett as "possibly the only person going who works on any but a worn out . . . principle . . . of versification" (*Letters*, p.79) and, a month afterwards, as "one of the few artists writing . . . who have a theory of their own upon which all their work down to the least accent is done" (*Letters*, p. 88).

Still, there are many moments when Frost's pronouncements on prosody reveal something more than his pride of mastery and analytical insight.[9] Consider, for example, his "new definition of a sentence," which he announces to Bartlett in February 1914 as "a sound in itself on which other sounds called words may be strung" (*Letters*, p. 110). With "a sound in itself" Frost puts grammar and logic aside for the moment to de-familiarize the written sentence. And, with these "other sounds called words," he even sneaks a backward glance toward the nature and origin of language itself—to the "expressiveness" that came "before words,"[10] the "brute tones of our human throat that may once have been all our meaning."[11] At the same time, Frost engages us visually, asking us to imagine some fact on which these abstracted sounds "may be strung," only in the next moment showing us why: "You may string words together without a sentence hypersound to string them on just as you may tie clothes together . . . and stretch them . . . between two trees, but—it is bad for the clothes" (*Letters*, p. 111).

In this washday image, Frost—buoyed by Flint's response to his poetic theories and a growing belief in his own poetic future—sets himself not only against the "worn out" prosodies of established contemporaries such as Robert Bridges, but also against the cultural pretensions that he felt in Pound and a whole aura of refinement that much of late nineteenth-century esthetics had cast over poetry. In this sense, just as Frost's concern with technique reveals itself as more than defensive, so it is more than technical. When he says that "An ear and an appetite for these sounds of sense is the first qualification of a writer" (*Letters*, p. 80) and that "The most original writer only catches them fresh from talk" (*Letters*, p. 111), Frost, like Wordsworth, is claiming a respect and an authority for the language of ordinary people from which poets, he felt, had too often set poetry apart. In doing so, he challenges an imbedded view of culture that gives precedence to the written word. Just a few years later, in distinguishing between "our everyday speech . . . and a more literary, sophisticated, artificial, elegant language that belongs to books," Frost would claim that he "could get along very well without this bookish language altogether" (*Collected Poems*, p. 694).[12] For Frost, who had found a touchstone for his craft in the talk of his Derry neighbors and who would always "say" rather than "read" his poems before audiences, ordinary speech was inseparable from those who spoke it, and the question of words not a question of words alone. When, for *North of Boston*, Frost avoided the singing harmonies of Tennyson and Swinburne that remained part of *A Boy's Will*, he was rejecting an estheticism largely English and upper-class in favor of a poetry that would speak to Americans, and for them, in a language that Americans spoke. It was a language of labor and use by which a literary culture could affirm the values of an oral, vernacular one, placing cultivation of the soil at least on a par with the cultivation of the drawing room.[13]

Once back on American soil, where such populist strains might sound more sweetly, and with his poetic investment in England paying well, Frost is more direct about the human and social dimensions of his book. Finding *North of Boston* actively promoted by Henry Holt and himself courted by editors who had ignored his work for a decade,[14] Frost may have felt less compelled to prove himself an artist and freer to claim the democracy of spirit central to his vision. After the painful experience of feeling unappreciated and misunderstood, he may also have been eager to expand or correct earlier statements of his artistic concerns. Thus he writes in March 1915 to William Stanley

Braithwaite of the Boston *Evening Transcript*, giving him material for his weekly poetry column:

> It would seem absurd to say it (and you mustn't quote me as saying it) but I suppose . . . that my conscious interest in people was at first no more than an almost technical interest in their speech—in what I used to call their sentence sounds—the sound of sense. . . . There came a day about ten years ago when I . . . made the discovery in doing The Death of the Hired Man that I was interested in neighbors for more than merely their tones of speech—and always had been. (*Letters*, pp. 158-59)

By placing this discovery in 1905, when he drafted the earliest *North of Boston* poems, Frost makes it a cornerstone of the volume itself. Later he would say that the realization that "I was after poetry that talked" had "changed the whole course of my writing" and would even call it "providential."[15] Aided by so weighty a term, Frost implies that, since any vernacular is rooted in its culture, a poetry that "talked" could never be a purely technical achievement. A poetry that "talked" would not only sound like conversation. It would really say something— something human, basic, and significant. Seeking a poetry that talked in the accents of his Derry neighbors gave Frost a way both to test and to convey such realities. In addition to evoking a specific culture in which to ground the human conflicts which he wished to explore, the search gave Frost a language free of false refinements in which anything inauthentic would prove weak or untrue.

While Frost is increasingly candid about the human and moral dimension of his poems after his return from England, these concerns reveal themselves even before his exit from obscurity. Writing from England in July 1913, as he was shaping the book for publication, Frost conveys this interest to Thomas Mosher, an American collector and publisher, when he describes the "volume of blank verse . . . already well in hand" with "some character strokes I had to get in somewhere" (*Letters*, p. 83). Feigning apology for having "dropped into an everyday level of diction that even Wordsworth kept above," Frost tries at once to tweak and reassure, prompt and flatter the fastidious Mosher:

> I trust I don't terrify you. I think I have made poetry. The language is appropriate to the virtues I celebrate. At least I am sure that I can count on you to give me credit for knowing what I am about. (*Letters*, pp. 83-84)

"The language is appropriate to the virtues I celebrate": this unqualified assertion stands definite and tall amidst Frost's more calculated postures ("I trust . . . I think . . . At least I am sure") and underlines the importance which he attached to the human substance of these poems.

We see much the same emphasis in Frost's note to F. S. Flint written earlier that July, after their first discussion of "sentence sounds." Delighted as he is with Flint's response to his thoughts on prosody, Frost makes clear his greater concern with what his language is saying when he asks Flint, who had read eight of the longer narratives:

> Did I reach you with the poems[?] . . . Did I give you the feeling of and for the independent-dependence of the kind of people I like to write about[?] . . . The John Kline[16] who lost his housekeeper and went down like a felled ox was just the person I have described and I never knew a man I liked better. . . . (*Writing*, p. 82)

A more pregnant comment on the kind of people whom Frost liked to write about—and on the way that character enacts itself through language—surfaces in the letter to Sidney Cox written in September 1913, after a family trip to Scotland. The passage is notable partly for Frost's first mention of the local stone walls that would soon prompt the writing of "Mending Wall." More remarkable still is the way it associates various facets of Frost's life—his experience of England and New England, his early exposure to Scots writers by his mother, his social and moral attitudes—with the volume in preparation and the hopes attached to it. He writes:

The best of the adventure was the time in Kingsbarns where tourists and summer boarders never come. The common people in the south of England I don't like to have around me. They don't know how to meet you man to man. The people in the north are more like Americans. I wonder whether they made Burns' poems or Burns' poems made them. And there are stone walls (dry stone dykes) in the north: I liked those. My mother was from Edinburgh. I used to hear her speak of the Castle and Arthur's seat, more when I was young than in later years. I had some interest in seeing those places. (*Letters*, pp. 94-95)

This web of associations makes clear enough that the Americans whom Frost has in mind are those in the poems that he is readying for publication—another "common people" who "know how to meet you man to man" and have made their mark in stone across another northern landscape. Equally revealing is Frost's comment about Robert Burns, another poet of democratic and vernacular impulse whom Belle Frost had read to her son from early childhood and whose 1786 *Poems, Chiefly in the Scottish Dialect* had also asserted the worth of a rural people and their language.[17] In the alchemy of Frost's memory and imagination—with thoughts of home stirred by the Scottish hills and people, and the whole process aided by his Scots mother and her literary legacy—Frost merges Burns's people with his own and, implicitly, himself with Burns. Perhaps most striking is Frost's surmise about the mutual act of making between one's poems and one's culture. When we realize how suddenly Burns's 1786 volume brought this farmer-poet to the attention of his nation's literary elite, we get a sense of the degree to which Frost's feelings of gratitude and obligation toward his Derry neighbors are entwined with his own poetic hopes: that their "making" of his poems would also "make" him as a poet, bringing him home to Boston and New York, just as Burns's second book had taken him to literary Edinburgh; that if they did so, these poems would impact the Derry neighbors to whose lives and speech they owed so much; that his book might bring their voices alive to readers who would not otherwise know them, gaining them a respect and recognition which they could never win for themselves, thus perhaps saving some part of their disappearing world. The poems might even show them some of their own substance and value, which Frost had seen and tried to capture in his poems.

Frost's concern for his human subjects and his wish to make them known is implicit in the book's dedication to Elinor—"to E.M.F. This Book of People"—and by the other titles that he considered for the volume: *New Englanders*, *New England Hill Folk*, or the one originally listed by his London publisher M. L. Nutt, *Farm Servants and Other People*. It may seem curious that, in the end, Frost chose a title that does not mention these people directly. Yet, as in so much of Frost's work, this reticence is eloquent. Like the book's language, the words "north of Boston" say something about its people not only by pointing to the region and culture that have shaped their lives, but by making clear what they are not. Posed against "Boston," with its history and urbanity, what lies "north" is simply out there, provincial and exposed, somewhere between the capital and the pole, so that, even before we have read the book, *North of Boston* suggests the fortitude of its people by hinting at the cold and emptiness that they face. And, by the time we have finished its poems about failed and failing farms[18] and the families who have left or will be leaving them, we see that their traditional way of life takes definition and value in opposition to the urban wealth and power to which it literally loses ground each year. With just a little help from his dedication, Frost's title trusts the poems to bring his people to our notice, just as he has trusted their language to shape his poetic voice, and just as the poems, with their sparing narration, trust so largely to the speech of the characters themselves.

It is both ironic and revealing that Frost took the phrase "North of Boston" from a real estate advertisement in *The Boston Globe* that he recalled in England.[19] For the sale of these once-working farms in an urban market confirms the change witnessed by the poems: a culture of independent farmers pushed toward extinction by an expanding, capital-driven economy. Yet this real estate heading, when converted to poetic use, becomes part of the book's assertion that what must be lost in fact may be saved in imagination and need not pass in silence—indeed, that a culture that might seem dead remains alive in Frost's poems and, through them, in us. In this way, Frost's use of the commercial heading "North of Boston" epitomizes the book it has named, enacting not only the "renewal of words" that Frost considered essential to poetry, but with it a renewal of values by recalling us to a world more manual in labor and more personal in scale than the culture of mass-production from which the phrase had come.

There is a further and complicating irony in the fact that this mass culture is precisely the one within which the poems would have to find a place if they were to be read as Frost hoped that they would be—from books printed by the thousands. In a letter to Bartlett in November 1913, he makes clear that for him all other forms of poetic recognition will be hollow without such large-scale economic gains. "[T]here is a kind of success called 'of esteem,'" Frost writes,

> and it butters no parsnips. It means a success with the critical few who are supposed to know. But really to arrive when I can stand on my legs as a poet and nothing else I must get outside that circle to the general reader who buys books in their thousands. I may not be able to do that. I believe in doing it—dont [sic] you doubt me there. (Letters, p. 98)

Frost's depreciation of a privileged class who is "supposed to know" about poetry in favor of "the general reader," who presumably knows economic necessity, corresponds with his feeling for the people of his poems—working people whose virtues he celebrates in a language that they could call their own. As Frost discounts the "esteem" of "the critical few," we may well be reminded of his claim that he could "get along very well without [their] bookish language" rejected in favor of "our everyday speech." To Bartlett, he continues:

I want to be a poet for all sorts and kinds. I could never make a merit of being caviare to the crowd the way my quasi-friend Pound does. I want to reach out, and would if it were a thing I could do by taking thought. (*Letters*, p. 98)

Here, as Frost slights Pound both for slighting the ordinary reader and for slighting him, we may think ahead to his later resentment at the condescension toward the people of his poems that he sometimes detected in college audiences. But as much as he would like to leave behind the judgments of a privileged class, he could not ignore them any more than he could, as a poet, wholly dispense with the more artificial, elegant language of books. And much as he might wish it, he cannot reach a wider general audience simply "by taking thought." To get beyond that exclusive literary world, he must go through it—must first get its attention. To get published, especially by an American house back home, he needed the help of "the critical few"—their referrals and introductions, their readings and reassurances, their favorable reviews; understanding that need, he sought and exploited such connections. Indeed, in the November 1913 letter to Bartlett, he is eager "to brag a bit" about the recent attentions he had been paid: an invitation to lunch with Poet Laureate Robert Bridges and growing friendships with Wilfrid Gibson and Lascelles Abercrombie, recognized English poets who had been drawn to Frost through the *North of Boston* poems which they had read in manuscript. Frost's "depreciation" of these poetic "exploits," interwoven as they are with his eagerness to report them, is perhaps a reminder to himself as much as to Bartlett that even this hard-won "success of esteem," however gratifying and promising, is only a step toward—and not to be confused with—the public success required as much by his personal principles and literary pride as by his economic need.

Frost, then, is connected to the people of his book in ways that reach both back to his personal past and ahead to his imagined future. For the Frost who had labored in schoolrooms, factories, and farmers' fields even before the move to Derry, his farming neighbors were, like him, a part of the country's working class. In the poems, they become an extension of himself, made to embody his convictions about character and self-reliance. Like them he felt the diminished power of the individual in an increasingly corporate economy, and like them he knew the elusive profits of small-scale farming, which in 1906 had returned him to teaching at considerable cost to his poetry. In 1913, as he assembled *North of Boston*, his sense of common cause with the people of this rural world could only have gained strength from the fact that even now, as a poet, he faced the same market forces that they did, for the publishing elite that controlled Frost's future[20] was ruled by the same economic interests that had decided the fate of his Derry neighbors.

But Frost also knew that to succeed as a poet—to gain a hearing for their voices and his own—he would have to make his way in this world antithetical to the values he idealized in his "people." Indeed, Frost's need to gain the support of a privileged class in which he would never feel at home both parallels and partly explains the tensions and conflict that structure every *North of Boston* poem. These oppositions are introduced as early as "Mending Wall," whose modernist speaker argues against the wall he helps to rebuild and at least seems unresponsive to the claims of a tradition honored by the volume as a whole. In the course of the book, the oppositions take many further forms—individual against corporate, country against city, feminine against masculine—weaving a texture of social and moral drama into the counterpoint of voices found in poem after poem.

"The Wood-Pile," the last of the book's blank-verse poems, brings this drama within a single consciousness, with a speaker who begins by debating whether to "turn back" toward old, familiar ground or to "go on farther" and "see." In this moment of hesitation and choice, Frost reproduces in almost abstract, spatial terms the conflict between old and new, tradition and change, that has structured the volume. The abandoned woodpile that the speaker finds by going on does not resolve the tension, but takes him again in both directions—vividly back to the "labor of [an] ax" that had "cut and split" this now-decaying wood, and vicariously forward with one imagined as "forget[ing] his handiwork" in "turning to fresh tasks." In offering this explanation for why this wood remains "far from a useful fireplace," the speaker skirts a more unsettling one, giving it emphasis by avoidance. Clearly, the woodcutter has left his work behind, either in living or in dying. But despite the speaker's optimistic assertion, death remains implicit in the "handiwork" on which the woodcutter has "spent himself" and in the ironic "burning" of the wood's "decay"—images of the exhaustion and loss that remain among life's inescapable facts.

The understated power with which "The Wood-Pile" develops this opposition is essential to its climactic role in *North of Boston*, for the terms of the drama both recapitulate and extend the mortal stakes at issue in nearly every poem of the volume. Whether the survival is literal or figurative—social and emotional or physical—these poems present a series of life-and-death alternatives for the individuals in them, for their relationships, and for their culture as whole.

In developing the tensions introduced by "Mending Wall," *North of Boston* shows that a central feature of our national story—the retreat of independent farming within a growing, impersonal, capitalized economy—took particular and poignant form in New England, the symbolic birthplace of our nation's individualism. Equally significant and intriguing, the tensions traced by this pivotal volume in Frost's career correspond to one within Frost himself, whose poetic and practical aims must somehow span worlds in social and economic conflict and whose move to Derry was a step toward that poetic future by way of our cultural past.

From *Journal of Modern Literature* 27, no. 1/2 (2003): 70-78. Copyright © 2004 by Indiana University Press. Reprinted by permission of Indiana University Press.

Notes

1. The exact date was 20 February 1915. Holt had learned of the book from his wife, Florence Taber Holt, who had a special interest in rural New England. In April 1915 he issued an American edition of *A Boy's Will* (Henry Holt, 1915).

2. Lowell, having brought *North of Boston* home from London, had tried to get Houghton Mifflin to publish it and, when she learned of Holt's plans to do so, arranged to write the review. Frost discovered that the book was out only when he landed in New York on 22 February and found Lowell's review in *The New Republic*. For further details, see Lawrance Thompson, *Robert Frost: The Years of Triumph* (Holt, Rinehart and Winston, 1970), pp. 3-6, 518-20, 573.

3. John Evangelist Walsh, *Into My Own: The English Years of Robert Frost* (Grove, 1988), p. 99.

4. Robert Frost, *Selected Letters*, ed. Lawrance Thompson (Holt, Rinehart and Winston, 1964) p. 84. Hereafter, this volume will be cited in the text as *Letters*.

5. My thanks to John Evangelist Walsh for this insight (*Into My Own*, p. 103). For a detailed and illuminating account of these events, see Chapter 6 of Walsh's book.

6. Elaine Barry, *Robert Frost on Writing* (Rutgers University Press, 1973), p. 83. Hereafter this text will be cited as *Writing*.

7. Frost called the people of *North of Boston* "my people, . . . the ordinary folks I belong to" and was offended when he detected condescension toward them in college audiences or, on one occasion, in the actors playing them. See "Poetry and Poverty," in *Collected Poems, Prose, and Plays* (Library of America, 1995), pp. 759-67. (Hereafter this volume will be cited in the text as *Collected Poems*.) The offense which Frost felt on behalf of "his" people is clearly related to the offense which he felt at being taken for a poetic primitive.

8. William Pritchard, *Frost: A Literary Life Reconsidered* (Oxford University Press, 1984), p. 76. Pritchard observes that Frost, in emphasizing his quite genuine originality, "declined to consider the more recent examples of Yeats, of Hardy, or of the Georgian poets with whom he was becoming friendly at the time"—all of whom had also departed from the principles of prosody exemplified by Tennyson and Swinburne. Walsh also notes the subtle exaggerations in Frost's assertions about the "sound of sense" (*Into My Own*, pp. 120-22).

9. Paola Loreto has pointed out that, on the matter of intonation, Frost anticipated by decades the work of linguists such as Dwight Bolinger and Kenneth Pike. See "'I'm Talking Not Free Verse but Blank Verse Now': Frost's Poetics of Sound in Prose and Verse," *The Robert Frost Review* (Fall 2000), pp. 146-48.

10. "Conversations on the Craft of Poetry" (with Cleanth Brooks, Robert Penn Warren, and Kenny Withers, 1959) in *Collected Poems*, p. 855.

11. Letter to John Freeman (English critic and poet) [November 1925?], rpt. in Barry, *Writing*, p. 80. Frost emphasized the pre-linguistic voice as an important resource for poetry and restated the idea in many ways over many years.

12. This remark comes from a transcribed talk, "The Unmade Word, or Fetching and Far-Fetching," that Frost delivered at the Browne and Nichols School on 13 March 1918.

13. Unsurprisingly, the rhythms and inflections of the New England vernacular found their way into Frost's own speech as well as his verse. According to Thompson, Frost's "habit of careful pronunciation, encouraged by his well-educated father and mother," had lasted through high school. "But during the Derry years, particularly after he had formed a brief friendship with John Hall, . . . Frost had gradually modified his way of talking. He deliberately imitated the manner in which his neighbors unconsciously slurred words, dropped endings, and clipped their sentences. By the time he reached Plymouth [1911], glad to be rid of the farm, he was still perfecting the art of talking like a farmer" (*Robert Frost: The Early Years* [Holt, Rinehart and Winston, 1966], p. 371).

14. Most notable is Ellery Sedgwick, friend of Amy Lowell and longtime editor of the prestigious *Atlantic Monthly*. Having since 1900 rejected poems by Frost, including three from *North of Boston* that Frost had sent from England, Sedgwick now greeted Frost effusively, took him home to dinner, and introduced him to literary friends in Boston (Thompson, *Years of Triumph*, pp. 12ff).

15. This remark is quoted by Peter Stanlis in "Robert Frost: The Conversationalist as Poet," *The Robert Frost Review* (Fall 1998), pp. 23-24.

16. As Walsh has pointed out, Frost clearly means not John Kline but John Hall, who is mentioned by name in "The Housekeeper" and who died in 1906, shortly after his common-law wife of many years left him for a man willing to take formal vows of marriage. Walsh reports that "the 'Kline' no doubt came from Klein's Hill, a rise which bordered one end of the Frost farm in Derry." See *Into My Own*, pp. 59, 238.

17. Frost's complex association among a people's character, its cultural productions, and its vernacular language is further confirmed by Douglas Wilson. Examining Frost's handwritten letter, Wilson confirms what he had suspected—that Frost uses the older, dialect form, "dry *stane* [not stone] *dykes*," when he inserts the local term for these unmortared walls. See Wilson's "The Other Side of the Wall," *The Iowa Review*, 10:1 (1979), pp. 72-73.

18. According to Daniel Boorstin—in *The Americans: the Democratic Experience* (Random House, 1973), p. 292—the moment when the growing urban population of the United States came to equal the rural was 1910, a midpoint for the creative process of *North of Boston*. But at this point, even rural life was radically altered. Where, in 1800, roughly eighty percent of American men were self-employed, mainly in farming, by 1900, eighty percent were working for wages. Significantly, even those who remained self-employed, including farmers, were now working mainly for money rather than subsistence. My thanks to Richard Wakefield for first calling my attention to these facts and this source.

19. Jeffrey S. Cramer, *Robert Frost Among His Poems: A Literary Companion to the Poet's Own Biographical Contexts and Associations* (McFarland, 1996), p. 28.

20. This was perhaps especially so in America, where Frost's true interest and audience lay. Frank Lentricchia suggests that Frost's decision to go to England in 1912 was influenced by his belief that, unlike their American counterparts, "English publishers . . . were not yet shaped fatally by . . . conventional taste and mass-market lust," and "had somehow found a way to balance economic necessity with the love of good letters." See Lentricchia's *Modernist Quartet* (Cambridge University Press, 1994), p. 102.

Robert Frost and the Politics of Labor_____

Tyler B. Hoffman[1]

It has long been assumed that Frost's relationship to American industrialism is straightforward: he wrote a pastoral poetry that either ignores the spread of new technologies and modes of work or stands opposed to them. Frost's conception of the American working class, on which industrialism depends, is viewed as similarly clear-cut, as most believe that he fails to consider the plight of the working poor in America's cities, preferring instead to focus on the rural people and cultures of New England.[2] Despite the confidence behind these critical commonplaces, the assumptions they make about Frost are not only simplistic but misleading. Although it is not immediately obvious, for reasons that I will explore, the fact is that Frost figures the wages of American industrialism in both well-known and obscured texts, and his responses to that social and economic organization are more complex than his reputation as a conservative political thinker and poet would suggest. In one set of poems written early in his career and later suppressed, Frost articulates a clear sympathy with the plight of industrial workers in opposition to an uncaring capitalist elite. In another group of poems composed during the New Deal, Frost disguises the toll that industrialism takes on the American working class in an attempt to resist what he perceived to be the unwarranted intrusions of the federal government, particularly as regards the labor movement. Yet another strain appears in poems of the 1930s, with Frost expressing his fear that Roosevelt's farm policy will mean the spread of industrialism to the sanctum of the country—a move that he believes would strip away both individual liberties and peace of mind.

In my effort to evaluate Frost's struggle with the issues raised by industrialism, I have resituated his poems in cultural context, attempting to show that Frost responds directly to contemporary historical developments and to the unique configuration of labor and the politics of labor in the U.S. during the first half of the twentieth century. While

Richard Poirier argues convincingly that in Frost's writing (and that of other Emersonian pragmatists) "the correspondence between physical work and mental work, between manual labor and writing (which is no less an operation of the hands), is expressed with an eagerness that effectively blurs the social and cultural distinctions known to exist between these different kinds of activity," Frost does not always blur such distinctions (*Poetry and Pragmatism* 81). In this essay, I want to turn away from such a correspondence—as useful as it is in understanding some of Frost's rhetorical strategies—and toward Frost's understanding and depictions of physical work in a mechanical age as separate and distinct from the work of writing. I will argue not only that Frost clearly saw the human costs of America's industrial economy, but that he carefully calculated these costs in his poetry.

* * *

In 1936 Frost published *A Further Range*. Although this collection of poetry went on to win the Pulitzer Prize, it drew scathing attacks from leftist critics at the time of its appearance. It is perhaps not surprising that the book came under heavy political fire, since Frost calls attention to his foray into "the realm of government" in his epigraph, a risky move for a poet to make.[3] Recalling *A Further Range* and the negative press it received on the basis of its political leanings, he later admitted: "it has got a good deal more of the times in it than anything I ever wrote before. . . . One well known paper called me a 'counter-revolutionary' for writing it" (*CP* 765). The "paper" to which Frost alludes is *New Masses*, "well known" for its leftist sympathies. In his review of *A Further Range* in *New Republic*, another liberal publication, Horace Gregory criticizes Frost for his lack of "social responsibility," calling several of the poems in the book "self-defensive" and "ill informed" (132-33). In terms of politics, Gregory goes on to observe: "[Frost's] wisdom may be compared to that of Calvin Coolidge," certainly not the social conscience that characterized America in the

1930s. In another review of the book by a prominent leftist critic, Granville Hicks extends Gregory's attack, claiming that Frost fails as a major modern American poet for much the same reason: "There is one thing, of course, Frost cannot do: he cannot contribute directly to the unification, in imaginative terms, of our culture. He cannot give us the sense of belonging in the industrial, scientific, Freudian world in which we find ourselves" (85). In a 1944 piece in *New Republic* Malcolm Cowley similarly chastises Frost for his anti-progressive stance: "He is too much walled in by the past. Unlike the great Yankees of an earlier age, he is opposed to innovations in art, ethics, science, industry or politics" (39).

What none of these critics seems to consider very carefully is that "A Lone Striker" is subtitled in the table of contents of *A Further Range* "Without Prejudice to Industry" and is a poem intent on giving us just such a "sense of belonging in the industrial . . . world," even as it stages one worker's vacation from it (*Poetry of Robert Frost* 557). It is a world, too, that Frost knew well: "I was brought up in a family who had just come to the industrial city of Lawrence, Massachusetts. My grandfather was an overseer in the Pacific Mills" (*CP* 759). As a young man, Frost himself was involved in the life of the mills: he worked at Braithwaite's woollen mill outside of Lawrence, where he pushed a bobbin-wagon among the rows of machines to collect empty bobbins, during the summer of 1891; after that, he worked as a clerical assistant to the gatekeeper at the Everett Mill in Lawrence, a job that required him to record absences and tardiness; and, finally, he took the job of light-trimmer in the Arlington Mill in Lawrence, working there from 1893-1894.[4] The different positions that he and his grandfather held in the mills in one of the leading textile cities in the U.S. shaped their responses to changes in the industry, specifically union gains for mill employees. Prior to the summer of 1891, hours stretched from seven in the morning until six in the evening, with a half-hour for lunch, six days a week. When the Lawrence mills were forced to grant employees Saturday afternoons off starting in the middle of that summer, reducing the working hours per week from sixty-three to fifty-eight, Frost was delighted; as his biographer Lawrance Thompson reports: "Never before had his mother's Socialist interest in the doctrines of Henry George or her deep admiration for Bellamy's recently published *Looking Backward* made so much sense to him" (*Early Years* 106). Frost's grandfather, on the other hand, was not so pleased, warning Frost that "In a few years these lazy louts will be at it again, trying to cut their time down to a fifty-hour week" (Thompson, *Early Years*, 106). These opposite reactions to this signal event in the history of labor in Lawrence prefigure Frost's own later ambivalence about industrial capitalism and the rights of workers in such a system.

"A Lone Striker" begins ominously enough, with the clanging of "the swinging mill bell" and the scurry of "tardy" workers through the mill gates (a sight Frost would have experienced first-hand as assistant to the gatekeeper at the Everett Mill). The "fateful" quality of the sound is not lost on Frost's speaker:

> The swinging mill bell changed its rate
> To tolling like the count of fate,
> And though at that the tardy ran,
> One failed to make the closing gate.
> There was a law of God or man
> That on the one who came too late
> The gate for half an hour be locked,
> His time be lost, his pittance docked.
> He stood rebuked and unemployed.
>
> (*CP* 249)

The metrical regularity here is made prominent by the lack of hard enjambment and almost total absence of caesurae (the one caesura in the penultimate line does not disturb the dipodic rhythm). In fact, there is no metrical substitution in the entire first two stanzas (a total of 35 lines), a prosodic sign of the unbending laws of industrial life that

---

clamp down on and take hold of these workers. When Frost's speaker states that "There was a law of God or man" that determined the lockout, he is being facetious, since it certainly is man-made; through the statement he is able to suggest the divine authority that the mill bosses have conferred upon themselves. Although he is the worker who has been barred, he refers to himself as "One," hinting at the anonymity of a cog in the wheel. Frost's use of the word "pittance" to describe the worker's wages indicates his comprehension of the bare sufficiency that colors this scene—the fact that men and women in these mills are subjected to harsh working conditions for meager gain.

The speaker goes on to conjure up a frightening image of the factory in the throes of operation with him locked outside it:

> The straining mill began to shake.
> The mill, though many, many eyed,
> Had eyes inscrutably opaque;
> So that he couldn't look inside
> To see if some forlorn machine
> Was standing idle for his sake.

Here Frost stresses the mill as inhuman and inhumane, as a disciplinary force. It appears as a glassy-eyed monster, one that looks at you but is unable to be looked at (a structure that suggests a panopticon). Frost concludes the stanza by saying that "He couldn't hope its [the machine's] heart would break," since he knows full well it has no heart and is completely incapable of such sympathies. In the second stanza, though, the speaker changes his tune, allowing himself to imagine the scene inside the mill from which he has been excluded. In his vision of women at their machines, his hope is restored: "That's where the human still came in." As he so benignly figures it, a spinner works happily in the factory, which is "full of dust of wool":

Her deft hand showed with finger rings
Among the harp-like spread of strings.
She caught the pieces end to end
And, with a touch that never missed,
Not so much tied as made them blend.

By way of this aesthetically pleasing image, Frost blocks out material reality, history in short. Like Wordsworth's "Tintern Abbey," which does not include the beggars and industrial pollution that would have marred that tourist site (a fact that Marjorie Levinson points out in her New Historicist reading of that poem), "A Lone Striker" veers from the actual circumstances of industrial life. If, as Levinson argues, "Wordsworth's pastoral project is a fragile affair, artfully assembled by acts of exclusion," Frost's "pastoral project" is achieved by his exclusion of the more oppressive labor practices (and social injustices) that define industrial America (and which he hints at in the first stanza) (25). Indeed, his idealizing strategies are nearly identical to Wordsworth's, with the difference being that Frost is explicitly making a political argument.

Despite his romanticizing of industrialization, Frost's speaker finds it "easy to resist" the pleasing scene he assembles, even as he credits "Man's ingenuity" for making such a scene possible. For the moment, though, he opts for personal freedom, affirming:

He knew another place, a wood,
And in it, tall as trees, were cliffs;
And if he stood on one of these,
'Twould be among the tops of trees,
Their upper branches round him wreathing,
Their breathing mingled with his breathing.
If—if he stood! Enough of ifs!
He knew a path that wanted walking;
He knew a spring that wanted drinking;

A thought that wanted further thinking;
A love that wanted re-renewing.
Nor was this just a way of talking
To save him the expense of doing.
With him it boded action, deed.

Here, for the first time in the poem, the dipodic rhythm is broken, through the use of caesurae and the additional unaccented syllable at the ends of eight of these lines, to denote the speaker's extravagance of spirit. The speaker concludes that "[t]he factory was very fine;/ He wished it all the modern speed"; it is just that he has had his fill, that it is time for him to liberate himself from such workaday constraints. Notably, he does not condemn the industrial enterprise from which he excuses himself; rather, he insists (with help from the subtitle) that he acts "Without Prejudice to Industry," that he is not a Luddite, but simply desires the release that unbounded nature provides.

First published in booklet form in 1933, "A Lone Striker" consciously resists the progressive political forces of the New Deal, and is based on his own experience as a mill worker in Lawrence, where, upon being locked out of the mill for being late, he "walked out of it all one day" (*CP* 760). He further explained its personal resonance and its relation to prevailing political winds at a public reading:

> Now suppose I read you a few things. Suppose I begin with that very poem about me and the mills in Lawrence. This one is called, "The Lone Striker." It is all right to be a striker, but not a lone striker. You might think that I might get in right with my radical friends, but the trouble with me is that I was a lone striker; if I called it a "collectivist striker," that would be another matter. This was the way it was to me, not a very serious thing. (*CP* 763)

It was perhaps "not a very serious thing" for Frost because he did not yet have to provide for a family. In "A Lone Striker" the privileged position that allows the young man to take so lightly his escape is especially telling in light of how one less carefree worker read that industrialized city: "'The mills are Lawrence and you cannot escape them'" (qtd. Goldberg 85). If Frost's representation of himself as "a lone striker"—not just someone who figuratively "strikes out" on his own, but one who literally goes on "strike"—is not biased against industry, it is biased against the workers in that system of production. In the same year that the poem appeared, the National Industrial Recovery Act set labor codes (bargaining rights, wage-hour protection, prevention of child labor) and encouraged labor unions to conduct large organizational drives. Prior to its enactment, employers could prevent bona fide unions of workers from gaining sufficient strength to establish collective bargaining. Irving Bernstein reports that the year was a watershed in labor politics: "Man-days lost due to strikes, which had not exceeded 603,000 in any month in the first half of 1933, spurted to 1,375,000 in July and to 2,378,000 in August. In fact, the whole year 1933 (mainly its second half) witnessed the largest number of work stoppages since 1921. . . . The overriding issue in these disputes was collective bargaining" (173). By letting these facts go unregistered, "A Lone Striker" asserts Frost's bias against unionization, his preference for individual, as opposed to collective, action.

Frost's return to the scene of his factory walkout forty years after the fact tells us much not only about his views of the American political landscape in the 1930s, but about the politics of labor as staged in Lawrence in the intervening years. By the time he writes "A Lone Striker," that city is well known as the site of some of the most violent labor protests in industrial New England, in 1912 and again in 1919. The 1912 walkout "earned Lawrence a national and even international reputation as a radical labor center," standing as "'the era's supreme symbol of militant struggle against industrial oppression'" (Goldberg 91). Frost is suspicious of that reputation, and sides with the owner of the Wood Mill, whom he names as "a great figure against Bill Haywood, his antagonist in the big Lawrence strike of 1910-11":

Now Wood was really a proletarian in my use of the word. As the swear-word is, he was really a son of a sea-cook—I mean it literally—a son of a Portuguese sea-cook. He grew up in New Bedford—and rose to be the head of all the woollen mills; the Woollen Association, or whatever they call it. . . . Then he had the tragedy, after patronizing the poor and doing every-thing he could for his employees—even giving them escalators in the mills. He got a strike on his hands and came out very badly in it. He lost the affec-tion of his people and committed suicide afterwards. He was the genuine proletarian, because he came up from nowhere. (*CP* 760)

Insisting on the victim status of the industrialist as opposed to the workers in his mills, who, it is implied, should have been more grateful for the improvements made, Frost inverts the classes, seeing Wood as "proletarian" and the "poor" as privileged. But his idealizing of Wood ignores certain stubborn facts. Steve Dunwell has shown that "Wood's actions during the strike suggest consuming greed and total insensitiv-ity to labor" (153), and Joe Hill's song "John Golden and the Lawrence Strike" begins with a punning denunciation of that man: "In Lawrence, when the starving masses struck for more to eat/ And wooden-headed Wood tried the masses to defeat, . . ." (Kornbluh 180). The announce-ment by American Woolen that a wage cut would accompany reduc-tion of the work week from fifty-six to fifty-four hours—a reduction required by law—prompted wildcat strikers to rampage through the Wood Mill, cutting belts and breaking machines. The local chapter of the Industrial Workers of the World (I.W.W.) called in Joe Ettor and Bill Haywood, highly regarded Wobbly organizers, and the strike grew to include twenty-three thousand workers. After sixty-three days, American Woolen surrendered and agreed to strike demands for wage increases and time-and-a-quarter overtime. Eugene Debs called the Lawrence victory "one of the most decisive and far-reaching ever won by organized workers" (Goldberg 91). None of these events enters into "A Lone Striker," however, since the poem is based on Frost's own ex-periences there, which occur prior to labor unrest; but by leaving the time of the action unnoted (he dates several retrospective poetic imaginings in *West-Running Brook*), the poem clearly is intended to make a case for quietude in the present.[5] Frost's response to Fred Beal's account of his experiences as a textile worker and, ultimately, a labor organizer in Lawrence in *Proletarian Journey* (1937) is telling. He says he identifies with the first half of the narrative, but that in the end Beal "went radical," falling into the communist camp (*CP* 760). In Frost's nostalgic journey back in "A Lone Striker," he bypasses the history of labor in that mill city, steadfastly refusing to go radical; in doing so, he attempts to reconcile us to industrialism in such a way as to obviate New Deal labor activism.

* * *

If Frost's evasion of the human costs of industrialism in "A Lone Striker" constitutes a rejection of sympathy for the working poor as a result of his fear of New Deal liberalism, other poems he wrote earlier in the century—poems that he later suppressed—express his full awareness of the grim conditions in New England mill towns and his solidarity with workers. In a sonnet that he wrote in 1906 or 1907 but did not publish, Frost represents the desperation of mill laborers, who are physically and spiritually exhausted and alienated from their labor:

> When the speed comes a-creeping overhead
> And belts begin to snap and shafts to creak,
> And the sound dies away of them that speak,
> And on the glassy floor the tapping tread;
> When dusty globes on all a pallor shed,
> And breaths of many wheels are on the cheek;
> Unwilling is the flesh, the spirit weak,
> All effort like arising from the dead.

But the task ne'er could wait the mood to come;
The music of the iron is a law:
And as upon the heavy spools that pay
Their slow white thread, so ruthlessly the hum
Of countless whirling spindles seems to draw
Upon the soul, still sore from yesterday.

(*CP* 511)

This poem strikes the same chord as the first part of "A Lone Striker," depicting the mill as most workers experienced it; however, it does not succumb to the fictions of that later poem ("Her deft hand showed with finger rings/ Among the harp-like spread of strings"). Perhaps this is not so surprising, since Frost's own stint as a worker in the mills—and the oppressive conditions of that space—would have been fresher on his mind, but it is also true that political conditions in the country are not what they will be in the 1930s, allowing Frost to display his sympathies openly and unapologetically. The "homicidal roar" of industrial machinery wrecks the workers, whom we see going through the paces as their lives wind down ("Their slow white thread") (*CP* 279). That Frost originally submitted this sonnet to the New York magazine the *Independent* suggests his awareness that there was a market for such "protest" poetry as of about 1906 or 1907 and his readiness to identify himself publicly with the cause of the mill worker at that time.[6] However, when the poem was not accepted, it did not resurface in Frost's lifetime.

Another early sonnet, this one written in 1905, also represents Frost's sharp sense of the oppression of the American working class. In "The Mill City" he takes account of his own relatively privileged position and expresses his sympathy for workers who are trapped in deplorable conditions:

It was in a drear city by a stream,
And all its denizens were sad to me,—
I could not fathom what their life could be—
Their passage in the morning like a dream
In the arc-light's unnatural bluish beam,
Then back, at night, like drowned men from the sea,
Up from the mills and river hurriedly,
In weeds of labor, to the shriek of steam.

Yet I supposed that they had all one hope
With me (there is but one.) I would go out,
When happier ones drew in for fear of doubt,
Breasting their current, resolute to cope
With what thoughts they compelled who thronged the street,
Less to the sound of voices than of feet.

(*CP* 509)

The octet of this sonnet imagines the working men as drowning victims; the water that powers the mill rushes over them and, at the whistle, they are dredged up from the stream bed ("In weeds of labor") to drift home as ghosts. The speaker is different from them ("I could not fathom what their life could be"), but sympathetic to their plight; he extends himself to them when other, "happier" people refuse to look for fear that their faith in industrial "progress" will be shaken. At the end of the sestet, Frost expresses his willingness to grapple with the problem of industrialized labor, to listen to the concerns of these oppressed workers. In short, the speaker of this poem does what the speaker of "A Lone Striker" steadfastly refuses to do, as the New Deal has not yet forced him to look away from such suffering in his effort to defend the claims of the individual against the state.

Frost's poem "The Parlor Joke," which is written a few years after these sonnets, expresses more vehemently his anger at the exploitation of the working class and specifically figures the labor conditions in

Lawrence in the years leading up to the 1912 strike. Although the poem is not included in any of Frost's books, it was published in Louis Untermeyer's *A Miscellany of American Poetry* (1920). Originally, Frost sent the poem to Untermeyer in a letter (March 21, 1920) with the following note indicating its date of composition: "Patented 1910 by R. (L.) Frost" (*CP* 991). Here he jokingly suggests to his anthologist friend—and committed socialist—that he has protected his poem against imitation by competitors, marking it as a commodity in a capitalist culture, despite the fact that the poem mounts a critique of capitalism. Frost's speaker begins by asserting that what he has to say is a well-kept (and dirty little) secret of that economic system:

> You won't hear unless I tell you
> How the few to turn a penny
> Built complete a modern city
> Where there shouldn't have been any,
> And then conspired to fill it
> With the miserable many.
>
> They drew on Ellis Island.
> They had but to raise a hand
> To let the living deluge
> On the basin of the land.
> They did it just like nothing
> In smiling self-command.
>
> If you asked them *their* opinion,
> They declared the job as good
> As when, to fill the sluices,
> They turned the river flood;
> Only then they dealt with water
> And now with human blood.
>
>   (*CP* 516)

The moralism of this passage is hard to miss: Frost exposes the arrogance of the corporate elite by showing with what callousness they treat immigrant laborers and points up the unnaturalness of their designs. As the polluted city grows, the mill owners cynically retreat with their families to live in the "hillside suburb." But to their consternation the strongholds that they erect cannot keep the poor at bay:

> As their tenements crept nearer,
> It pleased the rich to assume,
> In humorous self-pity,
> The mockery of gloom
> Because the poor insisted
> On wanting all the room.

This expression of the rich constitutes the "feeble parlor joke" of the title, and the speaker goes on to imagine that the compassionless words of "the gentlefolk" will dawn on them and serve as a self-administered "gentle retribution," one that encourages them to change their contemptuous attitudes and ways.

However, the situation does not resolve itself so simply, as the speaker notes an alternative form of retribution taking shape:

> some beheld a vision:
> Out of stench and steam and smoke,
>
> Out of vapor of sweat and breathing,
> They saw materialize
> Above the darkened city
> Where the murmur never dies,
> A shape that had to cower
> Not to knock against the skies.

They could see it through a curtain,
They could see it through a wall,
A lambent swaying presence
In wind and rain and all,
With its arms abroad in heaven
Like a scarecrow in a shawl.

The ghostly presence is interested in overturning the hierarchical order, as it is heard to say

Something about rebellion
And blood a die for wool,
And how you may pull the world down
If you know the prop to pull.

Frost defined this vision more clearly in a letter to Untermeyer in 1919: "Sometime I must copy you out a poem I did on Bolshevism in 1911 as I saw it spectral over Lawrence at the time of the strike. It will show you where I was" (*Letters* 80). The "lambent swaying presence" represents, then, the communist spirit energized by unfair labor practices, but it cannot help but resonate with political cartoons of the period that exposed police brutality in Lawrence. In one such cartoon that ran in *Collier's* (February 24, 1912), a giant policeman with club in hand—a figure that must "cower/ Not to knock against the skies"—bears down on the strikers and their huddled families; the caption points up the social disparities that have instigated the trouble: "Dividends for mill owners/ Starvation wages for workers."

That the image in the poem suggests the strong-arm tactics of the mill owners and state agents as well as the ominous force of communism attests to where Frost was politically when he wrote the poem. In the same 1919 letter to Untermeyer he vents his anger at the greedy industrialists but hesitates to align himself fully with the working class: "If the poor promised themselves no more than vengeance in the oncoming revolution I'd be with them. It's all their nonsense about making a better or even a different world that I can't stand. The damned fools!—only less damned than the God damned fools over them who have made and made such a mess of industrialism." The poem ends by harshly criticizing the capitalists who have provoked the workers' outrage and driven them into the communist camp in their effort to ensure greater profits for themselves:

> What to say to the wisdom
> That could tempt a nation's fate
> By invoking such a spirit
> To reduce the labor-rate!
> Some people don't mind trouble
> If it's trouble up-to-date.

Frost expresses the same concern in a notebook that he kept during this period, highlighting the xenophobic strain that also marks the poem: "A great many more than half the industrial class [i.e., working class] are where by a wise stroke of concession they can be detached from the party of dissatisfaction that threatens the state. We are of little faith not to see the simple way to save ourselves from the Russian contagion" ("Notebook" 159). As a result of his condemnation of the mercenary zeal of American industrialists in "The Parlor Joke," Frost was wary of how the poem would be received, telling Untermeyer that "as a friend you are going to be delighted with anything I give you no matter how damaging it may prove to me as an author and to you as an editor" (*Letters* 104). Obviously, Frost believed in 1920 that his national reputation as a poet might be jeopardized by any show of sympathy for the working class—a sympathy that could be read as an endorsement of a leftist political agenda—and in later years expressed his dislike of the poem, in effect distancing himself from it (Newdick 268).

Beginning in the 1920s, Frost grows quiet about the politics of labor and the intensifying class warfare in American society, just as he

---

comes to believe that communism presents a potent threat to American democracy. As Lawrance Thompson points out, Frost overlooks quite a lot of social history in his narrative poem "New Hampshire" (1923), screening out the labor problems of his day:

> He himself is able to play Pollyanna in his attitude toward political and so-
> cial conditions in the United States, at exactly the moment when he is pro-
> testing that the Russian people are being given the choice between getting
> shot or playing Pollyanna. Insisting that "life goes so unterribly" in the
> United States, with "nothing worse than too much luck and comfort," Frost
> was characteristically closing his eyes to some social facts. The adminis-
> tration of Warren Gamaliel Harding was currently developing a notorious
> reputation for graft, corruption, scandal; widespread poverty helped cause
> more than 3,000 strikes involving some 4,000,000 workers in 1919 and
> 1920; the coal-mine strike at Herrin, Illinois, cost 36 lives on 22-23 June
> 1922—a date very close to the night when RF wrote the first draft of "New
> Hampshire." (*Years of Triumph* 594)

Frost credits the inception of the poem to a series of articles that appeared in 1922 in the *Nation* under the heading "These United States"—articles that he considered primarily fault-finding, delineat-ing what was wrong with the country from a socialist perspective (Thompson, *Years of Triumph*, 230-31). He declined the invitation of the *Nation* to contribute to the series but wrote a poem that presents a positive image of New Hampshire—a promotional piece that refuses to examine strained relations between labor and capital in that state or in the country more generally.[7]

Frost's only poems from this period that suggest strife between rich and poor were published posthumously. In "On the Inflation of the Currency 1919," Frost meditates on the drastic halving of monetary value as it affects the standard of living of the American working class:

The pain of seeing ten cents turned to five!
We clutch with both hands fiercely at the part
We think we feel it in—the head, the heart.
Is someone cutting us in two alive?

Is someone at us cutting us in half?
We cast a dangerous look from where we lie
Up to the enthroned kings of earth and sky.
They know what's best for them too well to laugh.

                                             (*CP* 535)

The nation's monetary policy, the speaker asserts, is determined by an oligarchic few, without concern for the loss in purchasing power suffered by the average American. The "enthroned kings," by relaxing the money supply and increasing inflation, only have at heart solidifying their own economic base. At about the same time Frost wrote another poem, "A Correction," which figures the same fiscal slashing, but in veiled terms:

When we told you minus twenty
Here this morning, that seemed plenty.
We were trying to be modest
(Said he spitting in the sawdust)
And moreover did our guessing
By the kitchen stove while dressing.
Come to dress and make a sortie,
What we found was minus forty.

                                             (*CP* 535)

In this version of the financial crisis, "minus twenty" becoming "minus forty" is the equivalent of "ten cents turned to five." Although the tone is less bitter, the class antagonism is no less marked, as the "enthroned king" dictating economic policy ("he spitting in the dust") seems all too casual about the decision made. The surprise on walking outside (i.e., into a store) and finding that a dollar goes half as far as it did the day before does not prompt indignation, as the poem stops short of the politically charged second stanza of "On the Inflation of the Currency 1919." But the fact that men are merely "guessing" what effect policies will have indicates a grave indifference to the welfare of the working poor. These two takes on economic "correction"—both of which Frost suppressed—illustrate his ambivalence: he recognizes the pain that the people suffer, but does not want to reflect publicly on it for fear that such sympathy will lump him with those on the left.

Another pair of poems written earlier in the decade, however, represents Frost's staunch refusal to assert sympathy or solidarity with the proletariat when they seek to remedy their situation through collective action. In "Good Relief," a poem based on an experience of 1912 in the English town of High Wycombe and composed that same year, Frost dismisses striking colliers for their reform-mindedness, mocking what he refers to in his introduction to Edwin Arlington Robinson's *King Jasper* (1935) as "grievances against the un-Utopian state" (*CP* 742):

> Remember how two babes were on the street—
> And so were many fathers out on strike,
> The vainest of their many strikes in vain,
> And lost already as at heart they knew.
>
> . . . .
>
> But why like the poor fathers on the curb
> Must we be always partizan and grim?
> No state has found a perfect cure for grief
> In law or gospel or in root or herb.
>
> (*CP* 523)

Frost acknowledges that not everyone all the time will be wholly content, but refuses to concede that in the absence of "a perfect cure," "Good Relief" could come by forcing the hands of capitalists to improve wages and working conditions. Instead, he insists on seeing the strikers as political partisans attempting to right the wrongs of the world—a futile (because idealistic) quest. Frost sent the poem to Susan Hayes Ward, the literary editor of the *Independent* to whom he had sent his early sonnet "When the speed comes a-creeping overhead," knowing that she would be ruffled by its sentiments (she was a devout Congregationalist like her brother the Reverend William Hayes Ward, with whom she edited the magazine), but it was not published until 1935 in his daughter Lesley's anthology *Come Christmas*. Here, too, Frost's timing is carefully calculated: he unleashes the poem when he is piqued sufficiently by the New Deal notion that the role of government is to "cure" the woes of working-class Americans.

Frost's poem "My Giving," the companion piece to "Good Relief" written the year before and unpublished in his lifetime, seems on the face of it to assert a solidarity with industrial workers that the speaker of "Good Relief" cannot muster; in fact, though, "My Giving," which also is set during the Christmas season, mocks the idea of full-blown sympathy for the disaffected and dispossessed. At one point in the poem the speaker asserts his intention to share in the grief of the striking workers—a "grief that is rightly theirs"—and forsake "merrymaking," but his lament is insincere:

> Here I shall sit, the fire out, and croon
> All the dismal and joy-forsaken airs,
> Sole alone, and thirsty with them that thirst,
> Hungry with them that hunger and are accurst.
> No storm that night can be too untamed for me;
> If it is woe on earth, woe let it be!
>
> (*CP* 518-19)

The speaker pretends to suffer with them, but the ironic undertow suggests that he is pointing up the limits to sympathetic attachment, that just because others are out of work and starving on the streets does not mean we can or should do the same in a show of solidarity. While he takes the side of the workers in "A Parlor Joke," where there is only a glimmer of a general strike, he turns on workers when they band together in "Good Relief" and in "My Giving" resists those who would have him merge his interests with theirs.

* * *

Frost's antipathy toward the evolving politics of labor in the U.S. during the first half of the twentieth century is complicated further by major changes in farming practice and policy that occur between 1910 and the mid-1930s. Irving Bernstein has demonstrated that "by 1933 the family farm was in decay in many sectors of American agriculture and was being rapidly displaced by industrial agriculture—mash crops raised on large holdings with professional management, scientific methods, and heavy investments in machinery—by what Carey Mc-Williams called 'factories in the field'" (142). The rise of this system of agriculture, and the wide-scale displacement of family farmers that it engenders, deeply disturbs Frost, who believes that "Government's chief end [should be] to propagate small farmers" ("Notebook" 159). In his notebook Frost explains that this situation immediately bears on one's class sympathies: "You can't favor the industrial class as against the capitalist without doing it as against the agricultural, and so turning the agricultural industrial. . . . Abolishing the capitalist would mean abolishing the farmer included" ("Notebook" 148, 150). Frost sheds light on these statements in another entry in his notebook and does not hesitate to assign blame: "The socialist means to abolish the farmer by driving him to work in the cities, and when he has left the farms vacant he will send squads of city industrials on weekly wage into the country for spells to cultivate the land. The president is up to this" (150). Franklin D. Roosevelt, the president "up to this," becomes Frost's target, as he worries that his administration is intent on turning agricultural production from an individualist pursuit into a collectivist enterprise. As much as he suggests that he might like to side with the "industrial class" (i.e., city workers) in opposition to "the capitalist," he does not feel free to do so, because, to his thinking, he then would be endorsing socialism and, thus, be complicit in the extinction of the small farmer. What Frost fails to acknowledge is that "the capitalist" is responsible for the growth of corporate farms that by 1933 already endangered Frost's ideal of the husbandman tending his soil. Despite this fact, he trains his sights on what he regards as disastrous New Deal policies, no doubt in part spurred on by the eruption of unionism in agriculture (in 1933-34, there occurred in the United States 99 strikes involving 87,364 agricultural workers) (Bernstein 142).

In "Build Soil," a "political pastoral" that he delivered at Columbia University on May 31, 1932, before the political party conventions of that year and later published in *A Further Range*, Frost airs his opinions about the farm problem through the personae of Tityrus, the farmer-poet who voices Frost's personal politics, and Meliboeus, his farmer friend who has been dispossessed of his land. That he borrows his characters from Virgil's first eclogue would seem to suggest that he is evading the issues of industrialism in his own time, but the poem is as much about them as is "A Lone Striker." His use of that eclogue is apposite, too, since Virgil's ideal landscape is put at risk by an alien world encroaching from without (in Virgil's case, the government in Rome). In "Build Soil" the forces of industrialism that impinge on the farm threaten the bucolic environment on which Frost stakes so much. In conversation with Tityrus, Meliboeus wonders why things should not be "Made good for everyone—things like inventions—/ Made so we all should get the good of them—/ All, not just great exploiting businesses" (*CP* 291). His concern about the effects of untempered capitalism on the small farmer leads him to ask, "But don't you think more should be socialized/ than is?" to which Tityrus makes ironic reply:

None shall be as ambitious as he can.
None should be as ingenious as he could,
Not if I had my say. Bounds should be set
To ingenuity for being so cruel
In bringing change unheralded on the unready.

Tityrus does not advocate socializing ingenuity, even if he does see that new technologies will mean the end of a livelihood for some (he remarks that a hypothetical new wool substitute when "let loose upon the grazing world/ Will put ten thousand farmers out of sheep"). He mocks the notion that such a force could be bounded—that our ambition could or should be held in check so as to protect those who would be adversely affected. Refuting Meliboeus's distrust of big business and wariness of commerce, Tityrus claims: "To market 'tis our destiny to go./ But much as in the end we bring for sale there/ There is still more we never bring or should bring." He urges Meliboeus to adopt not a five-year plan like the one "That Soviet Russia has made fashionable," but his own plan of self-enrichment:

You shall go to your run-out mountain farm,
Poor castaway of commerce, and so live
That none shall ever see you come to market—
Not for a long long time.

The embargo that Tityrus proposes does not depend for its efficacy on collective political action (what he calls "general revolution"), but on action undertaken by a lone farmer: "I bid you to a one-man revolution—/ The only revolution that is coming." The New Deal solution to increase the standard of living of farmers was to levy taxes so that the price of crops at market would rise artificially, with the tax revenues then redistributed to the farmers in proportion to their crop production. In a May 1933 article in *Harper's* Benjamin Ginzburg labeled that plan a "radical socialistic remedy of state control and fixed prices" (670), an assessment with which Frost would have agreed, as evidenced by Tityrus's individualism and *laissez-faire* economics ("Were I dictator . . ./ I'd let things take their course/ And then I'd claim the credit for the outcome"). Lest Untermeyer mistake the "revolution" for which he was calling in "Build Soil," Frost plainly stated his vision to him: "It isn't rebellion I am talking. . . . It is simply easy ties and slow commerce" (Thompson, *Years of Triumph*, 432).

In a letter to Frost, Ferner Nuhn, a family friend who worked for a time in the Roosevelt administration, challenges that political vision, and Frost's response sheds more light on his struggle with the complex issues raised by industrialism—his opposition to New Deal liberalism and guarded sympathy for the proletariat. Nuhn tries to explain to Frost the inadequacy of Tityrus's prescriptions:

> [A]s once we changed modes from monarchy to democracy, so now we are changing modes from individual to corporate economics. . . . If any large proportion of farmers took the advice given Moloebeus [*sic*] and "dug in" and ate and wore their own products and didn't go to market to buy and sell more than a little dribble of excess, city people and easterners including poets and homilizers would pretty quickly be starved out, by the millions. . . . You'll excuse this finger-counting arithmetic, but you know, a westerner, a corn-belter, some times has to stand up and talk western farm arithmetic to Vermonters with their hankering for self-sustaining mountain farms which, however excellent as a way of life, are not sustaining the United States at present. . . . Farmers and poets and machine-tenders, we've all got beyond self-containment economically; the mode has passed; the emphasis is misplaced. . . . (Thompson, *Years of Triumph*, 457)

Nuhn finds that Frost "give[s] comfort to . . . the real surplus-grabbers, who want to see all the Moelebeuses [*sic*] stay contented and quiet," that by defending the times Tityrus in effect aids and abets the "fat boys, the cashers-in on the system as it works now." In a letter to

Untermeyer, Frost expresses his distaste for Nuhn's position, claiming that his subject is "not the sadness of the poor" (*Selected Letters* 467-68). However, in a letter of reply to Nuhn that he never sent, Frost seeks to moderate his hard-line stance, informing him that "Both those people in the dialogue are me" (Thompson, *Years of Triumph*, 460). Our ability to see Frost in Meliboeus is hampered, though, by Frost's own remarks outside of his poetry, which suggest a clearer ideological connection with Tityrus, whose concern about the New Deal solution to "send squads of city industrials on weekly wage into the country for spells to cultivate the land" is Frost's:

> Needless to say to you, my argument
> Is not to lure the city to the country.
> Let those possess the land, and only those,
> Who love it with a love so strong and stupid
> That they may be abused and taken advantage of
> And made fun of by business, law, and art;
> They still hang on.
>
> (*CP* 294)

In these remarks Tityrus vents Frost's hostility to the New Deal Resettlement Administration, one aim of which was to resettle urban slum dwellers in autonomous garden cities and submarginal farmers in new, productive farm villages. The idea made Frost see red (in both senses), and when Tityrus pronounces, "Let none assume to till the land but farmers," he inveighs against the plan to use agriculture to liquidate the industrial surplus.

In his poem "A Roadside Stand" Frost steps up his attack on New Deal farm policy—particularly on this matter of resettlement. At the beginning of the poem we see what might seem innocent enough—a stand selling wares to city dwellers out for a drive in the country. But for Frost the country folks' plea for city money symbolizes a dangerous desire to imitate city ways—including the ways of industrialism.

The speaker scorns the government solution to the problem of these submarginal farmers just as Tityrus does:

> It is in the news that all these pitiful kin
> Are to be brought out and mercifully gathered in
> To live in villages next to the theater and store
> Where they wont have to think for themselves any more;
> While greedy good-doers, beneficent beasts of prey,
> Swarm over their lives enforcing benefits
> That are calculated to soothe them out of their wits,
> And by teaching them how to sleep the sleep all day,
> Destroy their sleeping at night the ancient way.
>
> (*CP* 261)

The "beneficent beasts of prey" are the "good-doers" of the federal government who claim to want to make life easier and better for the people, but only by stripping them of their free will; their idea of resettlement is unnatural ("teaching them how to sleep the sleep all day"), Frost maintains, and the cooperative farms proposed will only make the people dependent on the welfare of the state. The speaker offers at the end of the poem to put these "pitiful kin" out of their misery to prevent such a fate (the original title of the poem was the not so subtle "Euthanasia") (Thompson, *Years of Triumph*, 439).

Frost's assault on federal government policies that he believed would erase the distinction between the city and the country follows from his view that the family farm represents a "natural," restorative space, an antidote to the "artificial" (i.e., mechanical) forces of industrialism in urban America. In an interview published in the magazine *Rural America* in 1931, Frost asserts the need for measure in our lives—a measure that requires the existence of both worlds: "I should expect life to be back and forward—now more individual on the farm, now more social in the city—striving to get the balance" (*Interviews* 76). When the boundaries between farm and city are blurred, the ability to strike this healthy balance is imperiled, and Frost notes the damage that the spread of industrialism has wrought:

> We are now at a moment when we are getting too far out into the social-industrial and are at the point of drawing back—drawing in to renew ourselves. The country life we are going back to I can't describe in advance, but I am pretty sure it will not be the country life we came out of years ago. Farming, what survives of it, has demeaned itself in an attempt to imitate industrialism. It has lost its self-respect. It has wished itself something other than what it is. That is the only unpardonable sin: to wish you were something you are not, something other people are. It is so in the arts and in everything else. . . . The farmer has industrialized to his own hurt right on the farm. He has entered into the competitive outside life. The strength of his position is that he's got so many things that he doesn't need to go outside for. The country's advantage is that it gives many pleasures and supplies many needs for nothing. The tendency of our day is to throw away all of these things and count them worthless. (*Interviews* 76)

Frost finds that the farmer has compromised his self-sufficiency by submitting to industrialism, and fails to give credence to Nuhn's statement that "we've all got beyond self-containment economically; the mode has passed." In the *Denver Post* (October 11, 1932) an article entitled "Robert Frost, Famous Poet, Praises Farm Strike Idea" quotes Frost as saying, "We Americans are doing everything in our power to narrow, industrialize and mechanize this [agricultural] base." Exhorting midwestern farmers to decrease productivity, Frost claims that "[i]f the farmers would go Robinson Crusoe and dole out just enough of their produce to keep the cities alive for purposes of visiting and recreation, the agricultural problem might be settled, without benefit of politics, politicians or congress, for the good of all." Here he crosses the line between "a one-man revolution" and "general revolution," asserting his interest in the latter, provided that the action is not tainted by "politics." Of course, the action is inevitably political, but, because it is the idea of farmers, and not of "politicians or congress," Frost sees it in a positive light. Later in the interview he speaks collectively: "We do not need to sacrifice individualism in the struggle for recognition and a living, nor do we need to take a chance on being industrialized or mechanized. We hold the weapons with which to create our own success and security. All we must do is to learn to use them." The *Denver Post* reporter traces Frost's remarks, particularly his call "urging farmers to plot together to save themselves," to his poem "Build Soil." This political reading of Frost's poem seeks to justify what midwestern farmers already had begun to do. Mary Heaton Vorse's article "Rebellion in the Cornbelt" in *Harper's* (December 1932) refers to the "banding together of farmers for mutual protection," and notes that "A Farmers' Holiday Association had been organized by one Milo Reno, and the farmers were to refuse to bring food to market for thirty days or 'until the cost of production had been obtained'" (3). Although Frost would not have quarreled with the spirit behind such action, he makes clear in the 1930s his suspicion of "movements" of any kind, and in "Build Soil" has Tityrus exhort, "Don't join too many gangs. Join few if any" (*CP* 296).

Even before the dawn of the New Deal, in his poem "The Egg and the Machine," which was first published in 1928, Frost addresses concerns about the rapidly changing economic landscape, depicting a struggle between invasive mechanical forces and one worker. The title itself announces an opposition between the natural and the unnatural, and in the poem the speaker blasts what Leo Marx calls "the machine in the garden":

> He gave the solid rail a hateful kick.
> From far away there came an answering tick
> And then another tick. He knew the code:
> His hate had roused an engine up the road.
> He wished when he had had the track alone

He had attacked it with a club or stone
And bent some rail wide open like a switch
So as to wreck the engine in the ditch.

(*CP* 248)

Here Frost activates "the trope of the interrupted idyll"—a trope that shapes the work of some nineteenth-century American writers responding to the new industrial power: "The locomotive, associated with fire, smoke, speed, iron, and noise, is the leading symbol of the new industrial power. It appears in the woods, suddenly shattering the harmony of the green hollow, like a presentiment of history bearing down on the American asylum" (Marx 27). Frost's locomotive is a steam monster reminiscent of the shrieking mill: "Then for a moment all there was was size/ Confusion and a roar that drowned the cries/ He raised against the gods in the machine." The speaker's "hate" prompts a belated wish that he had sabotaged the rails "So as to wreck the engine in the ditch," a statement that raises interesting questions about the man's identity. At the time Frost wrote the poem, it was widely believed that the I.W.W. sponsored acts of sabotage; Bill Haywood, Wobbly organizer in the Lawrence strike, is credited with saying, "Sabotage means to push back, pull out or break off the fangs of Capitalism" (Kornbluh 64). In addition, the poem was entitled "The Walker" when originally published in the anthology *The Second American Caravan* (1928), the same title as a poem by Arturo Giovannitti, an Italian-born writer and orator who came to Lawrence early in the strike to take charge of strike relief. Giovannitti wrote his poem in prison in Salem, Massachusetts, after being jailed for his involvement in the strike, and it was published in a pamphlet issued by the I.W.W. in 1913. It is quite possible that Frost's walker is meant to be an I.W.W. itinerant worker, especially in light of the fact that "Most of them beat their way by freight car from one place to another, and railroad companies estimated that there were half a million hoboes riding the rails, walking the tracks, or waiting at railroad junctions to catch onto a train, at any one time" (Kornbluh 66).[8]

The climax of the poem in the final lines holds in suspension Frost's attitude toward the "walker" and his intended act of sabotage. Following the track of a turtle (as opposed to the artificial steel track that the engine rides), the man finds a buried nest and arms himself with turtle eggs, preparing to throw them at the train engine's headlight upon its next approach:

> 'You'd better not disturb me any more,'
> He told the distance, 'I am armed for war.
> The next machine that has the power to pass
> Will get this plasm in its goggle glass.'

The "war" that he stands ready to wage conjures up the reality of warfare between labor and capital raging in America at the time, but his insufficient arsenal seems to mock his position. Yvor Winters faults Frost for expressing in the poem his "sentimental hatred for the machine," thereby associating the poet with the title figure (68). But just what is Frost's relation to the armed man? Does he identify with his desire to keep industrialism at bay—to keep it from making inroads into the country? Or is he trying to expose the futility (and hilarity) of union attempts to throw a monkey wrench into the industrial machine, which simply should be accepted without prejudice? The landmark Railway Labor Act of 1926 (two years prior to the publication of the poem) emphasized collective bargaining and mediation over settlement of wage disputes by a federal board, and Frost may be suggesting that such legislation is fruitless, that each individual must measure himself against industrial forces at work in the world. When asked about the poem, though, Frost refused to declare his sympathies, stating that he was not "taking sides," that whether he was leaning toward the organic or the mechanical "is for you to choose" (Cook 35, 49). As these remarks indicate, his is no "sentimental hatred of the machine," but rather a careful weighing—and ambivalent staging—of the impact of the new industrial order.

Frost's negotiation of industrialism and the politics of labor associated with it is much more complex than most imagine, even if some of his equations and assumptions are not. Poirier is right to see that for Frost the New Deal was to be resisted on the grounds that it was a socialistic plan "designed to relieve the individual of responsibility for his own fate," but Frost was not always as "blind to social systems" or as lacking in "historical vision" as Poirier suggests (*Robert Frost* 230-33). Frost sympathizes with the plight of industrial workers in his early writings; his elision of these woes in later years is quite deliberate, as he seeks to defend rural America from "unnatural" mechanical forces and the specter of Roosevelt administration farm policy. Although Frost claims in his introduction to *King Jasper* that poetry should deal with "griefs," not "grievances" (*CP* 742), he gives voice to both in a range of poems in his effort to come to terms with contemporary labor issues and, ultimately, to secure a site for the renewal of poetry and the self.

From *Modern Language Studies* 29, no. 2 (Fall 1999): 110-135. Copyright © 1999 by Susquehanna University Press. Reprinted by permission of Susquehanna University Press.

Notes

1. I wish to thank the anonymous reader at *Modern Language Studies* for insightful commentary and suggestions.

2. The poet Louise Bogan's 1962 assessment has gone essentially unchallenged: "Frost is never concerned (as many poets and men of letters have shown themselves to be, since the beginning of the Industrial Revolution) with the blighting results of industry upon human beings in general. His is a personal feud, with the machine as adversary" (178-79).

3. Robert Frost, *Collected Poems, Prose, and Plays*, 977. Subsequent references to this edition appear as *CP* with page number in the text.

4. See Thompson, *Early Years*, 106-07; 135; 154-58.

5. For instance, a note in *West-Running Brook* dates "Bereft" "*As of about 1893*" and "The Thatch" "*As of 1914*" (*Poetry of Robert Frost* 554).

6. See Thompson, *Early Years*, 516-17.

7. At the Amoskeag Mill in Manchester, New Hampshire, labor unrest marks the period leading up to the publication of "New Hampshire." Hareven and Langenbach

report that in 1919 "the UTW [United Textile Workers of America] organized the first strike to occur in the Amoskeag since an 1885 strike led by the Knights of Labor," although it was quickly settled (24). In 1922, after an announcement of an increase in working hours and a 20 percent wage cut, "the first long-term strike in the Company's history" ensued with disastrous consequences for the mills, which finally shut down in 1936.

8. Carleton Parker characterized the American I.W.W. member as "a lonely hobo worker, usually malnourished and in need of medical care [who was] as far from a scheming syndicalist, after the French model, as the imagination could conceive." His mind, Parker noted, was "stamped by the lowest, most miserable labor conditions and outlook which American industrialism produces" (Kornbluh 66). Rexford G. Tugwell, head of the Resettlement Administration, also depicted the migrant as "a rather pathetic figure . . . wracked with strange diseases and tortured by unrealized dreams that haunt his soul" (Kornbluh 66). Frost wrote several poems about this figure, including "Two Tramps in Mud Time" and "The Old Barn at the Bottom of the Fogs" in *A Further Range* and the posthumously published "A Bed in the Barn." In some the tramp appears as a pathetic individual, but also as a political agitator: "Trust him to have his bitter politics/ Against his unacquaintances the rich/ Who sleep in houses of their own, though mortgaged" (*CP* 264).

Works Cited

Bernstein, Irving. *Turbulent Years: A History of the American Worker, 1933-1941.* Boston: Houghton, 1970.

Bogan, Louise. *A Poet's Alphabet.* New York: McGraw-Hill, 1970.

Cady, Edwin H., and Louis J. Budd, eds. *On Frost: The Best from American Literature.* Durham, NC: Duke UP, 1991.

Cook, Reginald L. "Frost on Frost: The Making of Poems." Cady and Budd 39-49. "Robert Frost's Asides on His Poetry." Cady and Budd 30-38.

Cowley, Malcolm. "The Case against Mr. Frost." Cox 36-45.

Cox, James M., ed. *Robert Frost: A Collection of Critical Essays.* Englewood Cliffs, NJ: Prentice-Hall, 1962.

Dunwell, Steve. *The Run of the Mill: A Pictorial Narrative of the Expansion, Dominion, Decline and Enduring Impact of the New England Textile Industry.* Boston: David R. Godine, 1978.

Frost, Robert. *Collected Poems, Prose, and Plays.* Ed. Richard Poirier and Mark Richardson. New York: Library of America, 1995.

_____. *Interviews with Robert Frost.* Ed. Edward Connery Lathem. New York: Holt, 1966.

_____. *The Letters of Robert Frost to Louis Untermeyer.* Ed. Louis Untermeyer. New York: Holt, 1963.

_____. "Notebook: After England." Ed. Margot Feldman. *Antaeus* 61 (1988). 147-64.

_____. *The Poetry of Robert Frost*. Ed. Edward Connery Lathem. New York: Holt, 1969.

_____. "Robert Frost, Famous Poet, Praises Farm Strike Idea." *Denver Post* (October 11, 1932). 14.

_____. *Selected Letters of Robert Frost*. Ed. Lawrance Thompson. New York: Holt, 1964.

Ginzburg, Benjamin. "Farm Relief—And What Then?" *Harper's* (May 1933). 667-77.

Goldberg, David J. *A Tale of Three Cities: Labor Organization and Protest in Paterson, Passaic, and Lawrence, 1916-1921*. New Brunswick, NJ: Rutgers UP, 1989.

Gregory, Horace. "Robert Frost's New Poems." Wagner 132-33.

Hareven, Tamara K., and Randolph Langenbach. *Amoskeag: Life and Work in an American Factory-City*. New York: Pantheon, 1978.

Hicks, Granville. "The World of Robert Frost." Wagner 83-85.

Kornbluh, Joyce L., ed. *Rebel Voices: An I.W.W. Anthology*. Ann Arbor: U of Michigan P, 1965.

Levinson, Marjorie. *Wordsworth's Great Period Poems*. Cambridge: Cambridge UP, 1986.

Marx, Leo. *The Machine in the Garden: Technology and the Pastoral Ideal in America*. Oxford: Oxford UP, 1964.

Newdick, Robert. *Newdick's Season of Frost: An Interrupted Biography of Robert Frost*. Ed. William A. Sutton. Albany: State U of New York P, 1976.

Poirier, Richard. *Poetry and Pragmatism*. Cambridge: Harvard UP, 1992.

_____. *Robert Frost: The Work of Knowing*. New York: Oxford UP, 1977.

Thompson, Lawrance. *Robert Frost: The Early Years, 1874-1915*. New York: Holt, 1966.

_____. *Robert Frost: The Years of Triumph, 1915-1938*. New York: Holt, 1970.

Vorse, Mary Heaton. "Rebellion in the Cornbelt." *Harper's* (December 1932). 1-10.

Wagner, Linda W., ed. *Robert Frost: The Critical Reception*. N.p.: Burt Franklin, 1977.

Winters, Yvor. "Robert Frost: or, the Spiritual Drifter as Poet." Cox 58-82.

Robert Frost:
The Walk as Parable_____

Roger Gilbert

Robert Frost is the first American poet in the twentieth century to explore the formal possibilities of the walk poem. From his first volume, *A Boy's Will*, to his last, *In the Clearing*, Frost exhibits a special fondness for ambulatory plots, and this is not simply due to his preference for rural settings and subject matter. Although he was conscious of his affinity with Georgian poets like Edward Thomas, for whom the countryside presented an inexhaustible source of picturesque objects for representation, Frost is never simply concerned with landscape per se. His true origins are American, and while Emerson may ultimately have influenced him more profoundly, Thoreau provided his most immediate model. (By contrast he shows little interest in or influence from Whitman, whose transcendental stance with regard to ordinary experience may have seemed to Frost to touch on what he himself feared most, the state of "formlessness.")

Many of Frost's lyrics read like versified Thoreau; they are factual records of daily experience, moments in the life of a subsistence farmer and inveterate walker. Yet they are, after all, *poems*, whereas Thoreau's characteristic production is the journal entry, a form to which even his more finished works show their debt. How do Frost's poems differ from Thoreau's prose? At what point do they cross the line between journalism and poetry? That line, we have seen, has much to do with the canonical ambitions of a piece of writing. For Thoreau the journalist, the amassing of experience in verbal form is an end in itself; no single walk or passage is meant to stand alone, for each is part of an ongoing whole coextensive with experience. But Frost is a poet, and his concern is with the creation of aesthetic constructs that will reward repeated scrutiny. His aim is thus not simply to reproduce experience but to transform it into something compact, singular, and lasting: in short, a poem. Each poem must therefore constitute a unique artifact, not one of hundreds of similar accounts whose value lies in their exhaustive transcription of daily particulars. (In shaping his journals into books, of course, Thoreau shows a similar concern for bringing to his raw experience the singularity of art, as attested to by Frost's frequent citation of *Walden* as his favorite poem.)[1]

Frost is thus faced with the problem of translating a Thoreauvian attention to the minute fabric of experience into a form capable of the concentration and permanence that we expect of a poem. His solution is the parable, or rather a strange hybrid of anecdote and parable that he made peculiarly his own. Frost's best poems exhibit an uncanny ability to locate themselves precisely on the border between literal and figurative modes of representation. The parable is his favorite trope because it displays just this ambiguous status. Parables are generally less transparent than allegories, lacking the one-to-one correspondence between image and concept that characterizes allegorical figuration; yet they nevertheless insist on a level of interpretation that transcends the literal. They present themselves as simultaneously literal and figurative, rather than purely one or the other. By taking up the representational strategy of parable, then, Frost's poems are able to fuse description and revelation, fact and figure, so that they are virtually indistinguishable. Seldom do we question the literality of his images, their origin in actual experience; and yet over and over they assume a parabolic dimension that lifts them above the experiential, enabling them to participate in a higher "wisdom" that for Frost constitutes the true aim of poetry. Like Thoreau in his treatment of Walden Pond, Frost seeks to imbue his images with thematic resonance without robbing them of their brute substantiality, their thing-ness.

For Frost the walk offers an especially good basis for parable, because its form seems to mirror the kind of thematic or parabolic movement he favors. Like his poetic heir A. R. Ammons, Frost tends to conceptualize poems in terms of walks. Here, for example, are some passages from his famous essay "The Figure a Poem Makes":

No one can really hold that the ecstasy should be static and stand still in one place. It begins in delight, it inclines to the impulse, it assumes direction with the first line laid down, it runs a course of lucky events, and ends in a clarification of life. . . .

Step by step the wonder of unexpected supply keeps growing. The impressions most useful to my purpose seem always those I was unaware of and so made no note of at the time when taken, and the conclusion is come that like giants we are always hurling experience ahead of us to pave the future with against the day when we may want to strike a line of purpose across it for somewhere. The line will have the more charm for not being mechanically straight. We enjoy the straight crookedness of a good walking stick. [. . .]

Scholars get their [knowledge] with conscientious thoroughness along projected lines of logic; poets theirs cavalierly and as it happens in and out of books. They stick to nothing deliberately, but let what will stick to them like burrs where they walk in the fields.[2]

It should be evident that the idea of the walk informs much of Frost's meditation on the nature of the poem. The analogy is a buried one, not an explicit equation as in Ammons's essay, but it is no less significant for that. Like a walk, a poem is an act of exploration, a dynamic process that unfolds "step by step" and eventually finds itself in some new, unforeseen "place." It occurs without a plan, moves impulsively, and may take many detours before arriving at its destination. Although this account of the poem seems to emphasize composition rather than the finished work, Frost refuses to differentiate between process and product; for him the value of a poem lies in its ability to reenact the impulsive movements that brought it into being. Thus each reader relives the initial process on each reading. The poem preserves a movement without freezing or fixing it in amber.

As with Ammons, this figure of the poem as movement has a tendency to become literal in Frost's own poetry. Because Frost conceives of the poem as an exploratory process, his poems are especially receptive to the walk as a kind of governing plot. In effect the walk enables him to externalize the deep structure present to one degree or another in all his lyrics. Thus for Frost the walk poem is not simply a container to be filled with description and meditation, random thoughts and perceptions bound together only by their copresence within the frame of the walk. Rather, the walk functions in his poetry as a parable of enlightenment, beginning in delight and ending in wisdom, in a "clarification of life" that gives us "a momentary stay against confusion" (*Prose*, p. 18). Frost departs from purely descriptive walk poems by insisting that the walk is not merely aesthetic but cognitive, a finding of new knowledge. In this way he moves beyond the Wordsworthian impasse, the realization that any walk can be made into a poem and that therefore any given walk poem is merely one of thousands of potential poems, with no special claim to uniqueness. What makes Frost's walk poems unique are the insights they generate, the clarifications they achieve. Thought and experience are more closely knit than in previous walk poems; the walk and the process of discovery form a single whole.

For this reason Frost's walk poems generally lack the dense accumulation of particulars that characterize previous instances of the genre. He is interested less in evoking the experience in its entirety than in distilling its wisdom, the special story or parable it tells. For the most part they are quite short, often composed in stanzas rather than flowing blank verse like Wordsworth's. This insistence on lyricism, through compression and emphatic prosody, is a way of asserting the distance between the experience in its raw, unprocessed state and the poem it occasions. Scrupulously selective, he includes only those details that in some way contribute to the deeper movement from delight to wisdom that each poem maps out. As parable, the walk embodies its own meaning. That meaning or wisdom is never baldly signaled or openly stated; rather, it inheres in the walk itself, in the succession of images, the walker's movement from the familiar to the strange.

* * *

Frost's earliest walk poem is also arguably his purest, since it is the only one that labels itself as a walk in its title. Nonetheless, "A Late Walk" is not representative of Frost's mature manner. Little of anything that can be called wisdom is brought forward; the parabolic dimension that comes to play so prominent a role in Frost's later poetry is here but a faint whisper. Instead we are given a series of decorative, melancholy tableaux:

> When I go up through the mowing field,
>   The headless aftermath,
> Smooth-laid like thatch with the heavy dew,
>   Half-closes the garden path.
>
> And when I come to the garden ground,
>   The whir of sober birds
> Up from the tangle of withered weeds
>   Is sadder than any words.
>
> A tree beside the wall stands bare,
>   But a leaf that lingered brown,
> Disturbed, I doubt not, by my thought,
>   Comes softly rattling down.
>
> I end not far from my going forth
>   By picking the faded blue
> Of the last remaining aster flower
>   To carry again to you.[3]

The poem is most notable for the lack of any internal logic connecting the images into a coherent movement. Instead they are united as similarly wistful expressions of a mood projected by the speaker onto the landscape; indeed when it was first published in *A Boy's Will* the poem bore a gloss that read "He courts the autumnal mood." This sense of a willfully melancholy youth trapped within his own sensibility dominates the poem, and prevents any movement towards genuine insight or apprehension from occurring. The lack of movement is clearly acknowledged in the final stanza. "I end not far from my going forth"—this applies to the poem as well as to the walk, since the speaker remains caught up in the autumnal mood with which he began the poem. He has stayed within a closed space, a "garden ground"; he has not ventured beyond the confines of either his familiar terrain or his solipsistic consciousness.

Despite this lack of real movement, however, "A Late Walk" almost uncannily foreshadows the imagistic and thematic concerns of Frost's later walk poems, albeit in a vague, unrealized form. What appears as a sentimental mannerism here—the projection of human affect onto nature, what Ruskin named "the pathetic fallacy"—will become one of Frost's chief preoccupations, one he never fails to frame with a high degree of irony and self-consciousness. It could be argued that the addition of the gloss, "He courts the autumnal mood," is an attempt precisely to ironize the poem, to acknowledge the speaker's solipsism and in some minimal way to reflect upon it. If so, however, it only serves to distance us from the poem itself and the sensibility it depicts; we are not given the continuous movement towards self-awareness of a single mind that will be so characteristic of Frost's later poems, only a formal split between an ironic and a sentimental consciousness.

I want to call particular attention to the second stanza, since bird imagery will come to be a kind of trademark for Frost, serving as a recurrent symbol for the attempt to find a human voice in nature. "One had to be versed in country things/ Not to believe the phoebes wept"—evidently this speaker is not so "versed," since he has no compunctions about finding the "whir of sober birds . . . sadder than any words." The poem's most blatant instance of projection occurs in the next stanza, when the speaker indulges his belief in the power of mind over matter: "a leaf that lingered brown,/ Disturbed, I doubt not, by my thought,/ Comes softly rattling down." Again it could be said that the phrase "I doubt not" carries a certain irony, since it admits the possibility of skepticism in the very act of denying it. Yet the tone is too indeterminate to sustain such a reading definitively; Frost has yet to master the tonal subtleties that will eventually be the pillar of his art.

Perhaps the most striking premonition of Frost's later walk poems, though again one that remains entirely latent, comes in the final stanza, when the speaker picks "the last remaining aster flower/ To carry again to you." Aster, of course, means star, and while the image is a buried one it directly anticipates the closural function of stars in a number of Frost's later poems. There the star represents an alternative to the humanized nature represented most often by birds; here the aster flower simply adumbrates the dominant mood of lateness and regret, without providing a new perspective on the landscape. It is as though the speaker lacked the power to perceive the star within the flower, the hidden emblem of a higher vision free from delusive projections of self.

To a remarkable extent, then, "A Late Walk" contains all the key elements of Frost's later walk poems, while failing to assemble them into a thematically cohesive whole. In its evocation of mood rather than movement it remains embryonic; Frost has not yet learned to use the sequential juxtaposition of images for cognitive ends. The beauty of this principle is that it disguises deliberate substitution as mere succession; that is, it avoids the overt didacticism of a "turn" from one attitude to another by presenting what is on the surface a mere temporal sequence, but which on closer examination proves to be a deeper movement—in Frost's terms a movement from delight to wisdom, or as I would translate it, from play to knowledge.

We can observe this principle at work in two poems from Frost's second volume, *North of Boston*. "The Wood-Pile" and "Good Hours" are very different poems in both tone and form; yet I would suggest that they manifest the same essential structure, a progress from playful communion with an animate landscape to a more sober and detached enlightenment. Frost himself chose to juxtapose these poems in assembling the volume; "Good Hours" was printed at the end of the book in italics as a kind of epilogue immediately following "The Wood-Pile." In my reading I will follow Frost's own ordering, first considering "The Wood-Pile"'s chilly excursion, then its somewhat lighter revision in "Good Hours."

"The Wood-Pile" is written in the flexible and unobtrusive blank verse that dominates *North of Boston*. Most of the other poems that employ it, however, are dramatic monologues or narratives with a heavy proportion of dialogue; there it supplies a fluid medium for the capturing of those speech rhythms or "sentence sounds" that so fascinate Frost. "The Wood-Pile" has a more solemnly meditative sound; unlike the conversational blank verse poem "Mending Wall," which opens the volume, its language is pitched slightly above the idiomatic, lending it an almost Wordsworthian dignity. Its rhythm is not that of casual speech, but of a measured exploration of the self and its terrain, at once a physical and an inner foray.

"The Wood-Pile" immediately differentiates itself from "A Late Walk" by opening with an explicit moment of choice:

> Out walking in the frozen swamp one gray day,
> I paused and said "I will turn back from here.
> No, I will go farther—and we shall see."
>
> (Poetry, p. 101)

Unlike the speaker in "A Late Walk," this walker chooses to go *beyond* the point at which it seems natural to turn back, in a gesture that Richard Poirier, following Frost who himself follows Thoreau, aptly calls "extra-vagance," with its root sense of "wandering beyond limits."[4] This movement of transgressing the boundaries of the familiar, of entering into strange and possibly dangerous territory, recurs throughout Frost's poetry, always suggesting not a desire for escape so much as a desire for distance, for a kind of lucidly alienated perspective on one's home ground. By willfully continuing his walk despite his instinct to turn back, Frost explicitly hopes to "see"—that is, to *know* something that is unavailable within the confines of familiar or domestic space.

The very surface of this ground is precarious—"The hard snow held me, save where now and then/ One foot went through" suggesting the dangers that attend any movement out of bounds. (Already the analogy between walk and poem is being played on in the word "foot," whose sudden displacement coincides with a spondee that similarly interrupts the poem's metrical progress.) Just such a vertiginous caving in of one's accustomed ground will be the ultimate outcome of this walk, though in no literal sense. The onset of this dislocation is signaled by the absence of landmarks:

> The view was all in lines
> Straight up and down of tall slim trees
> Too much alike to mark or name a place by
> So as to say for certain I was here
> Or somewhere else: I was just far from home.

Although we are not told so explicitly, one of the disturbing implications of these lines is that the speaker is lost. He can only define this "place" negatively: it is "far from home," but otherwise it is nameless. As is so frequently the case in Frost, the literal situation here seems to resonate with a kind of parabolic meaning without ever becoming openly allegorical. This wood is not the "selva oscura" of the *Inferno*, yet at the same time the language Frost employs suggests that it is more than an aggregation of trees: it is the very antithesis of "home," of the place in which the speaker knows himself and his surroundings. In its barren linearity the landscape takes on a kind of abstraction, and we can hardly avoid associating the image of black lines on a white ground with that of a text. There is nothing legible about this scene, however, since the crucial signifying element of language, difference, is absent: the trees are "too much alike to mark or name a place by."

Yet even here, in this abstract, angular landscape, Frost manages to find an anthropomorphic presence:

A small bird flew before me. He was careful
To put a tree between us when he lighted,
And say no word to tell me who he was
Who was so foolish as to think what *he* thought.
He thought that I was after him for a feather—
The white one in his tail; like one who takes
Everything said as personal to himself.
One flight out sideways would have undeceived him.

Surely Frost means us to feel the strain in this rather too Disney-like attempt at personification. Unlike the humanized birds of Poe, Whitman, and Hardy, this bird is not invested with tragic dignity; rather, his motives are assumed to be absurdly literal. We can speculate that the elaborate fiction of the bird's paranoia is meant to account first of all for his disturbing silence: he would "say no word to tell me who he was." Curiously, by characterizing the bird's silence as an absence of speech the narrator manages to posit the *potential* for a human utterance emanating from this inhuman landscape; he can thus reassure himself that its muteness is circumstantial, not essential.

In imagining the bird's thoughts, however, the speaker does not truly deceive himself; unlike the speaker of "A Late Walk," he does not say "I doubt not." He knows he is playing with the bird, attributing more consciousness to it than it actually possesses. Yet the bird's fear is presumably real enough (although it may also be a projection of the speaker's own paranoia, as Richard Poirier suggests).[5] It is only through metaphor and simile that Frost turns the bird into a homely human type: "Like one who takes/ Everything said as personal to himself." Beyond this overt figure of speech, the very notion that the bird fears for its tailfeather rather than its life is essentially metaphorical, a reduction of the bird's survival instinct to a kind of anxious vanity, thereby substituting an amusing fiction for the more sober facts of nature. For Frost, of course, metaphor is the supreme form of play, a way of indulging the imagination without entirely losing sight of reality.

Here metaphor helps Frost to domesticate an alien and elusive presence, providing him with a kind of companionship where otherwise he might feel too helplessly alone; but it is difficult to say precisely how far the speaker lets the metaphor carry him from the truth of his situation, his solitude in a place that is "far from home."

Reality breaks into the poem in the form of the pile of wood that seems, grammatically as well as visually, to appear from nowhere: "And then there was a pile of wood." The unceremonious words "And then" seem to represent this transition as pure succession, not the kind of dialectical turn commonly introduced by the Stevensian "And yet"; but the effect is nonetheless a decisive shift in the poem's imaginative course. Similarly, Frost's use of the phrase "there was" rather than "I saw" emphasizes the sudden obtrusion of the wood-pile, the way it thrusts itself upon the speaker's consciousness almost against his will. It thus provides a striking instance of the kind of discovery essential to Frost's lyric program: "It is but a trick poem and no poem at all if the best of it was thought of first and saved for the last" (*Prose*, p. 2). Like the walker, the poet cannot know in advance what he will find; it is the element of surprise that validates the poem. Here the wood-pile disrupts the speaker's comforting fantasy of companionship and makes him aware of his own isolation. In its starkness and inanimacy it contrasts sharply with the bird, who disappears behind it as though unable to exist in the same frame.

At first all the speaker can do is describe it meticulously, as though still startled by its brute factuality.

> It was a cord of maple, cut and split
> And piled—and measured, four by four by eight.
> And not another like it could I see.
> No runner tracks in this year's snow looped near it.
> And it was older sure than this year's cutting,
> Or even last year's or the year's before.
> The wood was gray and the bark warping off it

And the pile somewhat sunken. Clematis
Had wound strings round and round it like a bundle.
What held it though on one side was a tree
Still growing, and on one a stake and prop,
These latter about to fall.

Like the speaker of the poem, the wood-pile seems strangely out of place. Indeed, though it is a product of human labor, intended for a human dwelling, its presence in the swamp serves as an ironic reminder of the scene's estrangement, its distance from home. The very fact that it has been standing so long, and that the stake and prop which hold it up are about to fall, suggests that not only space but time as well have come between it and whatever home it was meant to warm. As a kind of mute signifier, the wood-pile might be seen as the landscape-text's first and only "word," a difference created by the human act of displacing the lines that are the scene's basic constituents, shifting them from a vertical to an horizontal position.

In reading this word, Frost at first resorts to the same strategy he used in confronting the bird: he invents a fiction to explain an absence. In the case of the bird the absence was his lack of speech; here it is the absence of the wood-pile's maker, and of any sign that he had made use of his work:

I thought that only
Someone who lived in turning to fresh tasks
Could so forget his handiwork on which
He spent himself, the labor of his ax,
And leave it there far from a useful fireplace
To warm the frozen swamp as best it could
With the slow smokeless burning of decay.

Just as he posited the bird's paranoia to account for his lack of speech, so the speaker now posits a kind of vigorous amnesia to explain the wood-pile's presence in the swamp. The words "I thought," however, alert us that this image of the absentminded woodsman is not to be taken as fact; it is a conjecture, and while not an implausible one it is no more rooted in reality than the far more fantastic notion of the bird protecting its white tailfeather. Critics have taken the poem's ending as an unambiguous affirmation of human labor and the happy forgetfulness of "turning to fresh tasks"; but to do so they themselves must forget that this vision is entirely hypothetical.[6] In fact it is not difficult to supply a more likely explanation for the wood-pile's abandonment, one more in keeping with Frost's poetry as a whole: useful objects are abandoned because the person to whom they are of use no longer exists. By imagining a prolific energy of life responsible for this singularly lifeless object, the speaker evades the darker possibility of the woodsman's death; once more he chooses to let his imagination distract him from his solitude.

A passage from Hawthorne's *The Blithedale Romance* may lurk in the background here; if so, it confirms the buried suggestion that the wood-pile's maker is dead:

> In my haste, I stumbled over a heap of logs and sticks that had been cut for firewood, a great while ago, by some former possessor of the soil, and piled up square, in order to be carted or sledded away to the farm house. But, being forgotten, they had lain there, perhaps fifty years, and possibly much longer; until, by the accumulation of moss, and the leaves falling over them and decaying there, from autumn to autumn, a green mound was formed, in which the softened outline of the wood-pile was still perceptible. In the fitful mood that then swayed my mind, I found something strangely affecting in this simple circumstance. I imagined the long-dead woodman, and his long-dead wife and children, coming out of their chill graves, and essaying to make a fire with this heap of mossy fuel![7]

If this is a kind of pre-text for Frost's poem, as would appear to be the case, then his revision of it has centered on the speaker's sensibility, he is no longer gloomily attuned to the wood-pile's implications, but instead valiantly tries to imagine life rather than death as the cause for its abandonment. Thus an ironic tension is introduced, where Hawthorne gives us a simple convergence of mood and object.

One may well ask whether the speaker has progressed at all by the end of the poem. Although Frost the poet may intend us to recognize the inadequacy of the speaker's response to the wood-pile, we cannot dissociate him completely from the voice of the poem; it is not, after all, a dramatic monologue, and while it is filled with ironies at the speaker's expense, Frost's mastery of tone allows us to read the poem as the self-subverting utterance of a consciousness at once deluded by play and aware of its own delusions. If the poem had ended with the woodsman, this complexity would be lost; as it stands, the last three lines of the poem take us back to the wood-pile itself, leaving behind the cheerful image of the laborer, and demonstrate a starker understanding of the object. There is a grim irony in the notion of the wood-pile "warming" the swamp in its decay. The total absence of domestic comforts is made all the more apparent by the attempt to see the wood-pile fulfilling its destined function in so pathetically futile a way. Indeed, we should recall that the swamp is "frozen," and that the speaker has by now been cold a long time, so that the wood-pile has a very real, bodily significance for him; it is a potential source of heat, though one that cannot be used because, like the speaker, it is "far from a useful fireplace."

The highly Frostian vision conveyed by the final line is of decay as a gradual, inexorable process, one that produces no warmth, no smoke, only a slow absorption back into nature. The wood-pile becomes a small-scale version of the statue in Shelley's "Ozymandias," an artifact which in its stubborn survival points to human mortality, and in its gradual decay points to the mortality of human works. (Indeed the poem's closing cadence, together with the use of the word "decay," seems a furtive echo of the close of Shelley's poem: "Round the decay/ Of that colossal wreck, boundless and bare/ The lone and level sands stretch far away.")[8] The poem ends, then, with a wisdom that transcends the speaker's playful speculations about bird and woodsman; he finally confronts the absence of the human from the scene in all its intractable blankness. Ironically his "extravagant" journey away from the domestic and familiar has only returned him to a vision of domesticity that cruelly exposes its delusiveness. He has had to walk away from his own home, into the frozen swamp, in order to recognize the fragility of everything home stands for: life, warmth, labor. His domesticating imagination finally yields before the stubborn reality of the wood-pile, which tells him that his own house must also decay and fall.

Before leaving "The Wood-Pile," I think it is useful to consider the relevance and the necessity of its form. Why is it a walk poem? Could it exist in another shape? Thematically, of course, the walk is important in that it carries the speaker into the bleak, unfamiliar space where estranged vision is possible. But just as important is the walk's formal structure, in particular the principle of successiveness that I referred to earlier. Unlike other lyrics such as "Hyla Brook," "The Oven Bird," or "Mowing," in which Frost confines himself to his titular subject, "The Wood-Pile" is not simply about the wood-pile; rather, it is about the movement *toward* the wood-pile, a movement that includes the landscape and, most prominently, the bird. In a sense it is the transition from bird to wood-pile that is at the heart of the poem. By moving from an animate to an inanimate object, Frost arrives at a recognition of the landscape's silence and inanimacy that cannot be imaginatively deferred, and that ultimately points to death. As I have noted, this movement is not presented as a rhetorical "turn"; rather, it belongs to the poem's temporal plot or diegesis. Wisdom seems to emerge of itself, without the poet's conscious participation, and as a result we are given the tonal complexity of the speaker's resistance to the wood-pile's meaning, a resistance that finally only strengthens the impact of that meaning. A truth has been *arrived* at, one all the more authentic for its having forced itself upon the speaker despite his infatuation with play. The poem fulfills the speaker's initial prediction that "eve shall see," but in a way that dramatizes the intractability of genuine knowledge, its complete opposition to human will and desire. In Poirier's words the poem presents "a reductive process by which possibilities of metaphor—of finding some reassuring resemblances—are gradually disposed of.[9] It is of the essence of this process that it move from bird to wood-pile, since the difference between these objects is finally the difference between life and death. The sequential or temporal dimension of the poem is thus integral to the kind of knowledge it attains, a wisdom won from the jaws of delight.

In its placement in *North of Boston*, "Good Hours" seems intended as a deliberate sequel to "The Wood-Pile," one that recasts the previous poem in a different form, and in an utterly different mood. Jaunty where "The Wood-Pile" is brooding, "Good Hours" nonetheless presents the same basic pattern of a movement away from home that exposes the true nature of home more fully:

> I had for my winter evening walk—
> No one at all with whom to talk,
> But I had the cottages in a row
> Up to their shining eyes in snow.
>
> And I thought I had the folk within:
> I had the sound of a violin;
> I had a glimpse through curtain laces
> Of youthful forms and youthful faces.
>
> (*Poetry*, p. 102)

Once again the speaker is walking through a winter landscape, and this alone is a significant fact, since it implies that his motives are unlike those of a person walking in springtime; he is interested not in flowers but in the kind of knowledge that can only be had by testing the limits of one's terrain. Like the speaker in "The Wood-Pile," this walker is alone—he has "no one at all with whom to talk" yet he lets his imagination supply him with company. This time his companion is not a bird, but the houses themselves, which are explicitly personified in the line "Up to their shining eyes in snow." The eyes are of course windows; again the speaker is playfully projecting an excess of consciousness onto the landscape by means of metaphor. The repeated emphasis on the verb construction "I had" lays stress on the peculiar nature of this "having," which emerges as a deeply inward, imaginative mode of possession.

In the next stanza Frost turns from the houses to the "folk within," who are also imagined to be accompanying the speaker on his walk. As in "The Wood-Pile," the tenuous, conjectural status of the inhabitants is signaled by the phrase "I thought," a phrase which for Frost usually amounts to a covert denial of what has been asserted. What, after all, does the speaker "have" here? He has glimpses through curtains, sounds of music—stray impressions that create a congenial atmosphere, but impressions only. In effect the metaphor of "having" substitutes for the more expected verbs of perception: seeing, hearing. Again it is only through play that Frost converts these impressions into the more substantial "company" of his walk.

The speaker's actual isolation is confirmed in the next stanza, when he outwalks the houses and reaches a place not unlike the deserted swamp of "The Wood-Pile":

> I had such company outward bound.
> I went till there were no cottages found.
> I turned and repented, but coming back
> I saw no window but that was black.

The uninhabited void, it seems, was his destination all along; as pleasant and companionable as the cottages may have seemed, the speaker was bent on leaving them behind, on traveling "outward," away from the familiar and the domestic. The seriousness of this intent is indicated by the word "repented," which implies that the speaker's initial resolve was to continue and not to turn back; at the same time, the word carries a sense of guilt, as though in leaving the houses behind the speaker felt he had somehow betrayed them. Indeed there is a still subtler hint in the word "but" that the speaker's action has actually *caused* the blackening of the windows, and that his repentance has come too late to save them. The imaginative weight of this deed becomes clear when we recall that the windows were formerly "shining eyes"; the speaker has in effect killed them, destroying the signs of life that had previously provided him with companionship.

What does it mean to say that the speaker has "killed" the houses? Obviously there is no literal connection between his passing beyond the houses and the extinction of their lights. But we should note that metaphor itself has also disappeared; the houses are no longer personified, the windows have stopped being eyes and reverted to their purely physical identity. In leaving the houses behind, then, the speaker has also abandoned the fiction of companionship itself; he has been forced to assume a more literal mode of vision. Like the wood-pile, the houses have turned into lifeless physical objects that poignantly express the fragility of human dwellings and of human life. Here, however, there is a more willful element in the speaker's turn to the literal; he has brought this change on himself by walking out into the uninhabited void, and by carrying the void back with him.

"Good Hours" differs from "The Wood-Pile" also in the tone of its ending. The final stanza has none of the sober majesty of "The Wood-Pile"'s closing line; it seems to show little more than a cheerful disrespect for the stodgy habits of the villagers:

> Over the snow my creaking feet
> Disturbed the slumbering village street
> Like profanation, by your leave,
> At ten o'clock of a winter eve.

Yet even here the speaker remains an outsider, alone with only the sounds of his own footsteps for company, now unaccompanied by violin. His use of the weighty term "profanation" for this noise (immediately deflated by the slightly insolent and homely "by your leave," as though the speaker had to ask our permission to use such a Latinate word) subtly reinforces the sense that he has returned to a dead place, from which the living have vanished and in which the houses are corpses. The dark knowledge of "The Wood-Pile"'s close has been transmuted into a wry, joking awareness of the perilousness of our illusions of home and community. Having once achieved the perspective of an outsider, the speaker cannot return to the same friendly place he left; once again the landscape confronts him with his own solitude.

The poem's title tells us that these have been "Good Hours," and so they may well be; but if the first hour, outward bound, is good because of its cozy sense of community, the second hour, coming home, is good because it leads to a barer, starker vision that corrects the imaginative excesses of the first. The cottages do not have eyes, and the speaker does not "have" the people in them: this is the simple but vital truth that emerges from both the walk and the poem. Where "The Wood-Pile" centers on the uninhabited swamp and the single artifact the speaker finds there, "Good Hours" follows the walker back from the outer darkness and discovers the consequences of such an excursion for his perception of home itself. In effect the houses become the wood-pile; the implicit synecdoche that identified the wood-pile with home is reversed, and we are shown that home, as represented both by the village in which the speaker lives and by the individual houses that resemble his own, is itself little more than a pile of wood, a physical object without a soul.

As poems of "extra-vagance," both "The Wood-Pile" and "Good Hours" show Frost wandering beyond the limits of home ground; yet unlike Thoreau, who can lose himself in the nonhuman, Frost is never able to leave home behind entirely. Instead he moves to a vantage point from which home appears in a stark, denuded form, stripped of the cheerful pathos that had previously clung to it. Frost's tone, however, remains willfully homey, despite his apprehension of the void that surrounds and inhabits the home. Unlike Stevens, he is more interested in seeing nothing that is not there than the nothing that is. As Poirier says,

> For Frost's lonely walkers, far from "home," nothing can come from such nothing, and they therefore must try to speak again and in such a way as to make known an ordinary human presence. Frost in this mood is bleaker than Stevens. He resists the transcendentalist willingness to disentangle the self from the ties of "home" and from any responsibility to domesticate whatever might be encountered while one is "extra-vagant."[10]

In short, "extravagance," the will to walk out into the frozen swamp, brings not transcendental freedom but renewed responsibility. The special knowledge Frost achieves in walking keeps forcing him back home, although home itself can never be the same. His refusal to give himself over to Emersonian transcendentalism or Hardyesque fatalism, his persistently colloquial voice and anecdotal manner, indicate that for Frost the walk is a circuit, not a one-way trip. It is the movement of return that validates the knowledge achieved; only by coming back from the swamp, back to the familiar world of home and village streets, can he confirm what he has learned, while leaving room for new forays into the wilderness.

* * *

Both "The Wood-Pile" and "Good Hours" present the walker in the act of discovering the true nature of home. In both poems the speaker begins by imaginatively supplying himself with a kind of domestic companionship even as he wanders away from humanity. The recognition that home is subject to death and decay is therefore presented as an interruption or obtrusion, an insight forced on the speaker against his will. But as Frost became older, he naturally began to represent knowledge less as discovery than as confirmation. As this change occurs, his depiction of the walk also changes, becoming more static, less sequential. That shift is visible in another poem about nocturnal perambulations, the well-known "Acquainted with the Night." Like "Good Hours," this poem is about the sense of isolation and outsiderness that the speaker attains simply by staying up later than everyone else. It is one of Frost's rare city poems, and perhaps for this reason its tone is rather different from his usual rustic manner. Indeed it may at times seem reminiscent of Eliot, particularly in its repeated use of the "I have" construction, recalling such Prufrockian lines as "I have gone at dusk through narrow streets/ And watched the smoke that rises from the pipes/ Of lonely men in shirt sleeves, leaning out of windows."[11] Such grammar dispels the kind of precise sequential focus that the earlier poems display, instead creating a repetitive space in which constancy rather than change is emphasized.

Nonetheless, "Acquainted with the Night" has a number of elements in common with "The Wood-Pile" and "Good Hours." As in "Good Hours," the speaker makes a point of "outwalk[ing] the furthest city light," leaving behind the human markers and habitations that create a sense of community, and faring into a lonelier kind of landscape. And again his solitude is underscored by the sound of his own footsteps, which here enter his consciousness only when he stops making them. Most significantly, we are given a new version of the dialectic between companionship and detachment, one that makes use of terms developed more fully in other poems:

> When far away an interrupted cry
> Came over houses from another street,
>
> But not to call me back or say good-by;

And further still at an unearthly height,
One luminary dock against the sky

Proclaimed the time was neither wrong nor right
I have been one acquainted with the night.

(*Poetry*, p. 255)

The speaker's casual denial that the cry is addressed to him contrasts with the projections made by the speakers in "The Wood-Pile" and "Good Hours"; perhaps because this poem lacks Frost's characteristic playfulness he is never tempted to construct a fiction of companionship. Instead his labor is wholly negative, revealing a more austere sensibility than we have previously seen.

In the next line the image of the "luminary clock" seems to offer an alternative to the "interrupted cry." It too "proclaims," yet its utterance is impersonal, directed to no one in particular. As critics have pointed out, this dock is undoubtedly the moon, a fact reinforced by the burial of "lunar" in "luminary." Thus its face is blank, and can tell us only that the time is neither wrong nor right. A kind of detached neutrality, an impassiveness that can be achieved only from an "unearthly height," is the reward of the speaker's acquaintance with the night. Unlike the walkers in "The Wood-Pile" and "Good Hours," he is disenchanted from the start, and so we are not given a movement from play to wisdom, only a static portrait of alienation. The very grammar of the opening line portrays the self as a constant, fixed entity, "*one* acquainted with the night" (italics mine); the speaker is not undergoing a process of self-transformation in the course of the walk, but is simply confirming his initial sense of solitude. The poem's essential stasis is emphasized by the repetition of its first line as its last, thereby framing the intervening lines as an elaboration of a single sentence. This lack of true progression can be ascribed to the poem's synoptic temporality; its events all take place in the timeless space of "the night," and so do not possess the kind of narrative specificity we have seen in Frost's other walk poems.

Yet although its speaker, like the speaker in "A Late Walk," does not move beyond his initial expression of self-pity, the poem itself contains a succession of images, most saliently the cry and the moon, which do imply a dialectical movement. The turn from a human or humanized voice to an "unearthly" celestial object, be it moon or star, becomes an important motif in Frost's poetry, most prominently displayed in two poems that bear close comparison, "Looking for a Sunset Bird in Winter" and "Come In." In both these poems a walker turns his gaze from a bird to a star, and in so doing he crosses over to a new, colder mode of vision. Yet the speaker's relationship to bird and star is significantly different in the two poems, and provides a measure of how Frost's later poetry departs from the exploratory paradigm set forth in "The Figure a Poem Makes."

"Looking for a Sunset Bird in Winter" appeared in *New Hampshire*, Frost's fourth volume, and in form it resembles "The Wood-Pile" and "Good Hours." As in those poems, the speaker is brought against his will to a new perspective, although here he is confronted not with an image of decay and abandonment but rather, as in "Acquainted with the Night," with an image of lofty detachment He is on his way home when he sees something: "I thought I saw a bird alight." Again the words "I thought" warn us as to the nature of this perception. The speaker remembers a bird with an "angelic" voice that he heard in summer; but now, even though he goes twice around the tree, he can see nothing but a single leaf. The voice or song he desires is not there; only his own nostalgic imagination has led him to expect the bird.

In the beautiful closing stanza, however, the speaker receives a kind of compensatory vision:

> A brush had left a crooked stroke
> Of what was either cloud or smoke
> From north to south across the blue;
> A piercing little star was through.
>
> (*Poetry*, p. 233)

Unlike the closing images in many of Frost's poems, this last image is genuinely a surprise; nothing in the title prepares us for it. The poem dramatizes the process of coming upon something inadvertently, while looking for something else—a process, as we know, central to Frost's conception of poetry. Yet there is a curious relationship between this little star and the object of the speaker's search, summed up in the word "piercing," which can be used to describe both a sound, like a bird song, and an appearance. (The pun is reinforced by the apparent displacement of "piercing" from its position as a verb—"A little star was piercing through"—to its more ambiguous adjectival position.) The reference to the brush suggests that this image is another kind of aesthetic reward, though in a different medium from the song. The seasonal setting of the poem may help to explain the substitution of star for bird; in this wintry landscape a star is a more appropriate object of vision, colder and more distant, less subject to imaginative distortion.[12]

As the fourth stanza tells us, the speaker in some measure shares the star's perspective: "From my advantage on a hill." Like the moon in "Acquainted with the Night," the star is a figure for a kind of vision, one that remains poised above desire and gazes impassively at human suffering. Increasingly Frost will turn to emblems for such a stance, choosing to celebrate his own victory over mutability rather than to mourn its effect on others. His exhortation to "Take Something Like a Star" may be seen as his response to the tragic discoveries presented in early poems like "The Wood-Pile," and critics have complained that in his later poetry Frost at times too easily dismisses the reality of pain and loss, finding repose in a cold, smug detachment. Yet one might say that it is precisely the measure of Frost's sensitivity to pain that he must find refuge in the stars.

From this point of view "Come In" offers an illuminating contrast to "Looking for a Sunset Bird in Winter." Published some twenty years later, it revises the earlier poem's outing by showing the speaker as now impervious to a bird's melodic invitation:

Far in the pillared dark
Thrush music went—
Almost like a call to come in
To the dark and lament

But no, I was out for stars:
I would not come in.
I meant not even if asked,
And I hadn't been.

                              (*Poetry*, p. 334)

Where the bird in "Looking for a Sunset Bird in Winter" was wholly a
creation of the speaker's desire, here it is an assertive reality, demanding
the speaker's imaginative participation. But this time he is out for stars,
not birds, and refuses even to toy with the notion that the bird's song is
a "call to come in" and join the bird in lamentation. As in "Acquainted
with the Night," the speaker remains undeceived from the start, and as
a result "Come In" is also essentially static; that is, it does not dramatize
the speaker in the process of changing his mind. Certainly the last line
makes a powerful gesture of rejection, but there is little sign in the poem
that he is at any point truly tempted by the bird's call. The effect is rather
of a decisive reaffirmation of his continuing commitment to stars. The
hardening of Frost's sensibility is evident in the loss of the fluidity and
dynamism that enabled him to write the kind of poem he describes in
"The Figure a Poem Makes," one that "unfolds by surprise." To put it another way, the walk is no longer organic to the poem; because the walkers in "Acquainted with the Night" and "Come In" have already chosen
stars over birds, detachment over involvement, they have nowhere to go.
"No one can really hold that the ecstasy should be static and stand still
in one place," Frost writes; yet the poems of his later years *do* stand still
in one place, appropriating as they do the fixed perspective of a star.

    It is not until Frost's last great poem, "Directive," that he manages to
reconcile the desire to write a poem that moves *toward* wisdom or

---

"clarification" with his mature stance as one who has already achieved the wisdom of detachment. His solution is an ingenious one; the poem is written in the second person, in the voice of a guide. Thus it is the reader who enacts the process of moving from play to knowledge, while Frost himself maintains the perspective of an all-knowing sage. The walk described in the poem is a walk *we* are being asked to take, and while we may assume that our guide has covered this route himself, he evidently has no further need for it. "Directive" is thus like a late version of "The Wood-Pile" in which the speaker has retired from the scene to oversee the initiation of new walkers.

The poem's famous opening lines establish the coordinates and goal of the walk we are being sent on:

> Back out of all this now too much for us,
> Back in a time made simple by the loss
> Of detail, burned, dissolved, and broken off
> Like graveyard marble sculpture in the weather,
> There is a house that is no more a house
> Upon a farm that is no more a farm
> And in a town that is no more a town.
>
> (*Poetry*, p. 377)

Much has been said about the intricate syntactical ambiguities these lines present: should we read the first line, for example, as an imperative or a prepositional clause? And should the word "now" be taken as a substantive rather than an adverb? We are indeed being urged to "back out" of the "now" of present history, to embark on a journey into the past; yet even the status of this apparently "simple" time is uncertain, for its simplicity seems to be a function of erosion, rather than an inherent property of an earlier era. Indeed the very point of our excursion into this landscape may be to undermine nostalgia, as another version of the sentimentalizing pathos that Frost backs away from in his earlier poems. The simile "like graveyard marble sculpture" hints that

---

not simply attrition but death is the precondition for the kind of bare clarity of outline the poem is leading us to, recalling the image of the wood-pile that survives its maker. The series of riddling phrases that begin "There is a house that is no more a house" further confuses our understanding of time. Had Frost written "There *was* a house that is no more a house" the ambiguity would be dispelled; as it is we cannot tell whether we are being directed into a past moment imagined as present, or to a present site haunted by its past. We only know that the poem is leading us to a place in which present and past, life and death, being and nonbeing intersect.

The first part of the poem's itinerary abounds in the kind of playful personification also found in "The Wood-Pile" and "Good Hours," suggesting an initial phase of imaginative projection that must eventually yield to a more sober apprehension. But where the speakers in the earlier poems confined their personifying to relatively small objects, a bird and a row of houses, Frost here magnifies this impulse to include the landscape as a whole:

> The road there, if you'll let a guide direct you
> Who only has at heart your getting lost,
> May seem as if it should have been a quarry—
> Great monolithic knees the former town
> Long since gave up pretense of keeping covered.
> And there's a story in a book about it
> Besides the wear of iron wagon wheels
> The ledges show lines ruled southeast northwest,
> The chisel work of an enormous Glacier
> That braced his feet against the Arctic Pole.
> You must not mind a certain coolness from him
> Still said to haunt this side of Panther Mountain.

Vast forces of nature are tamed and domesticated by the poet's imagination, and geological histories of the region are turned into storybooks. As in "The Wood-Pile," there is an element of forced playfulness here that seems to call attention to its own excess; the almost cartoonlike portrayal of the quarry's knees and the glacier's feet, representing feminine culture and masculine nature (a typically American realignment of the traditional gender associations), creates an effect of Rabelaisian unreality which I think is meant to put us on our guard. What these fantastic figures hide is the essential destructiveness of this landscape, its tendency to wear away both at itself and whatever human community seeks to tame it. Once more Frost invents a humanized companion (the glacier is referred to as "him") to disguise his, or rather our, solitude in a barren landscape; and once more this gesture can be perceived as a defensive strategy for staving off tragic knowledge.

Frost is never more artful than in this part of the poem. The cleverness, the arch tone, the overelaborated conceits, all I think are *meant* to trouble the reader, to start us of our own accord towards the poem's ultimate destination, which is the antithesis of such distracted play.[13] As if to move us gradually towards our goal, Frost allows the landscape to darken slowly, permitting more ominous details to enter one by one:

> Nor need you mind the serial ordeal
> Of being watched from forty cellar holes
> As if by eye pairs out of forty firkins.
> As for the woods' excitement over you
> That sends light rustle rushes to their leaves,
> Charge that to upstart inexperience.
> Where were they all not twenty years ago?
> They think too much of having shaded out
> A few old pecker-fretted apple trees.
> Make yourself up a cheering song of how
> Someone's road home from work this once was,
> Who may be just ahead of you on foot
> Or creaking with a buggy load of grain.

The word "ordeal," with its overtones of quest-romance, flippantly points us to the true nature of this walk. It is a quest because, unlike the walker in "The Wood-Pile," we know that there is a goal ahead, the "house that is no more a house." At this point, however, only our guide knows why the house is a suitable object of our quest. Unlike us, Frost knows what is to come; having traveled this path many times before, he can no longer be surprised by what he finds. Yet he can still conduct us there in such a way that the full impact of discovery is maintained. To this end he distracts us with jokes, similes, garrulous tales, all meant to offset the stark knowledge to come.

Again there is a touch of imaginative projection in the reference to the forty "eye pairs," perhaps recalling the "houses up to their shining eyes in snow" of "Good Hours"; but even without the simile we are still "being watched from forty cellar holes," so that rhetorically only the firkins are overtly fictional (perhaps inspired by Ali Baba's forty thieves hidden in their barrels). The use of the simile deflects the walker's deeper fears and uncertainties about the landscape's inhabitants by turning to explicit figurations; yet the literal sense of being watched remains. More importantly, the image of the cellar holes looks forward to the single ruined house that we are seeking, a cellar hole somehow different from the rest, more isolated and more tragic.

Another blatant projection comes with the "woods' excitement over you," as Frost again offers a complete narrative to account for their humanized behavior. Now, however, the personification has the landscape responding directly to the walker's presence (we may recall the leaf that falls in "A Late Walk," "disturbed, I doubt not, by my thought"). Here of course Frost's tone remains wryly self-conscious; but the story he tells about the trees gives an oblique indication of the landscape's true history. They are "upstarts" because they are young; they think well of themselves because they grew tall enough to block the sun from an apple orchard, thus killing it. The implicit scenario, as throughout the poem, is of nature overwhelming culture, obliterating the products of human labor with frightening ease. The apple trees belonged to someone's farm, and we should remember that Frost himself wrote of apple picking with great authority. (The epithet "pecker-fretted" may provide a hint as to why the orchard was originally abandoned.) The speaker's playful characterization of the woods, then, is another shrugging off of tragedy, an attempt to portray nature as responsive to the humans whom in reality it overwhelms.

Frost's deadly encouragements reach a climax in his advice to "make yourself up a cheering song of how/ Someone's road home from work this once was." At last the motivations behind his jangling rhetoric become apparent: he, like us, is in urgent need of cheering. Indeed the first part of the poem has been nothing other than a "cheering song," made up to animate a landscape whose truth is too painful to face. The fact that the song we are instructed to make up only brings us closer to the landscape's history of ruin is an irony in keeping with what has gone before. The cheerful vision of the laborer "who may be just ahead of you" is very much a reminiscence of the forgetful wood-cutter in "The Wood-Pile," a human figure imagined as full of life when in fact the scene before us tells only of his death.

Why does Frost go through the motions of making fictions, endowing a landscape with life when he is only too aware of its desolation? There is something almost sadistic or taunting in the way he seems to offer comfort and reassurance while actually showing us the evidence of human failure at every turn. I would suggest that he is mocking his former self as much as us, the persona of "The Wood-Pile," the sentimentalist of "A Late Walk." He gives us a kind of savage parody of the playful imagination that has been his metier for more than forty years, the mainstay of Frost the whimsical old New England sage. If we miss the irony in this part of the poem, we cannot adequately confront the massive repudiation carried out in the poem's closing section, in which we are made to gaze steadily and remorselessly at an emblem of decay far more devastating than the wood-pile.

The poem's final movement begins as we reach "the height/ Of country where two village cultures faded/ Into each other." A crucial difference between this walk and the walk in "The Wood-Pile" is that here we are moving *upward*, toward a summit, a vantage point. This topographical revision is in large measure responsible for the salvational cadence of the poem's ending. Before that saving movement can take place, however, we must be brought to witness the scene of destruction in all its sorrow. We are not greatly moved, perhaps, to hear of how the two village cultures are now lost; loss on the scale of culture is difficult to connect with human suffering. But as we are told to "make ourselves at home," the scale shrinks down to the domestic. For it is precisely a home that we have been brought to see.

Even here, Frost brings us to our goal by degrees:

> First there's the children's house of make believe,
> Some shattered dishes underneath a pine,
> The playthings in the playhouse of the children.
> Weep for what little things could make them glad.

In the relationship between the playhouse and the house in earnest, Frost brilliantly epitomizes the central movement of the poem as a whole. It is difficult to avoid associating the "children's house of make believe" with all the fiction making and projection of the poem's first half; and the repeated emphasis on "play" in "the playthings in the playhouse" further underscores the relation between children's toys and that higher form of play called poetry.[14] But the dishes are shattered, and this surely suggests that the poem's play is also at an end, its cheerful fictions broken. We weep for the little things that made them glad because we know they will never make us glad again, and because we recognize how fragile and inadequate a shield such playthings provide before the destructive forces of time and nature.

And so we turn from the children's house of make believe to

the house that is no more a house,
But only a belilaced cellar hole,
Now slowly closing like a dent in dough.
This was no playhouse but a house in earnest.

The implicit riddle asked at the beginning of the poem—"when is a house not a house?"—is answered here: when all that is left of it is the cellar hole, the original excavation on which it was built. The image of this hole "slowly closing like a dent in dough" simultaneously captures the lost sense of domesticity associated with the baking of bread and the slow, inexorable process of decay evoked so memorably at the end of "The Wood-Pile." (Frost's source for this image is probably *Walden*, the chapter entitled "Former Inhabitants": "These cellar dents are all that is left where once were the stir and bustle of human life.") In the next line the phrase "a house in earnest" poignantly summons up all the serious, simple needs and wishes that the house once contained and partly satisfied. But the house and its inhabitants are gone, and we are faced with the ruins of their labors slowly blending back into nature. (We should recall that when this poem was written Frost had already buried his wife and two of his children, so that his own "house" had quite literally returned to the earth.)

Yet "Directive," unlike "The Wood-Pile," does not end with the image of a rotting human artifact. We have still not attained our goal:

Your destination and your destiny's
A brook that was the water of the house,
Cold as a spring as yet so near its source,
Too lofty and original to rage.
(We know the valley streams that when aroused
Will leave their tatters hung on barb and thorn.)

The house too, it seems, has only been a byway, part of the ordeal rather than the reward. It is the brook that has been our destination all along. Yet why bring us this far to see a brook? The answer lies, I think, in the *relation* between the brook and the house. As in Frost's other walk poems, meaning arises here from the succession of images, the movement from playhouse to house to brook. This sequence plots a deeper imaginative movement that begins by shucking off the playful defenses indulged in during the first part of the poem, confronts the bare evidence of human transience, and finally finds refuge in the lofty perspective Frost associates elsewhere with stars. This brook is not just a brook, but a figure for a kind of vision and a kind of poetry.[15] It is cold because it is near its source; translated into human terms, we could say that coldness, apparent indifference to human suffering, actually comes from being close to the sources of life, the natural forces that both create and destroy it. The line "too lofty and original to rage" is even more suggestive. Once more impassivity is imaged as height, as a starlike distance from worldly affairs. From this unearthly vantage point, as in "Acquainted with the Night," "the time is neither wrong nor right." The brook's loftiness, then, suggests a refusal to pass judgment on life, a refusal to rage at it for taking away all that it gives us. The parenthetical lines about the valley streams that "when aroused/ Will leave their tatters hung on barb and thorn" can be taken to represent both the self-lacerating effects of indiscriminate rage against our given condition, and the very forces that provoke such rage.

Even here, at the poem's climax, an element of playfulness intrudes as the poet offers us the "broken drinking goblet like the Grail," again an allusion to quest romance. (There is also a touch of personification in the reference to the old cedar's "instep arch," recalling the glacier's "feet" earlier.) Frost's awareness that these playful elements have been smuggled in illicitly is expressed when he tells us "I stole the goblet from the children's playhouse," thus implying that it too is only a prop or toy. Yet in the end it seems we cannot do without such toys, without the leaky vessels of metaphor and parable, although the true goal of our quest is the water itself, emblem of a perfect and inhuman lucidity.

> Here are your waters and your watering place.
>
> Drink and be whole again beyond confusion.

By drinking this cold water we may attain what Frost says is the aim of all his poems, "a clarification of life—not necessarily a great clarification such as sects and cults are built on, but a momentary stay against confusion" (*Prose*, p. 2). The costs of such a clarification are great, however; notice the way the word "whole" in the last line echoes the cellar "hole" that the house has become. Such wholeness requires that we empty ourselves of all our illusions, fictions, toys—except of course the one toy we keep to drink from. The cold wisdom Frost's poems attain can never be wholly purified of play, of the trappings of domesticity; rather, it is only *through* such play that knowledge can be held and tasted. Yet knowledge for Frost is always knowledge of that which shatters play, home, companionship, leaving us alone in an empty place, beyond confusion.

"Directive" differs from "The Wood-Pile" in that it takes us beyond the contemplation of decay, to the contemplation of the power of contemplation itself. The poem ends on a celebratory note, but what it celebrates is the ability to see the worst that can befall us without flinching. It is for this reason that the poem's trajectory up the mountain is significant; whereas the walker in "The Wood-Pile" travels outward, into darkness, in "Directive" we move up, attaining a height from which the landscape can be viewed in its totality. As an old man who has seen his own house fall, Frost may have felt he *had* seen everything, the fated end of every house and every human. Having attained the glacial cold of detachment himself, he becomes a guide in "Directive," ushering the less experienced through the landscape he has already traversed, ending at the water where each pilgrim will learn clarity and acceptance.

Poems like "The Wood-Pile" and "Directive" bring a new thematic weight to the walk poem. Frost reinvents the genre by building on the formal analogy between poem and walk; both travel from the familiar, the domestic, the human to a renewed sense of contingency and mortality. In Frost's hands the walk becomes a parable for the way the mind comes to knowledge, by encountering realities that resist its domesticating impulse. Thus the walk serves him as a vehicle for charting inner movements, adjustments in perspective, the temporal process of discovery and understanding. His primary goal is not description but what he calls "wisdom," and so each poem narrows itself around some image embodying an insight; facts that may originate in experience are infused with parabolic significance, losing their status as mere data. Yet the way in which wisdom is attained is as important to Frost as the nature of wisdom itself, so that his best poems are never simply statements. Poems like "The Wood-Pile" and "Directive" use the structure of the walk, with its rhythmic principles of movement, succession, and arrival, to illustrate the way wisdom can suddenly emerge in the midst of play, startling us into sadness and understanding.

From *Walks in the World: Representation and Experience in Modern American Poetry* (Princeton, NJ: Princeton University Press), pp. 49-74. Copyright © 1991 by Princeton University Press. Reprinted by permission of Princeton University Press.

Notes

1. See *Selected Letters of Robert Frost*, ed. Lawrance Thompson (New York: Holt, Rinehart and Winston, 1964), pp. 182, 278.

2. "The Figure a Poem Makes," in *Selected Prose of Robert Frost*, ed. Edward Connery Lathem (New York: Holt, Rinehart and Winston, 1966), pp. 18-20. Henceforth cited in text as *Prose*.

3. Robert Frost, *The Poetry of Robert Frost* (New York: Holt, Rinehart and Winston, 1969), p. 8. Henceforth cited in text as *Poetry*.

4. Richard Poirier, *Robert Frost: The Work of Knowing* (New York: Oxford University Press, 1977), p. 89. Poirier has some interesting remarks on the relation between "extra-vagance" and Frost's walk poems: "Wandering beyond boundaries of a household or a field is, in Frost, often the enactment of any search for possibilities greater than those already domesticated. His many poems of walking are thus poems of 'extravagance' in the most pedestrian sense while also being about the need, and advisability, of poetic 'extravagance'" (p. 89). In discussing "The Wood-Pile" Poirier contrasts the poem with "Tintern Abbey" and "Dejection," claiming that "it is more ran-

dom in its structuring and has none of the demarcations of the descriptive-reflective mode," and adducing as an alternative paradigm Ammons's series of analogies in his "A Poem Is a Walk," *Epoch* (Fall 1968): pp. 138-39.

5. Poirier, *Robert Frost*, pp. 141-42.

6. See, for example, Robert Narveson, "On Frost's 'The Wood-Pile,'" *English Journal* 57 (1968): pp. 39-40; Marie Borroff, "Robert Frost's New Testament: The Uses of Simplicity," in *Robert Frost*, ed. Harold Bloom (New York: Chelsea House, 1986), p. 78; and Poirier, *Robert Frost*, p. 143.

7. Nathaniel Hawthorne, *The Blithedale Romance* (New York: Norton, 1978), pp. 195-96. Frost may also be recalling a passage at the beginning of Chapter Two, in which Coverdale compares his faded memory of Blithedale's cheery fire to "the merest phosphoric glimmer, like that which exudes, rather than shines, from damp fragments of decayed trees, deluding the benighted wanderer through the forest" (p. 9). He then calls this glimmer a "chill mockery of a fire," a phrase that clearly anticipates "The Wood-Pile"'s closing lines.

8. *Shelley's Poetry and Prose*, ed. Donald Reiman (New York: Norton, 1977), p. 103.

9. Poirier, *Robert Frost*, p. 139.

10. Ibid., p. 144.

11. T. S. Eliot, *The Complete Poems and Plays* (New York: Harcourt Brace and World, 1952), p. 5.

12. The increasing prominence of star imagery in Frost's later poetry is noted by John T. Ogilvie in "From Woods to Stars: A Pattern of Imagery in Robert Frost's Poetry," *South Atlantic Quarterly* 58 (1959): pp. 64-76.

13. Poirier is severely critical of what he calls the poem's "self-conscious and self-cuddling mode" (*Robert Frost*, p. 100), and feels that it has been overpraised; but I think he fails to see the function of the poem's admittedly cloying rhetoric, which is to prepare our palate for the cold draught that awaits us.

14. A well-known remark of Frost's may be apposite here: "I like to leave my toys lying around where people will fall forward over them in the dark. *Forward*, you understand, *and* in the dark." This joke can be taken as an accurate description of the movement of "Directive," particularly since it is we, not the poet, who do the falling.

15. We might compare it with "Hyla Brook," another watery embodiment of the reality principle, though of a less lofty and original kind.

Nature and Poetry_____

Judith Oster

Encounters with nature, of course, are not always contemplative or symbolic. In "Storm Fear" the person encountering nature is not just fearing what it may represent, nor reading the storm for its significance; rather he expresses genuine fear of annihilation prompted by actual circumstances—a nature unleashing dangerous and untamed forces that have the power to destroy him and that, consequently, dramatize his helplessness and render him subdued and fearful.

> When the wind works against us in the dark,
> And pelts with snow
> The lower chamber window on the east,
> And whispers with a sort of stifled bark,
> The beast,
> 'Come out! Come out!'—
> It costs no inward struggle not to go,
> Ah, no!
> I count our strength,
> Two and a child,
> Those of us not asleep subdued to mark
> How the cold creeps as the fire dies at length,—
> How drifts are piled,
> Dooryard and road ungraded,
> Till even the comforting barn grows far away,
> And my heart owns a doubt
> Whether 'tis in us to arise with day
> And save ourselves unaided.
>
> (CP 13)

This is a nature hostile to human beings which pursues them even into the fortresses they have built against it. Just as Frost's poems of na-

_____

Nature and Poetry

179

ture's indifference prove to be less concerned with nature and more with a person's unsatisfied needs, so this poem is more concerned with a person's fears—fear of annihilation, of the cold and dark, of his own helplessness and his own isolation. Even though the danger is real enough, it is the speaker who has turned an unthinking storm into a malevolent beast, "working against" him in the dark. It whispers, barks, and creeps. The "pelting" snow adds to the visual image of the beast that even doors and windows cannot shut out, for as the fire dies out, the cold advances inside. The strengths of the house as physical protection against the cold, and home as spiritual protection—two and a child, love and family—seem increasingly inadequate. The fear is one that antedates buildings and institutions. We are in the grip of a primitive, elemental fear—back in a world in which fire gave temporary security against the cold and the dark and frightened away the beasts—until it went out.

We have, then, the solid strength of the man-made and the strength of human love and companionship against the wild strength of the storm. But as the snow obliterates gradations and distinctions, it makes all other buildings, and by implication all the rest of humanity, seem farther and farther away. Piling drifts spin a cocoon from which the family will draw no comfort, for this is not an isolation that protects and shuts out evil. This is being shut in with the enemy, isolated from anyone who can help in the battle. Eventually the speaker doubts whether it is in them to arise with day and save themselves unaided. In one sense the fear is very real: it is possible that they will not survive the night; it is because of this that they remain awake, mark how the cold creeps, and, for this reason, feel subdued by it. In another sense, the fear is hypothetical and points to the fact that a person—even one who is not alone—still needs more: perhaps society, perhaps God, perhaps a benevolent nature, to save him from nights like this.[1]

Such storms are a fact of life, especially life lived close to nature and far from town and neighbors. What is imagined and projected, however, is enmity on the part of a nature that does not seek to destroy any more than it seeks to invite. The storm is as unaware of the speaker as is the spider in "Range-Finding." It is the person who supplies intent as a reflection of his own feelings.

Intent or awareness notwithstanding, it is the person who has his life at stake and needs, therefore, to retreat to his fortress and barricade it as well as he can. In "Spring Pools," on the other hand, it is the human speaker and, behind him, human experience and knowledge that make the poem something more than a simple description of a natural scene:

> These pools that, though in forests, still reflect
> The total sky almost without defect,
> And like the flowers beside them, chill and shiver,
> Will like the flowers beside them soon be gone,
> And yet not out by any brook or river,
> But up by roots to bring dark foliage on.
>
> The trees that have it in their pent-up buds
> To darken nature and be summer woods—
> Let them think twice before they use their powers
> To blot out and drink up and sweep away
> These flowery waters and these watery flowers
> From snow that melted only yesterday.
>
> (CP 303)

What to the casual observer might be a scene of tranquil and delicate beauty—spring pools reflecting sky and flowers—becomes in this poem a struggle without struggle, a devouring of the weak by the strong, the process and development of the mighty at the expense of the fragile. The first line, with its qualifying "though in forests" and "still," signals the transitoriness of what will follow. Only now, when snow has melted and trees are still bare, can a forest pool reflect the sky. In reflecting the flowers, the pools become one with the flowers—they share with them the "chill and shiver" and share with them the source of their pending annihilation. Watery flowers and flowery waters seem interchangeable, as do substance and reflection.[2] Since they look the same at the present moment and will also share the same future, it is not the distinction between substance and reflections which determines what is real. Rather it is the distinction between the present scene and its future which determines "reality." The statement of the first stanza, which is the statement of the poem—the substance, is simply: "These pools . . . will . . . soon be gone." Everything else in the poem is a further reflection upon this. We are shown the beauty of the present and consequently the price that the future exacts, and this is the "reality" of the scene. But it is a reality that is perceived by the human speaker because of his awareness of the meaning of cyclical process; it is not a "reality" that the scene itself conveys.

It is the warning tone of the second stanza which makes this distinction between scene and speaker's view of the scene absolutely clear. The sentence is a strange one: "The trees . . . let them think twice before they use their powers." It is almost as if he began to speak about the trees and ended up exhorting them.[3] It is at this point that the metrics show a pronounced irregularity. Line 9 is the only one that begins with a stressed syllable. It seems to emphasize that giveaway, the use of the pathetic fallacy—let the trees think. The man who wrote "Range-Finding," "Come In," and "The Need of Being Versed in Country Things" is not the man to commit it. This use of the pathetic fallacy surely underlines for us that it is the human observer who erroneously attributes thought and intent to these trees. We are witnessing a play within a play wherein nature plays out its drama of the fragile against the mighty; but we are witnessing still another drama—a person's "dialogue" with nature, or rather, as we can see it, a monologue with a nature that neither listens nor answers.

The process under discussion is certainly "natural": winter snows melt into spring pools, which nourish spring flowers; sap will rise in the trees, utilizing all the moisture its roots can carry up toward trunk and then toward leaf, until the forest is green. The scene of the poem is, after all, still at the stage of bare trees. We normally look forward to leaves budding and opening; yet in this poem the trees seem sinister, menacing, and destructive. They "have it in their pent-up buds" to harm the pools. We usually think of the destructiveness of pent-up fury, for example, but what is actually pent up in the bud is the compressed flower or leaf, the potential beauty. To "have it in them" implies un-leashed strength: they will "darken nature." We normally think of foli-ation as beautifying nature, not harming it. Neither do we think of trees as "using powers," here to blot out, drink up, and sweep away—again, greedy and destructive, and appropriately expressed in angry spon-dees.[4] In another uniting of pools and flowers, we are told that the water will not go out "by any brook or river"—in other words, to en-large its own medium. It will be *used* and used in the transformation to something else. The method of its annihilation will be "up by roots," a term that brings to mind the uprooting of a flower. But in this context, it is the water that will be "up by roots"—the roots of the trees which will drink it. This poem, incidentally, is an excellent example of the way sound can function to reinforce content: the first stanza in particular is filled with the liquid "l" sound, which appears, appropriately, not in "brook" or "river," but in "foliage."

Yet if the process is indeed "natural," if we do want those trees to be leafy in summer, we wonder why they are made to seem so sinister. The answer, once again, lies in the fact that the human observer brings something of himself to the scene, that what is natural process in an un-comprehending natural universe is process at a price to the comprehend-ing human being. Because he is human and aware, he will see implica-tions in natural process which threaten him; because he fears death himself, he fears those trees in a way the flowers have not the wit to do.

Thus while the poem is about spring pools, fragile flowers, and foli-ation, it is also about a person's fear of nonbeing, his own destruction in the process of ongoing life. It shows a thinking human incapable of seeing the present without envisioning the future as well. As in "Ac-ceptance," we are shown the difference between wishing that "the dark night be too dark . . . to see into the future" and acknowledging our human inability to ignore the future and our fear of it. In "Spring Pools" we have one person's view of a scene—his own distortion (nowhere, for example, are we told that the pools reflected branches as well), the perspective he alone brings to it. Still, he seems to be representing a human view of natural process, man the analogist, as Emerson would tell us, finding in nature the lessons we can apply to our own vulnerability in the face of process; and the poem, in leaving even such analogy implicit, also leaves more for the reader of the poem to do.

"The Drumlin Woodchuck" is at once more simple and more personal: simple, in its explicit analogy; personal in that a very individualized voice speaks of his own personal need, and thus we move from nature representing larger philosophical or cosmic concerns to something specific in nature which illustrates a personal, psychological one. Certainly not one of Frost's complex poems, its very simplicity, its clear-cut analogy, helps us to understand the more complex Frost of unspecified or multiple referents. As we have noted, clear-cut analogy is the easiest and most comfortable relationship we can find with nature. To choose a point, or limited points, of comparison with an object in nature and to ignore all the other possibilities that are inherent in close identification is to keep a comfortable emotional distance. While the poem explains much, its tone remains light and jocular. What could have been made of the sinister psychological possibilities of subterranean retreat, for example, is simply not present in this poem. A woodchuck is no threat; here, it is not even a temptation to wildness as it was for Thoreau. The short rhyming couplets reinforce the patness and easiness of the emotional position.

More explicitly tied to personal emotion are poems in which the speaker finds analogies with nature because of his mood or his state of mind. Some aspect of nature corresponds with what he is feeling at the time, and for the moment he makes the connection between mood and nature. In "Bereft" the mood of the speaker affects his view of wind and wind-blown leaves.[5] Although there is far less actual danger in the situation of this poem than there is in "Storm Fear," the malevolence is even more pronounced. His aloneness and his grief cause him to see himself as a natural target for a sinister wind that roars animal-like, and for snakelike hostile leaves.

The motive he projects on the wind and the leaves is a projection *because* of his mood, not *of* his mood.[6] It is a temporary mood—one that is occasioned by a desertion, a being left alone. While his emotions are engaged, the speaker is clearly separate from those leaves. He feels no lasting affinity with them.

When we see leaves or trees, however, become more closely identified with more fundamental, more on-going traits, fears, or needs of the speaker, we lose the distance and separateness of clearly drawn analogy. It becomes more difficult to pinpoint the exact element in nature that corresponds to a precise element in the person. In a more open-ended way the leaves and trees are shown akin to the speaker in such nonspecifics as "darkness" or "dream"; in such nonleaflike gestures as flight or wanderlust, the fears that these trees express are lasting and fundamental to the speaker.

There is no specific comparison or identification made between the hill wife and the tree in "The Oft-repeated Dream." As in "Bereft," sinister motivation is projected onto the tree, yet we feel a connection between person and tree in this poem which we do not feel in "Bereft":

> She had no saying dark enough
> For the dark pine that kept
> Forever trying the window-latch
> Of the room where they slept.
>
> The tireless but ineffectual hands
> That with every futile pass
> Made the great tree seem as a little bird
> Before the mystery of glass!

It never had been inside the room,
    And only one of the two
Was afraid in an oft-repeated dream
    Of what the tree might do.

(CP 161)

Perhaps because the hill wife seems obsessed, perhaps because the experience is "oft-repeated," because it comes out in nightmare, we feel a genuine, lasting fear in this poem. That "dark" modifies something for which she did not have the words, and then also modifies "pine," adds dimensions to the darkness of the pine which go beyond color and light.[7] Not only is nonliteral darkness established, but a connection between that darkness she cannot express and that tree. The hill wife does not reach the level of perception that the speaker in "After-flakes" does as he poses the possibility that the darkness is in him; she does not relate the tree to her "darker mood" as does the speaker in "Leaves Compared with Flowers." She is only bothered by the tree, and by her inability to verbalize its motions and its darkness.

Once the nonphysical is attributed to the tree, so can voluntary, purposive motion be: it tries the window latch with its "hands"; therefore it is to be feared for what it might do.[8] The hill wife feels herself pursued by the tree (we could label the fear paranoid); yet to be pursued by a tree is tantamount to being pursued, victimized by one's own fears, one's own darkness, and thus, while there is no overt comparison made, we feel that somehow that tree has become, in its darkness and its persistent tapping on the window, a representation, or an extension of, something dark and urgent in the hill wife. The identification between them seems borne out by the phrase "only one of the two."

The immediate antecedents of "two" are the "one" who is afraid and "it," the tree. Thus we could assume that "two" refers to the hill wife and the tree. Since, however, there is a reference in stanza one to the fact that she is not alone in the bed ("the room where they slept"), "two" seems also to refer to the two in the bed, and read this way, it is the husband who is unafraid. So easy is it to miss the reference to him that we can only deduce he is not in any sense a help in the drama that is taking place between his wife and the tree. Probably unaware of it, probably asleep, he does not help her to "find a saying" for it; in his unawareness of her need, he leaves her alone with her fear. Neither is his physical presence any company, the opposite of the situation in "The Dream Pang," wherein the dreamer's anxiety is resolved solely because of the physical presence of his wife in their bed. One could, on the contrary, see sexuality as a source of the anxiety.[9]

The tapping of the branches is ineffectual and even seems birdlike before the "mystery of glass." In this poem, as in "Tree at My Window" and "Now Close the Windows," it is a window that provides a necessary barrier between person and nature, but here glass is called mysterious, probably because it creates the illusion of accessibility. One can only see through it, not reach through it. It also acts as a lens—a way to see and "read" the natural object without allowing complete (and frightening) entanglement with what is seen. It reminds the viewer that the identification is both made possible and controlled by means of that lens. In "The Oft-repeated Dream" one can as easily attribute to the tree the power to see as the power to manipulate the window latch, the power to "do." Therefore she feels exposed to the tree even though she is protected by glass, for glass is both transparent and fragile.

In "Tree at My Window" the speaker makes a distinction between window sash and curtain—he will lower the sash as it grows dark, but he insists that no curtain be drawn between himself and the tree.[10] While he is cautious about projecting human vision onto the tree ("*if* you have seen me when I slept"), he feels that he and the tree have their "heads together." While he goes on to show how he and the tree are different, it seems that those differences are complementary, a necessary balance to him. Therefore between what he sees as similar and what he sees as complementary, he needs the sight of that tree enough to say, "But let there never be curtain drawn/ Between you and me." Both of them are "taken" and pushed about by "weather." Both use their "tongues" to articulate their condition. Thus the tree, in one sense, externalizes and represents what is of major concern to the poet—dreaming, articulating, and being tossed by some force more powerful than tree or person. At the same time, the tree is so refreshingly external, so unselfconsciously physical. Its dream-head does not create dreams. Rather it is lifted out of the earth by the force and growth of nature. It seems dreamlike by virtue of its diffuseness and its looseness, not its subconscious mental activity. Its leaves seem to talk but cannot be profound.[11] The tree has height, but the man has depth. Likewise the tree's concern is only with outer weather, for only man can suffer "the tempest in [the] mind." The tree at the window becomes the window tree—part of the man's home, though safely outside it.

In these poems, and also, for example, "Misgiving" and "The Wind and the Rain," Frost has shown the human protagonist identifying in some way with the trees, feeling somehow related to them because of mood, emotion, fear, or desires that are being projected onto the trees, creating relationships that are more than analogy, that approach an expression of identity. "Leaves Compared with Flowers" explores a more complex association of trees with various stages and needs in human life and a progression, within the poem, to a closer and closer identification with the natural object. The poem moves from valuing and pursuing objects "out there" in nature toward recognizing affinity with objects in the natural world. The speaker does not deny the value of flowers. Nowhere does he say that leaves and bark *are* enough, only that they *may* be. He shows the same tentativeness about his own feelings and values: "I *may* be one who does not care." If one does not concern oneself with the particulars of beauty, with visual aspects such as color, shape, and form—or with perfume—if one is satisfied with a tactile discrimination that only distinguishes between smooth and rough, not concerning oneself with softness, for example, one may find leaves and bark enough. If one does not care about bearing, and prefers not to have the additional burdens of concern with yield,[12] then one will find reasons to be satisfied with leaves and bark.

There are three basic contrasts in this poem, the most obvious one introduced in the title: leaves as opposed to flowers. Related to this contrast are the contrasts between "once" as opposed to "now," "late in life" and its implied opposite, earlier in life; then there is night as opposed to day, dark as opposed to light. Flowers, then, are associated with youth ("petals I may have once pursued") and the light of day. Leaves, on the other hand, are preferred at night, and *seem* to be preferred at this time of life. It is never really so stated, and an examination of the last lines shows that the speaker does not end with leaves and flowers in exact opposition. Before he may have *pursued* flowers; now leaves *are* his darker mood. The first real difference between the two clauses lies between pursuing and being; the second between a subject/object relationship (I pursued petals) and a predicate nominative, renaming, therefore an identity relationship (leaves are my mood). To pursue is to go after something outside, removed from self. To be is to remain with self. Pursuit of anything is no defense against, or escape from, what is within; Frost has stated his recognition of this fact, but it is not a part of this poem. One can see in it, however, the difference between the need to *pursue* (the object in this case remaining extraneous, apart from the self) and the need to *identify* with something outside the self (in this case the object becoming related to the self), especially if the object seems to express what is within. The relationship then becomes a confrontation with self rather than an attempt to escape self in the pursuit of something outside and unrelated to self. The confrontation now seems part of the greater maturity, part of the spirit of resignation to realities that we noted in the preference for leaves. It illustrates once again that the way the natural object is "read" has everything to do with what the "reader" brings to the encounter, what he needs to see or sort out, or express.[13]

Whatever we have said of trees, whatever attraction, identification, fear, and invitation are associated with them, can simply be multiplied in woods, which are, after all, composed of trees. There is still another dimension to woods: not simply a multiplication of objects, individual trees, they create a place, and the place, composed as it is of so many trees growing densely, is dark; growth is wild and untamed—and often beautiful. It is inviting, but dangerously seductive,[14] an excellent hiding place, but at the same time a place in which one can become irretrievably lost.[15]

Even if we had never read any Frost poems of leaves calling a person to join them in flight, or threatening him, or trying to carry him deathward, never seen trees as representing one's darkness of mood, or woods as frightening or attractive, we would find in "Stopping by Woods on a Snowy Evening" the basic conflict between attraction toward these woods and conscious resistance to that attraction—to use the verbs of the poem—between stopping and going:

> Whose woods these are I think I know.
> His house is in the village though;
> He will not see me stopping here
> To watch his woods fill up with snow.
>
> My little horse must think it queer
> To stop without a farmhouse near
> Between the woods and frozen lake
> The darkest evening of the year.
>
> He gives his harness bells a shake
> To ask if there is some mistake.
> The only other sound's the sweep
> Of easy wind and downy flake.
>
> The woods are lovely, dark and deep,
> But I have promises to keep,
> And miles to go before I sleep,
> And miles to go before I sleep.
>
> (CP 275)

The speaker of this poem is recounting a particular incident that takes place at a clearly specified woods on a clearly specified evening. Yet the title of the poem refuses specificity and concreteness. "Stopping by Woods (with no article, no noun marker) on *a* Snowy Evening" generalizes the experience to imply that this is not only one man's particular and peculiar experience: this is the way it is when one stops by woods on a snowy evening. This is the nature of stopping at such a place in such circumstances. Snowy woods can *have* this effect.

What, exactly, is the effect? So moved is the traveler by the sight of woods filling up with snow that he stops. Conscious first of all of the owner whose house is in the village, safely and sensibly away from snowy woods, he seems to need to assure himself that the owner will not see him stopping there. For one thing, he would presumably prefer that the owner not see him trespassing;[16] but for another, sensitive as he is to the mentality of the horse, he would probably feel foolish were he seen by another man—especially by a man whose house is in the village. It would be difficult to explain why he is stopping on such a night at such a place. This need not to be seen adds to the feeling of isolation that the poem has already provided in showing the man's aloneness. Not only does he happen to be the only person on the scene, but he is doing what someone more sensible would not do, or what a less sensitive person would not do—stop at the worst possible time simply because a scene is so attractive.[17] In this sense the traveler welcomes his solitude, luxuriates in an experience he need not share or explain.

The judgment of "queerness" is his own, as he projects it onto his horse, and this further isolates him. Not only might he be judged by the man in the village, but even his horse thinks he is queer. Robert Penn Warren makes a very apt distinction between man, who is capable of dreaming and appreciating, and the horse, who is not. There is, however, another set of contrasts. The man in the village would judge him based on standards of sensible if unimaginative practicality. This traveler, though, chooses, for the moment at least, the world of nature, of snowy woods as opposed to the village. Why then this imagined judgment on the part of an animal? An animal, a creature of no imagination, will do what is instinctive for its safety. Wanting to get home, out of the snow, dictates the shake of the reins. A deer would have run into the woods. This horse, however, has his place of rest in a barn. Tamed, domesticated, this animal stands somewhere between woods and civilization. And the man, between horse and woods, stands there as well. Human though he may be, he is drawn toward those woods, just as that horse, animal though he is, is drawn home to the barn.

The woods are dark and deep. Not frightening, this dark, not nightmarish, this unknown, but lovely, attractive even in the depth of its darkness, perhaps because of it. Because this lovely darkness is so quickly counteracted by "promises," it has been easy to see the lure of this darkness as the lure of whatever dark and lovely thing stands in opposition to promises, with its overtones of obligation (perhaps to society, family, self, a higher power, or moral code) and which requires something as strong and binding as "promises" to break the spell and call the traveler back to the road.

We could name many things, but they would probably all have in common some version of freedom from that which binds us to promises, to obligation or duty, to a sense of right and wrong—a freedom from awareness of the boundary between woods and road, or of any boundaries at all. Fundamental to all aspects of the contrary pulls, even the literal one of going as opposed to stopping, is the sense of responsibility that obtrudes itself at the end, probably winning over the impulse to irresponsibility, or perhaps the more specific irresponsible impulse.[18]

Lawrance Thompson takes John Ciardi to task for inaccurate and unfounded theorizing on the composition of this poem.[19] Ciardi knew that Frost had written it after having worked all night on a long poem that he thought had never been completed; he did not know that the poem was "New Hampshire." What Thompson objects to is Ciardi's willingness to "stake [his] life that . . . that work sheet . . . would be found to contain the germinal stuff of 'Stopping by Woods,' that what was a-simmer in him all night . . . offered itself in a different form, and that finding exactly the right impulse proceeded to marry itself to the new shape in one of the most miraculous performances of English lyricism." In correcting Ciardi's errors, Thompson states: "There is no connection between either the themes or the subject matter of 'New Hampshire' and 'Stopping by Woods.'" The biographer proves himself to be the more reliable on the facts, but the poet seems better equipped to understand germinal ideas,[20] for "New Hampshire" has many ideas, many themes, many subjects. Among them is Frost's nonanswer to the question put to him by the "pseudo-phallic . . . New York Alec . . . 'Choose you which you will be—a prude or puke.'"

> I wouldn't be a prude afraid of nature.
> I know a man who took a double ax
> And went alone against a grove of trees;
> But his heart failing him, he dropped the ax
> . . . .
> He had a special terror of the flux
> That showed itself in dendrophobia
> . . . .
> He knew too well for any earthly use
> The line where man leaves off and nature starts,
> And never over-stepped it save in dreams.
> He stood on the safe side of the line talking;
> . . . .
> I'd hate to be a runaway from nature.
> And neither would I choose to be a puke
> Who cares not what he does in company.
>   (CP 210-11)

He has not really chosen; and pressed again for a choice, he will *choose* to be a farmer—a resolution that seems to evade but really does not evade the issue. He will work with nature, but with some measure of control over it; he will live in the country near the woods, not in the woods; he will not go *against* a *grove*, he will cultivate it. If he does use his ax, it will be on one tree at a time, and when he "oversteps the line" he will remember his promises.

"New Hampshire" is the poem in which Frost calls himself a "sensibilist," a word that can mean one who is sensible, has common sense, but it also can mean one who is sensible *to* the world, and it reminds us of the word "sensualist."[21] The teasing statement "the more sensibilist I am/ The more I seem to want my mountains wild" was not in the original manuscript, which reads "the more I seem to want my mountains awful."[22] Whether he meant bad or awe-full (which would certainly fit into the context of the discussion on wanting to make the people shorter and the mountains higher) or both, the substitution of wildness to complement sensibility seems apt, especially when he goes on to discuss pukes, prudes, overstepped lines, and cultivated farms.

The word "wild" does not appear in "Stopping by Woods," but because wildness stands in opposition to cultivation and tameness, to restraint, order, and predictability, it also stands in opposition to the boundaries, duties, and rules that are represented by "promises." We have seen that the wildness in Frost seems to have frightened him on occasion. He had also spoken of "wildness" in poetry in "The Figure a Poem Makes," opposing it to the steadiness that comes from theme and subject: "to have . . . wildness pure, to be wild with nothing to be wild about . . . [is] giving way to undirected associations." At a later date Frost related this passage to his own nature: "I lead a life estranged from myself. . . . I am very wild at heart sometimes. Not at all confused. Just wild—wild. Couldn't you read it between the lines in my Preface nay and in the lines?"[23]

Wildness in poetry linked to wildness in his nature, which is linked in turn to deep woods, appears in the letter, written five years before this poem, which was quoted from in the previous chapter. Underlying everything he speaks of, from conservatism to gloom, seems to be a fear of dangerous irresponsibility that waits to erupt chaotically if it can find an unguarded spot to break through. He expresses explicitly the fear of being "a party to the literature of irresponsible, boy—again freedom . . . there is nothing but me. And I have all the dead New England Things held back by one hand as by a dam in the long deep wooded valley of Whippoorwill. . . . I hold them easily—too easily for assurance that they will go with a rush when I let them go" (SL 193). In another reference to wildness and its effect on sanity, we remember Frost wrote that "we can make raids and excursions into the wild, but it has to be from well kept strongholds" (SL 193).

One thinks of the "two and a child" watching the snow from their stronghold, the closed farmhouse, hoping for aid against the beast of a storm creeping up—and in. "Come out!" it says, just as the lovely woods filling up with snow seem to say "come in." It is ironic that we feel a greater danger in the one invitation—the quiet, restful beauty of the woods in "Stopping by Woods"—than we do in the other. The major point of contrast between these two poems of inviting snow lies in the nature of the appeal and consequently the response. In "Storm Fear" there is no temptation to say yes to the invitation: "When the wind works against us in the dark . . . It costs no inward struggle not to go, ah no!" But there is a tacit recognition that there might, under different circumstances, be an inward struggle, that the "beast" saying "come out" might find a kindred spirit wanting to come out, or get out. It is only when the invitation comes from what is obviously "the beast," when it pelts, barks, creeps, and poses a threat of physical pain, that it becomes no struggle to refuse. The very ferocity of the beast that can kill physically can also save psychically and spiritually. It is significant that there is no fear expressed in "Stopping by Woods" of what is potentially a dangerous situation.[24] The woods are dark, deep, and filling with snow. Whereas in "Storm Fear" the threat of annihilation comes from the man's being overcome by nature, in "Stopping by Woods" it comes from his giving in. What causes the man to go on comes from within him, not from the woods. He remembers his promises, and these promises exert a pull that works in opposition to the attraction of the woods—against their beauty, against his desire to stop there and to relax.

Ease and relaxation are among the most remarkable features of this poem. Like those snowy woods, the poem can lull us into an unaware acceptance only of its loveliness. The linked rhyme scheme draws us on from one stanza to the next, culminating in the repetend this scheme demanded, the perfect repetition that simultaneously soothes, concludes, and opens up further extensions of meaning.[25] The rhyme contributes to the lulling effect, for this poem is a rare example in Frost of near-complete regularity—strict iambics with no caesuras, no pauses. The only exception occurs in the last stanza where we pause slightly at the comma after "lovely," as if we are being prepared for the slight jolt of "promises"—that decisive word on which the poem turns, and the man turns. One can read the line with metric perfection, but to do so is to violate what Frost considers so important: the tones of real speech. This line is an excellent illustration of "the possibility for tune from the dramatic tones of meaning struck across the rigidity of limited meter" (CP 18), and the tension between the two reflects perfectly the tension that "promises" exerts on the man and on the experience.

Were it not for the turn because of "promises," we too might forget what snow is associated with in other poems, and how cold it is in reality, for we are told nothing of this. Besides the harness bells, "the only other sound's the sweep of easy wind and downy flake." The softness of the repeated "s" and "n" sounds adds to the "ease" of the wind, the softness of the snowflakes. They are downy, like a bed, and the man is thinking of sleep. The temptation to give in is not only to give in to relaxation of rules—to abandon—it is to give in to rest, to cessation, to stopping, and surely by now the snow has obscured the clear lines that divide road from woods.

When asked in a television interview what he thought of this poem's having been interpreted as a suicide poem, Frost replied, "That's terrible, isn't it?"[26] The question may have referred to Ciardi's article, which was widely circulated and very well known. Ciardi called it unmistakably a "death wish," a statement he has since wisely revised to a question.[27] Thompson, however, only suggested that Ciardi recognize that the death wish is resisted, a rather obvious point. Indeed, the biography shows a great deal of evidence that Frost toyed with the notion of suicide throughout his life, perhaps most often during the Derry years. There was a frozen pond he used to pass coming from the village, and he did tell Elizabeth Sergeant of a "black 'tarn' . . . (for convenient suicide), and what a pang it cost the poet not to have chosen it" (EY 548, 267). Even more telling are two poems he chose never to publish: "Despair" is about suicide by drowning—a poem he knew by heart in his old age;[28] the other is "To Prayer I Go," about which he wrote to Louis Untermeyer at one time: "That is my last, my ultimate vileness, that I cannot make up my mind to go now where I must go sooner or later. I am afraid." And at another time: "I decided to keep the matter private and out of my new book. It could easily be made too much of. I can't myself say how serious the crisis was and how near I came to giving in." Whether the reference in these letters is to prayer or to death seems almost irrelevant, for the two go together in the third and final version of the poem, a going down to a crucified and penitential death in prayer.[29]

So much for expecting Frost to admit on television that "Stopping by Woods" is a "suicide poem." We must ultimately judge by returning to the poem, where once again we wonder how much can be loaded onto a delicate lyric.[30] Of course, as we have noted elsewhere, Frost has us, the readers, both ways: if we see nothing but snowy woods, we have been lulled by it; if we see every possibility, we have been lured by it into weighting it with possibly unwarranted meanings, or into exposing ourselves in our readings. It is precisely here that we see once again the artistry of Frost; while remaining the simple and beautiful lyric poem that it is, it opens itself to extensions of meaning that are possible—but only possible.[31] That dark, deep woods can be dangerously lovely, dangerously wild; that death is the ultimate relaxation, the ultimate destination, and the ultimate escape from the world everyone knows. Whether these are the subjects of the poem no one knows.

We have no right to say that this poem is about suicide, or moral or psychic wildness; only that it *might* be. We *can* say that it is about resisting an attractive invitation extended by the beauty of nature, an invitation to forget promises.

In the same way we can only conjecture whether the speaker feels any kind of identity with those woods, whether the pull they exert on him to enter corresponds with something within him that demands withdrawal into self and away from promises. In "Desert Places," however, the traveler explicitly relates the snowy scene to himself.

> Snow falling and night falling fast, oh, fast
> In a field I looked into going past,
> And the ground almost covered smooth in snow,
> But a few weeds and stubble showing last.
>
> The woods around it have it—it is theirs.
> All animals are smothered in their lairs.
> I am too absent-spirited to count;
> The loneliness includes me unawares.
>
> And lonely as it is that loneliness
> Will be more lonely ere it will be less—
> A blanker whiteness of benighted snow
> With no expression, nothing to express.
>
> They cannot scare me with their empty spaces
> Between stars—on stars where no human race is.
> I have it in me so much nearer home
> To scare myself with my own desert places.
>
> (CP 386)

This later poem makes a fitting companion piece to "Stopping by Woods." Even the rhyme scheme (aaba) is the same, although in this poem, the poet has not chosen to commit himself to the greater difficulty of linking his stanzas by means of rhyme. This speaker too is traveling through falling snow at nightfall. The woods are present in this poem as well, though we are more conscious of their darkness in "Stopping by Woods" and more conscious of whiteness here. While the opening line sounds soothing with its repetition of "s," and "f," and "o," we know as early as the second line that this speaker does not stop, even for a moment—the fields he describes are those he is "going past." What is not presented as frightening in "Stopping by Woods" is frightening in this poem. Nothing here makes one feel that the speaker finds this snowfall attractive, nothing draws him in, for this snowfall does not present a relaxing oblivion; it presents a concrete blankness. Because it is with blankness that he identifies, it presents no escape, only a reminder of self, a self that is not a welcome haven or wellspring. Withdrawal would not be "strategic" and self-preserving. It would be facing a desert.

The open space is surrounded by woods that "have it." They claim it, and the speaker willingly relegates it to them—willing not because of a decision he has struggled to make, but because he is too apathetic, "too absent-spirited to count." The structural ambiguity in this line and its seeming carelessness emphasize his absent-spiritedness, his apathy. We cannot be sure whether "count" is being used in its active sense (to count, to tell what is happening, to reckon up woods, animals and fields) or in its passive sense (to be counted, to count to anything or anyone else). The following line is also enriched by its apparently careless use of "unawares," which could modify "loneliness" or could modify "me." Again, the ambiguous use of the word illustrates that very unawareness, that carelessness that causes us to associate absent-spiritedness with absent-mindedness.

In the third stanza loneliness is in apposition to snow, and just as the snow will cover more and more, will leave nothing uncovered to relieve its smooth unbroken whiteness, so the loneliness will become still more lonely and unrelieved. That same whiteness—snow or loneliness—is what makes desert of a field, helps the woods to "have" the fields in that it obliterates clear boundaries between field and woods, raising, as it does in "Stopping by Woods," the dangerous prospect of boundarilessness. Even when the journey is into one's own desert places, one's humanity or identity is threatened, and loneliness, the apposition suggests, can do this too. What terrifies him so much, however, is not the fact that he is alone, without other people, but that alone with himself he may find nothing—no one and nothing within. Whereas "Stopping by Woods" presented an invitation to the solitude and inertia of snow, this poem presents the attendant fear that once giving in to the self, or going into the self, he will find that the journey has been for nothing. That there is nothing but loneliness, blankness, and absent-spiritedness in the sense of absence of spirit.

The "nothingness" that Frost fears is not the metaphysical void, it is the void he fears in himself. In relating this personal void to the spaces between stars, he suggests that a personal void can have—or seem to have—cosmic proportions, that it can seem at *least* as important, as vast and as frightening, as anything "out there." This speaker fears the void, but he does not seem, like Wallace Stevens's snow man, to be "nothing himself"; he is capable of beholding what is not there. He is not a man of snow because he has enough feeling to be afraid. His is not yet a "mind of winter," for he can still think about having one, fear that he might discover it if he explores inside himself. He has it "in him"—again, as in "Spring Pools"—the threatening potential of what lies within. The man with the "mind of winter" does not think, but to Stevens there are two kinds of nothingness—"the nothing that is" and "nothing," which is the absence of something. The greater lack is the latter—the absence of imagination in the man who "beholds nothing that is not there." In "Desert Places" the speaker fears blankness "with no expression, nothing to express." There is a difference between "nothing to express" and an expression of nothingness, as Stevens has shown us. The fear in the poem is of the former, but the act of the poem is the latter.

For the poet there is an additional terror in identifying his own "desert places" with the blank landscape: it is a "whiteness . . . with no expression, nothing to express." If there is nothing there, nothing showing or growing, if there is no spirit, what will he have to say? This fear of nothing to say was a constant one to Frost. To Untermeyer he once confided "a very damaging secret. . . . The poet in me died nearly ten years ago. . . . The calf I was in the nineties I merely take to market. . . . Take care that you don't get your mouth set to declare the other two [books] a falling off of power, for that is what they can't be. . . . As you look back don't you see how a lot of things I have said begin to take meaning from this? . . . I tell you, Louis, it's all over at thirty. . . . Anyway that was the way I thought I might feel. And I took measures accordingly. . . . I have myself all in a strong box" (SL 201-2). Having nothing more to say was what he assumed lay behind Hemingway's decision to commit suicide—a motive and a decision Frost defended (LY 294).

Even worse than having nothing to say, perhaps, is emotional poverty—feeling used up, both by the pain of events in life and by the demands of his art. He once wrote: "[Poets] are so much less sensitive from having overused their sensibilities. Men who have to feel for a living would unavoidably become altogether unfeeling except professionally" (SL 300). Whatever the basis, the poem ends with the fear of one's own emptiness, one's own nothingness. To traverse these spaces inside the self is to traverse the barren.[32]

At the same time, though, and characteristically, the fear is expressed with a kind of bravado: "they can't scare *me*!" The comparison between the interstellar spaces and his own desert places also serves to aggrandize the speaker and the importance of his personal desert. Then, also characteristically, Frost undercuts both the bravado and the self-importance, mainly by means of metrics. Where the speaker tries so hard to show strength the lines end weakly: they are the only feminine rhymes in the poem; the three rhyming lines of the last stanza all have an added, unstressed eleventh syllable: /əz/. The effect in lines 13 and 14 is to undercut the tone of confidence. By the last line, where bravado gives in to fear, the unstressed ending reinforces the fear by sounding weak in the face of what is feared. The ´ ˘ rhyme concluding the poem also works against a feeling of closure and resolution.

While the whole final stanza has its metrical bumps, line 14 jolts us the most and alerts us to other tensions with and within that line. For example, whereas "spaces" and "places" are both noun objects of prepositions, rhyming what is also structurally parallel, "race is," as a noun subject and verb, seems out of kilter with the other two. To focus more closely, though, on these words is to notice the possible pun "where no human races" and the tensions *that* produces between the two possible meanings: in one sense, the contrast between a place where people do not race—no rushing, no competition—and a world where the need to go forward quickly and competitively obtains even in one's private desert. Following on this contrast is another: the active verb of one reading—"races"—contrasts with the static "is" of the other, which creates further tensions. Grammatically, the two would be awkward together, as we do not coordinate an active verb with a stative one. Semantically, the difference is related to two conflicting needs: going, doing, rushing to compete and simply being. Such stasis, though, is located where there is no human life (a concept we will take up in another context in chapter 7). Seen this way, the poem presents another version of the conflict between going and stopping, motion and stasis. While in this poem the outward action is not stopping but going *past* the field (he races?), what inner desert it represents, of course, goes with him, and, as "Stopping by Woods" reminds us, we must go—move, do—if we are to be.

An obvious contrast in a similar setting is the poem Frost chose to end his final collection, "In Winter in the Woods Alone." Here he crosses the fields to go against the grove of trees and, as if realizing that one man cannot conquer an entire grove at once, fells one tree and promises himself to return "for yet another blow," with "yet" leaving open the possibility that there will be yet another and another until life or strength gives out. The need is to act *upon* those trees and that frozen landscape even if the action can make no great immediate difference. This need to act and exert some form of control in the face of destruction dominates "The Leaf Treader" as well:

> I have been treading on leaves all day until I
>   am autumn-tired.
> God knows all the color and form of leaves I
>   have trodden on and mired.
> Perhaps I have put forth too much strength
>   and been too fierce from fear.
> I have safely trodden underfoot the leaves
>   of another year.
>
> All summer long they were overhead, more
>   lifted up than I.
> To come to their final place in earth they
>   had to pass me by.
> All summer long I thought I heard them
>   threatening under their breath.
> And when they came it seemed with a will to
>   carry me with them to death.
>
> They spoke to the fugitive in my heart as
>   if it were leaf to leaf.
> They tapped at my eyelids and touched my
>   lips with an invitation to grief.
> But it was no reason I had to go because
>   they had to go.
> Now up my knee to keep on top of another
>   year of snow.
>
> (CP 388)

The leaves have invited him deathward, and he will not find it adequate simply to refuse the invitation (as does the speaker in "The Wind and the Rain"). He needs to act, to demonstrate, and in so doing he makes a futile attempt to obliterate what he fears.

In this poem, as in others, the speaker identifies with the natural objects, even feels invited by them, but when he perceives that their invitation is "to grief," he becomes "fierce from fear." He resists, at the cost of draining his strength. In this case, self-preservation is precisely this strong resistance to continuing identification and to the invitation: "But it was no reason that I had to go because they had to go."[33] In retrospect the summer rustling of the leaves has become "threatening" and endowed with will and intent to carry him to death. They tap at his eyelids and touch his lips as if they were caressing him, seducing him deathward. It is not in the leaves but in the speaker's resistance that there is violence. The threatening quality of the leaves is what he *thought* he heard all summer; the relationship between speaker and leaves, flight and death is as the speaker/reader of the scene perceives it, and it is this perception of the meaning of that deathward flight and invitation which impels his strong and angry, if futile, reaction.

The leaves stand in three basic positions with relation to the speaker: they are above him in the summer, they are level with him, touching him, in their fall flight; and as they land, they are on the ground, under foot as eventually they will be under snow. The present time of the poem is the time of flight, landing, and treading, and in the speaker's saying: "To come to their final resting place in earth they had to pass me by," he establishes a connection not only between himself and the leaves, but between time and those leaves. All summer long they seemed to be threatening, a verb that carries implications of futurity—a threat is what one says he will do at some future time. At present they are falling, passing the speaker by, but trying to carry him along. Those that reach the ground have already passed the speaker. He represents what is past to them; yet their state in their final place in the earth is the future to him. Flight and position, which occupy space, are in this sense representative of the passing of time, and it is as if to conquer time itself that the speaker is treading on those leaves.

His achievement has been that he has "safely trodden underfoot the leaves of another year," but what is it to stand on top of a pile of leaves—or even on top of what it is those fallen leaves represent? He has remained alive another year—he is on top in that he has outlived them; he has demonstrated that fact in grinding them under his feet, rather than allowing them to carry him off. They are the "leaves of another year." Another year victorious is also another year older, another year closer to death, locked captive still within the scheme of time. This idea may help to explain the curious final line of the poem. It makes sense as a grammatical sentence only if "up" is an imperative verb, an exhortation to continue the battle. The introduction of snow seems totally out of place here; yet in the context of passing time, we are reminded that winter follows autumn, that snow will cover the leaves. The snow, however, is not acting as an ally to the speaker, helping him conquer the leaves; rather it is another challenge to him, another threat that he must "keep underfoot." As in "They Were Welcome to Their Belief," there seems to be a connection between "all the snows that clung to the . . . roof" and "the one snow on his head," the conclusion of the poem being that neither grief nor care, but time was "the thief of his raven color of hair" (CP 390).

Both treading on snow and treading on leaves can be futile in that both are soft; one often treads in not on them. Despite the fact that the leaf treader ends by saying "up my knee to keep on top," one cannot quite escape the image prompted by a phrase so similar to this one as to obtrude itself upon it: up to my knees to keep on top.[34] The final image of the poem is a combination of that man stamping furiously on leaves or snow that will not stay "safely down," that cause him to keep sinking, and the fighter who will keep fighting, keep winning every battle until the final one that will lose him the war.[35]

Of course, all the man is doing is obliterating the sign, trying to kill the messenger, with no control whatsoever over the reality of the message that winter is coming, time is passing. In the absence of control over time, he works very hard to exert some control over the signs of its passing.[36] We can see at once the futility of the act on time, the glory of the attempt, and the possible meaning for a poet. If language and poetic reading and writing are the only means we have to exert any control over reality, or accommodate it to us, then acting on the metaphor is a saving act, a poetic one, illusory though that may be. It is at the very least a refusal to be passive.

But acting on or with nature need not be fighting or resisting it. There are poems in which a poetic speaker finds in nature a partner in creation, more than simply the artist's raw material but cooperating in creation. True to the convention of nature as teacher, nature is also a model for artistic transforming and creating. In "The Freedom of the Moon" the moon represents nothing; it is the artist's raw material, and as in "Now Close the Windows," the "freedom" lies in the ability of the observer to change his position and thereby his perspective and to form analogies if he wishes:

> I've tried the new moon tilted in the air
> Above a hazy tree-and-farmhouse cluster
> As you might try a jewel in your hair.
> I've tried it fine with little breadth of luster,
> Alone, or in one ornament combining
> With one first-water star almost as shining.
>
> I put it shining anywhere I please.
> By walking slowly on some evening later,
> I've pulled it from a crate of crooked trees
> And brought it over glossy water, greater,
> And dropped it in, and seen the image wallow,
> The color run, all sorts of wonder follow.

(CP 304)

The poet/observer is free to compare the moon to a jewel, as he is free to compare the branches to a crate. The point of the poem is that it is the artist who *does* by seeing and varies the arrangements by varying his modes of seeing. He cannot touch the moon or approach it, much less control it; yet he is the subject of every active verb and the moon their object for eleven out of the twelve lines. Even the exception that occurs in the last line and a half is not really an exception for the subject is the *image* of the moon—an image that he has arranged. He says of the moon: "I tried it . . . I put it . . . I pulled it . . . brought it . . . dropped it." He combines it with a star and watches its image in the water—noting that in the reflection of the moon there are still further possibilities for change of shape, color, consistency. Thus in viewing a part of nature, in arranging and composing with it, in playing with its reflection and in applying his own imagination to it, he, as artist, feels himself to be in control of an object that in natural fact is obviously impossible. The moon is as "free" of his control as he is "free" to create with it.

The speaker in "Evening in a Sugar Orchard" wants the fireman to "give the fire another stoke,/ and send more sparks up chimney with the smoke." More interested in the view of the sparks than in the maple syrup, he watches the play of sparks tangled in maple boughs and watches them rise toward the moon. The moon—here the means of illumination—shows the trees and shows the snow around them looking like a bear-skin rug; it remains superior to the sparks, higher than they are. Yet the sparks are "content to figure in the trees/ as Leo, Orion, and the Pleiades" (CP 289). They are not content to be sparks, nor do they aspire to being celestial bodies; somewhere between the two conditions lies the figurative condition: sparks seeming like stars. For them it is enough.

Being stars as opposed to seeming like stars is much more sharply drawn in "Fireflies in the Garden," wherein the "emulating flies" who can "achieve at times a very star-like start . . . of course, can't sustain the part"[37] (CP 306). No more can sparks. The difference in the two poems—that of praise and the content awarded to sparks and the disdain pointed at fireflies—lies in the attitude of the speaker and, indeed, his part in the illusion. The figure trying to be the real thing is doomed to failure. The figure content in being figure, and figure, of course, of an observer's imagination, has its own value, a value created in the mind of a human observer. Whatever will be "sustained" or made permanent lies in what the observer will remember, what the artist will create.

In all these poems, we do not deal simply with "figuring" but with creating that figurative view. The artist in all of them is very consciously arranging his figures, stimulating them. He is aware that his imagination plays a large role in the way he sees and in what he does with what he sees. Only slightly less conscious, and consequently slightly more self-deceptive, is "A Boundless Moment":

> He halted in the wind, and—what was that
> Far in the maples, pale, but not a ghost?
> He stood there bringing March against his thought,
> And yet too ready to believe the most.
>
> 'Oh, that's the Paradise-in-bloom,' I said;
> And truly it was fair enough for flowers
> Had we but in us to assume in March
> Such white luxuriance of May for ours.
>
> We stood a moment so in a strange world,
> Myself as one his own pretense deceives;
> And then I said the truth (and we moved on).
> A young beech clinging to its last year's leaves.
>
> (CP 288)

The only direct quotation in the poem—"'Oh, that's the Paradise-in-bloom'"—is the false statement, the illusion. The truth, "a young beech clinging to its last year's leaves," stands as a fact of the poem. It concludes the poem in a one-line phrase that is punctuated as a sentence[38] but is merely a visual image; we are not given a statement about anything. We are merely shown the object as it is: the truth. Still the fact that it is not *stated*, that it is self-evident but undeclared, can show a lack of faith in the fact or lack of commitment to it. The "he" of the poem is struggling between his thought and his knowledge of March, "and yet ready to believe the most." His receptiveness seems absolutely necessary to the "lie" that the "I" of the poem verbalizes. That receptiveness to illusion and pretense must be there because neither one of them is ever truly deceived. The poem shows no discovery; "had we but in us to assume" is in the conditional, the hypothetical, not the actual. The word "as" in line 10 gives away the fact that his own pretense could not really deceive him. This has been not the passive reader's "suspension of disbelief" but the active courting of the imagination by one who wishes to cultivate his illusion—to make a moment "boundless" by removing for that moment the bounds of time and fact.[39] As this is Frost, however, we are not allowed to be boundless in this manner for more than a moment. The poem ends with the truth.

In "A Hillside Thaw" nature herself rearranges and transforms, and the observer sees melting snow as analogous to live animals; yet before we reach the end of the poem, we feel that there is an interplay between nature, its transformations, and the artist/observer's thinking about *his* transformations of material. Nature models the creative process. Melting snow is compared to lizards, but the sun and the moon cooperate in their creation, and this creativity is obviously analogous to the various facets of the artist's creativity—the manner in which necessary conditions work now together, now against one another, to mold between them the finished work. The artist watches what the moon has done and despairs of succeeding as she has succeeded in "transfixing," in "holding" the lizards in her spell.

The poem begins in sheer exuberance at the beauty of a natural scene:

> To think to know the country and not know
> The hillside on the day the sun lets go
> Ten million silver lizards out of snow!
>
> (CP 293)

Inseparable from the appreciation of the scene's beauty, however, is the emotional effect of the thaw and what has loosed those lizards. That emotional response looses the imagination as well for, as Emerson says, "the quality of the imagination is to flow and not to freeze."[40] The human observer is thawing in response to the thaw. Warmed by the sun, he feels enthusiasm letting go commensurate with the snow's letting go, but it would be no use to try to catch these "lizards."

> It takes the moon for this. The sun's a wizard
> By all I tell, but so's the moon a witch.
> From the high west she makes a gentle cast
> And suddenly, without a jerk or twitch,
> She has her spell on every single lizard
> . . . .
> . . . the swarm was turned to rock
> In every lifelike posture of the swarm,
> Transfixed on mountain slopes almost erect.
>
> (CP 293)

What is let loose by "the magic of the sun" is held by the spell of the moon. The rush of life, the "breeding" of the animals out of snow, is checked by the coldness of the moon, and these "animals" are preserved only during the sovereignty of the moon, who "held them until day,/ One lizard at the end of every ray" (294).

That the speaker compares his abilities to "hold" or catch a lizard with that of the moon encourages us as readers to compare him with the moon. He "can't pretend to tell the way it's done" (293), that turning of the snow into lizards which the sun achieves; he knows that no matter

---

how he tried, even throwing himself "wet-elbowed and wet-kneed/ In front of twenty others' wriggling speed" he would "end by holding none." That takes the moon, and in comparing his ability to hers, he concludes: "The thought of my attempting such a stay!" (294).

It is only because these are not real lizards that he cannot catch them. Like the sparks and the glowworms they are "figures" and such illusions must either vanish or be transfixed, either by the moon on the hillside or by the artist in the work of art. This poem seems to be Frost's "cold pastoral," presenting as it does the paradox that only in freezing can we hold, and only in holding can we preserve. The continuing onrush of warmth—either the sun's or the hands of the speaker—would end by melting the forms, destroying the illusions. It takes the opposite, the cold, to mold, to transfix, and to hold.[41]

Yet there would have been nothing to hold had the sun not used its warmth to generate those lizards in the first place. Like Antony's "fire that quickens Nilus' slime," the sun breeds lizards in the snow, and it lets them go as well so that the moon-made sculpture captures a scene in which the lizards may be frozen, but frozen into "lifelike" postures— "across each other and side by side they lay" (293). Thus in this scene we feel not lifelessness, but frozen life and motion. As in "To the Thawing Wind," Frost seems to recognize that the artist and his work must be turned outside, melted, swung and rattled and scattered (CP 16), but that this emotion, this enthusiasm, this creative life force is not yet art, for that takes the transfixing power of the moon. Both sun and moon work mysteriously—the sun is magic, the moon casts spells; the sun is wizard, the moon is witch. It takes both to create the sculptured lizards out of snow. The sexual connotations of the language reinforce the creativity of the process, of uniting mind and scene to create a poem.[42]

Whereas the speaker in "A Hillside Thaw" is overtly concerned with how things are transformed and transfixed, the speaker in "Hyla Brook" seems to focus on the brook itself, especially on its diminishing into nothing. The poem does not speak *about* transformation; rather, transformation takes place within the observed natural context:

By June our brook's run out of song and speed
Sought for much after that, it will be found
Either to have gone groping underground
(And taken with it all the Hyla breed
That shouted in the mist a month ago,
Like ghost of sleigh-bells in a ghost of snow)—
Or flourished and come up in jewel-weed,
Weak foliage that is blown upon and bent
Even against the way its waters went.
Its bed is left a faded paper sheet
Of dead leaves stuck together by the heat—
A brook to none but who remember long.
This as it will be seen is other far
Than with brooks taken otherwise in song.
We love the things we love for what they are.

(CP 149)

We are not coaxed by the speaker into forming comparisons; therefore we do not necessarily grasp this poem as working analogically. The brook is a brook. The "drama" of the poem—everything that lies between the "our" of the first line and the "we" of the last line—is the change of the brook as it dries out and either gropes underground or flourishes in jewel-weed. It could be another poem about process, and indeed the actual facts of the poem resemble those of "Spring Pools." Yet how different the two poems are, for we feel in "Spring Pools" that the overriding concern is fear of annihilation. In "Hyla Brook," there is no overriding emotional concern; nothing acts on the brook, the brook acts. Whatever the change has been, it is not feared but accepted: "We love the things we love for what they are."

But something in that last line rings hollow. We may ask: What is it that they are? What is it that we love them for? Is it the fact of diminishment and nonexistence? Is it whatever things have become that we love, like the jewel-weed? Do we love them *for* being what they are or despite it? The line is so pat, so platitudinous, and it seems to stand in direct opposition to the fact that this is a brook only to those "who remember long." Rather than being an acceptance of the present reality that grows out of the poem, it seems almost like a non sequitur, like an "oh well," a resignation dutifully and gratuitously tacked on. It even stands as line 15 of what would have been a sonnet without it; nevertheless, we cannot remove the line, for the rhyme scheme depends on it.

These questions send us back into the poem to find out what *is*, and we find not only brook-into-jewel-weed but "a faded paper sheet," which is no longer a brook. The "paper sheet" is a brook only in memory, but it stands as a record of what *was*, and that is one of the "things" that "are." The paper metaphor need not be belabored; it seems obvious, but what is interesting is that what it records is accessible only by means of memory. The most beautiful and most memorable line in the poem—in fact one of the most beautiful in the Frost canon—is also "only" a memory: "Like ghost of sleigh-bells in a ghost of snow."[43] There is more beauty of sound in this line than we usually attribute to real tree toads. The haunting, evocative quality of the line seems to result from the perfect fusion of repeated sounds (an appropriate "s" for ghosts and snow, for example) and the image—both visual and auditory. Ghost not only evokes the white and mysterious, but remains unseen, merely suggested. The rhythm of the line contributes to the feeling of sound coming on and retreating:

The stress pattern shows that, from the center of the line outward, the spondee followed by two unstressed syllables, every syllable is likewise paired in exact opposition with regard to stress. This seems borne out by the fact that the line reads "[like] a ghost of snow" but *not* "like a ghost of sleigh-bells."

It is not actually sleigh bells, but a ghost of them in a ghost of snow;

the suggestion is that we are not certain of really hearing them or really seeing the snow, or perhaps we are not certain when the reality faded into memory—the heard sound became "aftersound" in its wake. The snow itself is ghostly because it obscures vision, and therefore we may hear the bells without being able to see the sleigh.

Of course we are not even speaking of sleigh bells; we are speaking of tree toads. In a poem almost shorn of metaphors, presenting only the facts (the way things are?), the two metaphors stand out: paper sheet for the brook's bed and ghost of sleigh bells in a ghost of snow referring to the sound of the Hyla breed "in the mist a month ago." The point of the comparison in the latter is sound whose source is difficult to see. Thus even the actual tree toads were audible and not visible. The sound is now a memory, expressed by a metaphor of sound obscured by snow, aided by a subsidiary metaphor, "ghost," with all that "ghostliness" evokes. This is a good example of the way in which metaphor works associatively.[44] As we apply ghostly sleigh bells back to tree toads, we find heightened the quality of disembodied sound, no longer actual, but still haunting us in memory.

This evocation by means of memory, and the combination of "memory" with the "faded sheet"—the "brook to none but who remember long"—brings us anew to the questions regarding the last line: What are these "things"? *This* brook does not go "otherwhere" (a word that seems to underscore Frost's contrast between the romantics' ever-singing brooks and his remembered brook). This brook either gropes its way underground or flourishes in a transformed state; or perhaps the groping must precede the transformation. At the same time, its leaving has made memory of factual reality, and it has created "paper sheets" of dead leaves. Nowhere is there an analogy between this process, this transformation, and artistic transformations; yet so interrelated are the present, the memories of the past, the wisps of imagination, and the concept of transformation that the connection seems unmistakable.

The connection between memory and reality and the attendant questions of what we love when we love things as they "are," how these things relate to the record of what was, and the understanding of the change by which things present have become something they formerly were not—all these considerations are stimulated by the last line and its opposition to line 12: "A brook to none but who remember long." The original draft, however, ends at line 11. We cannot know conclusively that the poet considered the poem finished, but the prospect is a fascinating one. In its original form, it stands as an example of process and transformation:

> By June our brook runs out of sound and speed
> Sought for much after that, it will be found
> Either to have gone groping underground
> And taking with it all the Hyla breed
> That shouted in the mist a month ago
> Like ghost of sleighbells in the ghost of snow
> Or flourished and came up in jewel weed,
> Pale foliage that is blown upon and bent
> In memory of the way its waters went.
> The bed is left a faded paper sheet
> Of dead leaves struck together by the heat.[45]

Memory is named within the context of the process, and the relationship of present reality to a very different past reality is simply not in question. Accordingly, in the first four lines of the poem the verbs are in the present—the transformation going on for the duration of the poem—to be completed by line 11. (In the copy book, above the poem, the initial false start reads: "our brook has run," which becomes "runs.") As it stands published, of course, the brook is no longer a brook except in memory. Many readers would still find the last line unacceptably platitudinous.

Frost, who loves the facts for their own sake, sounds for their own sake, and nature for its own sake, nevertheless sees art as fact remembered, transformed, and combined with imagination or thought into a new, more powerful reality. What *is* is inseparable from what was and from the associations our imaginations bring to it to give it new form.

Ultimately, the lessons of creating our realities, of seeing the lessons of transformation in the processes of nature, coach us also in the best answer an artist—or any human—can bring to that Socratic "teacher," the Oven Bird, when he asks what we can make of a diminished thing. We reply: we *make* of it.

From *Toward Robert Frost: The Reader and the Poet* (Athens: University of Georgia Press), pp. 137-174. Copyright © 1991 by The University of Georgia Press. Reprinted by permission of The University of Georgia Press.

Abbreviations
CP = *Complete Poems of Robert Frost*
EY = Lawrance Thompson, *Robert Frost: The Early Years*
I = *Interviews with Robert Frost*, ed. Edward Connery Lathem
LT = Lawrance Thompson, "Notes on Robert Frost"
LU = *The Letters of Robert Frost to Louis Untermeyer*
LY = Lawrance Thompson and R. H. Winnick, *Robert Frost: The Later Years*
SL = *Selected Letters of Robert Frost*
V = *Robert Frost: A Living Voice*, ed. Reginald Cook
YT = Lawrance Thompson, *Robert Frost: The Years of Triumph*

Notes
1. Emerson's "Snow-Storm" (*Complete Works* 9:41-42) provides a telling contrast with its radiant fire and cozy privacy; but Emerson may have been in the city, which allows a more "social" storm. Besides, his storm is an artist, not a beast; and we are, for the most part, given the point of view of the storm, not of the sighing farmer. The only reference to people is "come see." They are not facing it, really; rather they are observing it, and not feeling themselves in the presence of a dangerous adversary as in Frost's poem. Written during the Derry years when such storms must have seemed more immediately threatening, "Storm Fear" contrasts as well with Frost's later poems wherein a more philosophical speaker faces nature, for example, "Spring Pools," a discussion of which follows.

2. Poirier points out that while both flowers and pools may shiver, only pools have the power to chill. "This yoking of a transitive and a normally intransitive verb is a

grammatical indication of the forced effort to make things identical when they are only . . . similar." He sees this as an illustration of "the way the voice can be said to be victimized by its own energies . . . betrayed by grammar as much as by the logical implications of the metaphors" (*Robert Frost*, 17).

3. The first version read "may well think." Frost changed it to the imperative form and, in so doing, strengthened this note of warning (variant shown in *The Poetry of Robert Frost*, ed. Lathem, 552).

4. In a television interview Frost said of nature: "I know it isn't kind . . . nature is more or less cruel. . . . The woods are all killing each other anyway. That's where the expression came from, 'a place in the sun.' A tree wanting a place in the sun it can't get. The other trees won't give it to it" ("At Home with Robert Frost," 6). In 1947 Frost said that he was not a nature poet. He wrote one nature poem, however, when he lived in Ann Arbor. The reference was to "Spring Pools" (I 114).

5. While this poem appears in *West-Running Brook* (1928), it was written in 1893 when Elinor and her mother left their summer home, and Elinor went back to college (EY 153).

6. Griffiths has called the Frostian man a "cosmic paranoid" in imagining nature's slights, assuming nature's indifference to be antagonism. Griffiths then uses "Bereft" by contrast as a poetic example of a nature *who* knows (italics mine) ("Frost and the American View of Nature"). Griffiths, in using "who" as well as in ascribing knowledge to nature, or the speaker's view of nature, is too prone to take the poem straight. I feel that the wind and the leaves know nothing, that the speaker is being a trifle paranoid—not in any cosmic way—and Frost knows it.

7. In this connection it seems pertinent that Frost once planned his fourth book to be entitled *Pitchblende* (SL 202). Another title he had thought of using was "Melanism," which indicates the darkness of color resulting from an abnormal development of black pigment in the epidermis of animals. Thompson finds that this blackness could well be used as a metaphor, since another title Frost contemplated was "The Sense of Wrong" and since the word is not unrelated to "melancholy" (EY 402). A similar metaphoric extension of darkness seems to underlie these remarks of Frost in speaking about "Stopping by Woods": "I've had people say—someone who ought to know better—quote me as saying [in] that poem, 'the coldest evening of the year.' Now that's getting a thermometer into it. And 'The darkest evening of the year.' Now that's better—more poetical some way. Never mind why. I don't know. More foolish. . . . Got to be a little foolish. . . . But then it goes on and says 'The woods are lovely, dark and deep,' and then if I were reading it for somebody else, I'd begin to wonder what he's up to" (V 81).

Also pertinent is the following notebook entry labeled "Dark Darker Darkest": "Here where we are life wells up as a strong spring perpetually piling water on water with dancing highlights fresh upon it. But it flows away on all sides as into a marsh of its own making. It flows away into poverty, into insanity into crime. . . . There is a residue of extreme sorrow that nothing can be done about and over it poetry lingers to brood with sympathy I have heard poetry charged with having a vested interest in sorrow. Dark darker darkest. Dark as it is that there are these sorrows and darker still that we can do so little to get rid of them the darkest is still to come. The darkest is that perhaps we ought not to want to get rid of them. They may be the fulfillment of exertion" (absence of punctuation in the original) (Hall, *Robert Frost*, 39).

8. For representative examples of Frost's own terror of night and of a tree at his window which gave him nightmares, see EY, 279 and 309. The following entry appears in Lesley Frost's journal: "Papa once made up a story about being surrounded by birch trees and that makes us imagine that the birch trees were after us sometimes. Yesterday we really thought a birch tree was after us, any way Irma and Carol did, so I pretended I thought it, but really it wasn't. . . . The wind blew it back and forth and made it look as if it was walking but of course I knew it wasn't. I showed it to the children and they said 'let's run home,' so we went. . . . After that we went in the house but we didn't tell mama. We kept it a secret till now" (*New Hampshire's Child*, 82-83). In the biography, we see also his fear of tramps, another link between himself and the hill wife. See also his poem "The Night Light."

9. And also fear of assault (thus tying in with her fear of the stranger and his smile and his watching them in "Her Word"). The hill wife would then be very like Frost's sister Jeannie and his daughter Irma. Lentricchia, *Robert Frost*, 71, sees the dark pine as "decidedly phallic" and the house as representative of female genitals. He refers to an earlier version of the poem in which the pronouns referring to "tree" were masculine and third-person singular. One need not be quite so graphic in exact metaphoric correspondence, but her fear as sexual could also be supported by the ambiguity of the reference to "two"—whether the "other" one, the one unafraid, is the husband or the tree.

10. Edwards sees this poem not as a representation of nature as sinister, but as a portrait of human misrepresentation ("Pan's Song, Revised," 110).

11. In "Now Close the Windows" similar sounds are less welcome. The speaker consciously shuts out the sounds that the wind causes the fields and trees to make. It seems significant that whereas the poem reads "Now close the windows and hush all the fields:/ If the trees must let them slightly toss," the original draft, entitled "In November," had "winds" for "trees." Whatever part "trees" play in Frost's poetic imagination and in the expression of his moods, he saw fit to add it to this poem, introducing tossing trees, and the need to silence these trees, in a poem that would have had no trees in it at all.

12. Perhaps apropos here is Frost's writing: "One sickness and another in the family kept us till I could have cried out with the romantics that no artist should have a family" (LU 204).

13. What Dewey says of response to art can here be said of nature, and its becoming "expressive": "Expression is the clarification of turbid emotion; our appetites know themselves when they are reflected in the mirror of art, and as they know themselves are transfigured. Emotion that is distinctively esthetic then occurs . . . an emotion that is induced by material that is expressive, and because it is evoked by and attached to this material it consists of natural emotions that have been transformed. Natural objects . . . induce it. But they do so only because when they are matter of an experience they, too, have undergone a change similar to that which the painter or poet effects in converting the immediate scene into the matter of an act that expresses the value of what is seen" (*Art as Experience*, 77).

---

14. Contrast Emerson: "In the woods, we return to reason and faith. There I feel nothing can befall me . . . which nature cannot repair" (*Complete Works*, 1:10).

15. As might be expected, there has been much written on the subject of woods imagery in the poetry of Robert Frost. Lentricchia finds "the image of the 'dark trees' . . . obsessive. . . . Ultimately the journey into the immense dark wood becomes a metaphor for a journey into the dark immensity of the self's wildness which will finally stimulate, once again, the need for community" (*Robert Frost*, 26). He finds it to be a metaphor of the irrational, and goes on to say: "In his dark wood the self is damned, not redeemed, because what may be unveiled and unloosed there is everything in us which must be kept under tighter control" (88).

The "irrational appeal" of the dark woods is also discussed by Dendinger, "The Irrational Appeal of Frost's Dark Deep Woods," as it relates to other major American literature (e.g., *Huck Finn*, *The Scarlet Letter*, *The Bear*) in which the wilderness exerts similar fascination and brings with it the temptation to escape the human condition, an escape that is morally wrong as well as being impractical. Yet he points out that "the dark unfathomable core of human nature relates man most surely to his swirling, unmeasurable universe, to all its inhabitants, and to their common . . . environment, the lovely wood dark and deep."

In this sense of a greater tie with all humanity and with nature, the journey into the woods is not all "damned" and unredeemed, as Lentricchia has it. Some nod to wildness, some "retreat" into the dark self and into the freedom of woods is necessary for one's keeping in touch with oneself and one's humanity, necessary to creativity. This must be what Frost meant, when he defined poetry as being "like a wild-game preserve. . . . It's where wild things live. This is the ultimate in poetry, and it has to be there" (I 137).

As Rechnitz writes in "The Tragic Vision of Robert Frost," 140: "Keep the wildness down we have to; but if we keep it too completely down we shall discover it breaking out in us, ourselves."

Frost himself recognized our ambivalence toward keeping ourselves "under tightest control." In defining puritanism he said: "It is that in you that fears your own pleasure, that distrusts your own pleasure . . . there ought to be in you something that forbids yourself. . . . There ought to be something in you that hates to be checked . . . that you better not need to be checked—that ought to be self-checked. That's Puritanism, too" (V 90-91).

John T. Ogilvie, who also sees dark woods as a place where one can lose the self as well as find it, states that in the later poems Frost cannot be enticed into the woods at all; he projects himself outward and, to do so, shifts his imagery from woods to stars. Ogilvie finds the whole pattern demonstrated in "Come In" ("From Woods to Stars"). There is some risk in basing assertions on the order of the appearance in print of Frost's poetry, as he saved up poems to be used much later. There is a "star" poem in *A Boy's Will*, and a few "woods" poems are in *In the Clearing*.

Woods can lure us to our destruction, but as Poirier points out, "home" can destroy by stifling and smothering (*Robert Frost*, 89, 96, 125).

16. Thoreau speaks of a poet's "having" a landscape: "The crusty farmer supposed [the poet] had got a few apples only, Why, the owner does not know it for many years

when a poet has put his farm in rhyme . . . has fairly impounded it, milked it . . . got all the cream, and left the farmer only the skimmed milk" (*Walden*, 82-83). Emerson also speaks of such "ownership" (*Complete Works*, 3:42).

17. This distinction, as well as the one below about man's capacity to dream, is made by Warren in "The Themes of Robert Frost," 218-33. Warren finds as a recurrent theme in Frost man's need to accommodate his capacity to contemplate and dream with action.

18. Coale, in "Emblematic Encounter," 103, sees it differently: "'And miles to go before I sleep' in their repetition are a sleepy final attempt to deny what in fact is already happening. The speaker is stopping, coming to an hypnotic halt; the repetition of the final lines suggests that the poem has come to a full spellbound stop." (A similar view is expressed in the same volume by Carmichael, "Robert Frost as Romantic," 162.) Coale also feels that Frost has slipped into a sort of "self-hypnosis. Always before, he has resisted the spellbinding, seductive quality of the encounter with nature" (102). Coale seems, however, to be confusing the speaker with Frost (as he also does in his discussion of "After Apple-Picking"). Frost may be showing such seduction and, in the process, seducing the reader. The poem is not written at the moment of seduction. That is not to say, though, that the act of writing cannot cause seduction. This may very well be a poem about the hypnotic qualities of poetry—its writing and its reading.

19. Thompson's remarks on Ciardi are contained in the notes to EY, 595-97. The article in question is Ciardi, "The Way to the Poem," 147-57. The article first appeared in *The Saturday Review*, 12 April 1958.

20. Ciardi, however, must have felt himself chastised, for when he reprinted the essay in his poetry text, he omitted the paragraph in question (*How Does a Poem Mean?* 670-77). He later refers to a passage he had cut from that article: an analogy to scuba divers so caught by the "rapture of the deep" that they go further and further until they do not have enough air to come up, so hypnotized by beauty, they are drawn into oblivion. He cut this to the parenthetical death wish. He recanted on the death wish but still believed in the oblivion part of his discussion. So do I (Cifelli, "Ciardi on Frost," 483).

21. An interesting earlier use of the word "sensibilist" occurred when he was writing about his sister Jeannie's insanity: "She has always been anti-physical and a sensibilist. I must say she was pretty well broken by the coarseness and brutality of the world before the war was even thought of. This was partly because she thought she ought to be on principle" (LU 247).

22. MS of "New Hampshire."

23. Letter to Sidney Cox, 18 May 1939. Robert Frost Collection, Dartmouth College Library, Hanover, New Hampshire. Part of this is quoted in LY 377.

24. A valuable insight into the creative process is comparing the quiet loveliness of the poem with the actual incident that Thompson had from Frost: "A bleak wind began to blow fine flakes of the year's first snowfall and Rob could feel the chill penetrating to his bones so ominously. . . . As the darkness settled in the wind-blown snow felt like fine sand against his face. Snow began to pile and drift in the road just enough to hinder the tired horse and threaten serious difficulties. Rob lost his way in the dark, had to stop at a farmhouse to ask for directions, grew more and more miserable as he got closer to home, and finally drove into his barn near midnight sick with rage and disgust" (EY 266).

Bleau's account refers to the time Frost related to him that the incident took place on "the darkest evening of the year"—22 December; it was before Christmas, and there was no gift money. "I just sat there and bawled like a baby." Lesley confirms it was what he had told them ("Robert Frost's Favorite Poem," 175-77).

25. For discussions of the way this ending came about, might have come about, and how it works, see YT, 596, quoting R. C. Townsend. See also Cooper and Holmes, *Preface to Poetry*, 604-7, which draws on a discussion with the poet and prints a facsimile of the original draft. Interesting as conjecture and insight into the poetic process is Ciardi's article, cited above.

26. "At Home with Robert Frost."

27. Ciardi, as the article appears in *How Does a Poem Mean?*

28. EY, 267.

> I am like a dead diver after all's
> Done, still held fast in the weeds' snare below,
> Where in the gloom his limbs begin to glow
> Swaying at his moorings as the roiled bottom falls.
> There was a moment when with vainest calls
> He drank the water, saying 'Oh let me go—
> God let me go!'—for then he could not know
> As in the sun's warm light on earth and walls.
>
> I am like a dead diver in this place.
> I was alive here too one desperate space,
> And near prayer in the one whom I invoked.
> I tore the muscles from my limbs and choked.
> My sudden struggle may have dragged down some
> White lily from the air—and now the fishes come.

29. The letters to Louis Untermeyer can be found in SL, 270-71 and 497, respectively. The final version of the poem is in the latter:

> To prayer I think I go,
> I go to prayer—
> Along a darkened corridor of woe
> And down a stair
> In every step of which I am abased.
> I wear a halter-rope about the waist.
> I bear a candle end put out with haste.
> For such as I there is reserved a crypt
> That from its stony arches having dripped
> Has stony pavement in a slime of mould.
> There I will throw me down an unconsoled
> And utter loss,
> And spread out in the figure of a cross.

Oh, if religion's not to be my fate
I must be spoken to and told
Before too late!

30. At this point some of Frost's other remarks on this poem seem in order:
On the question of its being a suicide poem: "I never intended that, but I did have the feeling it was loaded with ulteriority" (I 188).

"That one I've been more bothered with than anybody ever has been with any poem in just the pressing it for more than it should be pressed for. It means enough without its being pressed. . . . I don't say that somebody shouldn't press it, but I don't want to be there" (V 52).

Frost once called this poem "my best bid for remembrance" (LU 163). But most significant of all is Frost's remark that "Stopping by Woods . . . contains all I ever knew" (quoted by Cook, "Robert Frost's Asides on His Poetry," 357).

31. Frost, in one of his Harvard lectures, spoke of "the evil search for synonyms." Thompson explains: "Robert Frost, in referring to 'the evil search for synonyms,' was expressing his prejudice in favor of using images which imply (rather than state) analogies, images and actions which merely hint metaphoric and symbolic extensions of meaning. A convenient example is the familiar poem 'Stopping by Woods'" (YT 647).

32. Langbaum, in "The New Nature Poetry," 329, says that Frost turns into a kind of consolation "that perception of an internal void which would be for another poet the most terrifying perception of all." Obviously I do not agree; for Frost too it is "the most terrifying perception of all."

Poirier, in *The Renewal of Literature*, 52, finds "carried into the poetry of Robert Frost" the "terror of blankness and lassitude" that Emerson and James expressed in their obsession with action (this despite Emerson's "admit[ting] that he is a cold fish"). In Frost, Poirier locates the fear in "Stopping by Woods." True, action is the antidote to lassitude in "Stopping," but the "terror of blankness" seems much more the subject in "Desert Places," and Frost's "action," the making of it into art.

33. In a letter to Untermeyer about his sister Jeannie's insanity, Frost expresses his grief and his feelings of guilt. Then he adds: "And I suppose I am a brute in that my nature refuses to carry sympathy to the point of going crazy just because someone else goes crazy, or of dying because someone else dies. As I get older I find it easier to lie awake nights over other people's troubles. But that's as far as I go to date. In good time I will join them in death to show our common humanity" (SL 247-48).

34. In the first printing of the poem, the line read "Up, my knee, to keep on top." In the *Complete Poems* it read "Up my knee to keep on top." Lathem, in his editing of the latest complete edition—*The Poetry of Robert Frost*—restores the commas, presumably "for achieving greater textual clarity" (256), but I find the ambiguity preferable.

35. See also "In the Home Stretch" for another poem wherein trees stand for passing time; there too they are threatening even as the couple is drawn to them.

36. We have spoken before (and cited Holland) on the importance for Frost of the gathering metaphor and its relation to the task of gathering leaves. But there is a subtle irony in that here Frost has the speaker crushing metaphors that the poet created.

He could be crushing what those metaphors, or romantic conventions, express or represent—the act, too, of metaphor-making and its frustrating limits of control.

37. The comparison between fireflies and stars shows up in 1906 in Lesley's journal (written at about age seven), which may be the result of Frost's having pointed the difference out to her, or it may simply be her own very fertile imagination:

> in the damp medows the fireflys
> go in and out and in the
> sky the stars look down at
> the fireflys that look up
> at them that never go in
> and out like the fireflys in the
> damp medows fly.
> (*New Hampshire's Child*, IV, 10)

38. This is not the case in an unpublished version at the Dartmouth College Library, wherein there is a colon at the end of line 11.

39. Originally the poem had been entitled "March Moment." This poem, in its conscious extending of bounds by means of imagination, seems to illustrate what Frost meant when he said "imagination . . . must be requisitioned" (121). The following excerpt from Lesley's journal shows this kind of "requisitioning" in action as Frost practices it and teaches his daughter to do so: "Papa and I make beleave we can see people on mars, and children and houses and everything ells on the earth. We say these things when we go after the cow at night, we say we will no more than the astronomers do with telliscopes. We say o what are those things climing those trees they look like snakes but they must be children. o there comes a man to tell them to come down because their mama said they might tear their stokings and when we go in we are interested in taulking about mars and teliscops and things" (*New Hampshire's Child*, 82-83).

40. Emerson, *Complete Works*, 3:34.

41. "Poetry is a measured extravagance of the spirit, but on a measure of beat, you know, *held*" (italics mine) ("Meet the Press," 4).

42. Thompson reports conversations with Frost wherein they tossed sexual metaphors of metaphor back and forth: Frost liked Thompson's "engendering," noting that some metaphors seemed sexual—a bringing together of a male and a female element to create propagation of thought (LT 544-45). He went on to call the process "pollenating" (550). My favorite, though, is: "There was something wrong with a writer who couldn't get into his subject and screw it to a climax: if you were going to find metaphors for the artistic process in the functions of the body, that was the way you ought to do it" (659).

43. "The most exquisite line in the poem," according to Brower, *Robert Frost*, 82.

44. This is also a good example of Black's "interaction" principle (see chapter 2 above).

45. Frost, "Hyla Brook," MS.

Works Cited

"At Home with Robert Frost." NBC, 23 November 1952. TS of videotape, Robert Frost Collection. Amherst College Library, Amherst, Massachusetts.

Black, Max. "Metaphor." In *Models and Metaphors*. Ithaca: Cornell University Press, 1962.

Bleau, N. Arthur. "Robert Frost's Favorite Poem." In *Frost: Centennial Essays III*. Edited by Jac Tharpe. Jackson: University Press of Mississippi, 1978.

Brower, Reuben. *The Poetry of Robert Frost: Constellations of Intention*. New York: Oxford University Press, 1963.

Carmichael, Charles. "Robert Frost as Romantic" In *Frost: Centennial Essays*. Edited by Jac Tharpe. Jackson: University Press of Mississippi, 1974.

Ciardi, John. *How Does a Poem Mean?* Boston: Houghton Mifflin Co., 1959.

_____. "The Way to the Poem." In *Dialogue with an Audience*. Philadelphia: J. B. Lippincott, 1963.

Cifelli, Edward. "Ciardi on Frost: An Interview." In *Frost: Centennial Essays*. Edited by Jac Tharpe. Jackson: University Press of Mississippi, 1974.

Coale, Samuel. "The Emblematic Encounter of Robert Frost." In *Frost: Centennial Essays*. Edited by Jac Tharpe. Jackson: University Press of Mississippi, 1974.

Cook, Reginald. *Robert Frost: A Living Voice*. Amherst: University of Massachusetts Press, 1974.

_____. "Robert Frost's Asides in His Poetry." *American Literature* 19 (1948): 351-59.

Cooper, Charles W., and John Holmes. *Preface to Poetry*. New York: Harcourt, Brace and Co., 1946.

Dendinger, Lloyd N. "The Irrational Appeal of Frost's Dark Deep Woods." *Southern Review* 2 (1966): 822-29.

Dewey, John. *Art as Experience*. 1934. Reprint. New York: Perigee Books, G. P. Putnam's Sons, 1980.

Edwards, Margaret. "Pan's Song, Revised." In *Frost: Centennial Essays*. Edited by Jac Tharpe. Jackson: University Press of Mississippi, 1974.

Emerson, Ralph Waldo. *The Complete Works of Ralph Waldo Emerson*. Biographical introduction and notes by Edward Waldo Emerson. Centenary Edition. 12 vols. Boston: Houghton Mifflin Co., 1903.

Frost, Lesley. *New Hampshire's Child: The Derry Journals of Lesley Frost*. With notes and index by Lawrance Thompson and Arnold Grade. Albany: State University of New York Press, 1969.

Frost, Robert. *Complete Poems of Robert Frost*. New York: Holt, Rinehart and Winston, 1949.

_____. "Hyla Brook." MS, in Copybook 5. Robert Frost Collection. Jones Library, Amherst, Massachusetts.

_____. *The Letters of Robert Frost to Louis Untermeyer*. New York: Holt, Rinehart and Winston, 1963.

_____. "New Hampshire." MS, Robert Frost Collection. Jones Library, Amherst, Massachusetts.

_____. "Now Close the Windows." MS, Robert Frost Collection. Jones Library, Amherst, Massachusets.

_____. *The Poetry of Robert Frost*. Edited by Edward Connery Lathem. New York: Holt, Rinehart and Winston, 1969.

_____. *Selected Letters of Robert Frost*. Edited by Lawrance Thompson. New York: Holt, Rinehart and Winston, 1964.

Griffiths, Clark. "Frost and the American View of Nature." *American Quarterly* 20 (1968): 21-37.

Hall, Dorothy Judd. *Robert Frost: Contours of Belief*. Athens: Ohio University Press, 1984.

Holland, Norman N. *The Brain of Robert Frost: A Cognitive Approach to Literature*. New York: Routledge, 1988.

Langbaum, Robert. "The New Nature Poetry." *American Scholar* 28 (Summer 1959): 323-40.

Lathem, Edward Connery, ed. *Interviews with Robert Frost*. New York: Holt, Rinehart and Winston, 1966.

Lentricchia, Frank. *Robert Frost: Modern Poetics and the Landscapes of the Self*. Durham: Duke University Press, 1975.

"Meet the Press." 25 December 1955. TS, Robert Frost Collection. Amherst College Library, Amherst, Massachusetts.

Ogilvie, John T. "From Woods to Stars: A Pattern of Imagery in Robert Frost's Poetry." *South Atlantic Quarterly* 58 (1959): 64-76.

Poirier, Richard. *The Renewal of Literature: Emersonian Reflections*. New Haven: Yale University Press, 1987.

_____. *Robert Frost: The Work of Knowing*. New York: Oxford University Press, 1977.

Rechnitz, Robert. "The Tragic Vision of Robert Frost." In *Frost: Centennial Essays*. Edited by Jac Tharpe. Jackson: University Press of Mississippi, 1974.

Thompson, Lawrance. "Notes on Robert Frost." TS, Thompson-Frost Collection (# 10044-a). Clifton Waller Barrett Library, Manuscripts Division, Special Collections Department, University of Virginia Library, Charlottesville.

_____. *Robert Frost: The Early Years, 1874-1915*. New York: Holt, Rinehart and Winston, 1966.

_____. *Robert Frost: The Years of Triumph, 1915-1938*. New York: Holt, Rinehart and Winston, 1970.

_____, and R. H. Winnick. *Robert Frost: The Later Years, 1938-1963*. New York: Holt, Rinehart and Winston, 1976.

Thoreau, Henry D. *Walden*. Edited by J. Lyndon Shanley. Princeton: Princeton University Press, 1971.

Warren, Robert Penn. "The Themes of Robert Frost." In *The Writer and His Craft: The Hopwood Lectures, 1932-1952*. Ann Arbor: University of Michigan Press, 1954.

The Resentments of Robert Frost_____

Frank Lentricchia

By 1919 Louis Untermeyer—Robert Frost's most assiduously cultivated (if unwitting) literary operative—could declare in the opening
sentence to the first edition of his soon-to-be influential anthology,
Modern American Poetry, that "'America's poetic renascence'" was
more than just a bandied and self-congratulatory phrase of advanced
literary culture: "it is a fact."[1] And on the basis of that fact or wish (it
hardly matters which) Untermeyer and Harcourt Brace made what
turned out to be a lucrative wager on the poetry market through seven
editions of the anthology, the latter of which entered the university curriculum and stayed there through the 1940s and 50s, bearing to more
than one generation of faculty and students the news of the poetry of
modernism and at the same time establishing well into the 60s a list of
modernist musts: Frost foremost, together with strong representations
of Pound, Eliot, Stevens, Williams, Hart Crane, and a long list of more
briefly represented—and now mostly forgotten—poets. What Untermeyer had succeeded in presenting in his later editions, against his own
literary and social values, was a stylistic texture of modern American
poetry so mixed as to defy the force of canonical directive. If the poetry
of modernism could include Frost, Stevens, Pound, Marianne Moore,
and Langston Hughes, then maybe the phenomenon of modernism embraced a diversity of intentions too heterogeneous to satisfy the tidy
needs of historical definition.

But the first edition of Untermeyer's book offered no such collage-
like portrait of the emerging scene of modern American poetry: No
Eliot, Stevens, or Williams, only a token of Pound and the avant-
gardists. Untermeyer's anthology of 1919 was in fact heavily studded
with names that had appeared a few years earlier in the anthology of his
chief genteel competitor, Jessie Belle Rittenhouse's *Little Book of
Modern Verse* (1912)—including the name of Rittenhouse herself. The
economic interests of Untermeyer and his publisher, as Untermeyer

would acknowledge years later, ensured that his declaration of the new be accompanied not by an avant-garde act of rupture but by a conciliating act that veiled his differences with the popular taste that Rittenhouse, then in her second edition, had so well played to.[2] The first edition of Rittenhouse's anthology had sold over a hundred-thousand copies, a fact never apparently lost on Untermeyer who through all of his editions managed to include poems that Rittenhouse would have admired and which, through no stretch of imagination, would be included under anybody's definition of modernism.

Rittenhouse, a major literary journalist in the American scene in the first two decades of this century,[3] published in 1904 what must have been the first book to attempt a characterization of *modern* American poetry (*The Younger American Poets*), though not one writer she took up has survived in recent accounts of American literary history (not even for a sentence). She made it her business to get to know the literary powers of the day in New York and Boston, interviewing many of them for major northeast dailies; became chief poetry reviewer for the *New York Times*; and a founder in 1910 of the Poetry Society of America. In her various writings and anthologies she could say who was in and who (usually by omission) was out, and though recent historians have not ratified any of her choices and do not know her name, she was a force who represented both in her female person and her taste the aesthetic grain that the emerging modernist male poets worked against: the principle of "the Feminine in literature," as Eliot[4] put it, which he was none too anxious to give space to in *The Egoist*; the "Aunt Hepsy" that Pound[5] saw as typifying poetry's contemporary audience in the United States; one of those—again Pound—who had turned poetry (for serious people) into "balderdash—a sort of embroidery for dilettantes and women."[6]

Like E. C. Stedman's *An American Anthology* (1900) and Francis Palgrave's *Golden Treasury* (1867), in its several editions a best-seller in America, Rittenhouse's *Little Book of Modern Verse* sustained an innocent lyric ideal of sweetness, the voice of unadulterated song. Nothing in her anthology contradicted the literary principles announced by Palgrave and Stedman in their respective prefaces, where they characterized lyric by what they excluded. No narrative, no description of local, regional cast; no humor (the antithesis of the lyric mode, according to Palgrave); no intellect at meditation; nothing occasional; nothing dramatic—no textures of blank verse because lyric in its purity excludes the dramatic voice in its speaking cadences; certainly no vernacular. Eliot would say that a real poet could amalgamate his experiences of falling in love and reading Spinoza because a real poet's sensibility was not dissociated; a real poet did not shrink from the impurities of heterogeneous experience.[7] Palgrave, Stedman, and Rittenhouse were champions of the dissociated lyric of exclusion, the homogeneity of the isolate, autonomous, unmixed feeling (no ironists allowed), and their books sanctioned and sustained that lyric ideal through the young manhoods of the modernists-to-be who would in some large part learn how to write a "modern" poetry by writing against "poetry" as it was underwritten by these major tastemakers and the mass circulation magazines which gave space to genteel lyric and precious little else.

Stedman summed up genteel America's poetic ideal most provocatively when, in an I-told-you-so aside, he noted that the Civil War had motivated no "little classics of absolute song."[8] Democratic cultures, as we know, are not supposed to venerate heroic ideals, the big epic literary classic is presumably beyond our reach—which leaves us with the little or lyric classic, but even that is imperilled by the forces of social environment, the penetration of lyric interiority by temporal immediacy. The unhappy result, in the embedded logic of Stedman's lament, is the birth of the impure or "partial" song, song not quite emptied of worldly interests and pressures—lyric too much with the world. Joyce Kilmer thought Rittenhouse had "raised anthology-making to a fine art."[9] Frost thought otherwise. He told one correspondent that her title was "silly."[10] He didn't explain what he meant, but he must have meant that she had no right to the word "modern," and, of course, by the governing aesthetic dicta of genteel anthology-making, she didn't. In the world of Palgrave and Stedman "modern lyric" is a contradiction in terms, not to mention a besmirching of the category of lyric. Lyric practice by male and female writers seemed to Pound and Frost an effeminate business, and cultural authority in the female person of Jessie Belle must have made it seem doubly so.

Aside from needing to make a buck, Untermeyer needed to make a point or two. If he was at veiled war with Rittenhouse and genteel culture, then he was at open polemics with Conrad Aiken over whose version of the new poetry would achieve cultural authority, which new poets would survive. For Untermeyer the modern moment was peculiarly American, its progenitors his benign versions of Whitman and Dickinson, its vision hopeful and democratic, its formal manner always submissive to its human content: art with positive social function. The decadence of Stevens, the assiduous internationalism of Pound, the tenuous inwardness of Eliot, all represented an unhealthy foreign strain, an elitist art-for-art's-sake plying of the craft for a coterie audience: undemocratic to the core, Untermeyer believed, because an art that only the culturally privileged could make any sense of.[11] *Modern American Poetry* was aimed at a mass audience for economic reasons, but its democratic ideology also demanded a mass audience, and as a perfectly blended capitalist/populist venture, Untermeyer's book stood against the coterie anthologies only recently put out by the New York avant-garde, by Pound, and by Wyndham Lewis (*Others, The Catholic Anthology, Blast*). So upon the economic success of *Modern American Poetry* hung Untermeyer's version of the future of the new poetry, his desire for a poetry rooted in diverse American cultures, and his hopes for the reading and dissemination of poetry in a democratic society. Upon the economic success of Untermeyer's anthology hung the cultural authority of the party of Van Wyck Brooks's nativist intellectuals, the cultural politics of "America's coming-of-age" of which *Modern American Poetry* was the anthological representative.

Untermeyer went polemically further in his companion critical volume, *The New Era in American Poetry* (also published in 1919), in which he characterized the work of Pound, Stevens, and their aesthetic companions published by Walter Arensberg's *Others* as "mere verbal legerdemain," effeminate and morbid.[12] Aiken, Eliot's college mate and longtime correspondent, counterattacked in a review of the book in the *New Repub*lic with the charge that Untermeyer's celebration in American poetry of "the unflinchingly masculine" (which he glossed with the words "Americanism" and "lustihood") was unwittingly a celebration of the most conservative of poetic and political values.[13] Poetry with the right message—the carefully monitored poetry of the ideal state, good for the education of soldiers—had been welcomed by Plato, after all, poetry's most celebrated historical enemy. Aiken argued that Untermeyer's soft socialist politics, grafted onto a happy version of Whitman, blinded him to the force of the true revolutionaries who were "throwing their bombs into the aesthetic arena": Not Frost, Sandburg, Masters, Robinson, and Lindsay (those low modernists who dominated the first edition of *Modern American Poetry*), but the formal innovators, the high modernists of "absolute poetry" to whom Untermeyer had given such short shrift.[14] Untermeyer never managed to, or could, say why the stance of virility or the politics of social democracy required poetic representation, or what difference it could make to virility or democracy that they be imagined in an aesthetic rather than in some other medium. Aiken, on the other hand, who declared himself on the side of literary experimentation as the agency of art-for-art's-sake, never managed to, or could, say what connection obtained, if any, between literary and social experimentation, or why he should be taken seriously when he described the literary avant-gardist as a bomb-throwing radical. What surfaces in this early argument within modernism is one of the most ancient topics in literary theory, that of the relationship of art and the commonweal, here, in the Aiken-Untermeyer clash, given what would become its definitive framing in the critical literature of modernism, where aesthetics and politics are typically forced by rhetorical heat to stand in opposition even as that same rhetoric of modernist polemic causes them suspiciously (because protesting too much) to lean toward one another, as if revolution in poetry and social change could not be imagined outside a relation of strong interdependence.

But if, in Aiken's view, Untermeyer's introduction to *Modern American Poetry* seemed in its immediate polemical context to cherish too chauvinistically the peculiarly American possibilities for poetic renascence and too eager to court insulation from European traditions; if Untermeyer appeared to be replaying Emerson's call in "The American Scholar" for an American literature free from servility to British aesthetic rule, rooted in the American common places, and therefore worthy of the American social experiment, then on Untermeyer's behalf it ought to be remembered that his distinguishing heritage was not Emersonian New England but German-Jewish immigrant stock and that his revision of Emerson's ideas on the relations of literary expression to their cultural matrix was worked out at the high tide of our heaviest period of immigration. What Untermeyer needed to see in the new poetry was aesthetic responsiveness to voices that were never heard at the cosmopolitan finishing schools of genteel America, voices which were virtually unrepresented in poetic traditions before Wordsworth because they were unworthy of the memorialization provided by traditional producers of literature, whose typical objects of representation were people like themselves, with privileged routes to the acquisition of literacy. Alongside genteel authors Untermeyer published a black poet, Paul Laurence Dunbar, several Jews, a Philadelphia Irish-American journalist, T. A. Daly, whose specialty was Italian-American dialect, and numerous poets from outside the Northeast corner of the United States. In his critical book he devoted an entire chapter to the Italian immigrant socialist admirer of Whitman, Arturo Giovannitti: America was changing and as an untraditional literary voice himself, Untermeyer, the literary historian as anthologist, found himself in the sensitive political position to disseminate his vision of an America in which poetry emerged not from one or two culturally elite centers but from everywhere; a poetry which, in refusing legendary, traditional, and classical poetic materials, and their generally economically advantaged authors, in choosing its *materia poetica* from everywhere but the traditional sources, was in effect fashioning itself as a revolutionary literature standing against what literature had been. From the traditional perspective, the new poetry was an antipoetic poetry that even the "conservative *New York Times*,"[15] as Untermeyer put it, had to acknowledge had dislodged poetic traditions in this country in favor of a writing that insisted on prosaic everydayness, not only as subject but as its very medium of expression: a poetry which in following the lead of Howells, Twain, and the new novel would spell the death of genteel aesthetic ideals and at the same time signal a larger death, that of genteel America's cultural and political authority.

* * *

Although Untermeyer probably tuned into much of this American cultural and social change on his own—he was a keen observer of the literary scene—his sensibility was nevertheless being shrewdly nurtured and directed by his correspondence with Robert Frost, his favorite poet of the new school, who by the time he returned home from England in 1915 had set himself against Pound and the self-conscious avant-garde and was fully engaged in the entrepreneurial process of staging his own image as a different, an American kind of modernist. The Frostian directives that got into both Untermeyer's anthology and the critical volume of 1919 must have sounded to Aiken like Wordsworth's Preface to *Lyrical Ballads* re-visited, an effort to finish off a poetic revolution that had got sidetracked by Tennysonian aestheticism and the various moods of the 1890s. What Untermeyer thought he saw emerging in American poetry—the discarding of a "stilted" (he meant a rare, rhetorical, ornate, *writerly*) vocabulary in favor of what he called a sincere, simple "daily vocabulary" (a vocal language of everyday situation)—appears to overcome the very mediation of print itself, so that we can virtually hear the speaker on the printed page. All of it amounted to the creation of a literature whose most powerful effect lay in the illusion it created of its unliterariness, in its refusal to borrow its verbal modes and tics from official poetic history, from poetry with a capital letter under the imprimatur of Francis Palgrave.[16] Modern American poetry, Untermeyer thought, would be recognizable by its unliterary (vernacular) borrowing directly from life itself. Like Frost and the realists he meant by "life" the lives of the historically unsung— therein lay the radical, the "modern," and the "American" character of "modern American poetry." But what this account of the new poetry left out (this, perhaps, is the root of Aiken's impatience with Untermeyer's downplaying of the aesthetic dimension) is that such radicality is mainly perceptible only to those with keen awareness of the history of English poetry, because only those (not the unlettered man celebrated by Untermeyer's Whitmanesque ideal) are in a position to grasp basic shifts in literary history; to grasp not a change from "literariness" to "lifelikeness" but a change from established kinds of literariness, and the social bases that supported such writing, to a new kind of literariness, presumably an organic expression of a new kind of social arrangement: Literary change, in so many words, as index of social change and proleptic glimpse and push in the direction American society might be heading. The historically startling idea that social change might be reflected in and directed by lyric poetry, of all things, as well as in the grungy bourgeois forms of prose fiction, where accounts of social conflict are to be expected—in a novelized poetry which (Untermeyer's words) "explores the borderland of poetry and prose"[17] and thereby, at that generic crossing, explores fundamental social differences: this was perhaps the most deeply buried issue of the relation of aesthetics and politics that lay unexamined between Untermeyer and Aiken, Frost's line of the modern and Pound's.

In his battle with inherited poetic diction, Frost believed that in *North of Boston* he had scored a decisive victory in literary history because there he had "dropped to an everyday level of diction that even

Wordsworth kept above"; there, in *North of Boston*, he had performed "in a language absolutely unliterary," and had barred from his writing all "words and expressions he had merely *seen*" (in books) and had not "*heard* used in running speech."[18] "Words that are the product of another poet's imagination," as he declared in his strongest avant-garde moment, "cannot be passed off again. . . . All this using of poetic diction is wrong."[19] This, he explained, was the essence of his "war on clichés," which he later described as a war on all structure, systems, and system-building.[20] But he didn't want to be misunderstood, as he believed Pound had misunderstood him, as "a spontaneous untutored child" because he was not "undesigning."[21] What Frost's design amounted to was an antinomian intention to undo all design (all intention, all structure) in its institutional incarnation and sanction. "What I suspect we hate," he wrote in 1937, "is canons, which are no better than my guidances insisted on as your guidances."[22] For canons are on the side of stabilization and tradition, and would give the rule of the dead over the living, once and for all. But literature, Frost thought, is the very spirit of insubordination, as such the anticanonical principle verbally incarnate. If nothing is "momentous," if "nothing is final," then, he concluded, literary canons and the critical generalizations which produce and sustain them are instruments of literary repression wielded by professors in Frost's constant institutional target of literary repression, the university or college.[23]

The logic of Frost's poetics equates literary insubordination with literature itself, and literature with modern literature, not as some specific historical style evolved in the early twentieth century but as something like the very spirit of literature finding its fullest incarnation in an American scene which provided its true (because democratic) political directive: No literature except in radically individualized expression. In his arguments on behalf of the vernacular as an intoned and intransigent locality, the basis of a vital and living literary voice, "entangled somehow in the syntax, idiom and meaning of a sentence," Frost named the multiheaded enemy of literary insubordination—that is to say the enemy of *literature*—as the professorial sentence, the dead, grammatical discourse taught at school; the poets of classical tradition, fawned over by professors who teach them as literary models but whose sentences in living speech are not accessible to us; and the re-iterated poeticisms of English tradition preserved and sustained by contemporary genteel anthologists like Stedman and Rittenhouse: all those enemies of a living (i.e., a "contemporary," a genuinely "mod-ern") literature who come at us from the feminized crypt of manliness, the book.[24]

"Words," Frost said in a striking proverbial moment, "exist in the mouth," their masculine origin, "not in books," their effeminate emas-culation.[25] He told his son Carol, in a startling letter of sexual-poetic self-evocation, that Carol had written "No sissy poem such as I get from poetic boys. . . ." (And note "poetic boys": the provocatively gendered responses of Frost, Pound, and other male modernists were to a literary style, a cultural feminization, at work in the writing of both sexes.) It seems that Carol (who with a name like that maybe needed to hear this) had managed to "ram" his writing "full of all sorts of things"; the poem he sent his father had been "written with a man's vigor and goes down into a man's depth."[26] The mark of Frost's own manliness lay (this a frequent boast in his letters) in the success he had in breaking through the genteel lyric, as if through a cultural chastity belt, a vernac-ular desert from which Stedman and other genteel cultural critics had outlawed the conversational voice. And it lay in his success in "bring-ing to book" tones never heard before in poetry.[27] Frost's sexual self-image as a writer would define him simultaneously as phallic insemi-nator (vigorous rammer which no sissy, feminized male was capable of becoming) and radical female creator ("bringing to book" was his liter-ary turn on "bringing to bed" with child), all for the purpose of pene-trating down—now the homoerotic image—into a man's depth.

Frost's ideal audience would not be composed of the Aunt Hepsies contemptuously alluded to by Pound as the real material base of recep-tion for genteel lyric. His ideal audience would be no feminized audience in need of feeling his "prowess" (a favorite term with Frost, describing his feats of literary "performance"); it would be, rather, a skeptical and even scoffing masculinized audience whose American cultural formation had made it resistant to poetic reception, but which might receive him in its depth if his was the verse of a writer who is all man and whose poetry does not present itself under the conventional genteel signs of poetry.[28] Often a sneering coded term in the critical reflections of the emerging poets of modernism, American "poetry" at the turn of the century constantly flies and flees into the circumambient gases, as one of the gurus of modernism, T. E. Hulme, put it in scornful dismissal of nineteenth-century soft lyric ideals.[29] Poetry, Hulme argued, must become instead "hard" and "dry."[30] It must cease being "the great passive vulva," as Hulme's intellectual brother Ezra Pound would write of the London literary scene at the turn of the century.[31] A real man's poetry would not be shamed by confrontation with the real if, as Frost insisted against various nineteenth-century idealist rhetorics of lyricism, he did not "create" but "summoned" voices from the quotidian in all their particularity.[32] The act of summoning voices from the vernacular would be the sign of masculinity in poetry, an invitation to poetic reading that real (economically earnest) men might find seductive because redolent with the odors of a world they knew and the new lyric poet's key technical liaison with the already powerfully emerged realist novel that might win for him, an American male lyricist, social acceptance in an American capitalist context which typically encoded economic and cultural roles in engendered opposition.

So Frost's struggle against canonical forces was a struggle carried out on behalf of a new lyric diction and therefore new (and low) lyric social materials (below even Wordsworth), for the purpose of re-engendering lyric for "masculinity," a word in Frost's and other poetic modernists' lexicons signifying not a literal opening of the lyric to actual male voices and subjects, but a symbolic shattering of a constrictive lyric decorum that had the effect, in Frost's America, of denigrating poetry as the province of leisured women in their land of cultural irrelevance. (Frost's experiments in fact often featured at their very center economically disadvantaged female voices.) Unlike the old lyric, the modern lyric (like modern America itself) would be (should be) indecorously open ("full of all sorts of things"); the old lyric, which Frost talked about as if it were coextensive with poetry itself and what it had been, "left to its own tendencies" "would exclude everything but love and the moon" in its decorously pure, homogeneous texture.[33] Frost's struggle against the traditional author and the traditional lyric was simultaneously a struggle against both social and literary exclusion. The new lyric would be "modern" because it would implicitly stand as a political rebuke to traditional literature: revolutionary because heterogeneous in form, style, diction, subject, social origin, and social reference. In Untermeyer's and Frost's America, the new manly lyric would be an expressive medium of the collage of cultures America was fast becoming, the literary resistance to the cultural melting pot, a genuinely American creation, true to the radical spirit of the American social experiment.

* * *

Frost made his points in letters, not in essays, but because his thought made an appearance in Untermeyer's critical prose and as the hidden genius of his anthology, it made its historical impact. Concurrent with Frost's gendered, socially expansive and novelized efforts to rethink and rewrite lyric, Pound and Eliot pursued parallel efforts to open up the lyric, but in more public ways, in essays of immediate critical impact which eventually gave rise to a codified theory of poetry, the critical representation of modernity that came to be known as the New Criticism. In one of its most elegant expressions, Robert Penn Warren in "Pure and Impure Poetry" (1943) provides at once a focus for the issues of the emerging new lyric around 1912 and the ironic costs of the institutional prestige it had achieved by the late 1940s when Warren,

Cleanth Brooks, John Crowe Ransom, and Allen Tate had secured the domination of T. S. Eliot's poetics and criticism.

Like Frost, and in a gesture typical of the drastically narrowed idea of poetic types that had taken hold early in the nineteenth century, Warren—following Poe's pronouncement that a long poem is a contradiction in terms—identifies poetry with the singular subjective intensity of the short lyric and its tendency to exclude everything but feeling anchored in nothing but its own self-regard. In a key allegorical moment of alliance with the very aesthetic ideals that he would critically revise, Warren says "Poetry wants to be pure, but poems do not."[34] The impurity that lyric would exclude—and that Warren would put back into poems—turns out to be coextensive with the world of "prose and imperfection," by which Warren means the everyday world represented in realist fiction—"unbeautiful, disagreeable, or neutral materials," "situation, narrative," "realistic details, exact description, realism in general."[35] Warren's list of excluded impurities is notable for its aesthetic conservatism. He doesn't really disagree with Poe that there is such a thing as poetic decorum: because if there are such things as inherently unbeautiful or disagreeable materials, then there must be an inherently beautiful object toward which "poetry" might properly yearn. And his list is notable as well for its interesting confusion of realms, with some elements in the list referring to things in the world that "poetry" (to its detriment) doesn't wish to take account of and other elements referring to the realist literary medium of their representation. The oddity of Warren's effort to liberate poets from the strait-jacketing decorum of "poetry" is that it must grant the genteel aesthete's point—that there is a realm of the beautiful which is poetry's proper object—precisely in order to establish the identity of the "poem," whose character would lie in its act of avoiding "poetry." Strong mixtures of subject, diction, tone, and allusion are the trademarks of the tough-minded modernist poem that Warren and other New Critics admired in Eliot and which they theorized in their essays as signs of highest literary value. But these signs of the new poetics bear a haunted, historical quality—an uneasy consciousness (ironic, nostalgic, some-times both at once) of the way things used to be, of what can no longer be written but which is nevertheless often evoked in gestures of mod-ernist farewell.

Like Frost's, Warren's account of traditional lyric (via romantic aes-thetics) would appear to identify lyric substance with unsituated feel-ings of love, a subjectivity whose object knows no history. Poe's beau-tiful dead woman would be something like the logical object and fulfillment of this aesthetic and affective drive, the essence of lyric ide-alism, not its deviation. Frost calls the traditional lyric object "love and the moon"; Warren's examples of lyric are almost all drawn from the literature of love. So Frost and Warren pursue, because they under-stand, the issue of lyric purity in its late nineteenth-century embattled generic context in which the contemporary genteel lyric was being pushed gleefully into the grave by the novel and the polemical defend-ers of realism. They implicitly define the modernist moment for poetry as the moment of realist pressure upon the lyric; both, but Warren more than Frost, hypostasize a lyric impulse drained of historical specificity in direct proportion to their sensitivity to the generic dominance of a kind of writing (realist fiction) whose central claim to cultural value was its historical density. The struggle for literary liberation in the early modern moment of American poetry was directed against genteel idealism and its Victorian and Romantic sources, but the seductive pull of that idealism in the embryonic moments of modernist literary cul-ture turned out to be greater, more insidious, more invasive than might appear at face value in modernist polemic and manifesto.

Frost's effort to destroy what Poe, Tennyson, and Swinburne had wrought (and Palgrave, Stedman, and Rittenhouse had institutional-ized) by dramatically adapting the rhythms and aural qualities of the traditional lyric to the cacophonous, speaking rhythms of voices in worldly situations is an effort to come to terms with the novel, as is his theory that everything "written is as good as it is dramatic—even the most unassuming lyric," which must be heard as "spoken by a person in a scene—in character, in a setting."[36] His desire to be known as a poet who had summoned (not created) tones and rhythms from actual speech is as good a sign as we have of how far down in prestige traditional notions of "poetry" had sunk in the rankings of the literary genres by the early twentieth century. If in middle-class societies the novel had displaced the epic of traditional culture, and if classic forms of drama were increasingly being "replaced" (Pound's acidic reflection) by more popular and economically feasible forms of theater, then what role could possibly be imagined for the lyric?[37] Only half kiddingly Wallace Stevens asked Elsie Moll to keep it a secret that he was, some ten years after his Harvard experiments in decadence, returning to the making of verses, a habit he described as "positively ladylike."[38] In a letter of 2 May 1913 Frost expressed similar male discomfort when he remarked on the ease with which English men, as opposed to their pragmatic American counterparts, could attend to their aesthetic inclinations without sparking a scandal of gender-decorum violated: "I like that about the English—they all have time to dig in the ground for the nonutilitarian flower. I mean the men. It marks the great difference between them and our men." In the same letter Frost goes on to nominate himself the rare exception among American males—a digger of the wild flower, like a man he knew who "was a byword in five townships for the flowers he tended with his own hand" (pansy!). With sardonic joy he links his cultivation of the poetic with that same nonutilitarian and—this is the American cultural logic—unmanly pursuit ("I have certain useless accomplishments to my credit").[39] So when twenty years later he praises his son for the manliness of his poetic style and adds that "You perhaps don't realize what this means to me,"[40] he is reflecting in the precisest terms possible the crisis in the genteel lyric that such as he, Pound, Eliot, and others had precipitated when they decided (after, in Frost's and Pound's cases, brief flirtations with the novel) to devote their literary energies to producing a new (manly) lyric mode.

This issue of manliness is the historical thread binding Frost and

Warren's New Criticism and an index to the difference between the historical situation of the new lyric at its emergence point and the historical situation of its triumphs of the 1920s and 30s, when it was difficult to see it anymore as new writing in struggle against official forms of literariness, when, in fact, by the early 40s, when Warren's essay appeared, the new lyric's open ("impure") and heterogeneous character was fast becoming no longer perceptible as an historically specific discourse because it had been thoroughly institutionalized as the way poems always had been at their best. Brooks's landmark of 1942, *The Well Wrought Urn*, in effect so canonized the modernist lyric by carefully explicating what he offered as examples of poetic discourse from all the literary periods; by projecting the modernist moment backward in time (*Modern Poetry and the Tradition* [1939] is the title of his first critical book) Brooks, in patient elaboration of the argument Eliot had tossed off in a few sentences in the essay "The Metaphysical Poets," thought he had found a poetics good for all time. Warren for his part had inveighed in his essay against locating the poetic in some specific subject which then becomes the sign of poetic essence here and everywhere and forever (love and the moon), but he ended by reifying, like his co-author Brooks, the heterogeneous lyric (contra all canons of decorum, presumably) as itself a poetic essence, the standard of a new ("modernist") literary decorum no less constraining than the old decorum enforced by Palgrave, Stedman, and Rittenhouse. And no less canonical in its effect, as the revolt of the Beats and various poets of the 60s in so many words testifies.

If love is lyric poetry's purest inherent tendency—in Warren's terms, lyric's "soft" subject, and the exclusionary principle par excellence—then the principle of impurity is embodied, in Warren's most resonant example, by Mercutio, the spirit of hard masculine wit who brings love back from the far empyrean to bawdy earth.[41] Mercutio, in lines cited by Warren, by carrying the news of the unrequited phallic urge to Romeo and Juliet becomes the representation of the principle of impurity who transforms "poetry" into a *complex*, *ironic*, and (key new critical word) *mature* "poem." In terms closer to the effete literary culture that the American modern poets would have understood because they grew up in it: the genteel yearning for a desexualized Keats—a superb blue moth as Stedman would have him, the genteel representation of the poetic itself, free from the Victorian scandal of the Fanny Brawne letters—this fairy-like Keats must be surrounded by an unidealized consciousness that so far from doing in and doing away with the purity of "poetry" actually acts as its world-toughened shield, the realist protector of airy romantic ideality, "poetry" safely tucked away inside the "poem"—Keats made safe for modernist tough guys. No poet dare not make his peace with Mercutio who, if he is not invited inside, will do his bawdy debunking work destructively from without, relegating "poetry" for the males who take it up to the self-embarrassed sphere of the lady-like (Stevens), the work of sissy boys (Frost), and to societies of leisured ladies who have nothing better to do, having left business and politics to their men, as Pound once roughly put it in allusion to Jessie Belle Rittenhouse.

So the lyric is culturally sanctioned in modernist polemic when what is culturally branded (and denigrated) as essentially female is not done away with but is married to the male principle: such marriage is the mark, for Warren, of heterogeneous or impure lyric *tout court* and not only of the historically circumscribed modernist lyric which is lyric's most recent incarnation. In context, however, the issue of poetic manliness in the first decade of the twentieth century in the United States was not just another chapter in an historical battle of genders and genres, and not just another testament of patriarchal authority asserted (though Warren's essay is open to this last charge). For Frost and other young poetic modernists, manliness was quite simply the culturally excluded principle in a life given to poetry that made it difficult for the modern American male to enter the literary life with a clean conscience. In the young Frost's case the prospect of a literary life in poetry could raise only the most bitter of issues. For his assumption of the culturally imposed, feminine lyric posture as seeker of the beautiful not only cut against the authoritative and rapacious male models of vocation that culture in the Gilded Age offered him, as ironic gifts of social acceptance; it also cut severely against the actual lives of the females closest to him: his mother and his wife, neither of whom was blessed with the role of privileged-class woman upon whom ideals of cultural feminization in America are typically based. Neither Frost's mother nor his wife could qualify in the technical sense as working-class, but both were tied to toiling joylessly and without hope of respite in jobs of no glamour and to lifetime grooves of family obligation that permitted no life in high cultural activity for themselves; no life certainly in the leisured class work of cultural promulgation and the taming of the materially driven spirit of men in the values of religion, poetry, and domestic commitment; no life, in other words, in the cultural work enshrined in America's sentimental nineteenth-century feminine tradition.

The accolade of manliness that Frost gave to his son and his desire to get rid of poetic diction altogether are the related acts of insubordination and resentment of an economically marginal American college dropout who enjoyed none of the social privileges of the great English poets he admired, and whose class formation permitted him not even the easy pleasures of idealizing the life of his women folk, for the women he knew best knew only the hardest of times. For Frost the fashioning of a new lyric mode was an opening to all that his social identity had declared out of bounds. The cultural issue of manliness had for him immediate, personal impact: it was what structured his relationship to his family, to himself as a male, and to literary history. It was not, as it would become for the institutionally powerful practice that Warren helped to initiate, a symbolic issue concerning associated sensibilities and the course of English literary history in the seventeenth century.

* * *

In his earliest efforts to open lyric by rejecting the heritage of official lyric diction preserved and passed on to his generation of poets by his anglophilic genteel culture, Frost in effect predicted the shape that his literary career would take. It was to be a career committed to nativist values. The struggle of any young American poet who would be an original, he often argued, must be against those custodians of culture who betray the American scene by directing him to write in a banalized, special language found only in books (and English books at that), a language with no sources in the "cave" of the "mouth," a language that "everybody exclaims Poetry! at."[42] The American sounds and rhythms in running speech would constitute Frost's newfound virgin land, the uncanonized territory that gave him refuge of aesthetic freedom because he could refuse, as "no one horse American poet" after Keats could refuse, the mimetic idolatry of Keats's yearning romantic diction. Frost offered the endlessly echoed word "alien" from the Nightingale poem as the exemplary piece of ironic evidence of American self-alienation, a denaturing of the American thing by poets who could not help indenturing themselves to Keats, and a continuing display of aesthetic servitude to British rule that Emerson and many others had lamented in the 1820s and 1830s in their call for literary emancipation.[43]

The generally conservative lyric practice of Frost's first volume, *A Boy's Will* (1913), was followed by the dramatic and narrative experiments in the blending of dialogue, storytelling, and a vocality "lower" than Wordsworth's, in his second volume, *North of Boston* (1914), which was in turn followed by his final major transformation into the sententious poet of public fame who comes to dominate most of what he writes after the publication of his third volume, *Mountain Interval* (1916). These neat divisions of Frost's career tell the familiar modern American tale of youthful genius emancipated from convention only to be seduced by capital and heavy media attention. But in this case it is a story which partially misrepresents because it segregates what at Frost's most original was the fusion from early on, in a single literary impulse, of lyrical, narrative, dramatic, and didactic moods. (In fact, all of *North of Boston* and some of *Mountain Interval* were written in the long apprenticeship preceding the publication of *A Boy's Will*.) His most radical moment as a new lyric poet is discernible not in the dramatic and narrative successes of *North of Boston* ("Mending Wall," "The Death of the Hired Man," "A Servant to Servants") but in the deceptive poems of *A Boy's Will*, where in a context of tame, historically recognizable lyric practice, which won him (before he travelled to England) some acceptances in mass circulation magazines, we come across "Mowing," a poem in which he thought he had gotten so close to getting down everything he wanted to get down, that he despaired of ever matching that effort again:

> There was never a sound beside the wood but one,
> And that was my long scythe whispering to the ground.
> What was it it whispered? I knew not well myself;
> Perhaps it was something about the heat of the sun,
> Something, perhaps, about the lack of sound—
> And that was why it whispered and did not speak.
> It was no dream of the gift of idle hours,
> Or easy gold at the hand of fay or elf.
> Anything more than the truth would have seemed too weak
> To the earnest love that laid the swale in rows,
> Not without feeble-pointed spikes of flowers
> (Pale orchises), and scared a bright green snake.
> The fact is the sweetest dream that labor knows.
> My long scythe whispered and left the hay to make.

Beginning with his title Frost plunges us into a poetry of work interrupted and obligation briefly stayed ("But I have promises to keep/ And miles to go before I sleep"), aesthetic satisfaction wrested from a context of labor which is at once the antagonist of the aesthetic moment and the trigger of its gratification. Labor: the grudging basis for poetry for those who have no traditional means of economic and cultural support for the writing of lyric—those whose lyricism, like Frost's, had better somehow be supported *by and in* the very course of the actual tasks of daily work because there is no alternative system of literary support available; those who somehow must be simultaneously poets and laborers. Frost's penchant for titles which feature the present participle promotes the biographically telling fiction that his is a writing coincidental with the actual processes of work it describes ("Mowing," "Going for Water," "Mending Wall," "After Apple-Picking," "Putting in the Seed"). These poems obliquely focus the biography of a writer who from his childhood was required by circumstances to work: between eight and eighteen as newspaper carrier, waiter, gate keeper at a mill, farmhand, and more than once, as assembly-line worker—first at twelve years old in a shoe factory, the second time at a woolen mill, at seventeen, for sixty-three hours a week.

Wordsworth often composed in his head, wandering at his leisure in the Lake District, and Stevens did likewise, walking purposively through the districts of Hartford, Connecticut, to his executive desk at the insurance company. Frost's most intriguing poems imply a different fiction about their author's social origins: that he did it as he worked, that their written forms are unnecessary—the gratuitous recordings of an act, antecedent to writing, of labor aesthetically intersected for a laborer who may never actually write, either because he will have no time for it or because he will have no skill to do so. The implicit poetics of Frost's lyric poetry of work makes the statement that this is a kind of writing which claims nothing special for its being written, or for the values of writing as such: an anti-poetics of work for those who may never have heard of poetics, or read a poet; a highly literate poetry, nevertheless, that needed, in sly guilt, to efface itself as literature—as if poetry were a high-falutin indulgence, yet for some reason necessary—and in such effacement give us access to life in the here and now; access, in other words, to "modernity."

Unlike Wordsworth's "The Solitary Reaper," upon which Frost's

"Mowing" mounts a critique empowered not a little out of resentment, there is no separation in Frost's poem of poetic and laboring voices. Wordsworth, a third-person observer, coolly notes "yon" Highland lass, reaping and singing. His poem's key rhetorical directives ("Behold her . . . Stop here or gently pass!") tell us that his physical distance from the reaper is an aid to the distance required for imaginative reflection. And distance, physical and contemplative, is in turn a figure for the class difference, hierarchy, and privilege which define Wordsworth's relation to the working presence named in his title. These social distances produce the very possibility of this poem and also this, its pivotal question: "Will no one tell me what she sings?" Frost, a first-person participant, answers Wordsworth's innocent question with a parodic allusion to it that amounts to a working-man's joke on a comfortable outsider whose purpose is manipulation of pastoral conventions, not knowledge of labor: "What was it it whispered? I knew not well myself." The reaper is the occasion for Wordsworth's imaginative excursion; Wordsworth is in part recollecting his experience as a literal tourist who doesn't speak the language, but it hardly matters. In fact his outsiderly perspective (linguistically, economically, and educationally inflected) is all to the good: he is not obligated to communication, only to searching his own inwardness. So just as fast as he can, and while seeming to honor the mesmeric power of the reaper's song, Wordsworth moves in his second stanza from the site of the reaper's work to faraway romantic places, "Arabian sands," "the farthest Hebrides." Through Frost's lens Wordsworth's poem becomes everything that Frost's is not: "a dream of the gift of idle hours." Frost's poem, in this dialogue of literary history, claims that this man who writes *is* working, he *is* the solitary reaper.

Wordsworth's polished displays of highly regularized rhythm and intricate rhyme pattern, sustained flawlessly from beginning to end, sound monological next to Frost, who moves between the effortless lyric grace of his opening two lines (with anapests, trochees, and iambs fluidly integrated) to the sudden interruption of an unscannable talking (not singing) voice at line three ("What was it it whispered?") and its playful prosy surmises (perhaps, perhaps), then on to the flat declarative and epigrammatic (yet still musically iambic) moment for which he will become famous in the penultimate line: "The fact is the sweetest dream that labor knows." Never a poet of discontinuities and fragments in the sense made famous, and made synonymous with modernist collage, by Pound and Eliot, Frost is yet, in his subtlest vocal experiments, a maker of the quiet vocal collage which more than anything else in his repertory of strategies is the mark of his mixed identity as writer-worker and of his difference from the traditional poet represented by Wordsworth.

Frost did what Wordsworth never had to do (worked lower-class jobs), but also what all those represented by Wordsworth's female reaper were not likely to do (write poems of literary sophistication). Frost's virtuoso vocal changes, worked through a heavily Anglo-Saxonate diction, flaunt his difference with Wordsworth, whose nondramatic, regularized lyric voice, bodied forth in high literacy, highlights the critical social difference between the poet who imagines and the object which is the cause of his imagining. The socially and economically comfortable male poet builds visionary stanzas tranquilly upon his recollection of a female laborer, who becomes a peculiarly modern muse for a socially sympathetic English lyricist, the very same who had gone officially on record in his famous polemical Preface that he intended to honor ordinary voices but who is himself no ordinary voice and whose poem "The Solitary Reaper" unintentionally acknowledges his privileged relation to the base of rural labor which inspired him.

While the poverty and the sex of the solitary reaper doubly and drastically inhibit her access to the ease of literacy that might eventuate in a career like Wordsworth's, and while Frost's male mower performs roughly the solitary reaper's kind of work—therein lie the connections of class across gender—at the same time Frost's male mower can do what Wordsworth's female reaper cannot (this is Frost's pact with

Wordsworth): make knowing allusion to literary tradition, here to a Shakespearean song in part about work ("Perhaps it was something about the heat of the sun"), thereby revealing his learned, bookish ways in the very voice of the ordinary worker. This laborer is an American who has had the advantage conferred by democratic commitment to education. And his whispering scythe talks not only Shakespeare but also more than a little Andrew Marvell, whose "Damon the Mower" Frost recalls in order deftly to send up—in his critical allusion to "fay or elf"—a patently literary device, an artifice out of touch with the quotidian of farm labor ("The deathless Fairyes take me oft/ To lead them in their Danses soft"). No fairies are taking Frost's poet-laborer anywhere.

More urgently, and closer to literary home, Frost's whispering scythe implies, through a criticism of W. B. Yeats, the dominant living poet in English in the first decade of the twentieth century, Frost's own self-critique: in denying "dream" and the work of "fay or elf" Frost, in the directness of his vernacular voice, mounts an internal commentary on the ninetyish poetic diction of a number of his own early dreamy lyrics in *A Boy's Will* while forecasting the colloquial richness and unpretentiousness of *North of Boston*. Frost stakes his claim to difference not only from Wordsworth's elite position but also from Yeats and Yeats's overt celebration of dream in his early poetry and plays which Frost knew intimately, having produced the plays of heart's desire while a teacher at Pinkerton Academy in 1910: difference from the Yeats who had famously declared in flight from the world of fact that the "dream" of the poets "alone is certain good." So "dream" becomes in Frost's poem a doubly coded term of criticism signifying both the leisured idleness of the British poetic classes and an unmanly contemporary aestheticist fashionability, a world-fleeing imagination whose diction Yeats would purify from his writing with the help of Pound's editing, but which Pound himself would have trouble getting out of his own system until after Frost, in his early-century obscurity at the Derry, New Hampshire farm, had succeeded in doing so, though without the proper critical organs at his disposal to declare his triumph of having made it new.

Boring from within Wordsworth's pastoral territory and Yeats's domain of dream-as-imagination, Frost reduces visionary dream to vision (as in visual) and imagination to the purest act of perception (as in image-making), a precious because fleeting knowledge of fact, and fleeting because labor will not permit leisurely lingering in aesthetic pleasure of natural detail strictly irrelevant to the task of labor. And it is a knowledge that Frost comes to have not as independent agent—the laboring agent knows little freedom—but as agent of *labor's* action. Labor, not Frost, in Frost's most radical identification of literature with work, "knows" "the fact" which is also and at the same time the ultimate dream of imagination; Frost may know only insofar as he labors. The act of labor as an act of imagination rescues dreaming (Yeats's synonym for poetry) from both Wordsworth and Yeats, in this context impractical "dreamers" in the worst sense of the word.

Frost routes dream into a riveted attention to the incidental fact unveiled in work: a glimpse of fact for itself alone opened briefly, in a throw-away moment of syntactical subordination, as if it would be a desecration of work to permit those images of flowers (only parenthetically named) and the "bright green snake" to take over center stage and distract the laborer from his real task. This moment of syntactical subordination in "Mowing" is the expressive sign of a culturally subordinated aesthesis, an American guilt of poesis, the image garnered for no profit, stolen from the process of work which—by opening the possibility of aesthetic experience, of a consciousness momentarily off the groove of its utilitarian routine—becomes the necessary economic ground of aesthesis. So: work, a ruthless end-directed activity, not in hostile opposition to an activity valuable in itself—as the story of nineteenth-century idealist aesthetics would have it—but work as both constraining and productive context of the aesthetic for those, unlike Wordsworth and Yeats, who find work inescapable, whose own labor, not someone else's, is their peculiarly modern muse.

Yet what comes seeping through this effort to write out of a sympathetic antipastoral of work—a sympathy that would mark his difference from the social and sexual hierarchy of Wordsworth's pastoral performance—is a social arrangement similar to the object of Frost's critique of Wordsworth. Social distance and its corollary attitude, the sentimentalizing of common country labor—an attitude virtually demanded by traditional pastoral—make a subversive return in "Mowing" in order partially to trip up Frost's intention and to reveal his own sentimentalizing impulse in his would-be realist antipoetics and his subtly conventional stance above labor. This literate farmer is more literate than farmer, but uneasily so. This is guilty pastoral, written not out of leisure class privilege but out of American social constraint by a man who wanted his work to be writing, not those other jobs he did that qualify officially in our culture as work—including farming—and that he found so dissatisfying. The "earnest love" of this farmer's "long scythe" that "laid the swale" (not just any meadow but a low-lying, moist depression of a meadow), this farmer's productive phallic love throws into even greater subordination the moment of aesthetic vision as an interiorized moment of pathos, a moment freed from the act of labor (which makes hay while the sun shines)—unproductive, masturbatory, the indulgent feminine moment. In "Mowing," the literal parenthesis of lyric impression.

The didactic force of Frost's difficult penultimate line yields its statement best against the background of the huge cultural claims for poetic function made by traditional theories of poetry from Aristotle to Wordsworth. The role of poetry for a poet who is constricted by inescapable labor, a poet without the classic advantages, is perhaps a diminished thing in light of the portentousness of those earlier claims. But perhaps poetic function is newly enhanced, after all, in this kind of modern setting of work. Poetry now becomes a pragmatic personal urgency, an aid to getting by in a social setting which for Frost (in this he is representative of the modern American writer) doesn't make getting by very easy. Frost's implied comparative and his explicit superlative condense a story of literary and social history: Dreams sweet and sweeter, the dreams of Marvell, Wordsworth and Yeats—the easy poetic gold of idleness—yield to dreams sweetest. Sweetest dream—the best dream of all—is a form of laboring consciousness, somehow and oddly identical with "facts"—what is presumably raw, informational, objectively there. But "fact" in that ordinary sense is turned by this poet into an extraordinary thing; this constricted laborer just happens (an American happening) to be schooled in Latin etymologies of English ordinariness. *Factum*: a thing done, or produced, a matter revealed by and for a laboring consciousness, for no end beyond the momentary refreshment of its own act. *Factum*: a feat, a kind of performance, a display of prowess, the virtuosity, the poetry of work, but also (how could aesthetic contemplation be otherwise for a practical American male?) a kind of crime, as in an accessory after the fact.

Notes

1. *Modern American Poetry: An Introduction*, ed. Louis Untermeyer (New York: Harcourt Brace, 1919), p. vii.

2. *From Another World: The Autobiography of Louis Untermeyer* (New York: Harcourt Brace, 1939), pp. 327-32.

3. For the relevant information see Margaret Widdemer, *Jessie Rittenhouse: A Centenary Memoir-Anthology* (South Brunswick, N.J., and New York: A. S. Banner, 1969).

4. *The Letters of T. S. Eliot*, Vol. 1, 1898-1922, ed. Valerie Eliot (New York: Harcourt Brace Jovanovich, 1988), p. 204.

5. *Literary Essays of Ezra Pound*, ed. with an introduction by T. S. Eliot (New York: New Directions, 1968), p. 17.

6. Ezra Pound, *Selected Prose, 1909-1965*, ed. with an introduction by William Cookson (New York: New Directions, 1972), p. 41.

7. T. S. Eliot, *Selected Essays* (New York: Harcourt Brace, 1932), p. 247.

8. *An American Anthology, 1787-1900*, ed. E. C. Stedman (Boston: Houghton Mifflin, 1900), p. xxxi.

9. Quoted in Widdemer, p. 23.

10. *Selected Letters of Robert Frost*, ed. Lawrance Thompson (New York: Holt, Rinehart and Winston, 1964), p. 174.

11. Louis Untermeyer, *The New Era in American Poetry* (New York: Harcourt Brace, 1919), pp. 206, 209-10, 317.

12. See Conrad Aiken, "The Ivory Tower—I"; Louis Untermeyer, "The Ivory Tower—II," *New Republic*, 10 May 1919, pp. 58-61.

13. *Ibid.*

14. *Ibid.*

15. *Modern American Poetry*, p. viii.

16. *Ibid.*, pp. viii-ix.

17. *Ibid.*, p. ix.

18. *Selected Letters of Robert Frost*, pp. 84, 102.

19. Edward Connery Lathem, ed., *Interviews with Robert Frost* (New York: Holt, Rinehart and Winston, 1966), p. 26.

20. *Selected Letters*, p. 343.

21. *Ibid.*, p. 84.

22. *Ibid.*, p. 444.

23. *Ibid.*, pp. 181, 191, 234.

24. *Ibid.*, pp. 106-08, 140, 159, 181, 191, 234.

25. *Ibid.*, p. 108.

26. *Ibid.*, p. 390.

27. *Ibid.*, p. 191.

28. *Ibid.*, p. 138.

29. *Speculations* (New York: Harcourt Brace, 1924), p. 120.

30. *Ibid.*, p. 126.

31. *Pavannes and Divagations* (New York: New Directions, 1958), p. 204.

32. *Selected Letters*, p. 80.

33. *Ibid.*, p. 182.

34. "Pure and Impure Poetry," in *Critiques and Essays in Criticism*, ed. Robert W. Stallman (New York: Ronald, 1949), p. 86.

35. *Ibid.*, pp. 86, 87, 99.

36. *Selected Prose of Robert Frost*, ed. Hyde Cox and E. C. Lathem (New York: Holt, Rinehart and Winston, 1966), p. 13.

37. See Pound's "Hugh Selwyn Mauberley": "The pianola 'replaces'/ Sappho's barbitos."

38. *Letters of Wallace Stevens*, ed. Holly Stevens (New York: Knopf, 1966), p. 180.

39. *Selected Letters*, pp. 71-72.

40. *Ibid.*, p. 390.

41. Warren, pp. 87, 90.

42. *Selected Letters*, pp. 191, 141.

43. *Ibid.*, p. 141.

We Are Sick with Space_____

Robert Bernard Hass

> Space ails us moderns: we are sick with space.
> Its contemplation makes us out as small
> As a brief epidemic of microbes
> That in a good glass may be seen to crawl
> The patina of this the least of globes.
>
> "The Lesson for Today" (1942)

When Isabelle Moodie Frost encouraged her son to acquire the telescope he had found advertised in the pages of *The Youth's Companion*, she had high hopes that his sudden enthusiasm for the stars might also awaken in him an equal enthusiasm for God.[1] For some time she had feared that her fifteen-year-old son was beginning to question his religion, so when the chance to rehabilitate his waning faith presented itself in the guise of scientific inquiry, she seized it almost immediately. She knew of course that Emerson, once a devoted amateur astronomer in his own right, had undergone a similar reaffirmation nearly a half-century earlier, and she was confident that given enough time and proper guidance, her son would eventually adopt her favorite philosopher's creed, expressed in *Nature*, that "observation of the stars" would "preserve for many generations the remembrance of the city of God."[2] Thus, after pestering enough relatives and friends into buying the requisite quota of magazine subscriptions so the telescope might be acquired at no charge, mother and son set up a makeshift observatory in an upstairs bedroom window and began searching the sky for the heavenly bodies that might inspire their religious sensibilities and bring them into the "perpetual presence of the sublime."[3]

At first, all went as Belle Frost had planned, and for a while, at least, she was pleased to see her son following the religious paths she had blazed for him. Having read about the wonders of Saturn and Sirius in

Richard Anthony Proctor's *Our Place among Infinities*, a popular account of contemporary astronomical discoveries, the young Frost, his curiosity aroused, borrowed the star charts from the Lawrence Public Library and began observing the celestial events that Proctor's book had predicted. Immersed in such an intriguing body of knowledge and genuinely fascinated by his own growing command of the magnitude, position, and motion of stars, Frost publicly sang praises for his new hobby in an editorial for the Lawrence High School *Bulletin* in December 1891. "Astronomy," he wrote, "is one of the most practical as well as theoretical sciences. It is a wonderful teacher of observation and cultivator of the practical imagination."[4]

Such persistent devotion to the heavens not only continued to please his mother greatly, as it seemed to bolster her son's spirits and restore his confidence in God; it also kindled in him a strong desire to compose the first of many "astronomical" poems, several of which would attempt to integrate cosmology and theology.[5] One of the most revealing of Frost's juvenilia, "God's Garden," for example, illustrates just how deeply Frost had enmeshed himself in his mother's religion in the decade prior to 1900. Published in the *Boston Evening Transcript* in 1898, the poem's final stanza exhorts its readers to turn away from material riches and toward the stars for proper spiritual guidance:

> O, cease to heed the glamour,
>   That blinds your foolish eyes,
> Look upward to the glitter
>   Of stars in God's clear skies.
> Their ways are pure and harmless
>   And will not lead astray,
> But aid your erring footsteps
>   To keep the narrow way.
> And when the sun shines brightly
>   Tend flowers that God has given

And keep the pathway open
That leads you on to heaven.
(*Collected Poems, Prose, and Plays*
[hereafter *CPP&P*], 504)

While it is impossible to tell exactly when Frost composed this poem—the style and tone indicate that it was well before 1898—its pedestrian subject, sentimental clichés, and youthful overexuberance immediately suggest why he denied writing it as late as 1946.[6] Clearly, he was embarrassed by the poem, but perhaps for reasons that had little to do with aesthetic criteria. As Lawrance Thompson has argued, Frost remained intensely guarded about his religious convictions, even long after he had modified his views, out of fear that his critical detractors might use his "antiquated" beliefs as evidence of a more pervasive intellectual shallowness.[7] Reluctant to supply his detractors with ammunition and genuinely confused about the issue himself, Frost not only hid from the public much of his early religious poetry but also habitually evaded the question of his religious faith by speaking in metaphorical tongues. Asked by John Sherrill about what God had meant to him in his poetry, Frost answered that "if you would have out the way a man feels about God, watch his life, hear his words. Place a coin, with its denomination unknown, under paper and you can tell its mark by rubbing a pencil over the paper. From all the individual rises and valleys your answer will come out."[8]

Questions of embarrassment and literary value aside, "God's Garden" is useful as a historical relic, if only because it indicates that between its composition and the publication of *A Boy's Will* in 1913 Frost descended into the first of his many valleys of despair and entered into a spiritual crisis equivalent to the one William James had experienced in the 1860s. Consider, for example, the polar differences between "God's Garden" and "Stars," one of the opening poems in *A Boy's Will*. Composed in Emily Dickinson's favorite stanzaic pattern, common measure, the poem also alludes to a Dickinsonian theological skepticism, which is reflected in the subtitle, "There is no oversight of human affairs":

> How countlessly they congregate
> O'er our tumultuous snow,
> Which flows in shapes as tall as trees
> When wintry winds do blow!—
>
> As if with keenness for our fate,
> Our faltering few steps on
> To white rest, and a place of rest
> Invisible at dawn,—
>
> And yet with neither love nor hate,
> Those stars like some snow-white
> Minerva's snow-white marble eyes
> Without the gift of sight.
>
> (*CPP&P*, 19)

How appropriate that Frost would choose Minerva, Roman goddess of wisdom, culture, and the arts, as a metaphorical emblem for a universe that he now perceived as incapable of generating either wisdom or sympathy. Although the stars might have seemed to Frost more stable and less immediately threatening than drifting and accumulating snow, it is obvious that by 1913 he had completely divested them of all religious significance. In the context of his whole career such an antipodal gesture is momentous for two reasons. First, it marks the decade in which Frost matured into a poet deeply concerned about his own existential fate; and second, his religious skepticism demonstrates a remarkable congruity with his developing anti-romantic attitudes toward the natural world. Just as Frost grew more and more reluctant to detect in spider webs, woodchucks, and orchids evidence of divine design, he was now confronted by the even harsher realities of a cosmos completely emptied of its divine attributes. By 1913 the starlight he saw through his telescope was not the light of God shining through holes in the firmament, as his mother had once intimated, but rather the inevitable and predictable by-product of simple elements that reacted with one another for no apparent purpose or human benefit. No matter how often he aimed his telescope toward the heavens, or how frequently he upgraded his lenses' magnifying power, by the time Frost turned thirty-five the Emersonian certainties his mother had once found in the heavens had disappeared into the cold black emptiness of infinite space.

While it is impossible to speculate about all of the factors that may have contributed to this spiritual reversal, two distinct causes jolted Frost out of his religious complacency. The first was the personal tragedy that plagued the Frost family between 1900 and 1906. In 1900, just two years after the publication of "God's Garden," Frost's four-year-old son, Elliot, contracted cholera, was misdiagnosed by the family physician, and died suddenly two days later, leaving Frost and his wife devastated by grief.[9] Four months later, Belle Frost, who had been diagnosed with cancer, died alone in a New Hampshire sanitarium, bereaving her son of the most important religious influence in his life.[10] These misfortunes, coupled with the death in 1906 of another child, two-day-old Elinor Bettina,[11] and his intermittent estrangement from Elinor, who Frost once claimed had "come out flat-footed against God,"[12] placed tremendous pressures upon his religious faith and seemed to confirm for him the nagging suspicion that the Darwinian ideas he had absorbed at Harvard were not invented fictions, as he would have liked to believe, but the most truthful accounts of nature he had yet encountered. With the slaughter of the innocents mounting rapidly before him, and continually beset with bouts of pneumonia so severe that he often feared for his own life, it is no wonder that Frost decided long before the trip to England that a change of scenery was in order.

The second and, in this context, more important cause of Frost's changing attitude toward the stars was the simple fact that he educated himself. In addition to reading Darwin and Lyell as a special student at Harvard, Frost diligently kept abreast of the most popular astronomical models of his day, gleaning much of his knowledge from Proctor's book and from the pages of *Scientific American*, a periodical he read avidly and once touted as his favorite magazine.[13] Neither of these sources approached scientific concepts with the kind of detail that Frost might have liked, yet they did provide him remarkably well with diluted versions of the new theories, most of which were still comprehensible to an audience of nonspecialists. In addition to furnishing Frost with an above-average layman's understanding of physics, these popular forums also discussed how new developments in physics might affect culture.

Its pages filled with wonderfully detailed pen-and-ink drawings, *Scientific American* dealt primarily with practical issues. At the turn of the century the magazine devoted much of its space to the spectacular successes of the dynamo, discussing how it would eventually eliminate the drudgery of back-breaking manual labor and reduce American dependency upon coal as a source of power. Articles on the electron, the vacuum tube, the triode, and the radio reinforced the bully, progressive spirit of the age and provided the American public with remarkable new evidence that science, with its ability to manipulate nature, had a much cozier relationship with physical reality than did any competing discipline in the arts or humanities.

In contrast to *Scientific American*'s emphasis upon practical issues, Proctor's interests lay in the realm of pure rather than applied physics. *Our Place among Infinities* discusses in detail the evolution of galaxies and stars and speculates about the possibility of life in other worlds, subjects far more appealing to Frost's religious sensibilities. Frost seems to have been affected most profoundly by Proctor's method of placing all of his scientific discussions in a religious context.[14] Proctor even went so far as to set boundaries for science, suggesting in his second chapter, inauspiciously entitled "Of Seeming Wastes in Nature," that

We may believe, with all confidence, that could we but understand the whole of what we find around us, the wisdom with which each part has been designed would be manifest; but we must not fall into the mistake of supposing that we can so clearly understand all as to be able to recognize the purpose of this or that arrangement, the wisdom of this or that provision. Nor if any results of scientific research appear to us to accord ill with our conceptions of the economy of nature, should we be troubled, on the one hand, as respects our faith in God's benevolence, or doubt, on the other hand, the manifest teachings of science. In a word, our faith must not be hampered by our scientific doubts, our science must not be hampered by religious scruples.[15]

This passage, which Thompson cites as evidence of why Frost treasured Proctor's book, could have been written in the eighteenth rather than the nineteenth century, as many of its arguments share affinities with Enlightenment rather than Victorian assumptions about God and nature. Like Galileo and Newton, Proctor asserts that behind the changing facades of matter lies an immutable divine force that resists transformation by either perception or material processes. Conceived in this manner, the material world for Proctor is essentially a realm that evades complete scientific understanding. Although random waste appears to us as the essential condition of the universe, such a condition, he asserts, exists only within the larger context of an unknown divine purpose. "We should be content to believe," he writes, "though at present we may be quite unable to prove, *that the waste is apparent only, not real*, and to admit that we see too small a part of the scheme of the Creator to pronounce an opinion on the economy or wisdom of the observed arrangements."[16]

This argument, which by 1900 had become a mainstay for those who still wished to preserve religious faith, gathers its authority by overtly challenging the supremacy of the empirical observer and by placing cognitive limits on perception. The passage also resonates with the distinctions between fact and value that Arnold, in his well-known defense of poetry, "The Study of Poetry," levied against T. H. Huxley just four years after *Our Place among Infinities* appeared in London. There, in an effort to keep humanistic studies at the center of a university curriculum, Arnold attempted to do for poetry what Proctor attempted to do for religion. Employing equivalent strategies, both men defended their most cherished institutions by attacking the very heart of what they perceived to be science's strength. Arguing that the scientific method, with its strict emphasis upon objectivity and precision, prevented the researcher from penetrating larger and more meaningful realms of experience, Proctor and Arnold sanctioned competing disciplines that embraced other forms of inquiry. While in their view science might tell us much about the world's physical fabric, it could neither explain why physical phenomena existed in the first place nor show how we might assimilate new scientific discoveries in our efforts to ennoble the human spirit and discover how life might be made more meaningful. Questions of value were best addressed, in Proctor's view, by religious speculation, and in the absence of religion, in Arnold's view, by the study of poetry.[17]

Although Frost was certainly attracted to this type of argument and sustained throughout his life an Arnoldian belief that the "best description of us is still in the humanities,"[18] as an attentive student of the conflict between science and religion he was also well aware that such arguments, however eloquently expressed, had done little to bolster traditional religious belief or to prevent science from usurping literature's lofty status in the university curriculum. In an intellectual milieu that had evolved to value fact more than emotion, truth more than beauty, and empirical evidence more than blind faith, Arnold's argument that poetry offered "the breath and finer spirit of knowledge"[19] was a weak defense, especially if one believed that religion could no longer be supported, as it once had been, by scientific inquiry. The same charges of irrationality could also be applied by scientists to Proctor's arguments for the existence of God. Indebted to Christian doctrine, Proctor's religious faith was in many ways incompatible with his own assessments of recent astronomical discoveries. As any Victorian scientist or clergyman would have immediately recognized, most of his book was devoted to several new astronomical theories, many of which actually militated against a traditional religious way of life.

In particular, two scientific undercurrents in *Our Place among Infinities* emerged as a source of severe anxiety for Frost. The first was Proctor's discussion of Pierre Laplace's nebular hypothesis, a widely accepted theory that saw the solar system as originating from the cooling and contracting of a large, flattened, slowly rotating cloud of incandescent gas.[20] At the time seemingly corroborated by Sir William Herschel's observations, Laplace's theory brought to a conclusion the demise of medieval Christian cosmology. The once undisputed conception of the universe as a closed, finite, and hierarchically ordered whole had finally yielded to a more comprehensive model that revealed the universe as one of unfathomable dimensions, bound together only by fundamental, mechanistic laws. Proctor's version of this theory, complete with an extensive description of how the earth had accumulated its mass by attracting matter cast off by stellar activity, reinforced rather than repudiated the more disturbing elements of cosmic mechanism. He enumerated the extent to which nineteenth-century cosmology had distanced itself from Newton and Paley's divinely ordained "clockwork universe" and, more significantly, corroborated Darwin's assertion in *The Descent of Man* that arguments for special creation lay outside the provinces of reason:

> Let it suffice that we recognise as one of the earliest stages of our earth's history, her condition as a rotating mass of glowing vapour, capturing then as now, but far more actively then than now, masses of matter which approached near enough [the earth], and growing by these continual indraughts from without. From the very beginning, as it would seem, the earth grew in this way. The firm earth on which we live represents an aggregation of matter not from one portion of space, but from all space. All that is upon and within the earth, all vegetable forms and all animal forms,

our bodies, our brains, are formed of materials which have been drawn in from those depths of space surrounding us on all sides. This hand that I am now raising contains particles . . . drawn in towards the earth by processes continuing millions of millions of ages, until after multitudinous changes the chapter of accidents has so combined them, and so distributed them in plants and animals, that after coming to form portions of my food they are here present before you . . . is not the thought itself striking and suggestive, that not only the earth on which we move, but everything we see or touch, and every particle in body and brain, has sped during countless ages through the immensity of space?[21]

As Frost's poem "The Lesson for Today" (1942) suggests, the nebular hypothesis, although certainly disturbing in its own right, was only one contributing cause of a larger problem that for Frost lay at the heart of modernity itself. Convinced that the universe was "expanse and nothing else,"[22] Frost understood that the dissolution of Scholastic cosmology weakened Christianity's philosophical authority. As scientists from Copernicus to Laplace had extended the dimensions of space to indefinite and even infinite proportions, it had gradually become absurd to suppose that God had created the earth solely for human habitation and benefit. The modern universe was far too extensive to support the Aristotelian beliefs that the earth was the center of the universe and that heavenly bodies were inhabited by independent anima that controlled the direction and duration of celestial orbits. If all of the material components in the universe could be considered as ontologically equivalent, then no longer could theologians rationally envision a Dantean ascent from the dark, imperfect earth toward the illuminating perfection of the heavenly spheres. There appeared to be no definitive hierarchy, and as nineteenth-century scientists learned more and more about the true nature of physical space, it became more and more doubtful that a convincing eschatology, one that left room for divine providence and transcendent sources of value, would ever be recovered. Speaking of the shift from the "Ptolemaic geo-centric universe to the Copernican no-centric universe," Frost wrote; "It has taken me some years of my life to accept our position; but I see no way out of it. There is apparently not a soul but us alive in the whole business of rolling balls, eddying fires, and long distance rays of light. It makes any coziness in our nook here all the more heartwarming."[23]

Frost may also have been deeply troubled by Proctor's discussion of the second law of thermodynamics, the law of entropy—the "universal cataract of death," as Frost describes it in "West-Running Brook"— which demonstrated mathematically that kinetic energy within a closed system eventually dissipates in every conversion process until it finally becomes immeasurable.[24] Originally employed practically as a means for engineers to measure the horsepower and efficiency of coal-fired machines, the second law of thermodynamics, when translated to the solar system, also predicted the inevitable exhaustion of the sun's fuel, the certain cooling of the solar system, and, as a consequence, the eventual death of all organic life on earth. Although it would be nearly four decades until modern physicists, writing in the wake of Georges Lemaître's big bang theory, would postulate the thermodynamic equilibrium of the cosmos, the so-called heat death of the universe, the entropic forecast for the cosmos was just as bleak in the 1880s as it was in the 1930s. In the aftermath of entropy it became clear that despite science's profound ability to predict and sometimes control nature, humans could never completely immunize themselves against cosmic extinction. In his own discussion of entropy Proctor offered little consolation to those who were concerned about such issues. "When we look forward to the future of this earth on which we live," he wrote, "we find, far off it may be, but still discernible, a time when all life will have perished from off the earth's face. Then will she circle around the central sun, even as our moon circles, a dead though massive globe, an orb bearing only the records and the memories of former life, but, to our conceptions, a useless desert scene."[25]

In nearly every regard, then, except for a few tentative declarations of faith, *Our Place among Infinities* is not an optimistic book. Contrary to Thompson's depiction of it as a positive agent of Frost's spiritual and psychological recovery, *Our Place among Infinities* merely articulated Frost's most important philosophical problem: the growing estrangement between the human world, which emphasized moral necessity, and the natural world, which was completely indifferent to moral concerns. If the Victorian version of a godless universe was accurate, then perhaps the most rational moral response available was to "amend" nature, as John Stuart Mill suggested,[26] or, as Huxley asserted even more passionately, to "combat" nature so as to mitigate the traumatic consequences brought about by the death, disease, and predation that cosmic mechanism inevitably guaranteed.[27] The only other available alternative was to adopt the intuitive stance of the mystic, who, calmly accepting death and other cosmic absurdities as the essential conditions of the universe, saw no distinction between the civilized and natural worlds and so bridged the gulf between them.[28] In many respects, it was this latter position that Proctor unsuccessfully tried to adopt for himself. Yet despite his genuine effort to reconcile science and religion, his mystical belief had been so compromised by his scientific knowledge that he merely reaffirmed the problem Tennyson had found so disconcerting in the 1840s. God and nature were at strife, as Tennyson declared in *In Memoriam*, and the physical universe as revealed by science implied that God could not be located in the material components and mechanistic processes of nature.

Of course, had Frost been Whitman, he might have accepted Proctor's diluted romanticism with remarkable aplomb. It was Whitman, after all, who dismissed the calculations of "Learn'd Astronomers" as arrogant and then, without any vacillation, wandered "unaccountable" into the "mystical moist night-air" to "look up in perfect silence at the stars."[29] Frost, however, had none of Whitman's capacity for accepting death and "all the things of the universe" as "perfect miracles,"[30] nor could he consciously ignore the abundant scientific discoveries that had seemingly rendered a religious vision of the universe untenable. As an inheritor of a late Victorian moral sensibility, Frost was much more profoundly aware that the fin-de-siècle cosmos, newly expanded and mechanized by science, was now more than ever capable of reducing human aspirations and achievements to an almost total insignificance.

That the huge gulf between moral desire and natural fact had become for him one of the most conspicuous conflicts in his life is evident in one of his most dispiriting poems, "Desert Places" (1934). One can hardly imagine a starker contrast between Whitman's expansive, life-affirming catalogs and Frost's fear that the universe would eventually consume him:

> Snow falling and night falling fast, oh, fast
> In a field I looked into going past,
> And the ground almost covered smooth in snow,
> But a few weeds and stubble showing last.
>
> The woods around it have it—it is theirs.
> All animals are smothered in their lairs.
> I am too absent-spirited to count;
> The loneliness includes me unawares.
>
> And lonely as it is that loneliness
> Will be more lonely ere it will be less—
> A blanker whiteness of benighted snow
> With no expression, nothing to express.
>
> They cannot scare me with their empty spaces
> Between stars—on stars where no human race is.
> I have it in me so much nearer home
> To scare myself with my own desert places.
>
> (*CPP&P*, 269)

As in the earlier poem "Stars," both winter and the heavens have conspired to assault the poet's sensibility; he cannot "count" either as a significant human being or as a poet, who by "counting" out the metrics of his verse might engage the imagination to amend nature and transform it into a comprehensible, less menacing place. In such a bleak moment of absent-spiritedness, the only recourse left is for Frost to engage his keen sense of detached irony; he can deflect the external threat only by conjuring up an equivalent internal threat that might neutralize the other's impending danger. As a last resort, perhaps taking his cue from Wallace Stevens, Frost summons "the violence from within" to protect himself "from the violence without."[31]

Unfortunately, however, this strategy also fails, for contrary to the apparent bravado in "They cannot scare me with their empty spaces/ Between stars," the falling rhythms and faltering extra syllables of the last stanza betray the poet's posturing as his confidence gives way to a more comprehensive fear. Here, fear is not merely a projection of an overactive imagination but a highly rational response by one who has full knowledge of a world informed by science. The terrestrial and extraterrestrial environments are so threatening that the poet can no longer mentally forge adequate protective structures against them. Paralyzed by the desert places surrounding it, the mind, too, has become a desert place—notice the echo of Proctor's description of cosmic decay as "a useless desert scene"—where hope and redemption remain impossible and the threat of annihilation seems imminent.

The idea that the external universe might transform the mind from a sanctuary into a source of terror is further underscored by Frost's conscious revision of the famous quotation from Blaise Pascal's *Pensées*, "Le silence eternal de ces espaces infinis m'effraie" (The eternal silence of these infinite spaces frightens me), where Pascal describes how terror, rather than destroying his belief in God, actually leads him to ecstatic moments of religious faith.[32] As evidence of faith's rationality, Pascal offered his famous wager: If we believe in God and God does not exist, then we have lost nothing. Conversely, if we do not believe in God and God does exist, then we have committed ourselves needlessly to a lifetime of suffering. Because this argument shares strong affinities with James's belief that religious faith has a beneficial psychological component, one might assume that Frost would have welcomed Pascal's argument as an attractive complement to James. As the tone of resignation in "Desert Places" ultimately suggests, however, Pascal's wager was untenable for Frost. His fear of a barren cosmos is here so pronounced that it has crippled his ability to imagine a more secure future. Instead of leading him to religious insight, the "empty spaces between stars" lead him only to the stark realization that he is unable to reconcile the natural world's destructive processes with his own desire to preserve his ego.

While "Desert Places" suggests that hostile landscapes can transform the mind from a source of redemption into a source of terror, it would be unwise to take "Desert Places" or "Stars" as Frost's final word on the perils of astronomical phenomena. As always in Frost's poetry, discernible thematic countermovements often neutralize ideas that at first glance appear absolute. This deconstructionist propensity, which Richard Poirier has astutely identified as the "central achievement of Frost's poetry from the first volume onward,"[33] evinces itself in other poems that mediate seasonal or astronomical threats. In well-known poems such as "The Onset," "Tree at My Window," and "Take Something Like a Star," Frost stresses the idea that even though we are irreparably separated from nature by our own consciousness, it is paradoxically that same consciousness that allows us to navigate the gulf between "inner" and "outer" weather so we can "amend" nature and make it more compatible with our own needs. If nature is a destructive force that can annihilate the ego, it is also, to Frost's way of thinking, a restorative force that has paradoxically equipped us with a mind capable of creating ample protective structures. The imagination—whose volitional processes condition the mind to select the objects it wishes to perceive, to discriminate among them, to judge them good or bad, to change them for the better, or to make among them sound, responsible choices—enables us to imagine a better and more congenial future. The act of writing is thus for Frost not only the first step toward coming to terms with a hostile cosmos but also the first step toward erecting the saving structures of community, marriage, and religious faith.

In a 1961 interview with the novelist Mark Harris, Frost expounded his voluntarist tendencies, many of which had influenced his thinking since his first encounter with William James:

> The most creative thing in us is to believe a thing in, in love, in all else. You believe yourself into existence. You believe your marriage into existence, you believe in each other, you believe that it's worthwhile going on, or you'd commit suicide wouldn't you? . . . And the ultimate one is the belief in the future of the world. I believe the future *in*. It's coming in by my believing it. You might as well call that a belief in God. This word God is not an often-used word with me, but once in a while it arrives there.[34]

The will to believe, the capacity to transform imaginatively the disturbing elements of one's life, including threats fostered by the natural world, became for Frost such a useful redemptive method that he argued for its validity for the rest of his life.

While Frost's uncompromising belief in free will and an autonomous ego contradicts postmodern arguments that the author is nothing more than an articulator among the various discourses by which he or she is written,[35] it is necessary to remember that Frost's desire to defend free will stems partly from his profound need to rescue himself from the processes of mechanistic determinism. If human consciousness is a mediating process of continual invention, Frost reasons, then psychic activity cannot logically be bound by the same determinate laws that govern matter. Because psychic activity helps us to create rather than discover the laws of the physical world, mental processes partially elevate themselves beyond the reach of the mechanical law. Our capacity for make-believe and a deep awareness of our constantly changing subjectivity liberate us from determinism and help us create the moral foundations of our own humanity.

There is nothing terribly original in Frost's romantic faith in the autonomous ego; surely emphasis upon the poet as a maker and shaper of reality can be traced from Santayana, James, and Nietzsche all the way back to Coleridge and Wordsworth and, finally, Kant. What makes Frost's insistence on free will so surprising is that he was one of the few modernists in America to defend both free will and individual genius against the panoply of psychological, sociological, scientific, and linguistic systems that would explain them away. As Frost well knew, the laws of thermodynamics and evolution implied that people were not active agents in the world but were shaped by natural contingencies that brought them under the control of the external environment. In such a deterministic system, where physical law exerted its machine-like regularity upon people exactly as it did upon planets, combating nature's most destructive forces by imaginative processes remained impossible. Nature would run her course despite any human intervention designed to change its direction. As the scientific historian Carl Snyder wrote in 1904, "So far as the outer world is intelligible to us, the immediate portion in which we live our lives is simply a machine, so orderly and compact, so simple in its construction, that we may reckon its past and gauge something of its future with almost as much certitude as that of a dynamo or a waterwheel. In its motions there is no uncertainty. . . . This is the first fact which modern science has to offer the philosophic mind."[36]

As Thompson and Poirier have argued, it was this kind of scientific thinking that Frost found so repugnant because it failed to acknowledge the prominent role that free will and imagination played in the construction of knowledge. What Frost desired most from his immersion in science was not so much a refined knowledge of his exact relationship to the physical world but rather a version of the discipline that would be more amenable to the free play of the imagination. If it could be demonstrated, for example, that the human mind, as both Wordsworth and Coleridge argued, partially constructed rather than discovered its own universe, then a universe of constantly changing particulars might be shaped and reshaped into a realm more thoroughly compatible with one's desires for permanence and value.

To anyone familiar with the history of thought in the early twentieth century, the version of science that Frost had been looking for since his Harvard days was already well under way, even as Snyder was busy singing the praises of scientific certitude. As the nineteenth century came to a close, a revolution in physics was beginning to undermine not only the assumptions of classical physics, whose Newtonian principles had laid much of the essential groundwork for the widespread belief in cosmic mechanism, but also the two most sacred principles of the scientific method: causality and objectivity. In a span of forty years, three successive events—the refutation of a luminiferous ether as a medium for the transmission of light, the theory of special relativity, and the quantum theory of energy—corrected nearly all the core conceptions of Newtonian mechanics. Although concepts such as absolute space, time, mass, and motion could not be construed by the emerging paradigms as wrong per se, the new physics clearly demonstrated that traditional Newtonian concepts were valid only within a limited domain of experiential phenomena.[37] These unimaginable and strangely original accounts of nature also seemed to reveal the universe as one of emergent novelty and unpredictability, thus reducing the once dominant idea of cosmic mechanism to a historical oddity.

Taken together, these three events revolutionized physics. Modern scientists suddenly found themselves in a natural realm much more complex than the one the Victorians had envisioned, and as the billiard-ball model of the universe yielded to one that viewed uncertainty as an incontrovertible fact, the limitations of perception became more and more apparent, especially to the scientists themselves. Perhaps even more telling of a shift in thought was the restoration of chance and freedom to philosophical inquiry. If the universe did not depend upon a perfect determinism for its processes, then free will and chance, both of which had been accepted as conditions of the universe until Darwin, might be reconsidered in light of the new physical discoveries.

It was therefore not long before the popular press began to discuss the impact of the new physics, often distorting basic science in order to validate particular ideological, theological, or aesthetic viewpoints. Relativity and quantum mechanics, for example, were enlisted in various circles to sanction the idea that all truth was relative, that empirical observation was completely subjective; that poetry, if it was to reflect reality accurately, had to be a poetry of motion and process; and, finally, that a spontaneous free will, one that mirrored the physical world's quantum leaps, was a genuine component of humanity. Einstein himself became a celebrity almost overnight, and although only very few people actually understood relativity, a popular magazine such as the *Nation*, which once had declared relativity a theory that "psychologists, priests, and poets had known all along," could claim with impunity that the "difficulty of the subject" was greatly exaggerated and that anyone who did not "understand it [relativity] at a glance" was nothing but a "dunce and a simpleton."[38]

In addition to magazines, the most widely read newspapers also devoted ample space to Einstein, relativity, and quantum mechanics. In 1919, after Arthur Eddington proved that light could be deflected by a gravitational field, the *New York Times* ran sixteen articles and editorials in November alone, one of which declared that "light was all askew in the heavens."[39] With these and other popular accounts distorting the new physics so severely, most people failed to recognize the huge contrast between Einstein's relativity theory, which attempted to establish a new framework of absolute relations rather than relative ones, and quantum mechanics, which suggested that complete scientific certainty was untenable. Nevertheless, despite these and other misconceptions, most educated people thought that the new century's revolutionary physical paradigms had somehow reunited science, art, and philosophy after years of separation and specialization. The new physics, rather than solving the persistent physical problems of the nineteenth century, had merely created several new ones that required an entirely new set of scientific and philosophical lenses. A Pandora's box had been opened, and no one, not even Einstein, seemed able to close the lid.

One scientific popularizer who did understand relativity as well as Einstein was Arthur Eddington, a professor of astronomy at Cambridge and perhaps, with the exception of Niels Bohr, the single most important scientific influence upon Frost's later career. In a groundbreaking essay dealing with Frost's indebtedness to Eddington, Heisenberg, and Bohr, Guy Rotella argues that the source for much of Frost's astronomical knowledge was Eddington's *Nature of the Physical World* (1928), a widely popular account of the new physics that explored the impact of the new science upon social values and particularly upon religion.[40] According to Rotella, Frost was attracted to this book primarily because Eddington recognized the limitations of scientific inquiry and wrote about physics in a witty style that often employed allusions to classical poetry. A severe rationalist as well as a devout Quaker, Eddington doubted the authority of mechanistic laws and often claimed in his books that science offered an incomplete picture of reality because its conclusions were cognitive creations based upon epistemological principles, not empirical data. "All the laws of nature that are classified as fundamental," he claimed, "can be seen wholly from epistemological considerations. They correspond to *a priori* knowledge, and are therefore wholly subjective."[41] In a famous quotation, Eddington, echoing Kant's idea that we can never know the noumenal world, boldly challenged Einstein's widely shared belief that physical theories were merely economical descriptions of observed natural phenomena. Suggesting instead that theories were free creations of the human mind that were imposed upon the world in a "complex of metrical symbols," Eddington suggested that humans had found "a strange footprint on the shores of the unknown" and had "devised profound theories, one after the other, to account for its origin. At last, we have succeeded in reconstructing the creation that made the footprint. And Lo! It is our own."[42]

Taken a step farther, Eddington's idea that scientific conclusions were constructed rather than discovered meant that given the flexibility and ingenuity of the human imagination, theoretical permanence of any type was highly unlikely. Anticipating our contemporary predilection for scientific skepticism, Eddington recognized that the historical context of an era could direct the course of future scientific activity and thus exclude from the realm of possibility all ideas that had not already been partially forged in the furnaces of scientific tradition. Indeed, thirty years before Thomas Kuhn popularized the concept of the scientific "paradigm," Eddington asserted that revolution was an integral component of science and speculated that the theoretical knowledge he possessed might one day become as obsolete as Newton's theories:

> It is not so much the particular form that scientific theories have now taken—the conclusions we believe we have proved—as the movement of thought behind them that concerns the philosopher. Our eyes once opened, we may pass on to yet a new outlook on the world, but we can never go back to the old outlook.
>
> If the scheme of philosophy which we now rear on the advances of Einstein, Bohr, Rutherford and others is doomed to fall in the next thirty years, it is not to be laid to their charge that we have gone astray. Like the systems of Euclid, of Ptolemy, of Newton, which have served their turn, so the systems of Einstein and Heisenberg may give way to some fuller realization of the world. But in each revolution of scientific thought new words are set to the old music, and that which has gone before is not destroyed but refocused.[43]

One of the consequences of limiting science to a small domain of experience was that Eddington, like James and Bergson, could then postulate the existence of an unseen spiritual world that lay beyond the realm of observed physical reality. According to Eddington, if we were to know the spiritual world, we had first to attend to the "symbols of our personality" rather than to the "symbols of the mathematician" and thus develop an intuitive relationship with the spiritual world that would "not submit to codification and analysis."[44] Similar to Bergson's advice on how to recover real duration, Eddington delineated distinct boundaries for all forms of symbolic knowledge. In order to gain access to the spiritual world, we had to admit that feeling, emotion, intuition, and memory contributed to the totality of each moment of lived experience: "We recognize a spiritual world alongside the physical world," he wrote. "Experience—that is to say, the self *cum* environment—comprises more than can be embraced in the physical world, restricted as it is to a complex of metrical symbols."[45] Attention to the nonquantifiable aspects of reality reinforced the very qualities of life that made man most human. "We all know," he wrote, "that there are regions of the human spirit untrammeled by the world of physics. In the mystic sense of the creation around us, in the expression of art, in a yearning towards God, the soul grows upward and finds the fulfillment of something implanted in its nature."[46]

In addition to finding in Eddington credible arguments to support the possibility of a divine reality, Frost was also drawn to Eddington's belief that determinism could not hold true at the quantum level. As Rotella has pointed out, clear evidence that Frost was fascinated by the possibility of a flexible, indeterminate universe can be found in "Education by Poetry," an ars poetica that Frost delivered to the Amherst College Alumni Council on 15 November 1930.[47] There, in a talk that lauded metaphor as the cognitive foundation for all knowledge, Frost enlisted several physical theories to demonstrate how science, like poetry, depended upon figurative juxtapositions to explain the inexplicable complexities of natural phenomena.

In particular, references to two major developments in particle physics served his arguments well. The first was a discussion of quantum probability. Comparing quantum leaps to actuarial science, Frost rationalized that quantum events were random occurrences and could not be predicted: "You know that you can't tell by name what persons in a certain class will be dead ten years after graduation, but you can tell actuarially how many will be dead. Now, just so this scientist says of the particles of matter flying at a screen, striking a screen; you can't tell what individual particles will come, but you can say in general that a certain number will strike in a given time. It shows, you see, that the individual particle can come freely."[48]

Why Frost concentrated his attention on the "freedom" of the "individual particle" Rotella never suggests. A closer look at *The Nature of the Physical World*, however, reveals at least one plausible explanation. In the penultimate chapter, a polemical essay entitled "Causation," Eddington tackled the problem of free will and predestination. Arguing that "physics is no longer pledged to a scheme of deterministic laws," Eddington appropriated Heisenberg's famous indeterminacy principle to show why quantum action necessitated a revision of materialist explanations for human behavior. Although Eddington was often reluctant to enlist science as proof for religious arguments, he nevertheless postulated in this chapter that human volition and free will were the natural outcomes of physical processes. The "emancipation" of the mind, however, also required a concomitant emancipation of material, which for Eddington was not an obstacle:

> The materialist view was that the motions which appear to be caused by our volition are really reflex actions controlled by the material processes in the brain, the act of will being an inessential side phenomenon occurring simultaneously with the physical phenomena. But this assumes that the result of applying physical laws to the brain is fully determinate. It is meaningless to say that the behaviour of a conscious brain is precisely the same as that of a mechanical brain if the behaviour of a mechanical brain is left undetermined. If the laws of physics are not strictly causal the most that can be said is that the behavior of the conscious brain is one of the possible behaviours of a mechanical brain. Precisely so; and the decision between the possible behaviours is what we call volition.[49]

If Frost actually read this passage, he may have noticed in Eddington a familiar reluctance to formulate reality into either a purely deterministic or a purely random cosmos. Like Frost, Eddington desired a universe that admitted to the simultaneous existence of predetermined causation and random chance. The universe could not be too rigid, or else emergent novelty in both natural forms and ideas would be absurd. Conversely, however, the universe must have had some causal antecedents that could give rise to a material reality, including the human brain. For both men, then, humans' most propitious engagement with the physical world occurred in the dynamic interplay between matter and spirit, form and flux, necessity and chance. The "freedom to work in one's material," as Frost often described his poetic process, was naturally offset by the retarding forces of the material itself, and no matter how much the physical world might limit volitional choice, it was paradoxically that material confinement that awakened the opportunity for metaphorical activity. Freedom could be measured only by the magnitude of its constraints; tennis could only be properly played, as Frost liked to assert in his famous statement on free verse, with a net.

In addition to using quantum mechanics to demonstrate his ideas about metaphor and science, Frost also enlisted Heisenberg's uncertainty principle to explain some of his ideas about poetry. Although Heisenberg had formulated the uncertainty principle only three years prior to the composition of "Education by Poetry," Frost understood the principle well enough to use it as an example of another "charming mixed metaphor right in the realm of higher mathematics and higher physics." Comparing the uncertainty principle to Zeno's problem of the arrow, Frost described one of the problems long associated with consciousness. As Frost well knew, the arrow's flight, in Zeno's frame of reference, was a series of positions without any corresponding motion. For Heraclitus, however, the arrow itself was pure motion, and its discrete positions, merely a fixed series of illusions. For Frost, the paradox was easily resolved by limiting the domain of velocity to time and the domain of position to space. Referring directly to Heisenberg, Frost explained the problem by suggesting that measurements were constrained by an experimental context in which time and physical space were incompatible frameworks:

> The other day we had a visitor here, a noted scientist, whose latest word to the world has been that the more accurately you know where a thing is, the less accurately you are able to state how fast it is moving. You can see why that would be so, without going back to Zeno's problem of the arrow's flight. In carrying numbers into the realm of space and at the same time into the realm of time you are mixing metaphors, that is all, and you are in trouble. They won't mix. The two don't go together.[50]

To Frost, who had spent most of his life searching for rational ways to resist scientific naturalism, the idea that Eddington and Heisenberg might limit the scope and domain of science was indeed a happy discovery. For the first time in Frost's life, scientists, not theologians, provided him with solutions to the problems of faith and volition that he had been struggling with since first encountering Darwin, nearly forty years earlier. Here were men who were willing to challenge the foundations of nineteenth-century science and offer the world a completely modern version that demanded new theoretical lenses. In Eddington he found rational arguments for belief in both God and free will. In Heisenberg he found evidence that human perception ultimately encountered physical limits that could not be crossed. And in both he recognized an unqualified acceptance of uncertainty as a paradoxical feature of existence.

To be sure, Eddington and Heisenberg were not the only scientists to reassert belief in God as a valid response to the problems of existence. In contrast to the biologists, who were then formulating the neo-Darwinian synthesis, physicists such as Max Planck, Alfred North Whitehead, Louis De Broglie, Erwin Schroedinger, James Jeans, and Wolfgang Pauli—among the most gifted scientists of the day—were in various ways contemplating the existence of God, whom they often described as a "perfect" rationality. Planck, for example, emphasized faith and intuition as integral components of scientific inquiry.[51] Heisenberg, who was heavily influenced by Pauli, advocated a Neoplatonic theory of forms and suggested that "just as in Plato, it therefore looks as if the seemingly so complicated world of elementary particles and force fields were based upon a simple and perspicuous mathematical structure."[52] Perhaps echoing the sentiments of all of these figures, James Jeans summarized the significance of the movement as follows:

> The most outstanding achievement of twentieth-century physics is not the theory of relativity with its wedding of space and time, or the theory of quanta with its apparent negation of the laws of causation, or the dissection of the atom with the resultant discovery that things are not what they seem; it is the general recognition that we are not yet in contact with an ultimate reality. To speak in Plato's well-known simile, we are still imprisoned in our cave, with our backs to the light, and can only watch the shadows on the wall.[53]

The view that shadows did exist in the realm of higher physics was also prominent in the thought of Niels Bohr, whom Frost met and dined with at Amherst College in 1923. As Thompson describes their encounter, Frost asked Bohr several questions about the structure of the atom, most of which, Thompson claims, were "far more penetrating than those questions asked by professional scientists in the dinner group."[54] What the two talked about is open to speculation, but strong circumstantial evidence suggests that they talked about recent developments in physics and how those developments reinforced the idea of free will. Given that Bohr himself had read extensively from William James, Frost may even have prodded the physicist on several Jamesian issues. In "Education by Poetry" Frost mentions Bohr in relation to the freedom of the individual particle: "I asked Bohr that particularly, and he said, 'Yes, it is so. It can come when it will and as it wills; and the action of the individual particle is unpredictable. But it is not so of the action of the mass. There you can predict.' He says, 'That gives the individual atom its freedom, but the mass its necessity.'"[55]

Just how much of this statement can be attributed to Bohr and how much to Frost is guesswork. Rotella has correctly noticed, however, that Frost alludes in this passage to Bohr's correspondence principle, an epistemological model that Bohr developed from his recognition that macroscopic classical laws broke down when they were applied to microscopic quantum numbers.[56] In the absence of a theory to unify microscopic and macroscopic phenomena, Bohr conceded that one had to accept the efficacy of both scientific frameworks. One system did not have to replace the other or assume a dominant epistemological position; both, in fact, were necessary and *complementary* descriptions of an elusive totality that could not be fully explained by the same measuring tools.[57]

We have no way of knowing whether Frost fully understood the significance of Bohr's correspondence principle. What is important here is that Frost saw in Bohr, as he did in so many other well-known physicists of the time, an epistemological skepticism incommensurable with the professed certitudes of nineteenth-century science. Scientific concepts, he learned, were not literal transcripts of reality but rather mental constructions—mathematical symbols, as Eddington called them— imposed upon matter to serve as useful guides through chaotic sensory experience. Even if supported by reasonable observation, scientific models were still only forms of thought, metaphors, as Frost so often called them, that mediated between conceptual abstraction and concrete experience. Although each of these scientists would readily admit that scientific law provided humans with the most practical means for orienting themselves to the natural world, the epistemological integrity of those laws was still a matter open for debate. Bohr himself suggested that causality might be considered just another "mode of perception by which we reduce our sense impressions to order."[58]

Frost expressed the idea a little differently. Appraising Amy Lowell's poetry just after her death, he formulated some of his most profound statements concerning scientific knowledge: "The most exciting thing in nature is not progress, advance, but expansion and contraction, the opening and shutting of the eye, the hand, the heart, the mind. We throw our arms wide with a gesture of religion to the universe; we close them around a person. We explore and adventure for a while and then we draw in to consolidate our gains. The breathless swing is between subject matter and form."[59] Composed in 1925, this brief passage amalgamates the several instrumentalist accounts of knowledge that Frost learned from James and Bergson and later found verified in theoretical physics. Here one can immediately recognize the familiar nonteleological account of creative evolution, the Promethean desire to impel spirit deeply into matter, the futility of religious certitudes, and, finally, the hard-won belief that constructed forms can provide us with the only meaning possible in a world irreducible to rational formulation. The "breathless swing between subject matter and form" is, as always for Frost, indicative of our daring struggle to fend off death and limit nature's threat. In spite of these redeeming qualities, however, Frost acknowledges that forms, no matter how useful or beautiful, are temporal illusions, "strange apparitions of mind," as he describes them in "All Revelation," that can never assure us of their truthfulness (notice the allusion to King Hamlet's ghost) or guarantee the fulfillment of our deepest desires about how the world should be. The best they can do is provide us with brief revelations of insight, or as Frost stated more simply in "The Figure a Poem Makes," "momentary stays against confusion."[60]

The idea that poetry and science can never penetrate the surface forms of everyday experience to uncover a deeper, more meaningful realm of existence is a feature of nearly all of Frost's books from the mid-twenties until his death in 1963. That this theme did not emerge until after his encounter with Bohr, Eddington, and modern physics becomes clear when one compares Frost's account of science in "Birches" (1915) with the pervasive scientific skepticism that informs later poems such as "The Bear," "Skeptic," "All Revelation," and "Any Size We Please." The most striking difference between the earlier poem and the later group is that in the former Frost nostalgically yearns for a pristine, divinely inhabited world not yet violated by the encroachment of scientific knowledge, while in the latter, seeing no threat from science, Frost enlists its help to demonstrate an epistemological equivalence between science and poetry.

As most commentators have noticed, the controlling metaphor of "Birches" centers on the malleability and resistance of nature as it comes under the influence of the manipulating processes of human will.[61] The opening lines yoke the poem's central conflict, namely, the speaker's struggle between accepting a naturalized world immune to the human forces exerted upon it and his desire to subdue that world by imaginative reverie. The alternating pattern of natural and imaginative processes attests to the speaker's desire for balance between the two forces so that one will not dominate the other:

> When I see birches bend to left and right
> Across the lines of straighter darker trees,
> I like to think some boy's been swinging them.
> But swinging doesn't bend them down to stay
> As ice storms do.
>
> (*CPP&P*, 117-18)

As Frank Lentricchia has noticed, the speaker knows that his imagined explanation for the birches' bend cannot compete with the more believable empirical explanation. The final shape of mature birch trees cannot be attributed to human causes but rather must be attributed to natural causes such as ice storms, which subdue nature more permanently than human figuration.

The speaker's awareness that his fictional world is ephemeral, a condition that Lentricchia has labeled Frost's "ironic consciousness,"[62] becomes even more evident as the poet extends his description of material causes, in effect pleading with his readers to verify what he already knows to be true. Ultimately his scientific explanation of the

birches' bend expands into a description of a modern, scientific world
that has shattered religious sentiment:

> Often you must have seen them
> Loaded with ice a sunny winter morning
> After a rain. They click upon themselves
> As the breeze rises, and turn many-colored
> As the stir cracks and crazes their enamel.
> Soon the sun's warmth makes them shed crystal shells
> Shattering and avalanching on the snow crust—
> Such heaps of broken glass to sweep away
> You'd think the inner dome of heaven had fallen.
>
> (*CPP&P*, 117)

The spondaic rhythms in line ten unmistakably call attention to the
double entendre of the sun as the source of both artistic inspiration and
religious decay. Initially comparing the ice-coated trees to pottery,
Frost also simultaneously employs images of sun and light to remind
us of the consequences of material causation. One cannot help recalling here Keats's despair over Newton's prismatic diffraction of light—
an experiment that, for Keats, destroyed the rainbow's beauty forever—or Copernicus's heliocentric model of the cosmos, at one time a
heretical idea that discredited medieval cosmology. In a scientifically
informed culture where transcendent sources of hope have been discredited, the poet must rely upon his metaphorical resources to transform the harsh objective world into an imagined reality bathed in the
life-enhancing qualities he desires:

> You may see their trunks arching in the woods
> Years afterwards, trailing their leaves on the ground
> Like girls on hands and knees that throw their hair
> Before them over their heads to dry in the sun.
>
> (*CPP&P*, 117)

Although nature in this section stands briefly humanized by the manipulating powers of mind and will, the speaker is all too aware that his metaphorical re-creation of the world is merely a fleeting fictional gesture. As in traditional pastoral, where political strife and civic duty eventually invade the *locus amoenus* and destroy it, in this modern pastoral, science, with all of her "matter of fact about the ice storm," interrupts his reverie and demands capitulation to an empirical explanation. The speaker seems to resent science's intrusion, however, and once again he embarks upon another reverie, this one even more fantastical and teeming with images of a single, human will braving alien entanglements:

> I should prefer to have some boy bend them
> As he went out and in to fetch the cows—
> Some boy too far from town to learn baseball,
> Whose only play was what he found himself,
> Summer or winter, and could play alone.
> One by one he subdued his father's trees
> By riding them down over and over again
> Until he took the stiffness out of them,
> And not one but hung limp, not one was left
> For him to conquer.
>
> (*CPP&P*, 118)

Frost's attempted return to a Wordsworthian childhood, an imagined world in which the childlike vision of nature's munificence has not yet been corrupted by knowledge or doubt, obviously cannot provide him with any lasting psychological relief. Instead, far from revealing a benevolent cosmic order "recollected in tranquillity," the isolated boy who finds happiness in an activity of his own making becomes a metaphor for our necessity to subdue by any means possible an inimical natural world whose romantic possibilities have been eradicated by science. The necessity of this reparation can arise only from a poet who is entirely self-conscious about how ineffective his fictional reveries are in the face of scientific truth. While imaginative forms allow him for a brief moment to elevate his mental processes beyond the reach of cosmic mechanism, he knows that even as he imposes his fictions upon reality, nature's hard facts undermine his constructs, thus making an equivalent redeeming countervision nearly impossible.

Frost's rarely discussed later poem "Any Size We Please" (1949) serves as a strong rebuttal to the scientific positivism of "Birches." A sonnet divided into two equal parts by the period in the syllabic middle of line seven, the poem formally mirrors the radical shift in cosmology that occurred during Frost's own lifetime. The first half is clearly influenced by Euclid's parallel postulate, an idea that led not only to an unquestioned acceptance of infinite space and absolute time but also to Newton's belief in the intricate order of God's clockwork universe. Here the narrator, feeling insignificant as part of the natural order (the "he" and the "I" are the same person), holds his arms out parallel in "infinite appeal" to a universe that refuses to respond to his entreaties:

> No one was looking at his lonely case,
> So like a half-mad outpost sentinel,
> Indulging an absurd dramatic spell,
> Albeit not without some shame of face,
> He stretched his arms out to the dark of space
> And held them absolutely parallel
> In infinite appeal.
>
> (*CPP&P*, 359)

The consolations to be gathered from this appeal are minimal, even as the speaker seems perplexed by an exaggerated posture that he can assume only in private. In the second half of the poem, the narrator, finding this lack of celestial response a portentous "hell," immediately draws his arms around him in an effort to contain the immense size of the universe and transform it into a more manageable size:

Then saying, 'Hell'
He drew them in for warmth of self-embrace.
He thought if he could have his space all curved
Wrapped in around itself and self-befriended,
His science needn't get him so unnerved.
He had been too all out, too much extended.
He slapped his breast to verify his purse
And hugged himself for all his universe.

(*CPP&P*, 359-60)

This exploratory gesture "between subject matter and form" might have been unremarkable had Frost not grounded the sonnet's final seven lines in Einstein's curved space-time dimension, a theory based upon Riemannian geometrical models, which set limits on the boundaries of physical space. Frost's shift from one paradigm to another also suggests knowledge of Gödel's theorem, which states that while a geometrical proof validates an initial set of postulates, the postulates themselves cannot be proven within the mathematical system itself.[63] Geometrical proof in no way guarantees the truth of any set of axioms. Scientific paradigms are so prone to revision and collapse that the best we can do is explore and adventure for a while, draw in to consolidate our gains, and accept the idea that uncertainty need not paralyze our quest for meaning and purpose in the world, however unstable our answers might ultimately be.

The pervasive scientific skepticism that informs "Any Size We Please" is also a prominent feature of "The Bear," a poem that reveals how knowledge mediates among several extremes, none of which can be regarded as truer than any other. On the surface, the poem addresses a conflict between our desire to return to an unbridled primordial state and our equally strong desire to erect artificial barriers or landmarks that can guide us through the wilderness. Upon closer inspection, however, "The Bear" demonstrates how intellect, rather than liberating us from nature, merely defines the boundaries of our perception. From the outset, the poem laments the fact that human beings possess an innate curiosity and simultaneously celebrates the unbridled instinct that drives the bear's forays through the wilderness:

> The bear puts both arms around the tree above her
> And draws it down as if it were a lover
> And its choke cherries lips to kiss good-by,
> Then lets it snap back upright in the sky.
> Her next step rocks a boulder on a wall
> (She's making her cross-country in the fall).
> Her great weight creaks the barbed-wire in its staple
> As she flings over and off down through the maples,
> Leaving on one wire tooth a lock of hair.
>
> (*CPP&P*, 247)

In contrast to "Birches," "The Bear" focuses upon a creature that, endowed by nature to master its environment, subdues natural and artificial barriers by brute physical force. Relatively invulnerable to any structures standing in its way (hence leaving nothing but a lock of hair), the bear appeals to the speaker's desire to abandon the corrupting influences of an intellect that has imposed upon nature too many patterns, mores, and traditions. Despite the speaker's knowledge that the bear's own natural urges negate autonomous choice, he, like the bear, seeks a more direct, instinctive relationship to the natural world than he has yet encountered through scientific or philosophical inquiry. Emphasizing the inability of either discipline to provide any secure forms of knowledge, Frost chronicles the futility of our intellectual efforts to comprehend a natural world:

> Man acts more like the poor bear in a cage
> That all day fights a nervous inward rage,
> His mood rejecting all his mind suggests.
> He paces back and forth and never rests

The toe-nail click and shuffle of his feet,
The telescope at one end of his beat,
And at the other end the microscope,
Two instruments of nearly equal hope,
And in conjunction giving quite a spread.
Or if he rests from scientific tread,
'Tis only to sit back and sway his head
Through ninety odd degrees of arc, it seems,
Between two metaphysical extremes.
He sits back on his fundamental butt
With lifted snout and eyes (if any) shut,
(He looks almost religious but he's not),
And back and forth he sways from cheek to cheek,
At one extreme agreeing with one Greek,
At the other agreeing with another Greek
Which may be thought, but only so to speak.
A baggy figure, equally pathetic
When sedentary and when peripatetic.

(*CPP&P*, 247)

Pacing back and forth like a caged, raging animal, Frost's frustrated man demonstrates that truth does not reside in the literal correspondence between concepts and reality but rather in the movement between two metaphysical extremes. Platonic idealism (our "sedentary" truths) and Aristotelian processes (our "peripatetic" truths) inform our knowledge in any given historical moment and condition our interpretation of life and nature. Failing to find the correct interpretation of life through the use of one philosophical framework, we become aware of our diminutive place in space and are forced by our desire for certainty to shift our gaze to the other. Intellectual history, the poem implies, is merely a process of shifting emphasis, in which we turn from idealism to naturalism, or vice versa. In the absence of any permanent or satisfying correspondence between nature and knowledge, the best Frost's modern bear can do is "reject all his mind suggests" and begin searching anew for more comprehensive truths, which unfortunately will forever elude him.

The antipositivist account of science that informs "The Bear" invites comparison with one of Frost's most complete rejections of astronomical certainty, the perplexing poem "Skeptic" (1949). Perhaps more fully influenced by modern physics than any of his earlier astronomical poems, "Skeptic" not only doubts the hard facts of science but also offers an alternative method for comprehending the world more clearly. To understand the full significance of these esoteric stanzas, it is first necessary to understand the scientific theories that inform this poem.

Early-twentieth-century astronomers had no clear evidence that observed astronomical objects lay outside our own Milky Way galaxy. In 1912, however, the work of V. M. Slipher proved that objects resided not only outside our galaxy but a great distance from it.[64] Basing his measurements of stellar distance upon what later came to be known as the "red shift," Slipher observed that light emitted from distant stars and galaxies always shifted toward the red spectrum. In 1929 Edwin Hubble, using Slipher's theories, concluded that the red shift was proportional to a stellar object's distance from our galaxy and that the greater the distance between any two galaxies, the greater the speed at which they were separating.[65] This important observation, later termed Hubble's law, was seen by many as a confirmation of Georges Lemaître's controversial big bang theory (1927), which saw the universe as originating from a singular cosmic explosion. Although Lemaître and his theory were ridiculed by many scientists, Hubble's law implied not only that the universe seemed to be expanding uniformly toward higher states of entropy but that cosmic expansion must eventually end in thermodynamic equilibrium, the so-called heat death of the universe. Confronting these disturbing theories, Frost's speaker attempts to reconcile diminutive human experience with the vast dimensions of an indifferent cosmos:

Far star that tickles for me my sensitive plate
And fries a couple of ebon atoms white,
I don't believe I believe a thing you state.
I put no faith in the seeming facts of light.

I don't believe I believe you're the last in space,
I don't believe you're anywhere near the last,
I don't believe what makes you red in the face
Is after explosion going away so fast.

                                            (*CPP&P*, 353)

As in "Any Size We Please," Frost's speaker once again tries to contain the immense size of the universe by challenging the epistemological status of the poem's informing concepts. The idiomatic expression "I don't believe I believe" reflects the poet's teetering vacillation between belief and doubt, as well as his inability to discern whether the "seeming facts of light" can be attributed to either particles or waves. The dual nature of light, coupled with his own recognition that the light he sees is already far older than the light currently emitted by the star, casts doubt upon the veracity of his observations and thus prevents him from accepting any theory that claims the universe will die a "heat death."

The pervasive doubt that informs our understanding of light spills over into the second stanza, where the poet vacillates even further. While he seems able to accept the idea that the far star is not the "last" alternative galaxy in the universe, he appears reluctant to accept that the universe is continually expanding in the "after explosion" of the big bang. Calling all prior evidence into question, the speaker abandons his search for definitive answers and once again draws in to consolidate his gains:

> The universe may or may not be very immense.
> As a matter of fact there are times when I am apt
> To feel it close in tight against my sense
> Like a caul in which I was born and still am wrapped.
>
> (*CPP&P*, 353)

Evocative and completely appropriate for his need to contain space, Frost's comparison of the universe to the womb's protective membrane once again satisfies his need to transform a threatening environment with metaphorical activity. Unlike "Birches," however, where Frost's imaginative transformations are rudely interrupted by scientific knowledge, "Skeptic" maintains an easy stasis between fact and fiction, or more accurately, between one fiction disguised as science and another fiction disguised as poetry. In either case, what Frost describes here is a means by which he can satisfy his thirst for real knowledge. By calling into doubt the truth claims of all scientific theories and metaphorically transforming them into protective enclosures, Frost reveals that the only way for us to understand the universe is to measure it by its responsiveness to human need. Although scientific evidence may or may not inform us that both organic life and the universe are expanding toward an entropic death, imaginative reverie and common sense transform those discomforting "matters of fact" into more congenial ideas that rescue us from fear.

Frost elaborates upon this idea in "All Revelation" (1938), perhaps his fullest poetic meditation on the futility of speculation about the origin of matter, thought, and knowledge. An elaborate fertility ritual, the poem's union of mind and matter plays with history's most important ideas regarding the construction of knowledge. It also ponders whether the world of sensory experience can be an adequate object of knowledge if our modes of perception continually change.

In the first ten lines of the poem Frost examines at least four different epistemological theories, none of which attains prominence as *the* definitive account of how we formulate knowledge. Neither wholly ac-

tive nor wholly passive, the natural world and human consciousness
interact with one another, breaking down the traditional nineteenth-
century dichotomy of a penetrating scientific consciousness and pene-
trated natural object:

> A head thrusts in as for the view,
> But where it is it thrusts in from
> Or what it is it thrusts into
> By that Cyb'laean avenue,
> And what can of its coming come,
>
> And whither it will be withdrawn,
> And what take hence or leave behind,
> These things the mind has pondered on
> A moment and still asking gone.
> Strange apparition of the mind!
>
> (*CPP&P*, 302)

As the first five lines make plain by their obvious sexual diction (*thrust*
occurs three times in the opening lines), knowledge can be conceived
of as an instinctual urge, the origin and end of which must necessarily
remain a mystery. Partially determined by an unknown natural force
that impels consciousness into uncharted territory (the Darwinian position), cognition appears initially to be a bodily function, a purely practical mechanism that allows us to negotiate the environment in a manner that satisfies our immediate needs, values, and desires. Viewed in
this manner, the rational intellect for Frost is an adaptational tool of
survival. The end of our contemplation is not arbitrary; rather, nature
directs our thought toward those material objects that can serve us in
the most productive and protective ways.

The suggestion is strong here, however, that problems arise once
mind and matter begin to interact with one another. Whether the medi-

ating subject constructs the object of its knowledge (the romantic position), whether the subject "withdraws" from its object to complete the necessary separation of mind and matter (the empiricist position) or whether the mind will "ponder" constructs that exist independently of empirical data (the rationalist position), the end result remains ambiguous. As both the object and the subject of its contemplation, the mind can know neither its own cognitive processes nor the noumenal world that exists beyond the boundaries of perception and rationality. Frost makes clear that each method sets limits on the type of knowledge the mind can comprehend, thus relegating to the provinces of illusion ("strange apparition of the mind") any concept formulated outside one particular method. What counts, Frost seems to suggest, is not so much the integrity of our concepts as the processes by which we derive whatever meaning we can from a mysterious and "impervious" natural world.

The third and fourth stanzas extend the abstract inquiry of the first stanzas and offer a Jamesian account of how sensation actually stimulates conceptual activity. Here our excursive mediating consciousness, metaphorically compared to a "cathode ray," and the objective "geodesic" world upon which it operates conspire to produce the conceptual offspring that emerge in the poem's final lines. Frost's choice of the cathode ray to describe the interplay between conceptual abstraction and immediate experience is an exceptionally accurate illustration of Jamesian pragmatism. By using this figure, Frost implies that we have been equipped by nature to direct our mental activity toward a freely chosen object of contemplation:

> But the impervious geode
> Was entered, and its inner crust
> Of crystals with a ray cathode
> At every point and facet glowed
> In answer to the mental thrust.

Eyes seeking the response of eyes
Bring out the stars, bring out the flowers,
Thus concentrating earth and skies
So none need be afraid of size.
All revelation has been ours.

(*CPP&P*, 302-3)

Just as a directed beam of electrons might illuminate a phosphorescent screen, so too does intellect illuminate, or "bring out," the world's more salient features. The illuminated crystals, however, constitute only a small part of the geode's interior cavity. Unable either to penetrate beyond the material world's negligible surfaces or to expand its inquiry to encompass an adequate scientific breadth, the mind is limited to concepts that are in part predetermined by environmental exigencies.

This obvious shift from abstraction to sensation reveals not only the futility of all metaphysical speculation but also the inherent wisdom of our attempts to shape the local features of experience. Our innate curiosity to know a sentient being, whether human or divine, forces us into conceptual innovation, which in turn leads to greater experiential revelation.[66] By "bringing" out the "stars" and "flowers," Frost "concentrates"—both mentally and physically—the inexplicable world and transforms it into a genial realm where he can find his bearings and contemplate life's transient beauty. As the title "All Revelation" ultimately implies, knowledge is a product of both invention and discovery, a process of creating the useful forms that reveal our relationship to the material world. And while we cannot fully recover certainty through either philosophy or science, we must nevertheless "reveal" the forms of existence to ourselves in a manner that responds to our deepest psychic needs. Only then can we begin to prosper in a difficult, immense world and strengthen, as Frost once claimed, our tentative "hold on the planet."[67]

The same epistemological skepticism keeps repeating itself in

Frost's work after 1925. Scientifically based poems such as "The Star-Splitter," "A Star in a Stoneboat," "On Looking Up by Chance at the Constellations," and "Lost in Heaven" recapitulate in one form or another the antipositivist attitudes that Frost cultivated in the years following his encounters with Heisenberg and Bohr. In their metaphysical suspicion, in their exploratory mediation between abstraction and experience, and in their strong affirmation of our ability to amend the reality we perceive, these poems exhibit the means by which Frost transformed the immense, chaotic, and dark worlds that he so often conjured. Perhaps the most important distinction one can make between these and the earlier poems is that in the later poems, rather than cowering beneath science, Frost paradoxically makes use of science to surmount his anxiety over the heaven-shattering materialism that pervades so many of his earlier poems and letters. Indeed, far from being the obsessed antagonist of physics and biology that many commentators describe, Frost demonstrates in his later poems a remarkable tranquillity in the face of those disciplines. Science, he suggests, has not made the world safer or less mysterious, and, as he makes clear throughout his later work, he believes such prospects are highly unlikely.

Lack of ultimate certainty, however, need not paralyze our efforts to find meaning and value in the world. As Frost continually reminds us, uncertainty can awaken in us an unlimited opportunity to produce the radiant forms—the beautiful myths, models, and fictions of our imagination—that bring order and meaning to existence. Although we can never be completely sure whether our propositions are true, we can measure their "truthfulness" by the extent to which they guide us successfully through the chaotic flux of experience. Neither wholly optimistic nor wholly pessimistic, this two-fold attitude—an acceptance of our limitations and an acknowledgment of our life-affirming capabilities—underlies Frost's mature approach toward all orders of knowledge, including science, thus marking him as one of the most eloquent spokesmen of the humanistic tradition. This skeptical attitude also helped to restore Frost's belief in divine purpose, what he often called in private moments of religious speculation a "wisdom beyond wisdom." As Frost grew older and settled his quarrel with scientific materialism, he found more reasons to be confident about the intellectual integrity of his own religious beliefs. "I despise religiosity," Frost once stated in 1949. "But I have no religious doubts. Not about God's existence, anyway."[68]

Such bald statements of belief are difficult to ignore, and one can do so only at the peril of neglecting the mature philosophical position that Frost adopted in the mid-1920s and maintained for the rest of his life. Occupying a stance that mediates halfway between the epistemologies of Bergson and James, Frost believed that man's anthropocentric creations were deceiving illusions that served as barriers to a deeper reality, ultimately hidden to consciousness (the Bergsonian view), or that man's invented forms were synecdochical parts of a much larger unity whose purpose and magnitude remained imperceptible (the Jamesian position). In several respects, Frost's vacillation between these two positions reflects his perpetual struggle over whether to relocate the fallen, pristine realm of Platonic perfection in the transcendent realm of some preconscious unity or in the immanent creative surge of Bergson's *élan vital*. This problem seems to have preoccupied Frost's thoughts toward the end of his life, and whereas early in his life he denied being a "Platonist," in his old age he admitted that many of his ideas exhibited certain Platonic characteristics. In a 1961 address to the Greek Archaeological Society in Athens, Frost explained that many of his late "romantic tendencies," as he called them, were derived from Plato. "I like to think that I'm not quite a Platonist," he claimed, "and then all of a sudden I find myself saying something that I myself trace right back to Plato. For instance, I say there's more religion outside the church than in, there's more love outside of marriage than in, and there's more wisdom outside of philosophy than in."[69] Frost's enduring faith that a larger or more benevolent reality exists beyond our intellectual creations clearly indicates that he saw religious conventions both as catalysts for civic order and as limiting orthodoxies that had to be overcome in the name of intellectual freedom. Adhering to the latter demand, Frost challenged the religious dogma he inherited from his mother, and he ardently disputed the scientific ideas that had given rise to materialism and atheism. If the truthfulness of man's invented concepts could not be grounded in anything beyond the self, Frost reasoned, why was it not possible to discredit the concepts that had purged the modern world of its religious belief?

Perhaps, in the final analysis, one can best describe Frost's poetry as an art of equipoise, his lasting achievement a body of work whose emotional gravity and formal temperance enable us always to find small moments of hope amidst life's abominations. Virtually every feature of Frost's work, from his elegant metrics to his heroic themes, from his imaginative excursions to his imaginative withdrawals, is free of the emotional excess that characterizes so much of his generation's poetry. The means by which Frost reconciled his early quarrel with science might best be described as controlled moderation. Speaking with Jonas Salk in 1956, Frost, seven years removed from his own death in 1963, offered one of his most eloquent and inclusive statements on how he regarded science and religion:

> I think a scientist and anybody with an active mind lives on tentatives rather than tenets. And that you've got to feel a certain pleasure in the tentativeness of it all. The unfinality of it. And that's what you live [and]—when I say that you hang around until you catch on, that doesn't mean you hang on until you get the final answer to anything, that you hang onto—the spirit in which we live, in which this is to be taken, the tentativeness of things, the process of things, of the little certainties that we get among the uncertainties, the little place we make, the little formula we make. And those—there's faith in it, of course, the faith that those all some way are related and may be tumbled together somewhere, that they may make something, may make something.[70]

Perhaps Frost took this final cue from Einstein, that enigmatic, optimistic, and dominating spirit of the age, who, only two weeks before his own death in 1955, had confided to Bernard Cohen that because our "physical theories were far from adequate" the fundamental mysteries of physics might always be with us.[71] To Frost, who read this account and praised it in one of his Bread Loaf lectures,[72] Einstein's words must have been a source of incalculable comfort. Coming from a man who had spent his whole adult life searching for a unified theory for all physical phenomena, this admission of a "great attempt" that had so far failed must have joyfully confirmed for Frost what he had suspected all along: that the wisest man, as Socrates once declared, was wise simply because he knew he did not know.

From *Going by Contraries: Robert Frost's Conflict with Science* (Charlottesville: University Press of Virginia), pp. 89-124. Copyright © 2002 by The University Press of Virginia. Reprinted by permission of The University Press of Virginia.

Notes

1. See Thompson, *Robert Frost: The Early Years*, 90-93.
2. Emerson, "Nature," 23.
3. Ibid.
4. Frost, in *Lawrence (Mass.) High School Bulletin* 13, no. 4 (December 1891): 4.
5. Frost once claimed that nearly a third of all of his poems were "astronomical." Thompson records that Belle Frost, as a way of coaxing her son toward astronomy, often quoted a line from Edward Young's *Complaint or Night Thoughts on Life, Death, and Immortality*: "An undevout astronomer is mad" (see Thompson, *Robert Frost: The Early Years*, 92-93).
6. Thompson claims that Frost admitted authorship of this poem to Charles R. Green, the librarian of the Jones Public Library in Amherst, Massachusetts, and then retracted that statement, out of embarrassment, in 1946. Most Frost scholars, including Richard Poirier, now attribute the poem to Frost (see Thompson's note on this poem in ibid., 540).
7. Ibid., 593-94.
8. Lathem, *Interviews*, 149.
9. Thompson, *Robert Frost: The Early Years*, 258.
10. Ibid., 265.
11. Ibid., 340.

12. The sharp contrast between Robert's and Elinor's religious views is highlighted in a letter Frost wrote to Louis Untermeyer on 21 March 1920 (see Frost, *Selected Letters*, 244).

13. Mertins, *Robert Frost*, 326.

14. Much of the evidence that Frost liked Proctor's book comes from a letter Mrs. Frost wrote to Mrs. Edna Romig on 4 February 1935, in which she noted that Frost, attracted to the book's religious element, had read *Our Place among Infinities* several times about 1890 (see Thompson, *Robert Frost: The Early Years*, 501). In spite of Frost's attraction to *Our Place among Infinities*, his obsession with science in his prose and poetry clearly indicates that Proctor did not resolve Frost's conflict with science. Not until Frost encountered Bergson in 1912 and Eddington, Heisenberg, and Bohr in the early 1920s did he begin to find plausible arguments against materialism.

15. Proctor, *Our Place among Infinities*, 37-38.

16. Ibid., 39-40, emphasis added.

17. Arnold, *Works*, 4:2.

18. Frost; "The Future of Man" (unpublished version), 870-71.

19. Arnold, *Works*, 4:2-3.

20. In 1796 Laplace published *Système du Monde* (World system), which contained his nebular hypothesis as well as a general account of Newtonian mechanics. Though the nebular hypothesis had been postulated earlier by Swedenborg and Kant, Laplace's theory had become the dominant cosmology by 1820.

21. Proctor, *Our Place among Infinities*, 9-10.

22. Frost, quoted in Mertins, *Robert Frost*, 326.

23. Frost, Notebooks, Special Collections, Dartmouth College Library.

24. Postulated by Rudolf Clausius in 1865, the second law of thermodynamics states that all processes must operate at less than 100 percent efficiency because of wasted heat thrown off through the processes of friction. Mathematically, the concept of entropy can be stated as $\Delta S = \Delta q/t$, where S is the increase in entropy, q is the amount of heat added, and t is the absolute temperature. Frost often talked about the concept of entropy by invoking Yggdrasil, the great ash tree in Norse mythology, which extended its roots and branches through the universe, holding it together: "But all growth is limited—the tree of life is limited like a maple tree or an oak tree—they all have a certain height, and they all have a certain life-length. And our tree, the tree Yggdrasil, has reached its growth. It doesn't have to fall down because it's stopped growing. It will go on blossoming and having seasons—I'd give it a hundred or two hundred million years" (Frost, "The Future of Man" [published version], 868).

25. See Proctor, *Our Place among Infinities*, 41-44.

26. Mill, "Nature," 381.

27. Huxley, *Evolution and Ethics*, 83.

28. I am indebted here to Christopher Clausen's ideas concerning what he terms the moral and the mystic imagination, which he claims are two distinct but antithetical responses to nineteenth-century science. Viewing the later Hopkins as representative of the moral imagination and Whitman as the supreme representative of the mystic imagination, Clausen explains Whitman's influence on Hopkins and why Hopkins, harbor-

ing severe misgivings about finding god in the natural world, repudiated his earlier mystical stance ("Whitman, Hopkins, and the World's Splendor," 175-78).

29. Whitman, *Leaves of Grass*, 228.

30. Ibid., 18.

31. Stevens, "The Noble Rider and the Sound of Words," in *Wallace Stevens: Collected Poetry and Prose*, 665.

32. Pascal, *Pensées* 61.

33. Poirier, *Robert Frost*, 267.

34. Lathem, *Interviews*, 271.

35. I am speaking chiefly of Michel Foucault, who describes the author as a function within the larger discourse of poststructuralists who deny the author agency (Foucault, "What Is an Author?").

36. Snyder, *World Machine*, 465.

37. According to Newtonian mechanics, once the forces and initial conditions are specified, it is possible to calculate the motions of particles into the indefinite future. Basing his predictions upon his law of force, $F = ma$ (force equals mass times acceleration), and his inverse square law of gravitation, $F = G(m_1m_2)/r^2$ (force is directly proportional to the product of the masses and inversely proportional to the square of the distance between them), Newton postulated that the course of the universe was fixed and calculable. Newton, however, had difficulty specifying an absolute state of motion or rest, a fixed frame of reference, which was necessary in order to observe these conditions. To solve this problem, Newton argued that God had provided him with the absolute frame of reference necessary for his mechanics to work. Einstein disputed this claim by suggesting that there could be no absolute state of motion or rest, only relative motion. While Newtonian mechanics worked well to describe the motions of relatively slow-moving objects, it failed once those objects approached the speed of light. For an excellent general discussion of the differences between Newtonian and Einsteinian physics, see Jeremy Bernstein's *Einstein*, 29-31.

38. I am here indebted to Carol Donley and Alan Friedman's informative discussion of the impact of physics on popular culture in *Einstein as Myth and Muse*, 13. The issue of *The Nation* they refer to is that of 7 April 1920, p. 503.

39. Donley and Friedman, *Einstein as Myth and Muse*, 10.

40. Rotella, "Comparing Conceptions," 174.

41. Eddington, *Philosophy of Physical Science*, 56.

42. Eddington, *Space, Time, and Gravitation*, 201.

43. Eddington, *Nature of the Physical World*, 353.

44. Ibid., 353.

45. Ibid., 288-89.

46. Ibid., 327.

47. Rotella, "Comparing Conceptions," 167.

48. Frost, "Education by Poetry," 721.

49. Eddington, *Nature of the Physical World*, 311.

50. Frost, "Education by Poetry," 720.

51. Planck, *Where Is Science Going?* 214.

52. Heisenberg, *Across the Frontiers*, 26.

53. Jeans, *Mysterious Universe*, 150-51.

54. Thompson, *Robert Frost: The Years of Triumph*, 617.

55. Frost, "Education by Poetry," 721.

56. Rotella, "Comparing Conceptions," 179-80.

57. Bohr's earliest elucidation of the correspondence principle occurs in "Über die Anwendung der Quantentheorie auf den Atombau" (On the application of quantum theory to atomic structure), 141.

58. Bohr, *Atomic Theory and the Description of Nature*, 116-17.

59. Frost, "The Poetry of Amy Lowell," in *CPP&P*, 712.

60. Frost, "The Figure a Poem Makes," 777.

61. To my mind, the best reading of "Birches," to which my own reading is indebted, is still Frank Lentricchia's explication of the poem in *Robert Frost*, 107-12.

62. Ibid., 7.

63. This idea may be indebted to Kurt Gödel's Incompleteness theorem (1931), which states that the axioms in any given mathematical system cannot be proven from the axioms within that system itself.

64. Bernstein, *Einstein*, 157.

65. Ibid., 158.

66. Frost's ideas here are very similar to Derrida's notion that throughout history Western philosophy has attempted to find a privileged truth, what Derrida terms the "transcendental signified," which exists outside of language, consciousness, history, and time. For Derrida, such an attempt is futile, as no self-evident truth or metaphysics of presence can exist outside of discourse.

67. Frost, "Our Hold on the Planet," in *CPP&P*, 317.

68. Frost, quoted in Rodman, "Robert Frost," 41.

69. Thompson and Winnick, *Robert Frost: The Later Years*, 291.

70. John Lancaster, curator of Amherst College Special Collections, reports that the original transcript of this interview, upon which this version is based, was loaned to Amherst by William Britton Stitt, Amherst College class of 1918 (see Frost, "Interview with Jonas Salk," Archives and Special Collections, Amherst College Library, 15).

71. Cohen, "Interview with Einstein," 69.

72. See Cook, *Robert Frost: A Living Voice*, 100.

Works Cited

Arnold, Matthew. *The Works of Matthew Arnold*. 15 vols. London: Macmillan, 1903-4.

Bernstein, Jeremy. *Einstein*. New York: Viking, 1973.

Bohr, Niels. *Atomic Theory and the Description of Nature*. Cambridge: Cambridge University Press, 1934.

_____. "Über die Anwendung der Quantentheorie auf den Atombau" (On the application of the quantum theory to the structure of the atom). *Zeitschrift für Physik* 13 (1923): 117-65.

Clausen, Christopher. *The Place of Poetry*. Lexington: University of Kentucky Press, 1981.

_____. "Whitman, Hopkins, and the World's Splendor." *Sewanee Review* 105 (1997): 175-78.

Cohen, I. Bernard. "An Interview with Einstein." *Scientific American* 193, no. 1 (1995): 61-74.

Cook, Reginald. *Robert Frost: A Living Voice*. Amherst: University of Massachusetts Press, 1974.

Darwin, Charles. *The Descent of Man and Selection in Relation to Sex*. Chicago: Rand, McNally, 1874.

Donley, Carol, and Alan Friedman. *Einstein as Myth and Muse*. Cambridge: Cambridge University Press, 1985.

Eddington, Arthur Stanley. *The Nature of the Physical World*. New York: Macmillan, 1933.

_____. *The Philosophy of Physical Science*. Cambridge: Cambridge University Press, 1939.

_____. *Space, Time, and Gravitation*. New York: Harper & Brothers, 1959.

Emerson, Ralph Waldo. *Selections from Ralph Waldo Emerson*. Edited by Stephen E. Whicher. Boston: Houghton Mifflin, 1957.

Foucault, Michel. "What Is an Author?" In *Language, Counter-Memory, Practice*, edited by Donald F. Bouchard, translated by Sherry Simon, 113-38. Ithaca, N.Y.: Cornell University Press, 1977.

Frost, Robert. *Collected Poems, Prose, and Plays*. Edited by Richard Poirier and Mark Richardson. New York: Library of America, 1995.

_____. *Selected Letters of Robert Frost*. Edited by Lawrance Thompson. New York: Holt, Rinehart & Winston, 1964.

Heisenberg, Werner. *Across the Frontiers*. Translated by Peter Heath. New York: Harper & Row, 1974.

Huxley, Thomas Henry. *Evolution and Ethics*. London: Macmillan, 1894.

Jeans, James. *The Mysterious Universe*. Cambridge: Cambridge University Press, 1931.

Lathem, Edward Connery. *Interviews with Robert Frost*. New York: Holt, Rinehart & Winston, 1966.

Lentricchia, Frank. *Robert Frost: Modern Poetics and the Landscapes of Self*. Durham, N.C.: Duke University Press, 1974.

Mertins, Louis. *Robert Frost: Life and Talks-Walking*. Norman: University of Oklahoma Press, 1965.

Mill, John Stuart. "Nature." In *The Collected Works of John Stuart Mill*, edited by J. M. Robson, 10:373-402. Toronto: University of Toronto Press, 1969.

Pascal, Blaise. *Pensées*. Translated by W. F. Trotter. New York: Dutton, 1958.

Planck, Max. *Where Is Science Going?* Woodbridge, N.J.: Ox Bow, 1981.

Poirier, Richard. *Robert Frost: The Work of Knowing*. New York: Oxford University Press, 1977.

Proctor, Richard Anthony. *Our Place among Infinities*. New York: Longmans, Green, 1876.

Rodman, Selden. "Robert Frost." In *Tongues of Fallen Angels*. New York: New Directions, 1974.

Rotella, Guy. "Comparing Conceptions: Frost and Eddington, Heisenberg, and Bohr." *American Literature* 59, no. 2 (1987): 167-89.

Snyder, Carl. *The World Machine*. New York: Longmans, Green, 1907.

Stevens, Wallace. *Wallace Stevens: Collected Poetry and Prose*. Edited by Frank Kermode and John Richardson. New York: Library of America, 1997.

Thompson, Lawrance. *Robert Frost: The Early Years, 1874-1915*. New York: Holt, Rinehart & Winston, 1966.

——————. *Robert Frost: The Years of Triumph, 1915-1938*. New York: Holt, Rinehart & Winston, 1970.

—————— and R. H. Winnick. *Robert Frost: The Later Years, 1938-1963*. New York: Holt, Rinehart & Winston, 1976.

Whitman, Walt. *Leaves of Grass, and Selected Prose*. Edited by Sculley Bradley. New York: Holt, Rinehart & Winston, 1962.

The Need of Being Versed:
Robert Frost and the Limits of Rhetoric_____
Shira Wolosky

Robert Frost's boast about his notable craftsmanship[1] has never quite been made critically good. Most Frost criticism continues to center upon issues—thematic, philosophical, religious, historical. Relatively few essays address formal matters,[2] and those tend to restrict themselves to rhyme scheme, sound patterns, and above all to prosody—to how natural speech rhythms, in accordance with Frost's own prosodic discussions, play with and against traditional meters. As to the significance of form in Frost's work, most discussions reiterate his definition of poetry as "a stay against confusion." Form acts to contain chaos: its order both presupposes and opposes disorder.[3] Rarely is this general rule particularized in pursuit of form as articulated within specific texts, or as constituting a text's very utterance, elements, and textuality. Yet there are in Frost's poems events taking place on the linguistic level beyond such initial formal surfaces as sound and meter, events which implicate the whole notion of form as a penetrating poetic concern. An approach to Frost through his language moreover yields a somewhat different understanding of other thematic concerns more usually the subject of Frost studies. This is the case most notably for his irony, and for his place in and relation to a tradition of American poetics and concerns.

Frost's verse is often so apparently paraphrasable as to seem the précis for some short story: a domination of plot that takes up the slack seemingly left by an overly straightforward, homey, and blunt language. "The Need of Being Versed in Country Things" is in these, as in other ways, prototypical. Comprised of all the expected Frostian elements—the rural setting, the nostalgic or elegiac identification with nature then punctured by the almost equally nostalgic retreat from such identification—the poem even may be said to take Frost's own typical themes as its theme, a metapoem exactly thematizing

Frost's usual thematics. And yet the textual life of the poem not only exceeds such stated themes; it significantly complicates them—in their "plot," their conduct, and above all their outcome and implications. Through Frost's exacting craft, the language of the poem enacts a drama of its own that reframes the entire relation to nature and the irony such relation generates, which is the text's explicit subject:

> The house had gone to bring again
> To the midnight sky a sunset glow.
> Now the chimney was all of the house that stood
> Like a pistil after the petals go.
>
> The barn opposed across the way,
> That would have joined the house in flame
> Had it been the will of the wind, was left
> To bear forsaken the place's name.
>
> No more it opened with all one end
> For teams that came by the stony road
> To drum on the floor with scurrying hoofs
> And brush the mow with the summer load.
>
> The birds that came to it through the air
> At broken windows flew out and in,
> Their murmur more like the sigh we sigh
> From too much dwelling on what has been.
>
> Yet for them the lilac renewed its leaf,
> And the aged elm, though touched with fire;
> And the dry pump flung up an awkward arm;
> And the fence post carried a strand of wire.

For them there was really nothing sad.
But though they rejoiced in the nest they kept,
One had to be versed in country things
Not to believe the phoebes wept.

The compelling aspect of this poem's theme and thematizing is amply registered in its many paraphrases. In these the mistaken anthropomorphism is described, with concomitant moral lessons: "Men may weep to see a home abandoned where there had been so much life, but the birds' springtime duty is nesting and they rejoice in it." "The [birds'] murmuring may sound like weeping to man unless he is versed in the understanding that the task at hand takes all one's energy in country life."[4] "It is up to man himself to comprehend and accept nature on its own terms if he is to achieve any real contact with it. . . . That the phoebes nesting in the barn are not really lamenting the burning of the house for they are part of the natural world, rather than man's . . . [reveals] that nature is independent, self-sufficient, and often brutal: this is what man is to learn from the ironic contrast between his expectations and nature's fulfillment of them."[5] "The birds are oblivious in their homemaking to the destruction of the once productive human household. . . . We 'need to be versed' for the sake of certain realities that belong specifically to human consciousness, the difference between human love and homemaking and the mating of animals."[6]

Such anthropomorphism on the thematic level in turn functions, on the level of imagery, as pathetic fallacy—a force and concern in so many Frost poems. The poem not only enacts, but also reflects upon the tendency to project onto nature—here the birds—human feelings, concluding with a rejection of or resistance to this tendency, in an ironic move characteristic of Frost. What is masterful in the poem's craft is how this concern with pathetic fallacy informs its linguistic events, and how this linguistic level finally changes if not the nature, then the target of the irony. It does so via the trope of personification. The poem in fact may be read as a study in personification: a trope extending well beyond the birds who are its most explicit subject to include almost every element in the poem in a steady, although various, succession. While personification is without question the poem's governing trope, its power is far from uncontested. As the poem proceeds, the trope not only evolves, but underscores itself, ultimately to question its own claims and finally to reject them.

This process commences in the poem's first line, which contains its first two personifications—albeit almost inaudible ones: "The house had gone" and "to bring again." "Had gone," although somewhat dead as a figure, nevertheless suggests some animate motion. "To bring" similarly need not be more than a sentential complement, equivalent to "and brought." Yet the infinitival form, here and elsewhere in the poem, insinuates a sense of intentionality, carrying within it an implicit purposive: in order to. Here, the two phrases taken together strengthen this impression of both animation and intentionality. "The house had gone to bring again" in its syntax invites an animate subject, and urges joining the first action in purposeful sequence with the second.

These personifications are the opening gestures in a rhetorical strategy conducted throughout the poem, a strategy that distributes different levels and kinds of personification through the text. The poem in fact pursues an exquisite range of personification's possibilities. Often—and this seems to be one of the poem's points—the reader must pause to determine whether or not a personification is even present. Although most of Frost's formal remarks—and certainly those most often cited—underscore prosodic questions, Frost as rhetor is not a surprising figure. As he pointedly remarks in his *Paris Review* interview, he had read "more Latin and Greek than Pound ever did."[7] He had been himself a Latin teacher, and most allusions in his prose are to the classics. In "The Need of Being Versed," Frost accomplishes with personification the "speech with range" he praises in "Education by Poetry" as having "something of overstatement, something of statement, and something of understatement."[8] There are mild personifications, such as those of the opening, and about whose status the reader must hesitate. There are extreme personifications, so extreme that they underscore and make unmistakable their status, but ultimately thereby also call that status into question. And there are hidden personifications. The search for and sensitivity to these different tropological kinds is one of the poem's effects, just as the hesitation regarding whether a personification is even present works to throw attention back onto the whole nature and notion of personification as such.

The first stanza concludes, as it opens, with just such questionable and hidden instances. Is there any personifying force in the assertion that the chimney "stood" or the petals "go"? Or are these dead personifications bereft of force, as perhaps are "had gone" and "to bring" in the first line? The second stanza, however, traces a movement in the opposite direction, toward personifications increasingly unmistakable and yet whose force is also questionable exactly in their being extreme. The barn "opposed" across the way implies nothing more than its spatial placement in relation to the house, with no intentional resistance. That it "would have joined" the house could perhaps also register nothing more than spatial juncture, as when a river joins the sea. The conditional mood, however, with the phrasal complement "in"—"would have joined the house in flame"—nudges the verb in the direction of a sense of choosing to take part, as in the expression "to join in" a country dance. Such encroaching animation then becomes explicit and decisive with "had it been the will of the wind." This near cliché, recalling Frost's first volume title and its echo of Longfellow's "A boy's will is the wind's will," emerges within a context of repeated attributions of intent so subtle as to border on unconscious assumptions, serving in its overtness to bring these to consciousness. But at the very moment the trope achieves clarity it also loses credibility, as do the preceding personificatory gestures of which it is the culmination. The wind simply does not will a barn to decide to join in with a house on fire and burn down too.

The direction and sweep of imagery thus is brought to a momentary halt, as the undercurrent of personificatory projection comes instead to the surface, exposing itself to view and therefore to critical questioning. This is a pattern the poem will repeat. Here it is merely proleptic; and exactly because "the will of the wind" borders on cliché, it is ultimately accepted, allowing the poem to proceed after its discrete pause to pursue descriptions that, however, within the context of encroaching suspicion, vacillate between personification and some possible literal rendering of the scene. Thus the barn as "left/ To bear forsaken the place's name" also comes to seem equivocal. The phrase avers that the barn alone remained of the farm. But, following as it does the asserted will of the wind, does "left" acquire an intentional force? Is "forsaken" a predicate adjective describing the barn as simply the last vestige of farmstead, an adverb (colloquially misinflected) expressing the observer's impression of how the sole remaining barn bears the farm's name, or a (direct) adjective indicating the barn's own sense of abandonment? The infinitive especially becomes suspicious in a poem where it repeatedly appears with equivocal functions and whose patterning pursues an escalating personification. "To bear" hovers between sentential complement whose function is merely participial— the barn as left bearing—as against a purposive barn as (purposely) left (in order) to bear—a reading amplified by the object borne: the "place's name," the essential human marker.

The third stanza pursues this pattern of infinitives, no longer with regard to inanimate objects but in terms of animate but unconscious creatures. This stanza is in many ways transitional. The barn is here openly personified, but only as a metonymic substitute for the human agents who open barns for teams: "The more it opened with all one end/ For teams." "To drum" and "to brush" are infinitives of habitual action that need impute no intention either to the barn as admitting or to the teams as entering in order to brush or drum. Yet both brushing and drumming seem, as activities, to occur at some boundary of the human: each verb originates in actions peculiar to the human sphere, the first to music, the second to cleaning. In descriptions of activity, at least, human categories remain in force. "Scurrying," in contrast, compares one kind of beast to another—the wild forest creatures who perhaps have come to inhabit the abandoned barn, as opposed to the oxen or horses for which the barn was constructed. The farmstead, in being described exactly as depopulated, nonetheless constantly projects a human presence through the poem's categories of description. But the barn is itself a transitional place, situated between the human house now almost completely absent and the wild life of creatures who have come to make the once-farm their home.

It is only in stanza four that these personifying constructions and foci of stanza three fully emerge. Stanza three remains within properly human territory, concerned with domestic animals—albeit absent ones—whose activities are quite properly defined in human terms. Applying to them human categories thus remains plausible, both logically and rhetorically. With stanza four the poem moves expressly out of the human sphere, past the implied "scurrying" creatures to explicit wild birds who now inhabit the barn. Now the crossing of human and non-human involves traversing a much wider distance, so that applying human and sentient terms to the non-human world—as the poem persists in doing—creates a greater and greater rhetorical strain which it is the final act of this poem to snap.

The first step into this different sphere is registered in the "to it" with which the birds, flying through windows, enter the barn (there are presumably no windows left in the house):

> The birds that came to it through the air
> At broken windows flew out and in,
> Their murmur more like the sigh we sigh
> From too much dwelling on what has been.

Like the infinitives threaded through the text, the preposition "to" (and also "for") takes its place within a continuous textual network. And both infinitives and prepositions together constitute in the realm of syntax a corollary to the rhetorical pattern made up by tropes of personification. In this sense, the poem is about—indeed, textually it turns about—the word "to": the "to" of an infinitive; "to" as preposition, and thus as directional; and the differences between these usages, their fields of force as they approach and recede from one another in implication. These differences, as the text probes, exactly mark differences in intentionality—the very intentionality which distinguishes the trope of personification. The preposition "to" implies direction, reference, transfer. But it does so in terms of placement and location without entailing any animation or consciousness. The "to" of an infinitive may similarly be merely a neutral construction for providing a sentence with a verbal form. But the infinitive, at least within this poem's patterns, seems ever to carry with it the purposive construction the infinitive also commands. And the prepositional/directional "to" also becomes infected with suggested purpose. This is the case from the poem's very outset, which offers the first coupling of these two uses of "to." "To bring again/ To the midnight sky a sunset glow" plays with an implicit purposive sense of "in order to bring again" that moves toward a trope of personification. This implicitly purposive "to bring" is then matched with a second "to," one no less sly in its running counter to normal syntactic expectations. Completing the infinitive phrase, "To the midnight sky a sunset glow" implies the intentional movement of an object to an intended and specific place. Instead, both object and place dissolve into the near oxymoron of midnight-sunset, so that "to" itself becomes almost figurative. The "midnight sky" is not a circumscribed location to which things may be brought. A "sunset glow" is not a graspable object one may bring.

Within this context of the poem's unfolding rhetorical and grammatical patternings, "The birds that came to it through the air" of stanza four already suggests some intention to the birds' movement. And while the preposition "at" and the adverbs "out" and "in" of "At broken windows flew out and in" reassert the function of pure placement, the detail of broken windows frames the birds' entry and exit in a sense of disruption entirely the property of the human observer. Stanza four's "to it" in fact marks a moment in the poem at cross-purposes: the world of humanized pathos is exactly the domain that, with the wild birds, has been crossed out of. Yet the preposition "to" continues to resist its purely neutral function of placing and locating. The impulse to project the human instead reasserts itself with revitalized and explicit force: "Their murmur more like the sigh we sigh/ From too much dwelling on what has been." The poet's identifying with the birds—or rather, his identifying them with himself and assimilating them into the human state—is expressly asserted. Like man, they murmur and sigh. Moreover, like man they dwell—and indeed do so in a specifically figurative and personified sense: not only in constructed shelters, but in the past, for which the current, damaged farmstead is itself merely a figure. For what is this abandoned barn but a sign for the formerly intact, but now absent farmhouse, its surrounding buildings, and the life once lived there? A movement of figuration has overtaken and determined the surviving farmstead, the notion of "dwelling," and also the prepositions "From" (too much dwelling) and "on" (what has been), which indicate relation to "place" only when place represents some non-spatial psychic "territory."

It is precisely this unchecked movement of figuration and personification that it is the task of the following and penultimate stanza to disrupt:

> Yet for them the lilac renewed its leaf,
> And the aged elm, though touched with fire;
> And the dry pump flung up an awkward arm;
> And the fence post carried a strand of wire.

Here, as the poem's turning point, the entire movement of projection, personification, and intentionality is exposed exactly to be such. Until this moment the poem's rhetoric has been realizing and enacting the poem's humanizing point of view. The human mourning for the lost farmstead first infuses the landscape and, in the next stanzas, is shared by nonhuman creatures as well. The very site is seen to mourn—the solitary chimney, the forsaken barn; while the birds in their "murmur" speak with the speaker's voice, their "sigh" like our "sigh," their "dwelling" like our dwelling. But are they indeed like? In a problematic common to much Frost poetry the similarity reveals itself not to be valid. As with the "thrush music" that calls to the poet in "Come In," the poet finally will "not come in . . . even if asked,/ And I hadn't been." Here too he resists an invitation based upon a likeness which he ultimately sees not to exist. The likeness itself is instead recognized, not as drawn between differing realms but only as based in a humanizing point of view and realized through a personifying rhetoric. This rhetoric now splits open and apart, as the two like things instead prove divergent. From this moment, the poem pursues two paths, speaks with two voices—or rather, shows itself as having done so from the outset. The human voice recognizes itself as representing nature in terms of human categories, as it has done from the poem's start. It equally recognizes that the birds and nature have, and have had, an independent and divergent stance, and wishes somehow to attest to this. But how is it to do so? The scene of desolation, as the poet experiences it, is for the birds another scene altogether. Yet there is an immense difficulty—indeed an impossibility—in rendering this other scene, this scene as "for" the birds. The very preposition "for" carries with it an unfounded attribution, as though the scene either exists teleologically "for" the birds or is being construed intentionally and intelligently by them. Yet neither "for" is within the power of the birds to assert; neither "for" is "for" them. The only legitimate "for" in nature is entirely positional. All others are only "for" the human observer, who however he tries, is unable to extricate himself from human categories—who in the very act of trying to do so only can reassert them.

Nor will this doubling between the human and non-human easily be resolved by yielding to division according to figurative and literal senses. This very difference is called into question. The pun on "dwelling" resolves into a figurative representation of human memory and nostalgia, while the birds from their own point of view may be dwelling only literally. But a problem remains as to how memory and nostalgia can be represented at all except in the spatial imagery of inhabiting or, as in the "nostos" of nostalgia, returning. For memory, there is no literal level—the figurations of space are, for memory, literal. Not literal/figurative distinctions, but levels within figuration are at issue, as is also the case in "Their murmur more like the sigh we sigh." There, the sounds of birds are triply figured. In order to compare it to nostalgic human sighs the speaker must first liken it to a human sigh as such: like the sigh we sigh. "More like" then serves to distinguish a nostalgic human sigh from some other kind. But even "murmur," the supposed ground in nature out of which the figure is built, is figurative. Bird sound murmurs only in likeness to human sound, so that the description of birds is finally only the figuring of three kinds of human utterance.

The poem thus resists its divisions as falling into literal/figurative, natural/human. What emerges instead is a doubling of forces: one personifying, and in counterforce against it, one of depersonification. By the very nature of man and of language, a direct and unmediated presentation of the non-human cannot be accomplished. Inevitably humanized for man through the human categories that mediate it, nature-in-itself as beyond or outside these categories remains inaccessible. Its independent and autonomous status therefore can only be indicated by way of detour—not via an impossible non-personification but rather through a depersonification. Stanza five offers such a detour. The speaker there makes his most concerted effort to adopt and present the birds' experience from the birds' point of view. In this he inevitably fails. "Yet for them the lilac renewed its leaf" raises the problem of "for"'s ascriptive powers, both teleological and perceptual, a problem carried through the zeugma in which "for them" constitutes the missing yet controlling phrase of the verse's extended ellipse, a phrase exactly emphasized through its absence. "The aged elm" registers a sense of time, "touched with fire" a sense of space that birds do not possess.

The fence post can not traverse for birds the metaphor and personification by which it may be said to "carry" wire. But above all, "The dry pump" could not for them have "flung up its awkward arm."[9] This double personification, ascribing to the pump intent in action and anthropomorphic body can simply not be "for" the birds. And yet its effect in a peculiar way turns back to the birds, exactly in its so impossibly evading them. For the far-fetched and almost grotesque quality of the pump's personification is so especially and expressly striking that one cannot help but take note of it. Personification in fact here verges into catachresis—displaying a truncated arm that asserts the human body only in a manner that dismembers and reifies it. And catachresis, rather than convincing us of its illusions, instead forces us to take note of them. By thus underscoring its own rhetoricity, the trope's affect shifts from persuasion to a recognition and consciousness of rhetorical functions, claims, and powers; as a rhetoric that is self-exposing and self-unmasking it is more involved with exploring its own implicit claims than in advancing them.

This technique had in fact made its first appearance earlier in the poem, with the "will of the wind." In taking the attribution of intention to nature too far, there too the trope had drawn attention to itself, forcing the reader toward a consciousness of the claims being made. Such self-betrayal, rather than accomplishing a metaphoric transfer, points to the relation between terms as visibly straining. In so straining, the trope in one sense fails. And yet it is only by such strain that a realm independent of trope can even be indicated. The human language which would ascribe such independence must inevitably compromise it by the very fact that it is in language the attempt is being made. But if language's tropes become so catachrestic as to expose their own effects, these effects can be in a sense negated, leaving open in the space of cancellation a sense not of an extra-linguistic world directly represented without mediation, but of such a world existing where language, in its self-limitation, has withdrawn. "The will of the wind" in this sense so lacks credence that the trope's effect, rather than to personify "wind" by attributing to it intentional "will," is to depersonify "will," making it the wind's random attribute rather than its intentional faculty. Only such space of defiguration—a space not at all equivalent to the "literal"—leaves an opening by which the extra-linguistic world may be indicated.

This will be the strategy controlling the poem's final stanza. "For them there was nothing really sad" is really a very peculiar declaration. It is strangely tautological to say that birds do not experience human emotions when they in fact could not possibly do so. Yet such a denial of a false ascription may perhaps be the most direct and only route of releasing them from the human. The only way to present birds-in-themselves in language may be to release them from the language that has first appropriated them. Releasing the birds from a human emotion only after having ascribed one to them alone can create an affect of extra-human and extra-linguistic bird life. This in no way belittles language; it is still by way of language that the affect of release must be orchestrated. Yet such release remains the sole avenue for indicating what lies without the human world—not through direct apprehension but reflected via retraction.

In this way, "For them there was really nothing sad" offers a tautological doubling which, because empty, serves to retract and negate the human sadness imposed on birds; thus released from pathetic projection, they attain a kind of autonomy. And in so doing, the line constitutes a move into irony characteristic of Frost. The sentimental identification of nature with human feelings, and particularly with elegiac feelings of loss, turns back on itself through self-exposure, the poem itself recognizing that it has been engaged in just such a project of projecting the human onto the non-human world.

Yet the nature of Frost's irony here also shifts. Classical or dramatic irony may be said to consist in a disparity of knowledge: characters or audience each exclusively possess facts denied the others. Romantic irony may be said to consist in a disparity of consciousness: as in a sudden shift from consciousness to self-consciousness, such that, as in

Schlegel, the fragmentary and partial status of art becomes itself an object of reflection, or, as in a breaking of illusion, the fictional status of a fiction is exposed.[10] Both of these ironies occur in Frost, the first commonly in dramatic dialogues, and also in lyrics where, however, it is sometimes difficult to locate exactly what knowledge will resolve what problem, or even to determine whether it is knowledge that is lacking at all. The second, romantic irony is perhaps even more prevalent in Frost, and certainly accounts in part for the irony of "The Need of Being Versed in Country Things." The pathetic fallacy with which the poem has proceeded is at last exposed to be just that, the projection onto the things of nature emotions which properly belong to human beings. But there is in the poem a third kind of irony, what might be called an irony of language. In this there is a disparity between the claims implicit in specific linguistic constructions and what these constructions in fact accomplish. This irony need not depend upon a particular acquisition of knowledge or accession to awareness as a narrative event or overt authorial recognition of the nature and status of his art. Rather, such irony explores the implicit assumptions in specific rhetorico-linguistic constructions—grammatical, dictional, tropic—exposing and exploiting them, making them explicit and thereby inevitably altering their effect. In one sense such linguistic irony recalls the traditional verbal irony that Frost interestingly assimilates to metaphor as such, when in "Education by Poetry" and also "The Constant Symbol" he declares metaphor to be "saying one thing and meaning another."[11] But it is language that says and means otherwise. Yet at issue is not necessarily the kind of aporia implied in Paul de Man's theory of verbal irony, which pits literal against figurative, sign against meaning in an unresolvable structure of mutual negation, such that linguistic claim becomes incompatible with either reference or logic, and linguistic knowledge becomes an impossibility.[12] At issue in Frost seems instead the finer definition of language's powers, not a radical contradiction within its parameters but rather their proper demarcation and limits—as "The Need of Being Versed in Country Things" finally makes evident.

In "The Need of Being Versed in Country Things," all three ironies—classical, romantic, and linguistic—are at play, each augmenting the other. Classical irony is perhaps slightly complicated in that being versed in country things involves not a further knowledge gained, but a false one relinquished. This correlates, on the level of romantic irony, with the self-conscious recognition of pathetic fallacy. And the unmasking of and resistance to pathetic fallacy on the level of romantic irony opens in turn into the unmasking of and resistance to personification on the linguistic and rhetorical level—which, however, introduces its own concerns and its own distinct framework. For, unlike both romantic and classical ironies, exposing the disparity between personification's claims and the existence of a sphere beyond its legitimate reach does not resolve this disparity. The recognition of linguistic projection does not make possible its transcendence. However we try to resist language's personifying tendencies, as through techniques of its exposure, we are ultimately unable to rid our language of personification. A realm without human figuration or fictionalization remains the supreme fiction. Even discussions of language—and this essay's discussion is no exception—cannot escape the tendency to personification, ascribing to language itself human action, intention, volition. However, the shape or boundary of an extra-linguistic realm can be traced by the space left when, having offered a linguistic construction, we then retract it, so that language in a sense is made to retreat from itself: not by impossibly avoiding personification but by exposing it through double or triple figures which dramatize its presence; by the tautologies and double negatives of depersonification which expressly retract the figures they cannot help but obtrude; by self-indicating catachresis; or, at the pole opposite to catachresis, by the hesitation as to whether a figure is personified at all, making us conscious of both the extent and the limits of linguistic claim, as this poem shows us we should be.

The final stanza of the poem offers instances of most of these strategies and serves to recapitulate and repose the issues the poem has hitherto raised. From the opening tautology of "For them there was really nothing sad," it goes on to propose the mildest, most questionable personification, "Though they rejoiced in the nest they kept." Naming the birds' busy activity and full-throated song rejoicing may not represent a projection; but it may. The poem makes us hesitate. And the final two lines then reintroduce the poem's main syntactic features, once again in terms of their rhetorical functions:

> One had to be versed in country things
> Not to believe the phoebes wept.

This poem, with its pathetic fallacies and personifications, had begun not by being versed in, but rather by versing country things. It has been about incorporating the natural into the human—into the verse of the poem, into language, and indeed into the figure of the farmstead that is the poem's subject. It is remarkable that what is taking place here on a linguistic level matches and echoes the struggle that defines both the poem's setting and its narrative action. The effort to domesticate nature is the very activity of farming; and nature's resistance to such effort is the event this poem, in tracing the return of the farmstead to its precultural state, traces.[13] The vicissitudes between nature and culture are felt in the poem through such images as the "stony road," the "dry pump," and the solitary chimney. "Stony road" at first suggests a tautology in the human sphere, where stone is an obvious material out of which farm roads may be made; but it comes to seem an oxymoron in the natural sphere, the yoking together of forces eternally at odds. So "dry pump" is only paradoxical from the standpoint of human technology; and the cold chimney is only the re-sorting of nature and culture into their respective categories as the farmstead resorts to its natural state. But farming is itself a trope for the question that personification enacts as a linguistic activity. It too humanizes reality by incorporating nature into human categories; it too is a kind of personification. At its turn, the poem attempts to pull away from the assimilation of the natural into the human categories of agriculture and linguistic culture. From the pun on "dwelling," with its intrusive insistence that birds live a nostalgic life such as man does, the text becomes one in which the human rage to verse resists itself and reverses itself, in an attempt actively to withdraw in order to leave free some territory not under its hegemony. Just as the birds reclaim the farmstead, so they reclaim their own voice, at least as much as this is possible in a poem humanly uttered: which is to say they speak, but by way of indirection, through the withdrawal and self-negation of utterance as it retreats from an active versing to a grammatically passive being versed.

Such negation is paramount in the poem's close, and is so in a way that resonates and reiterates patterns dominant throughout. "Not to believe" does more than signal a return to the infinitival form with the purposive implications it has carried throughout the poem. It represents in a sense the very archetype of this form: to believe is a specifically human act, and one that entails and asserts the whole question of paradigms and of purpose. Here, moreover, questions of ends, purposes, teleologies especially arise. For it is exactly the belief in and paradigm of conclusion that is at issue here—that has provided the categories for the poet's mis-humanization of the birds and of nature. To him the scene has been an emblem of finality—the finality of the desolate farm engulfed by chaotic natural forces. But in nature itself, the scene instead takes place within a process of continuous reproductivity that exactly confutes such notions of endings by its uninterrupted endlessness. What had been to the speaker a scene of desolation is "for" the birds—and through them as synecdoche, for nature in general—the setting for renewal. What from the human point of view represents an event of finality and closure, from the point of view of nature represents no break in process, no lapse in fertility. The need to be versed in country things is in this sense a need to be versed in country matters, in the sexuality by which nature, through and against whatever traumas, insists on their normalization in an uninterrupted reproductive venture.[14]

The crux of difference between the birds' activity and the human view of it is just this question of closure—a question imposed by human categories, by the human need for categories. Closure is exactly the category governing the discrepancy, misrepresentation, and misinterpretation of the scene, construing it in terms of disruption, finality, and terminus as opposed to a continuous and normal reproductive cycle. And it is exactly this imposition of category that the poem must retract and from which it must retreat—a retreat which in fact shapes the text's movement from first to last. In this regard the poem proceeds inversely. The vision with which it opens is one of radical and even apocalyptic finality—in which not only the human farm is utterly desolate but indeed nature is: sunset at midnight suggests the disorder of the very cosmos, even to an apocalyptic degree. Similarly, the first stanza's comparison of the chimney to "a pistil after the petals go" presents as a simile for the farmstead's depletion toward decline and demise what in nature points in quite other directions. For certain plants at least the petals "go" not merely to their death but as part of the flower's reproductive cycle.[15] The misrepresentation of this dissemination as dissolution registers how fully the human viewpoint intrudes into and distorts the scene that meets its eye, by construing it in accordance with its own preestablished paradigms of conclusion.

From these opening superpositions of human ends on nature's continuities, the poem pursues a way of retraction to arrive at its final "not to believe." And in the end, this locution's force implicates not only the particular belief in pathetic fallacy from which the poet finally withdraws, but the whole intentionality of belief, with its grammar and its rhetoric, and all that this in turn implies regarding human categorization. On the one hand, the negation signals that man cannot simply extricate himself from human experience and human language, to apprehend directly a non-human nature. He can only pursue his linguistic path and then double back on it. Language can indicate the space beyond language only by its self-erasure.

On the other hand, the negation introduces one of the poem's most

complicated twists. In this poem, Frost arrives at the sense of difference and distinction from nature which has long been recognized as
central to his stance—where, as Robert Penn Warren early described it,
poems which seem "to celebrate nature, may really be . . . about man
defining himself by resisting the pull into nature."[16] Yet, the many discussions of nature as "other" in Frost assume the configuration of difference to be one in which nature is the sphere of disorder and source of
"confusion" that it is poetry's task—not least formally—to "stay." And
the recognition of difference is itself often described as a regrettable
concession on Frost's part, if not a betrayal of a Romantic longing for
identity and harmony with the natural world.[17] In "The Need of Being
Versed," however, it is not nature that acts as the source of disruption. It
is man who does so, with his vision of the scene as desolate. Nor is this
quite the ambivalence to imagination that has also been remarked in
Frost studies, most fully by Frank Lentricchia. Lentricchia sees Frost
as asserting limits for imagination's power; but only in that the artist,
first, must respect the "crudity which is rawness" that provides him, as
Frost wrote in one letter, with the material from which he then wrests
his form. His art must preserve its contact with "the ugly pressures and
messiness of the empirical world," a task Lentricchia asserts that Frost
accomplishes by countering every assertion of imagination with a
skeptical ironic consciousness.[18] Second, imagination is to be distrusted in that it may be "impelled by a disturbed consciousness," when
"the fictive is projected by the neurotic and the obsessed."[19]

In "The Need of Being Versed," however, it is not pathological
imagination but imagination in its normative role that is problematic.
Not the mind's chaos but the mind's order proves to be the disruptive,
destructive force, reversing the direction and effect of the relation
Lentricchia outlines between imagination and irony. For it is, ironically, irony—the exposure of pathetic fallacy, the retreat of mind—
that, instead of deflating, proves to be welcome, salutary. The nostalgic
mourning for the lost farmstead seemed, by way of disappointed pathetic fallacy, to give way to a nostalgic mourning for a lost identity

with nature. Instead, the release of nature from human identity also releases man. This by no means endorses an independent, innocent nature ordered beyond human experience and human representation: nature is inevitably mediated by and for the human. But it suggests dangers inherent in the activity of mind, especially as mind, in asserting its paradigms for apprehending the world, employs to that purpose a sense of ending. It is not accidental that closure provides the interpretive paradigm for a misreading which is also in this poem a misfortune; for Frost's poem reveals how the interpretive activity itself can imply closure, how the mind's act, closing in on meaning, can involve closure as such. The act of interpretation, that is, carried on and through without limitation, is itself in a sense apocalyptic, and not only when the vision is of apocalypse.

But, with these questions of interpretive paradigms and their consequences, Frost's unobtrusive and unassuming text raises issues whose complexities and enormities shape the American experience throughout its history and the various modes of its several heritages. In personifying nature, in interpreting landscape as his own state, and in projecting the finality of this vision, Frost has not been pursuing a solitary walk on a less travelled road. He has been traversing and tracing one of America's commonest byways, with implications extending beyond this particular and presumably New England farmstead into the general American territory as grasped by American tradition. From the Puritan literalization and historicizing of typology, through the political assertion of identity between American destiny and American territory, and into the economics of settlement and expansion, nature's nation has laid particular claim to the continent it inhabits, in the name of ultimate visions of New Jerusalems attained, paradises regained, and fulfillments of history, sacral and secular. These several and intertwined concerns have been the subject of much scrutiny from various scholarly and critical points of view. Sacvan Bercovitch in a series of studies and collections has explicated the relation within Puritan hermeneutics between what he calls natural theology and federal eschatology, in which the Bible provides not only general insights into spiritual states but the intricate plot, detail by detail, of the Puritan coming to America, which pronounces the realization of the divine promise unfolded in the Bible anew and at last. But this history, with all its millennial import, was no less inscribed for the interpretive gleaning in the Book of Nature, whose every nuance no less encoded an elaborate, and indeed eschatological, significance.[20] Leo Marx, Richard Slotkin, and Myra Jehlen, to name a few, each explores how images of the land impelled, and indeed determined, the social/political forms the nation, as the land's natural expression, came to take.[21] In each case, the confrontation with uncivilized nature—of which, in America, there was so very much—gave rise to an ambivalent response, as at once something to be conquered and something to be obeyed, a world to be imposed upon and yet drawn from. Yet both these impulses are finally forms of possession: identifying the national destiny appropriates the land to human purpose, even if it appears to base the human in the natural. Whether, as Jehlen debates with regard to Emerson, taking nature "as a metaphor for the human mind" curtails or releases man's creative powers, "man is still the focus of all creation," and nature is conceived in man's image. As Emerson himself declares, "Man is placed in the centre of beings, and a ray of relation passes from every other being to him."[22] But to posit reciprocity between mind and nature such that nature provides man with the very basis of his language—as Emerson famously claims in "Nature," calling words the "signs of natural facts"—is still to assume nature-as-construed according to human presuppositions, needs, and above all expectations.[23]

"The land was ours before we were the land's," Frost writes in his perhaps most national poem; but its symmetry of chiasm disguises the asymmetry of possession. And, as Frost shows—in a stance no less familiar to the American tradition—this hermeneutic possession in which the land is ours carries with it an apocalyptic twist. Accounting for everything, appropriating everything into human relevance is ultimately an act of consumption leaving over exactly nothing. As Bercovitch remarks of Emerson's "philology of nature" in which "nature must be the vehicle of his thought," "The real force lies in the relation to . . . Emerson's teleology of nature. His exegetical approach is above all prophetic, his Romantic apocalypse of the mind a guide to vaster prospects ahead." Emerson, equating landscape with redemptive history, appeals to the millennium as manifesting itself immediately and at once in Young America.[24] But neither does the dark side of this apocalyptic vision go unnoticed in American letters. Bercovitch cites Melville's *Pierre* as transforming this hermeneutic vision into "an epiphany of the New World landscape as the apocalypse."[25]

The totalization of meaning can take the aspect of madness: apocalyptic, paranoid, violent, possessive. But the irony of "The Need of Being Versed" offers a welcome release from this tyranny of meaning, this tyranny of the human as it appropriates the non-human without end toward its own ends. Divesting of belief, it institutes possibility. Yet this is an astonishing position: the human is supposed to be that which articulates meaning, and endings, since at least Aristotle, to provide a sense of sense. But here it is the release from the human, from human ends, that is liberating; it is the limitation of the human power to mean and to interpret that permits positive assertion. Yet such a positive retreat poses language against itself, against the very categories that constitute it and which it in turn constitutes. Nietzsche, in *The Will to Power*, warns that "all purposes, aims, meaning are only modes of expression and metamorphoses of one will . . . the will to power," that they are "only an expression for an order of spheres of power and their interplay." But in this interplay language is far from innocent. Cause and effect, aims and ends in fact find their basis "in language, not in beings outside." And conversely "linguistically we do not know how to rid ourselves of them."[26]

Within Frost's canon, the problem of teleology has long been recognized and debated.[27] But just as his stance toward nature may be less a question of Romantic identifications with nature than of specifically American appropriations of it, so the problem of teleology may be, within his poetic, not generally philosophical and thematic only, but rather specifically placed within the venture of American destiny as enacted within an American hermeneutic—where it in turn implicates language as such. In "Education by Poetry," Frost, in a rhetoric less exotic than Nietzsche's, proposes the metaphoric nature of all knowledge, the radically figural nature of human access to the world. "I have wanted in late years," he remarks, "to go further and further in making metaphor the whole of thinking . . . all thinking, except mathematical thinking, is metaphorical." But, he goes on to warn, "unless you are at home in metaphor . . . you are not safe anywhere. Because you are not at ease with figurative values: you don't know the metaphor in its strength and its weakness." For "all metaphor breaks down somewhere. That is the beauty of it. It is touch and go with the metaphor."[28] This insistence on the limits of metaphor in no way negates language's power. Rather, it directs toward language's fuller exercise, less appropriating, more appropriate. "The Need of Being Versed in Country Things" thus concludes with an accomplishment that, grammatically, isn't even certainly asserted—"One had to be versed in country things" does not necessarily entail that one is so versed[29]—and with its positive statement of continued rejoicing cast as a negative one: "Not to believe the phoebes wept." But this is not to declare language as limited in the sense of inadequate to its proper tasks. Rather, the self-demarcation of language, in the space it leaves by retraction and its acknowledgment of its own boundaries, releases man from his own foreclosures, his own totalizations, his own tyrannies. Limitation is then a creative act, a recognition of boundaries in order to affirm linguistic power, to engender its possibilities, and properly to embrace them.

From *Essays in Literature* 18, no. 1 (1991): 76-92. Copyright © 1991 by Western Illinois University Press. Reprinted by permission of Western Illinois University Press.

Notes

1. Robert Frost, letter to John Bartlett, 4 July 1913, *Selected Letters of Robert Frost*, ed. Lawrance Thompson (New York: Holt, 1964) 79-81.

2. As John A. Rea remarks, "It is surprising that of well over 2000 items of Frost scholarship, only a handful have set out to treat formal matters despite the poet's own repeated comments on them." "Language and Form in 'Nothing Gold Can Stay,'" *Robert Frost: Studies of the Poetry*, ed. Kathryn Gibbs Harris (Boston: G. K. Hall, 1979) 17.

3. See, for example, James L. Potter, *Robert Frost Handbook* (University Park: Pennsylvania State UP, 1980) 128. Potter describes form as "one means of resisting the confusion of existence." Basing his discussion on Frost letters of 19 Sept. 1929, 21 Mar. 1935, and 7 Mar. 1938, Donald J. Greiner similarly characterizes "form as a resisting the confusion. Confusion is a boundary against which man can act by creating form. Chaos is what you create form out of." "The Difference Made for Prosody," *Robert Frost: Studies of the Poetry* 5. Karen Lane Rood concurs: "Tension between sentence sounds and form . . . appears to be a direct reflection of Frost's world view. For if Frost admires freedom or wildness in the rhythms of poetry because wildness mirrors the confusion of this world, he also stresses the need to impose some kind of order upon it." "Robert Frost's Sentence Sounds: Wildness Opposing the Sonnet Form," *Robert Frost: Centennial Essays II*, ed. Jac Tharpe (Oxford, MS: UP of Mississippi, 1976) 196.

4. Kathryn Gibbs Harris, "Lyric Impulses," *Robert Frost: Studies of the Poetry* 146.

5. William H. Pritchard, *Frost: A Literary Life Reconsidered* (New York: Oxford UP, 1984) 168.

6. Potter 62, 77.

7. *Interviews with Robert Frost*, ed. E. C. Lathem (New York: Holt, 1966) 199.

8. Robert Frost, "Education by Poetry," *Selected Prose of Robert Frost*, ed. Hyde Cox and Edward Connery Lathem (New York: Collier, 1966) 36.

9. Potter sees the anthropomorphizing in this stanza as undercutting "by a gentler and more sentimental flavor" Frost's realistic assertion of difference between man and nature (77). In *Robert Frost: Modern Poetics and the Landscapes of the Self* (Durham: Duke UP, 1975), Frank Lentricchia understands the narrative perspective in the line "The dry pump flung up an awkward arm" as "an act of sympathetic imagination . . . which leads the self into the fictive world . . . where the precious state of serenity is restored" (83). He therefore sees the anthropomorphizing as a genuine attempt on Frost's part to "link human artifice and nature," but he also argues that the poem finally checks such identification through an ironic consciousness that it exists only in the figures of the poet's language (83-84).

10. Friedrich Schlegel, *Dialogue on Poetry and Literary Aphorisms*, trans. Ernst Behler and Roman Struc (University Park: Pennsylvania State UP, 1968). See, e.g., aphorism No. 108. See also the discussion on Schlegel in Rene Wellek, *History of Modern Criticism* (New Haven: Yale UP, 1955) 2:15.

11. *Selected Prose* 36, 24.

12. For a discussion of Demanian irony, see especially Paul de Man, "The Rhetoric

of Temporality," *Interpretation: Theory and Practice*, ed. John S. Singleton (Baltimore: Johns Hopkins UP, 1969) 191 ff.

13. Leo Marx offers a full discussion of the central place that the farm, as the center of an agrarian economy, held in the American conception of itself as a "middle state" of harmony between primitive nature and civilization. *The Machine in the Garden* (New York: Oxford UP, 1964) 100.

14. Richard Poirier notes this Shakespearean pun in *Robert Frost: The Work of Knowing* (New York: Oxford UP, 1977) x.

15. Lentricchia notes the discordance of these images, but sees them as a false projection of nature's rebirth onto "the artificial human enclosure: the house will come back even as the flowers shall bloom again" (84).

16. Robert Penn Warren, "The Themes of Robert Frost," *The Writer and His Craft: The Hopwood Lectures 1932-1952* (Ann Arbor: U of Michigan P, 1954) 223.

17. For an overview of Frost's relation to nature as "other," see Donald J. Greiner, "Robert Frost as Nature Poet," *Robert Frost: The Poet and His Critics* (Chicago: American Library Association, 1974) 207-48.

18. The quotation from Frost appears in *Selected Letters* 465; it is cited in Lentricchia 145-46. This argument adopts terms familiar to Frost criticism. See, for example, Potter's argument that man needs to achieve the right relationship with confusion, one poised between giving in to it and resisting it too much by the artificial imposition of form (157).

19. Lentricchia 157, 163. Cf. Patricia Wallace, who notes in "The Estranged Point of View: The Thematics of Imagination in Frost's Poetry" that "in Frost's poetry characters possessed of imaginative power are often more cursed than blessed." But she sees its curse as inhering in its disruptive, not ordering aspect, as represented in asocial, violent, nightmare figures. *Robert Frost: Centennial Essays II* 177-78. Lentricchia's argument actually vacillates between attributing imagination's dangers to potential pathology and seeing such dangers as inherent in the act of making "monolithic, absolutizing" visions as such, which is closer to my own argument.

20. See in particular Sacvan Bercovitch, "The Myth of America," *Puritan Origins of the American Self* (New Haven: Yale UP, 1975) 136-86. Also Emory Elliott, "From Father to Son: The Evolution of Typology in Puritan New England," *The Literary Uses of Typology*, ed. Earl Miner (Princeton: Princeton UP, 1977) 204-27. Perry Miller makes the question of nature's religious significance, with the contradictions this entails, a topic in *Nature's Nation* (Cambridge: Harvard UP, 1967) 152-57, 200-04.

21. Marx; Richard Slotkin, *Regeneration Through Violence* (Middletown, CT: Wesleyan UP, 1973); Myra Jehlen, *American Incarnation* (Cambridge: Harvard UP, 1986).

22. Jehlen 106, 110.

23. Jehlen 102; see also Bercovitch 159.

24. Bercovitch 159-60.

25. Bercovitch 162.

26. Frederick Nietzsche, *The Will to Power*, ed. and trans. Walter Kaufmann (New York: Vintage, 1967) sections 675, 552, 562, 551.

27. Nina Baym's early "An Approach to Robert Frost's Nature Poetry" asserts that

Frost "is consistently uncommitted . . . on all such final and teleological questions." *American Quarterly* 17 (1965): 720. George W. Nitchie sees Frost's failure to commit himself as a failure of nerve, a culpable uncertainty. *Human Values in the Poetry of Robert Frost* (New York: Gordian, 1978) 37, 148.

28. *Selected Prose* 37, 41. Compare his remark in his *Paris Review* interview that he could "unsay" just about anything he does say, in an art of "talking contraries." *Writers at Work: Paris Review Interviews*, 2nd Series (New York: Viking, 1963) 28.

29. Pritchard points out that the poem "does not end with positive security, potentially complacent, of being so versed" (168).

National Forgetting and Remembering in the Poetry of Robert Frost_____

Jeff Westover

"Forgetting," wrote the French historian Ernest Renan, "is a crucial factor in the creation of a nation." "Indeed," he continues, "historical enquiry brings to light deeds of violence which took place at the origin of all political formations, even of those whose consequences have been altogether beneficial. Unity is always effected by means of brutality" (11). In the case of the United States, the conquest of Native Americans exemplifies the violence that according to Renan must always be forgotten in the formation of a nation. A number of Robert Frost's poems reflect the necessary forgetting that Renan describes, but many of them engage in acts of remembering that honor the past without subverting any particular ideology. As a poet, Frost is both settled and unsettling, a writer who composes without resorting to simplistic moral categories or the easy romanticization of Indians as noble savages. At the same time that his poems testify to their conflicting positions within the Joycean nightmare of history, Frost himself "distrusted progressive models . . . and was apt to see certain of his inheritances as natural and unchangeable" (Rotella, 242). In his thinking about national history and empire, Frost adopts a Virgilian perspective, assuming that tears are in the nature of things and that in the long-term perspective of human history, the European conquest of the Americas merely gave rise to the world's most recent empire, which in its turn, too, would someday fall. In particular, Frost's treatment of the theme of the American Indian shows that despite the willed forgetting entailed by national narratives, the memory of the brutality that founds the nation persists in the imagination of European Americans. Many of Frost's poems show the ways in which that memory can haunt otherwise confident expressions of patriotism, troubling complacent formulations of American history as a straightforward progress toward freedom and equality.

Benedict Anderson explicates a particular passage from Renan's essay in order to convey the odd temporality of the process of "national forgetting." "The essence of a nation," writes Renan,

> is that all individuals have many things in common, and also that they have forgotten many things. No French citizen knows whether he is a Burgundian, an Alan, a Taifale, or a Visigoth, yet every French citizen has to have forgotten the massacre of Saint Bartholomew, or the massacres that took place in the Midi in the thirteenth century. (11)

Anderson zeroes in on the French phrase that is rendered in this translation as "has to have forgotten," pointing out that Renan wrote "obliged already to have forgotten" instead of "obliged to forget." To him, the phrase "suggests . . . that 'already having forgotten' ancient tragedies is a prime contemporary civic duty. In effect, Renan's readers were being told to 'have already forgotten' what Renan's own words assumed that they naturally remembered!" (200). Anderson accounts for this paradox by arguing that the citizens of modern nations must undergo "a deep reshaping of the imagination of which the state was barely conscious, and over which it had, and still has, only exiguous control" (201). This reshaping exacts a forgetting in order to reconfigure the bloody events of the past as disputes between common members of a nation—as fratricidal or civil conflicts instead of wars between enemies unrelated by blood. This remembering-through-forgetting gives birth to a conception of the nation as an extended family. In his effort to account for the necessity of already having forgotten something one may be expected to know, Anderson writes that

> the creole nationalisms of the Americas are especially instructive. For on the one hand, the American states were for many decades weak, effectively decentralized, and rather modest in their educational ambitions. On the other hand, the American societies, in which "white" settlers were counterposed to "black" slaves and half-exterminated "natives," were internally

riven to a degree quite unmatched in Europe. Yet the imagining of that fraternity, without which the reassurance of fratricide cannot be born, shows up remarkably early, and not without a curious authentic popularity. In the United States of America this paradox is particularly well exemplified. (202)

Forgetting past events in order to reconfigure the nation as a family, the citizens of the United States nonetheless confront themselves (as the plural name of their country suggests) as a diverse population that is anything but a family. Despite American society's being more *gesellschaft* than *gemeinschaft,* Anderson suggests, the need for a sense of national unity is so great that it overcomes (or seeks to overcome) fragmentation by figuring the social contract (*gesellschaft*) of the U.S. Constitution in the kinship terms of family or tribe (*gemeinschaft*). The conflict between these two views of social relations may inform the conflict in Frost's poetry between the dutiful forgetting that accepts the metaphor of the nation as a family and the sometimes less sociable act of remembering that troubles that metaphor. However, unlike Anderson's examples of fraternal partnerships from nineteenth-century American literature (Natty Bumppo and Chingachgook, Ishmael and Queequeg, or Jim and Huck Finn), Frost's poems offer no soothing view of American history as "reassuring fratricide" or a peacefully fraternal companionship (199-203). Frost's speakers might at times sympathize with Native Americans, but they ultimately avoid the sentimentality of transfiguring them from threatening "others" into comforting brothers.

As Frost insisted in his reflection upon his practice as a poet, the category of the nation was fundamental to his identity as a writer. "'Nationality,'" he told an audience at Middlebury College in 1943, "'is something I couldn't live without'" (Cook, 34). For Frost, nationality and individual personality were parallel terms. In "Education by Poetry," he explains what he means:

Look! First I want to be a person. And I want you to be a person, and then we can be as interpersonal as you please. We can pull each other's noses—do all sorts of things. But, first of all, you have got to have the personality. First of all, you have got to have the nations and then they can be as international as they please with each other. (*Collected Poems, Prose, and Plays*, 727)[1]

Similarly, in a letter to Régis Michaud, Frost wrote that

I am as sure that the colloquial is the root of every good poem as I am that the national is the root of all thought and art. It may shoot up as high as you please and flourish as widely abroad in the air, if only the roots are what and where they should be. (*Selected Letters*, 228)

Such comments suggest that the matter of knowing one's national and metaphysical bearings—knowing who and where one is, as "A Cabin in the Clearing" puts it—intimately informs Frost's practice as a poet. This knowledge, as Frost's work also shows, emerges from the dialectic between remembering and forgetting the circumstances of one's country's origins.

Frost reflects his interest in national matters in a number of poems throughout his career. For example, some of his juvenilia ("La Noche Triste," "The Sachem of the Clouds") as well as a few of his mature poems ("The Vanishing Red" and "A Cabin in the Clearing") and one unpublished poem ("Genealogical") deal with the subject of Native Americans, while one of his most famous poems, "The Gift Outright," addresses the matter of the nation's origins, demonstrating the way in which key elements of colonial history are obliged to be forgotten in the process of constructing a grand narrative of national development. In Frost's poetry, remembering becomes a way of both articulating national responsibilities and critiquing forms of patriotism he found too easy.

Frost "once remarked" to Sidney Cox that "one of his passions in boyhood was angry sympathy with the American Indians" (Cox, 21). Two poems among Frost's juvenilia reflect this early interest in Native Americans. "La Noche Triste" (1890), his first published poem, recounts the attack on the Aztec capital Tenochtitlán by Cortez and the rout of his army by Montezuma's army. The other poem, "The Sachem of the Clouds" (1891), clearly evinces the sympathy for American Indians that Frost also articulated in a class debate the same year he published the poem in a local newspaper. In that debate, Frost defended "a bill for removing the Indians from Indian Territory to more fertile districts and ceding said districts to the tribes forever; and for giving them some compensation for the losses already suffered," drawing on "extensive factual information from Helen Hunt Jackson's impassioned indictment, *A Century of Dishonor: A Sketch of the United States Government's Dealings with Some of the Indian Tribes*" (Francis, 10). Subtitled "A Thanksgiving Legend," "The Sachem of the Clouds" acts out a gothic fantasy of revenge on behalf of the Indians. Its commemoration of American aboriginals reflects the white speaker's mournful regret concerning their defeat at the hands of his ancestors. The poem communicates this mourning through the voice and behavior of the sachem, who commands the elements and calls upon them to enact his vengeance on behalf of his people:

> "Come, O come, with storm, come darkness! Speed my clouds on
>   Winter's breath.
> All my race is gone before me, all my race is low in death!
> Ever, as I ruled a people, shall this smoke arise in cloud;
> Ever shall it freight the tempest for the ocean of the proud.
> 'Thanks!' I hear their cities thanking that my race is low in death.
> Come, O come, with storm, come darkness! Speed my clouds on
>   Winter's breath!"
>
> (*CPPP*, 494-95)

As in later poems by Frost (and in such nineteenth-century poems as Lydia Sigourney's "The Cherokee Mother" and "The Indians Welcome to the Pilgrim Fathers"), the voice of the Indian haunts the Poe-like landscape of "The Sachem of the Clouds," unsettling the complacency of his white usurpers: "Thus his voice keeps ringing, ringing, till appears the dreary dawn" (*CPPP*, 495).[2] Yet the enthusiasm for warfare and the awareness of the injustices of the Aztec empire evident in "La Noche Triste" also reappear in Frost's later work, so that contradictory perspectives on Indians and European colonization persist throughout his writing.

Assuming the perspective of "The Sachem of the Clouds" in the later "Genealogical" (1908), a poem he included in a letter but never published, Frost demonstrates something of this "boyhood" passion by writing about his ancestor, the "Indian killer" Charles Frost. In a letter dated January 1908 to Susan Hayes Ward, Frost ironically refers to his forebear as "my bad ancestor the Indian killer" and calls the poem "some Whitmanism of mine" (*Selected Letters*, 42). In addition, in a letter dated December 19, 1911, Frost refers to the poem again, calling it "that authentic bit of family history I once promised you" (*Selected Letters*, 43). The poem links Frost's national and family history in a comic and ironic bond that evokes without resolving the tensions between Native Americans and European settlers:

> It was my grandfather's grandfather's grandfather's
> Great-great-grandfather or thereabouts I think—
> One cannot be too precise in a matter like this.
> He was hanged the story goes. Yet not for grief
> Have I vowed a pilgrimage to the place where he lies
> Under a notable bowlder in Eliot, Maine,
> But for pride if for aught at this distance of time.
> Yearly a chosen few of his many descendants
> At solemn dinner assembled tell over the story
> Of how in his greatness of heart he aspired

To wipe out the whole of an Indian tribe to order,
As in those extravagant days they wasted the woods
With fire to clear the land for tillage.
It seems he was rather pointedly *not* instructed
To proceed in the matter with any particular
Regard to the laws of civilized warfare.
He wasted no precious time in casting about
For means he could call his own. He simply seized
Upon any unprotected idea that came to hand.

(CPPP, 514)

The clearing of land here, extravagant though it is, corresponds to the
title and theme of the later "A Cabin in the Clearing." Like that poem, it
also subtly implies a connection between the cutting down of trees and
the mowing down of men.[3] "Genealogical" contemplates a "pilgrimage" "for pride" to the "notable bowlder" marking the tomb of the ancestor and articulates at the same time a mock repudiation of the colonial ancestor's deeds. The poet's imagined pilgrimage instead turns out
to be an account of the ancestor's grim pillage of the Indians and their
land. His already ironic pride turns into an amused chagrin.

With his joking repetition of ancestral grandfathers, his admission
that "One cannot be too precise in a matter like this," and his colloquial
aside ("He was hanged the story goes"), Frost suggests the legendary
character of the narrative that follows. Given the vagaries of oral transmission resulting from the changes that creep into a story as it gets
passed from generation to generation, Frost's casually dropped remark
turns out to be more significant than it may first appear. It hints at the
fictive quality of the entire narrative, evoking (or provoking) the
reader's desire for an entertaining tale at the same time that it subtly undercuts the veracity of the events to be recounted. Like "The Vanishing
Red," "The Witch of Coös," and "Paul's Wife," "Genealogical" has an
air of the tall tale about it; the narrator of this poem delivers his account
with a nod and a wink. Part of the pleasure of the poem is in the narra-

tive performance, including any touches of excess that may embellish the story line here and there. In the process of that performance, inherited views about the colonization of North America and the origins of the United States are scrutinized, challenged, and reshaped.

"Genealogical" is thematically linked not only to Frost's youthful "Sachem of the Clouds" but to his more mature poem "The Vanishing Red." Significantly, the association of eating with murder occurs in both "Genealogical" and "The Vanishing Red," an association that figures colonial dispossession as a form of cannibal savagery. The angry rapacity of the Miller in "The Vanishing Red," which I will discuss later, figures the colonial dispossession of indigenous inhabitants by white invaders. In "Genealogical," Frost represents his ancestor's massacre of the Indians at the banquet to which he has invited them. Once they arrived, Frost writes,

> he fell upon them with slaughter
> And all that he didn't slay he bound and sold
> Into slavery where Philip the Chief's son went.
>
> (*CPPP*, 515)

Motivated as it is by the desire for the lands they inhabit, Charles Frost's ruse of a "barbecue" (a word derived from Taino, a Caribbean Indian language)[4] also represents his assault as a devouring violence, for after the ambush, we are told, he remained a "good sleeper and eater" and "serenely forgot" those who escaped his power. Frost undercuts the "heroism" of this betrayal by following up the report with the offhand remark that "He doubtless called the place something and claimed the victory" (*CPPP*, 515). The intentional vagueness of "doubtless" and "something" deflates the significance of the event, translating the victor's ritual from a sublime naming that affirms the heroism of action into a satiric travesty of triumph, while the second half of the predicate ("claimed the victory") may be read as a buoyant announcement of conquest or a doubting account of the ancestral Major's version of events. As so often in Frost's poems, the imagined tone of voice is crucial, for a stress on "claimed" suggests that what the Major claimed as a great victory was in fact a grave ignominy. And the claim he stakes is for the land formerly used by the Amerindians he has vanquished.

While Charles Frost's ruse of a dinner is echoed in the Miller's treachery in "The Vanishing Red," it also makes his ambush a murderous violation of the rites of hospitality. This violation is on the disastrous order of the grisly feast Atreus gave his brother Thyestes, for it too entails a long and painful legacy that persists over the course of many generations. In provisionally conceiving of American history as family history, Frost's burlesque acts out the consequential events of another family's ancient tragedy. In the same way that Atreus's betrayal of his brother left a curse on their family for many generations to come, Frost's "Genealogy" records a curse that indelibly marks the history of the United States. The dinners Charles's scions sponsor in his honor ritually repeat his treachery. In this regard, Frost's reference to his family's banquet echoes "The Sachem of the Clouds" by ironically revising traditional Thanksgiving narratives of pilgrim-Indian cooperation, replacing their falsifying solace with a less felicitous but perhaps more perspicacious version of the nation's misremembered origins.

Frost's burlesque rendering of his ancestor Charles's death, burial, exhumation, and reburial in "Genealogical" suggests that he very much enjoys debunking his remembered progenitor: the poet evokes the figure of his forebear, kills him off, grants him a sodden resurrection in the form of a desecrating disinterment and posthumous hanging, and finally returns him to the earth of his "eternal" rest. "All that detracted from the glory of" the Major's "achievement," Frost writes,

Was the escape of a few of the devoted tribesmen
Either by running away or staying away
An awkward remnant that would have lain, methinks,
Even upon my somewhat sophisticated conscience
Given to the sympathetic fallacy of attributing to savages
The feelings of human beings,
More heavily than those who were slain.
He good sleeper and eater serenely forgot them.
But here again he just missed greatness as a captain.
For these waylaid him one Sunday on his way home
From the proper church completely edified
And slew him in turn with great barbarity
And left him outspread for filial burial.
His sons with dignity dug him a decent grave
And duly laid him to rest.
But the Redskins, not quite sure they had done enough
To satisfy the eternal vengeances,
Returned and had him out of the ground and hanged him up.
And so he was hanged!
The indefatigable sons cut him down and buried him again,
And this time to secure him against further disturbance,
With the help of their neighbors at a sort of burying bee
They rolled a stone upon him that once it was sunk in place
Not strong men enough could come at together to lift it.

(CPPP, 515-16)

Frost satirizes the self-righteous and perhaps puritanical religion of his ancestor when he reports that the survivors of his attack "waylaid him on Sunday on his way home/ From the proper church completely edi- fied" (515). Frost means us to share his delight in the "great barbarity" of the Indian reprisal and his scorn for "the proper church" from which Charles exits (and that no doubt countenanced the white mistreatment of the Indians). Whereas the dead obtrude on the living as an eerie irruption of the nether world in Robert Lowell's "At the Indian Killer's Grave," a poem which shares a similar theme but which treats it somewhat differently, "Genealogical" is an irreverent exhumation, for it digs up the dead ancestor (not once but twice) in order to defame him. Frost performs his own revenge against his ancestor by evoking a poetic effigy of him in order to malign and shame it. The poem reverses the conventions of elegy by denigrating the achievement of the dead man. Instead of simply honoring Charles Frost through his poetic commemoration, Robert Frost looks back at his example with a mixture of chagrin and humor: "And there he lies in glory the ancestor of a good many of us./ And I think he explains my lifelong liking for Indians" (516). Although it is a private joke fraught with oedipal impudence, "Genealogical" also squarely plants Frost the poet in "the bloody loam" of his nation's history. For in a sense he is the descendant of his ancestor's deceit. While the poem remained, as I have indicated, a *private* joke or entertainment in the corpus of Frost's writing, a piece he consciously excluded from his published work, its appearance in a letter might suggest, if we follow the logic of Mark Richardson, that it offers a less diplomatic but more "sincere" version of Frost's view of the relationship between poetry and society than his published poetry does (54-75).

Frost's reference to his "somewhat sophisticated conscience" explicitly conveys the guilt regarding colonial injustice against Native Americans that often remains unspoken in his published works. Given the stylized humor of the phrase, Frost makes clear his sense of irony regarding the putative superiority of his conscience to that of his ancestor, poking fun at his own self-righteous stance even as he exposes the racism that regards Amerindians as "savages" who lack "the feelings of human beings." Frost's wry phrase suggests that he is aware of historicity as well as history. He seems to imply that his sense of things may in the end be no better than that of his ancestor or his contemporaries, recognizing how easy it is to condemn aspects of a past in which one has not personally participated but from which one has nonetheless benefited. As Richardson observes, Frost acknowledges that "It is a *fallen* world" in which we live, one "not subject to any but a 'divine redemption'—and that, one gathers, is *not* forthcoming" (159). Charles Frost's atrocity was only one in a larger pattern of sinful dispossessions upon which the possessions of his scion's famous poem "The Gift Outright" depend. Frost the poet also knows the story he inherits is not an unusual one. The poet's relation to the account demonstrates his larger-than-American sense of man's inhumanity to man, which puts him at odds with the view that the American empire is somehow exceptional. For him, the American imperium is neither more nor less monstrous than previous forms of empire. The poet's emphatic commemoration in "Genealogical" of the brutality of colonial history demonstrates his awareness of the unsettled, conflicting nature of his country's origins and history. It provides an account of the dispossession of Native Americans that "The Gift Outright," with its self-conscious ceremony and celebration, will be obliged to forget.

In "Genealogical" Frost situates himself as a reader of his forefather's act by comparing his own identity as a poet to the Major's identity as "renegade" statesman and de facto soldier:

> I will not set up the claim for my progenitor
> That he was an artist in murder or anything else
> Or that any of his descendants would have been
> Without the infusion of warmer blood from somewhere.
> Were it imperative to distinguish between statesman and artist
> I should say that the first believes that the end justifies the means
> The second that the means justify the end.
>
> (*CPPP*, 515)

The rhetoric here ("an artist in murder or anything else") is comic, suggesting that Frost is joking as much about his own artistry as his progenitor's military maneuvers. The "infusion of warmer blood" he deems necessary to account for his poetic temperament separates him from the cold-blooded killing of "the Major," but it also draws on stock racial stereotypes that associate southern climates such as those found in the Mediterranean region and in Latin America with passionate dispositions. Moreover, the strategic scheming Charles Frost displayed in laying his ambush is not categorically different from the cool-headed calculation his descendant mustered in the practice of his craft as a poet. Frost's phrase betrays his sense that art is in fact a kind (but *only* a kind) of murder. Perhaps he was thinking of his wife Elinor's dislike of his publishing when he composed the line (Meyers, 160-61, 165).

More significant, perhaps, is the chiasmus Frost relies on to define the differences between politics and poetry and between Charles Frost and himself. The Major does not quite earn the title of "statesman," but the poet's identification of him as such nonetheless reflects the careers of the many soldier-statesmen who won U.S. elections after having served in wars against the Indians. According to the poet's discriminating definitions, the "statesman" "believes that the end justifies the means," whereas the "artist" believes the reverse, that "the means justify the end." If the poet doesn't quite achieve his desired end in "Genealogical," it is the fault of his artistic means and not of his maverick ancestor's bloody ends. The Major's dispossession clears the ground for his people's settlement, but the unsettling memories of colonization persist even in the midst of the benefits the settlers bequeathed to their descendants. In "Genealogical," the logic of a lineage becomes the figure for a nation's history, though this logic works differently from the mythology that Renan and Anderson describe, which recasts conflicts between conquerors and conquered as conflicts between kin. The war Frost depicts is not a civil one.

Frost's arch homage to his family patriarch ends up honoring the Indian victims of his ancestor more than the ancestor himself. This unsentimental twist leaves as its legacy a sense of the Indian's persisting presence in America even at the moment of his supposed eclipse. In this respect "Genealogical" serves as a thematic counterpart to "The Vanishing Red," while its meditation on the issues of settlement and dispossession link it to the later poems "The Gift Outright" and "A Cabin in the Woods" as well.

In "The Vanishing Red," published in the 1916 collection *Mountain Interval*, Frost renders a shocking gothic portrait of racial hatred in 29 brief but compelling lines. The voice of the poem's narrator is extraordinarily intimate and colloquial. In the first two lines, the narrator repeats the verb phrase "is said to" twice, affirming the second-hand basis of the narrative that follows, a fact that Karen L. Kilcup observes when she says that Frost's repetition "highlights the poem's 'made' quality, its legendary framework" (56). The rumored report that the narrator gives is precisely the stuff from which legends develop, and the details with which the narrator tells his story make it memorable enough to last as legend as well.

Both the poem's title and the hedging declaration of its first sentence refer to the genocidal decimation of Amerindian peoples at the hands of their white supplanters. They simultaneously remember and forget, in other words, the colonial displacement that lies at the center of American history. Alluding to the nineteenth-century commonplace that the Indians were dying out, the poem's title makes its reference metonymically, by virtue of its racial designation. This identification by color is of course reinforced and clarified in the first line of the poem with the phrase "the last Red Man," but it also implies that the vision of the Miller in the poem is colored by blood. As Sidney Cox writes, "He saw red," not only in his assessment of the Indian according to the color of his skin rather than the content of his character, but in the bloody visions of his murderous plan (22-23). The narrator introduces his two chief characters in the evasive language of the first three lines of the poem:

> He is said to have been the last Red Man
> In Acton. And the Miller is said to have laughed—
> If you like to call such a sound a laugh.
>
> (*CPPP*, 136)

The reductions of the characters of the story to the racial and professional designations that identify them establish the legendary anonymity that characterizes the poem as a whole, indicating (despite its meter) its ballad-like quality. It also throws into relief the violent tension that will erupt between them.

The Miller's defensive repetition of the interrogative phrase "Whose business" in the following passage characterizes his as-yet-undescribed deed in terms of a familiar idiom that associates the murder of the Indian as part of his profession, his own personal "business":

> But he gave no one else a laugher's license.
> For he turned suddenly grave as if to say,
> "Whose business—if I take it on myself,
> Whose business—but why talk round the barn?—
> When it's just that I hold with getting a thing done with."
>
> (*CPPP*, 136)

The Miller is indeed a man of business; he prefers action to troublesome mincing words. For him, business is a thing whole, while words reduce reality to confusing and disjointed pieces. The Miller, in repeating his rhetorical question regarding the interest of others in his affairs ("Whose business . . . ?"), insists that his murderous activity is clearly his *own*. In rendering the Indian a literal grist to his mill, Frost figures the white man's act as an expression of commercial voracity. Frost's answer to the Miller's question would be the same he attributes to Terence in "The Constant Symbol": "all human business is my business" (*CPPP*, 787). Frost proves this claim in the text of his poem, for part of the artist's ethics is to reveal to his audience all dimensions of human experience—even those we label "inhuman." Frost's fable tropes the industrial capitalism of his own day as a murderous machine that a white proprietor turns to his own racist ends. It is in this sense that the fate of "The Vanishing Red" is most fully consumed in the Miller's personal business.

In the second stanza of the poem, the narrator explicitly sets his tale in the context of the historical conflicts between European invaders and Amerindian inhabitants. Yet in doing so, the narrator just as explicitly, if deceptively, insists that the story about the Miller is the result of something more personal and complicated than the ongoing conflicts "between the two races." In reporting his tale, the narrator seems to invite a sympathetic or at least nonjudgmental perspective towards the Miller. "You can't get back and see it as he saw it," the narrator insists.

> It's too long a story to go into now.
> You'd have to have been there and lived it.
> Then you wouldn't have looked on it as just a matter
> Of who began it between the two races.
>
> (*CPPP*, 136)

The narrator contradicts himself in claiming that "It's too long a story to go into now" and then denying that the murder was "just a matter/ Of who began it between the two races." On the one hand, the narrator's first *it* would appear to refer to the relationship between Europeans and Amerindians in all its sweep and complexity. Hence the pronoun implicitly *remembers* the dispossession of Native Americans inaugurated by the establishment of the United States. On the other hand, the second *it* is much more clearly delimited, apparently referring to the specific act of the Miller, and so it represses the memory of that original dispossession. That second pronoun, however, is literally circumscribed by syntax that refers to the colonial conflict between whites and reds: "This story that is 'too long' 'to go into now,'" writes Kilcup, "is in fact what the poem unfolds" (56). Despite the mystifying apologia of the narrator, then, the appalling history of relations between conquering pioneers and indigenous occupants clearly contributes to the animosity of the Miller. In a manner that conforms to the pattern described by Renan, his animosity at once evokes the origin of the United States and willfully forgets it.

That his animosity takes a *bodily* form, moreover, is a testament to the powerful sway of racist ideology over the individual mind. In this case, the Miller's visceral response to the "guttural exclamation" of his Indian visitor, perhaps corresponds to an ideology of race as a matter of blood. If over time the conception of race as a biological category has fallen into scientific disrepute, it nevertheless exercises a powerful hold over the Miller's imagination. It is noteworthy that the Miller's disgust is triggered by a not fully verbal expression on the part of the "Red Man," a noise that connotes the bestial:

> Some guttural exclamation of surprise
> The Red Man gave in poking about the mill,
> Over the great big thumping, shuffling millstone,
> Disgusted the Miller physically as coming
> From one who had no right to be heard from.
>
> (*CPPP*, 136)

The indirect discourse of the last line of this passage registers the Miller's prejudice, as does the description of the Red Man's inspection of the mill, an act that the Miller clearly regards as offensive. Masking his umbrage, the Miller invites him to have a closer look. Like the narrator of Poe's "The Cask of Amontillado," the Miller ushers the Indian "down below a cramping rafter," leading his guest to an unsuspected but carefully premeditated death.

While the narrator's details are lavished upon the circumstances of the Miller's disgust and the spectacular dash of the mill's "water in desperate straits like frantic fish,/ Salmon and sturgeon, lashing with their tails," he characterizes the "Red Man" only very sparingly, rendering through such reticence a figure of almost complete inscrutability. This inscrutability proves to be a cynosure of the Miller's prejudicial malice, for he ascribes to the Indian an emptiness that he fills with his own bigoted beliefs about him. Because of his preconceptions about Indians in general, he attributes to this specific individual an unflattering innocence and lumbering imbecility.

The Indian, moreover, does not even speak; his "guttural exclamation of surprise" at the sight of the mill, about which he surreptitiously pokes like an awkward animal, suggests that in the view of the Miller he is not even capable of "real" speech. In attributing to the Indian a bestial or childlike speechlessness (a true form of infancy, if one recalls that the Latin root of that word, *infans*, means "speechless"), the Miller reduces the Indian to something like a cipher of the white man's prejudice (Kilcup, 56). The Indian is not even granted a distinguishing appellation; one feels that the Miller's addressing him as "John" is done with a total disregard for the man's actual name (although this anonymity may of course also be part of the generic conventions of the poem). When the narrator makes his grisly report in the closing lines of the poem, he reinforces the suggestions of cannibal commodification evoked earlier by the Miller's vocabulary of "business":

> [The Miller] took him down below a cramping rafter,
> And showed him, through a manhole in the floor,
> The water in desperate straits like frantic fish,
> Salmon and sturgeon, lashing with their tails.
> Then he shut down the trap door with a ring in it
> That jangled even above the general noise,
> And came upstairs alone—and gave that laugh,
> And said something to a man with a meal sack
> That the man with the meal sack didn't catch—then.
> Oh, yes, he showed John the wheel pit all right.
>
> (*CPPP*, 136)

While the Europeans, as Eric Cheyfitz and others point out, convinced themselves that there were cannibals to be found everywhere among the Amerindians they had "discovered," such beliefs were not accurate. The disparity between expectation and actuality did not, however, prevent Europeans from corrupting the designation *Carib* into *cannibal* and thereby inventing a phenomenon through a process of willful misnaming (Cheyfitz, 41-44). Such misnaming, of course, reflects the way in which European assumptions shaped colonial assessments of the New World. Like the "tapestried landscape" of expectation to which Elizabeth Bishop alludes in "Brazil: January 1, 1502," the conventions of Indian behavior and of relations between Amerindians and Euro-Americans that Frost evokes and reconfigures in "The Vanishing Red" conform to familiar preconceptions.

Jeffrey S. Cramer points out that Frost used a local tale as the basis of "The Vanishing Red." "According to an annotation made by Frost in a copy of *Mountain Interval*," Cramer writes, "the story was told to him by someone from Acton" (59). In this tale that Frost recasts in poetic form, the Miller reverses that earlier pattern in which whites accused Indians of being cannibals, for in his unreported remark "to a man with a meal sack," the Miller suggests that he has converted the Indian from grist to gristle, making him into a food commodity, a horrible flour of bone meal and blood. The Miller moves, then, from the physical disgust he felt before the living Indian's "guttural" outburst, to a grotesque appetite for his dead and mutilated body. The Miller's "wheel pit," writes Robert Faggen, is Frost's "metaphor for a machinery that inexplicably allows one creature to extirpate another" (121).

The narrator of Frost's poem does not merely reproduce some more or less expected prejudice against Native Americans, however. Just as he identifies "the last Red Man" by his race, he names the white man by his occupation. Hence both red and white men are identified by something other than personal categories. In the language and generic conventions of the poem, both men remain types, distanced from the reader by a mist of time and anonymity. In addition, the narrator modifies his opening description of the Miller's reputed laugh with the modifying line "If you like to call such a sound a laugh." That parenthesis finesses even further the narrator's already tentative report. The narrator's hedging rhetoric suggests the limitations of his knowledge about the tale he so carefully retails (or, as the etymology of this verb intimates, "cuts up" into the meaty parcels of a poetic account for his readers' eager consumption).

The narrator does not even know what the Miller "really" thinks. He has to infer his motives and emotions from his laughter and his sudden gravity, for we are told that "he turned suddenly grave *as if* to say,/ 'Whose business,—if I take it on my self,'" not that the Miller actually said these words. The poem evokes a series of expectations from its readers that are based on a shared knowledge of American culture and history—and it plays with them with an intensely gothic glee in order to expose them. The poem resists the reader's efforts to pin down the perspective of the narrator at the same time that it invites its reader to condemn or condone his perspective rather than the Miller's racial bigotry—or even the reader's own prejudices. For this reason, a reader risks misreading the narrator's function in the poem—which is to elicit the reader's emotions about the event he describes without "committing" himself too demonstratively to either the position of "John" or "the Miller." This aspect of the poem's diegesis, or account of events, constitutes not only part of the wit and fascination of the poem but also a large part of its political content. While it is not clear, as Kilcup argues, that the narrator speaks "from the point of view of someone who has not only heard the story but also been present during its actual enactment" (maybe he was, maybe he wasn't), her claim that "the narrator intimates the responsibility of the voyeuristic audience, himself included, in the murder that transpired" does seem accurate. The poem implies the Miller's murder of the red man, but the narrative of that murder itself "remains painfully unspoken" (57). "If in 'The Vanishing Red' John is hardly noble," Kilcup writes, "then, in a supremely ironic twist, the Miller becomes the savage" (59).

In a poem that bespeaks the genocidal plight of Amerindians without presuming to speak for them (either those who are dead or their survivors), Frost articulates a central tension of American history through a powerfully telling silence. If for the Miller, John's "guttural exclamation" signifies his insuperable distance from language, for Frost's reader, the poem turns on the Miller's (initially) "illegible" laugh. Articulation disappears down the well of his laughter. But it disappears only momentarily, to reappear with a vengeance in the implications of the poem as a whole. Frost's articulation in "The Vanishing Red" resides as much "between the lines" of the poem as it does in the words that constitute it.

Hayden Carruth may be right to argue that "the heart of the poem is the Miller's laugh," but if he is, it seems to me that he makes this argument for the wrong reason (34). Carruth reads the Miller's laugh as an existential response to the absurdity of "Man destroying himself, held in the absolute need to destroy himself," but that laugh is in fact the sign of something much uglier and more reprehensible. After all, the poem depicts one man destroying another man, *not* himself. The laugh—or something approaching that ("If you like to call it a laugh")—actually expresses the Miller's defensive complacency regarding his murderous "business": "the Miller is also uncomfortable, of course, laughing off his own feeling of guilt. What he has done is more savage than anything the red man . . . ever did" (Cox, 23). In this sense, "The Vanishing Red" temporarily buries language in a cacophonous cackle. Carruth's perceptive reflection on the role of New England "understatement" in the poem shows how language is both defeated and redeemed, or made to speak beyond its limitations, in "The Vanishing Red." "There is rarely a shriek in Frost," Carruth writes. "The Red Man just vanishes—not a word. The trap door says it, and then the Miller's laugh" (35).

Kilcup also comments on the poem's curious silences, but she does so in order to decipher the moral and political issues it both bespeaks and obscures. "The ultimate horror of the murder," she writes, "is its concealment, both concretely and linguistically" (58). In that concealment, the narrator's attempt to maintain some sort of objectivity fatally fails:

The speaker himself intimates and covers the violence with ostensibly detached and shockingly ironic language like "a *manhole* in the floor" (emphasis added). Next it is muffled by the noise of busyness, of business, and then the final line of the poem buries the Miller's guilt in a metaphoric and linguistic hole that renders it even more abhorrent because of the vacuum of moral responsibility it conceals: "Oh yes, he showed John the wheel-pit all right." The auditor inside the poem—like the speaker and the reader—shares the Miller's guilt, for he "didn't catch" what the latter tells him until much later. (Kilcup, 58)

Like Kilcup, Cox reads the poem as an indictment of the reader's complicity in the Miller's act: "those who shared the Miller's civilization," he points out, "never did anything about the murder of the Indian" (24). In its dissolution of the narrator's attempted distance between himself and his story lies the performative power of Frost's poem. It undoes the appropriative lust figured by the Miller's macabre mill.

In "A Cabin in the Clearing" (circulated in 1951 as his Christmas poem to friends), Frost evokes the pioneer tradition and colonial settlement that characterize U.S. history. By relating the issue of place to the matter of self-knowledge, Frost repeats the trope of "The Gift Outright" (first published in 1942) and suggests that the settlements of American history are vexed ones that need to be worked out in a more satisfactory way. Although the question of knowing who and where the cabin dwellers "are" would appear to be ultimately metaphysical, Frost explicitly grounds the psychological considerations of his poem in the local and material settings of a representative American "clearing." National heritage and the pioneer ethos, after all, provide the basis of the metaphors in "Cabin." In "A Cabin in the Clearing," writes J. Albert Robbins, Frost "employs a metaphor uniquely American," even though he means that metaphor to speak "for all men" (62). In "Genealogical," as I have shown, Frost considers the life and behavior of a family ancestor in relation to the Native Americans whom that ancestor displaces and kills. Frost daringly interrogates national history through the metaphor of his individual ancestry, revealing the internal divisions of the nation and calling attention to its bloody origins. In "The Vanishing Red," which functions as a fable of white-red relations in North America, Frost shows that the still unresolved tensions of settlement persist in the "unsettling" specter of the subjugated Indian. The resonant metaphors of possession in "The Gift Outright" can be related to the historical dispossession of the Indians of North America, and the experience of existential displacement in "The Gift Outright" and "A Cabin in the Clearing" is symbolically linked to the bodily "displacement" acted out in "The Vanishing Red," which represents the wholesale displacement of Indians from their "land of living" at the hands of the European colonizers.

This phrase, "land of living," is a biblical one that Frost uses in "The Gift Outright," and I use it here to refer to the land that American aborigines cultivated in order to get their living before they were pushed into other regions or defeated in battle by settlers. At one end of the social spectrum, the colonial rapacity for land reflected the wealth and prestige of land ownership in European culture, while on the other, the tenure of land by pioneer farmers simply represented their need for sustenance—for "making a living." Both conditions account for the pathos commonly associated with the pioneer homestead. The figure of the settler is so powerful in the symbolic iconography of America because it embodies the quintessentially American ideal of independent self-sufficiency, the autonomy on which American freedom is based ideologically. Nevertheless, Frost's poems often remind us that the rugged individual of the American frontier won independence through violent displacements that have not only hurt Amerindians but have haunted the conscience of the pioneers' descendants ever since. In this way, Frost's poems continually raise the unsettled questions of American settlement.

"A Cabin in the Clearing," for example, presents its reader with a pioneer vista discussed by the personified smoke and mist surrounding the cabin. As Robbins notes, "the metaphor of wilderness and clearing is made to carry much of the poet's meaning, whether we read the lines psychologically, historically, or spiritually" (73). Frost uses dialogue form to make statements that are in one sense about the metaphysical "place" of the cabin's inhabitants and at the same time about those inhabitants' sense of themselves as participants in a distinctive nation among other nations. Frost links the human and natural world by characterizing Smoke as the by-product of the domestic activities of the cabin-dwellers; in the course of the poem, Smoke is both a sign of domestic warmth and the airborne matter given off by human efforts to win a "living" from the fruit of the now-tilled American "wilderness." It is also the by-product of clearing land by fire. Similarly, Mist is the hovering cloud of water that "cottons to their landscape." It saturates that landscape, furnishing one of the ingredients necessary to the growth of the foodstuffs that sustain the dwellers in the cabin.

The representative of doubt, Mist, begins the poem by asserting, "I don't believe the sleepers in this house/ Know where they are." Smoke, the defender of the cabin's inhabitants, adopts a more optimistic outlook, stressing the accomplishments of the people whom Mist only recognizes as "sleepers." Smoke points out that

> They've been here long enough
> To push the woods back from around the house
> And part them in the middle with a path.

Mist, the inveterate questioner, repeats his claim: "And still I doubt if they know where they are./ And I begin to fear they never will" (427). The debate broached by Frost's two speakers turns on their view of the settlers who inhabit the cabin and the clearing over which the speakers hover. As "the guardian wraith of starlit smoke,/ That leans out this and that way from their chimney," Mist's interlocutor literally flows from the interior, domestic space of the settlers he describes. Smoke's defensive posture derives from his closer proximity to the cabin-dwellers, but it turns out that Mist, too, is involved in their lives and livelihood. Although Mist's existence is external to their hearth, he is

> the damper counterpart of smoke
> That gives off from a garden ground at night
> But lifts no higher than a garden grows.

Mist may be outside the house but, as he tells Smoke, "I cotton to their landscape" and "I am no further from their fate than you are" (*CPPP*, 428). Taken together, then, Frost's interlocutors represent products of the labor of the cabin's inhabitants and natural features of the landscape. These forces speak from a vantage "above" that of the human beings they discuss. The perspective Frost attributes to these personified elements is more encompassing than that of the silent (if overheard) humans of the poem. And fond as the speakers might be of these human settlers, they also see their shortcomings.

At one point, for example, Smoke remarks of the cabin-dwellers that "They must by now have learned the native tongue./ Why don't they ask the Red Man where they are?" (428). Smoke's question, alluding perhaps to the cliché of Indian smoke signals, implies that the Indian offers a clue to the identity and destiny of the cabin's inhabitants. Mist's reply—"They often do, and none the wiser for it"—provides an ironic rejoinder that hints at the possibly misguided outlook of those inside the cabin. Mist's remarks affirm the characterization of the Indian as a knowledgeable forebear whose relationship to the land offers an important form of wisdom that could mitigate the spiritual disorientation of their dispossessing successors. "A Cabin in the Clearing" explicitly associates the Amerindian with the genius loci of the New World, but it also satirizes the effort to recapitulate the Indian as a trope for indigenous national culture by portraying the pioneer inhabitants of the cabin as "none the wiser" for having sought out the Native American for his wisdom. "Cabin" shows that the Native American is a permanently haunting feature on the landscape of the American consciousness, but it shows at the same time that the pioneers inhabit a world that is not commensurate with the Native American one. The ghost of the Amerindian can roam through the dreams of Americans only because, as D. H. Lawrence argued, their numbers have so dramatically dropped (40-41).

Smoke's response is less a rebuttal of than a meditative concurrence with Mist's speculations, for he agrees that the cabin-dwellers may never clearly comprehend their identity and their destiny. The settlers, it seems, have lost their bearings, and this fundamental disorientation may prove to be permanent. Mist concedes that the occupants of the clearing spend a lot of energy trying to learn the qualities of their location and the nature of their relationship to it, and he ambiguously characterizes their piecemeal approach as "fond," meaning both foolish *and* affectionate. Taking up the thread of Mist's thought, Smoke goes on to consider the history of these newcomers. "If the day ever comes when they know who/ They are," says Smoke,

> they may know better where they are.
> But who they are is too much to believe—
> Either for them or the onlooking world.
>
> (*CPPP*, 428)[5]

In an interesting shift that approximates Mist's skepticism, Smoke observes that such people "are too sudden to be credible." As latecomers to the stage of world history, Americans remain blind to their true status in the world (for "who they are is too much to believe"—their status outstrips their credibility). Yet in another sense, too, are they beleaguered by being "too sudden," for "sudden" in this context can mean both "historically belated" and "spontaneous" (or "impulsive"). Being "too sudden" implies belated youthfulness but also reckless immaturity. No opprobrium attaches to the fact of their late emergence in the world, however abrupt, but the want of tact and deliberation associated with immaturity is a more serious matter. The ambiguity of Frost's phrase both grants and withholds its sympathy, for it at once countenances and condemns the anonymous inhabitants it describes. On the one hand, these pioneers are "too sudden" in appearing in the clearing and before the audience of "the onlooking world" through no fault of their own, but on the other, their "too sudden" behavior is embarrassingly precipitate.

Mist concludes the colloquy by inviting his partner to "listen" in on the settlers "talking in the dark." This scene dramatizes Frost's exemplary scenario in an important letter to John Bartlett, in which he tells his friend that "The best place to get the abstract sound of sense is from the voices behind a door that cuts off the words. . . . It is the abstract vitality of our speech. It is pure sound—pure form" (*Selected Letters*, 80). If the sleepy speech of the inhabitants ultimately amounts to so much "haze," their words are nevertheless all they have, for in this context they approach what Frost calls "the abstract vitality of our speech," which he conceives of as a Platonically "pure form." Frost's witty play on "eavesdropping" pleases him so much he repeats it. In doing so, he underscores his characterization of the poem as a critical but baffled inquiry into the meaning of the inhabitants' location and identity in the rhyming couplet that rounds it out: "*Who*" is "*better*" equipped, asks the newly introduced narrator, "*than smoke and mist*" to "*appraise/ The kindred spirit of an inner haze*" (*CPPP*, 428). Frost's choice of verb is quite precise, and yet the judicious connoisseurs this verb prompts one to expect turn out to be the murky interlocutors of the poem. Smoke and mist "appraise," or search out and evaluate, the moral worth of the cabin's inhabitants. The "inner haze" of the cabin dwellers corresponds to the material haze of Smoke and Mist.

One way to read this short dialogue is in the context of the other poems I have discussed—that is, as a meditation on the nation and its history, including the people's sense of itself, its location, and its position in the world beyond its borders. As a dialogue, it involves some give and take, and although it ends on a negative note, it at least offers a modicum of sympathy and hope regarding the inhabitants of "the clearing." Frost's decision to include "A Cabin in the Clearing" as the title poem of his 1962 book indicates the personal significance that the myth of the pioneer held for him. Despite the widespread urbanization of the country by the 1950s and the imperial forays that multiplied in the wake of the second world war, the picture of the nation as a wilderness inhabited by a hardy people lingers as a powerful icon for the poet and his readers.

Yet Mist's insistence that the cabin's inhabitants know neither where nor who they are makes "all the difference" to one's understanding of the poem, for that insistence transfigures received notions of the nation. At the same time that the poem evinces an affection for the people inside the cabin, it questions and criticizes their circumstances. As I have suggested, although these circumstances have cosmic and existential dimensions, they also have more local and political ones. Frost's language is broad enough in its implications to allow for all of these meanings. "A Cabin in the Clearing" figures the cultural and political issues associated with the country's settlement in the simple image of an isolated cabin. Frost's homestead resonates more or less immediately within American political culture—or at least it did so for a period of time that extended through Frost's cultural moment. Because of that legacy, it is still possible to interpret the poet's cabin and clearing as a representative American settlement, and therefore as a space that engages the issues of national remembering and forgetting.

While the cabin-dwellers that Mist and Smoke discuss may be interpreted as the American common man and woman, Frost portrays contemporary Americans as the descendants of pioneers much more explicitly in "The Gift Outright." The voice the speaker of this poem adopts is confidently representative, for there is no breach between the national "we" inscribed in the poem and the individual who pronounces that "we." In fact, the poem dramatizes the nation's constitution of the speaker as well as the reader as citizens:

The land was ours before we were the land's.
She was our land more than a hundred years
Before we were her people. She was ours
In Massachusetts, in Virginia,
But we were England's, still colonials,
Possessing what we still were unpossessed by,
Possessed by what we now no more possessed.
Something we were withholding made us weak
Until we found out that it was ourselves
We were withholding from our land of living,
And forthwith found salvation in surrender.
Such as we were we gave ourselves outright
(The deed of gift was many deeds of war)
To the land vaguely realizing westward,
But still unstoried, artless, unenhanced,
Such as she was, such as she would become.

(316)

As in Louis Althusser's formulation of interpellation, the poem "hails" its "hearer," and in the act of the listener's response to that invocation, he knows himself to be the person addressed—in this case, that is to say, he "remembers" his identity as an American citizen.

Because the poem takes for granted the centrality of the English perspective on "the American colonial experience," it presents its compressed account of U.S. history as normative. As Harold K. Bush, Jr. observes, Frost's

> narrator immediately incorporates the reader into some sort of social grouping or identity. The paradoxical nature of that co-optation recalls the simple opening of the U.S. Constitution: "We the people." The immediate assumption must be that "we" represents all true Americans, past, present, and future, and from the beginning of the poem a consensus is posited. The act of positing that collective group, or naming that "we," is

a speaking into existence, such as God did at the Creation: "Let there be light." (175-76)

In the poem, the speaker's contradictory "we" is meant to embrace all the members of the nation, but this embrace conceives its audience as a homogeneous community divided only by its colonial connections to England. A certain blindness informs the speaker's perspective, for his words subordinate the losses of Native Americans, enslaved blacks, and non-English immigrants to the grander narrative of colonial pilgrimage and freedom. In its commemoration of national origins, the poem "forgets" the bloody history that features so prominently in "La Noche Triste," "The Sachem of the Clouds," "Genealogical," and "The Vanishing Red." By assuming its readers' assent to its implicit hailing, "The Gift Outright" deftly pressures or persuades one to accept its representation of the national constituency, into seeing oneself in the lineaments of its particular formulation of "America." Frost's "we" dramatizes the constitution of its readers as citizens by the national polity. Its assumption of national unity implies that the constituency that it both describes and enacts is a synergistic whole that cannot be fully comprehended.

In declaring that "This land was ours before we were the land's," Frost both invokes his readers' already established sense of themselves as American citizens and calls that citizenship into being. The line enacts its version of the national community in its evocation of a "we" defined by what is held in common as "ours." The poem presumes that its audience is unified by common proprietary ties. In order to forge its vision of national unity it must "forget" the manner in which it became "ours." Frost first presented the poem in public just days before Pearl Harbor was bombed, and the rhetoric of the poem either reflects the strong sense of national unity that the attack solidified among Americans, or it promotes such a sense by repeating a defining narrative in a contemporary climate of threatening aggression. Regardless of the date of the poem's first draft, Frost made it public at a moment when, because of potential threats from the Axis powers to U.S. interests, security, and sovereignty, the value of national unity was especially high.

As some readers of the poem point out, however, the definition of the national that Frost assumes in "The Gift Outright" comes at a price. For those readers who cannot claim English heritage, the poem demands an imaginative identification with—and fealty to—those founders, so that the audience addressed by the poem must affiliate with the English by proxy, as it were. Since for some groups of U.S. citizens this is presumably easier to do than it is for others, Frost's poem "forgets" something of the cost of the symbolic identification it asks of its readers. Whereas the poem aims to communicate a sense of the unity of the nation through the metaphors of possession, salvation, and surrender, it can only do so by requiring the imaginative affiliation of all its citizens with the mythic pilgrims who laid the foundations for the latter-day republic. In this respect, the poem conforms to the drama described by Anderson, whereby disparate citizens become filiated kin.

In addition, the poem ironically transfigures the several military surrenders of the Amerindians into the psychic surrender of all "colonials" to America. That gesture unites citizens not only to the land of the New World, but to one another in the imagined community that constitutes the "nation." Frost reverses expectations when he makes the possessors become the "possessed." Indeed, as Reuben Brower observes, the entire "poem is an expanded pun on 'possession'" (202). Unlike "The people along the sand" in "Neither Out Far Nor In Deep" who "turn their back on the land" and "look at the sea all day," Americans must look inland to find their meaning and their place (*CPPP*, 274). They must turn from "a conformity of dull staring" backward toward the shores of England (Poirier, 244). The progeny of the uprooted colonials had to learn to think of themselves as belonging to America as much as they thought of America as belonging to them. As soon as this process of identifying American rather than English soil as "home" got underway, the poem argues, the first real Americans were born. In the words of William Carlos Williams's lyric "By the road to the contagious hospital," a "profound change/ has come upon" such settlers and their descendants. In the process of this change, in fact, Frost's fellow citizens—like the stubborn "stuff" of Williams's poem—become one with their new land, and achieve a consciousness not hitherto available: "rooted, they/ grip down and begin to awaken." (*Collected Poems*, 1, 183). In Frost's poem, however, the pioneers' surrender to the soil of America paradoxically corresponds to the military surrenders of Indians it leaves unreported. In the process of becoming "rooted," Americans "grip down" into a soil stolen from others; if the sleepers of "A Cabin in the Clearing" ever "begin to awaken" to themselves and their new power in the world, they must—sooner or later—also "awaken" to their part in the continuing nightmare of history. By suggesting the continuities as well as the disparities between the forms of forgetting and remembering required to make and sustain a nation, Frost's poems indicate the threatened and threatening relationships of American history to longer and more complex spans of human history. U.S. history is embedded in human history as a whole, so that it participates in the problems and triumphs of that history in ways that are detrimental or beneficial not only to its own interests but to those of other nations and groups as well.

In the syntax of Frost's poem, the military conflict entailed by the colonials' salvific "surrender" is relegated to parentheses: "Such as we were we gave ourselves outright/ (The deed of gift was many deeds of war)." In this formulation, one kind of surrender erases or covers over another kind. In the topsy-turvy whirl of meaning enacted by the poem's puns, colonial surrender becomes an act of possession and Indian dispossession goes unmentioned. Yet the parenthetical line that implies such dispossession glosses it over in the extravagance of its wordplay, for Frost's punning repetition of *deed* and *deeds* modulates in meaning from a legal document conferring or affirming possession to acts of military conquest. Nevertheless, Frost's artful ambiguity keeps in play the unmentioned menace of Indian inhabitants: in the end, the significant political and historical links between the two meanings are underscored *as well as* obscured by the equivocation.

The poem's identification of surrender as salvation further compounds the complexity of the metaphor. The colonist's self-discovery follows upon the European "discovery" of the Americas:

> Something we were withholding made us weak
> Until we found out that it was ourselves
> We were withholding from our land of living,
> And forthwith found salvation in surrender.
>
> (*CPPP*, 316)

The finding of salvation of course presupposes the need for it. The poem suggests that salvation is a form of deliverance from the dilemma of physically living in one place while spiritually inhabiting another. "'The Gift Outright,'" writes Brower, "is . . . a compact psychological essay on colonialism. . . . Contradictions that run deep in our history and in our national mind—part of being an American is the feeling that we also belong to the country our ancestors came from—are imaged in contradictions of poetry" (202). The conflict between the heritage associated with the colonist's remembered place of origin and his commitments to his current circumstances prevents him from achieving a true sense of home: "mere presence," writes Hamida Bosmajian, "was not enough to achieve national identity. The colonial American was still in an existential limbo" (98). Of course this has not changed, and this limbo is part of what enables the United States to achieve whatever unified pluralism it ever does achieve.

This unsettling aspect of settlement is perhaps conceptually akin to Homi Bhabha's theory of the "unhomely moment" he finds in contemporary "postcolonial" experience (9-18). Referring to Freud's original German word for the uncanny in his essay of that name, Bhabha's version of the *unheimlich* names a specific kind of unwelcome irruption. It designates the intrusions of the public upon the private, the improper upon the proper, and the foreign other upon the native self. Frost's poem evokes all of these intrusions in one way or another. In the speech of the poem, for example, the private individual assumes the voice of the public *we*, the puns on *possession* signify ideological allegiance and affiliation on the one hand as well as the colonial ownership of property on the other, and the colonist is at once a foreign other and a native self. Occupying both a land that is foreign and remembering a distant nation that is no longer home, he feels himself disinherited, spiritually dispossessed. Yet he feels this way even though his colonization has entailed the dispossession of an indigenous population he experiences as alien.

Frost's poem dramatizes the legal enactments behind the European conquest of the Americas. The acts of naming and mapping various regions of the New World were part of the colonial process of "taking title to" the region—a process Frost figures through his puns on "deed." Naming and mapping are ways of laying claim. From a Foucauldian perspective, these instruments of knowledge double as the disciplinary technology of power—the means of securing and maintaining possession.

A deed is something done, but in the plural form which it takes in the poem ("many deeds of war"), it is also the record of things done. In this regard, the word registers the two principle meanings of history. On the one hand, history refers to the sweep of actual events through time, but on the other, history is the preserved record—either oral or written (as in the text of the poem itself)—of those past events. Frost's first use of the word *deed* to refer to a legal document conferring possession roughly corresponds to the definition of history as document, as preserved record. His reference to *deeds of war*, however, corresponds to history as event, the actions of a person or group that affect the course of future events. As a document, a deed has an illocutionary effect—it is a speech act, an example of language that can make something happen. A legal deed extends title to its bearer, and Frost's line makes it clear that the price of that transfer of ownership is paid in military deeds. Given the correspondences I have outlined, it follows that the poem implies that such acts of aggression make up an important part of a nation's history. Such acts engender history, inevitably impelling it towards the future. As the documented record of these acts, the poet's text becomes the "entitling" deed of his nation, its virtual performance in the medium of language.

As Richardson points out, Frost explicitly linked poetic performance and deed in a brochure of 1923 entitled *Robert Frost: The Man and His Work*: "Sometimes," Frost wrote,

> I have my doubts of words altogether, and I ask myself what is the place of them. They are worse than nothing unless they do something; unless they amount to deeds, as in ultimatums or battle-cries. They must be flat and final like the show-down in poker, from which there is no appeal. My definition of poetry (if I were forced to give one) would be this: words that have become deeds. (*CPPP*, 701)

As Richardson observes, such "brief remarks provide a fine example of a public persona that Frost often adopted as a poet" (51). Frost's mixing of the categories of language and action in these statements clearly corresponds to the language of "The Gift Outright," and it just as clearly evokes the linguistic and theoretical concepts of the performative. The martial rhetoric of the prose passage matches that of the poem, too, suggesting that Frost's sense of poetic creation as a form of competitive, athletic, and manly prowess was also profoundly martial. In the context of his recitation of "The Gift" at John F. Kennedy's presidential inauguration, the words of Frost's poem became a deed, registering the importance of the poem's meaning in a specific political and social context and repeating the story of the nation's coming-into-being. But the poem also plays with categories in a way that suggests the partialness of such equations.

The rhetorical parallels and repetitions of the poem, its appeal to the common man ("Such as we were we gave ourselves outright"), and its evocation of a common, unifying heritage, also give the text an oratorical character. It is as if a politician or local figure of authority were reciting the words of the poem as a speech, so that the poem already "inscribes" Frost's historic recitation of the poem at Kennedy's inauguration *avant la lettre*. The fictive situation of the poem is that of a public address.

Frost's reading of his poem at Kennedy's inauguration provides an important example of the performative quality of his poetics in terms of its political meaning and social ramifications. Frost had composed his poem about 20 years before the inauguration and had read it in public for the first time "before the Phi Beta Kappa Society at William and Mary College, December 5, 1941," and he first published the poem in *The Virginia Quarterly Review* in 1942 (*Poetry of Robert Frost*, 565). When Frost recited the poem from memory at the inauguration, he delivered a text that had been rendered public many times, in the published form of his various selected and collected poems (1946, 1949, 1954, 1955) and in the oral form of his many public readings. "In one sense," Philip Gerber writes, "this recital was the very peak of his long career" (27). Although Gerber's hedging phrase "in one sense" is of course a very important mitigation of an otherwise overstated claim, a remark about the occasion that Jean Gould attributes to Frost might confirm this view: "It is a proud moment," Frost beamed, "to have poetry brought into the affairs of statesmen" (4-5). From one perspective, Frost's publishing and performing career exemplifies the kind of "performative iteration" Judith Butler has in mind when she discusses the duration and renewal of social structures (13-14).

Indeed, Frost became as famous for his crafty public persona as for the careful craft of his poetry. "Like the ancient bards and troubadours," his biographer Jeffrey Meyers writes, "Frost performed his poetry and brought it directly to this audience" (181). "He was certainly," Meyers adds, "a first-rate actor, liked performing and was excited by appearing on stage" (185). Frost himself attests to his view of poetry as a skilled performance. As he told Richard Poirier in an interview published in the *Paris Review*, "I look on poetry as a performance. I look on the poet as a man of prowess, just like an athlete. He's a performer. And the things you can do in a poem are very various" (*CPPP*, 890). Poirier's own commentary on Frost handsomely expands on this statement: "Poetry is not life," he writes, "but the performance in the writing of it can be an image of the proper conduct of life. The exercise of the will *in* poetry, the *writing* of a poem, is analogous to any attempted exercise of will in whatever else one tries to do" (9). For Frost, "A poem is an action, not merely a 'made' but a 'making' thing" (64).

Frost had of course attained his national prominence before Kennedy's inauguration. In a famously controversial speech, Lionel Trilling acknowledged Frost's status as a national myth in 1959:

> We do not need to wait upon the archaeologists of the future to understand that Robert Frost exists not only in a human way but also in a mythical way. We know him, and have known him so for many years, as nothing less than a national fact. We have come to think of him as virtually a symbol of America. . . . [W]e do indeed honor him as a poet, but also as a tutelary genius of the nation and as a justification of our national soul. (448)

Despite the stir Trilling's speech engendered, it is unlikely that any of his critics would have carped at these comments. Bernard DeVoto, for example, gushed that "Frost" was "'the greatest living American'" and "the quintessence of everything I respect and even love in the American heritage" (Meyers, 270). Indeed, whereas his fellow poets promoted American culture and aspired to contribute to it, Frost came to *embody* it. During his 1961 visit to Israel, Frost displayed his confidence in his status as a "national fact"—and perhaps his solipsism as well—when he "publicly announced that he did not intend to talk *about* American civilization because," as he put it, "'I *am* American civilization'" (Meyers, 325). Its extravagant humor and hubris aside, the statement perhaps has a grain of truth to it.

In any case, Frost clearly styled his image with the same care that he invested in his poetry, and his sense of poetry as a performance is of a piece with his knack for sparkling conversation and his vocation of "barding around." Frost clearly associated his public image and his work with American culture by evoking the stereotypes of Yankee independence and hardihood as themes that resonate within his work and his audience. The view that Frost's reading at Kennedy's inauguration was the summit of his career emphasizes the performative aspect of poetry, and it dramatizes the process by which a national tradition is formulated and perpetuated over time. Just as Frost's historic recitation disseminated an inherited narrative of his country's experience, every reading and rereading of "The Gift Outright" presents a new opportunity for either accepting and perpetuating or rethinking and adjusting its version of national history. The ceremonial context for Frost's delivery of his poem to a television audience imparted to its speech an authoritative power it would not otherwise "possess," but the poem also lent the considerable power of its eloquence to the drama of the new president's inauguration.

While "The Gift Outright" narrates the genesis and development of the poet's nation, it also looks beyond the past and the occasion of the poem's presentation to an open-ended future. The repeated formula of "Such as we were" in line 12 and "Such as she was" in line 16 echoes the phrase "Such was our land" in line two and builds up a sense of continuity between the past and present that culminates in a vista of the future that is presented as both hopeful and uncertain. The final line's stately declarations—"Such as she was, such as she would become"—draw the poem-as-speech to a conclusive end, but they also look forward with confidence to a promising future. At the same time, the poem's closing statements characterize an end that, precisely because it is projected into the future, remains necessarily clouded in doubt. Such declarations leave the details of American history vague in ways that recall the forgetting they permit and require. Frost's account of U.S. and colonial history must suppress the injustices that the nation perpetrated in the very process of its constitution.

If such poems as "The Gift Outright" and "A Cabin in the Clearing" seem to ignore or momentarily "forget" the Indian genocide entailed by American settlements, the ghosts of these Indians nevertheless haunt their landscapes, while other poems by Frost overtly acknowledge the founding barbarities of American democracy. Because the figure of the oppressed and defeated Amerindian haunts the collective psyche of the colonizers' heirs, the figure of the Native insists upon itself in various ways in the works of American writers. "Inheriting both the guilt of the conquerors and the deprivations of the conquered," writes Benjamin T. Spencer, "the American has thus become the split and fearful soul of which his national literature, if astutely read, is the reflection, ineluctably pervaded with haunting imagery of Indians, forests, and the night" (116). The Amerindian may be "The Vanishing Red," but the memory of him stubbornly persists, while the cabin of the settlers' clearing remains haunted by "the native tongue" to the point that its inhabitants must "ask the Red Man where they are" (*CPPP*, 428). If the new dwellers in the land pursue such inquiries to no avail, they nevertheless express their mingled helplessness and guilt in the land they came to govern. The speaker of "Genealogical" eschews the violence committed by the settlers against the Indians and attempts to atone for it. Despite this Whitmanesque effort to share the position of the disinherited, the poem is brought up short against itself, limited by the fact that it originates in its creator's guilt and concomitant longing for reconciliation.

These poems reflect the tensions that constitute settlement and hence the central experience of the nation, and they show that the unsettling aspects of national history inhabit the lives and minds of the conquerors as well as of the conquered. If the colonizer dispossesses his indigenous rivals, his descendants remain nonetheless dogged by the ghosts of their displaced victims, and their consciousness of those ghosts constitutes as vital a part of the nation as the declarations and documents of the country's famous white "fathers." If "the Indian, from the start, was invisible" to his white conquerors, these poems bring his disavowed specter into sharp and haunting relief (Beaver,

11). They show that the imperial enterprise that forged the nation and that has pervaded its subsequent existence also fractures it from within by dividing the lives and allegiances of its citizens in the process. In doing so, they lend paradoxical support to Kennedy's posthumous tribute to Frost. "In serving his vision of the truth," he wrote, "the artist best serves his nation" (54).

From *Texas Studies in Literature and Language* 46, no. 2 (Summer 2004): 213-244. Copyright © 2004 by the University of Texas Press. Reprinted by permission of the University of Texas Press.

Notes

"Genealogical" quoted by permission of the Estate of Robert Lee Frost.

This article will appear in a revised and expanded form in a chapter of my book, *The Colonial Moment: Discoveries and Settlements in Modern American Poetry*, to be published in Fall 2004 by Northern Illinois University Press.

Thanks to Robert Kern, Guy Rotella, and Suzanne Matson for their advice concerning the revision of this essay.

1. All subsequent quotations from this volume will be cited in the text in the abbreviated form as *CPPP*.

2. For discussions of the trope of the vanishing Indian, see Bellin, Bergland, Huhndorf, Maddox, Scheckel, and Walker.

3. The relationship between "Genealogy" and "A Cabin in the Clearing" is perhaps like the relationship Mark Richardson sees between Frost's letters and his poetry. In his reading of "Good Hours," which closes *North of Boston*, Richardson argues that Frost accommodated himself to the utilitarian contempt for poetry that he found common among fellow New Englanders and Americans in general. Although in "Good Hours" Frost overtly registers his dissent from the townspeople he passes on the walk he records in his poem, he also ironically accommodates himself to it. For Richardson, the poem is "about intransigence, but it is also about propriety and accommodation." Richardson finds a correspondence between the cryptic propriety of published poems and the more openly dissenting attitudes Frost expressed in letters to his friends, both in the United States and in England. In the letters Frost is less accommodating in his defense of poetry and his involvement with it, but in his published poems, he adopts a tone that allows him to differentiate himself from his fellows in a way that will not give offense. Similarly, "Genealogy," which Frost included in a letter and chose not to publish, conveys a relatively critical commentary on ancestral white mistreatment of Indians in comparison with "The Vanishing Red" and "A Cabin in the Clearing." Be that as it may, the violent clearing described in "Genealogy" finds its eerie echo in the more peaceful and domestic "clearing" on which Frost raises his later "Cabin."

4. Thanks to Guy Rotella for pointing out the origin of this word to me.

5. Together with Mist's earlier dictum, Smoke's comments clearly echo a remark Job makes to God in *A Masque of Reason*, which was first published in 1945 (*CPPP*, 956). In exasperation, Job "confesses" (though not without evident irony) that "We don't know where we are, or who we are" (*CPPP*, 381). In that context, the saying emphasizes the existential and metaphysical resonance of the terms. In joining the two sayings in a single line with the paratactic "or," Frost shows them to be parallel versions of one another.

Works Cited

Anderson, Benedict. *Imagined Communities*. Rev. ed. New York: Verso, 1991.

Beaver, Harold. *The Great American Masquerade*. London: Vision; Totowa, N.J.: Barnes & Noble, 1985.

Bellin, Joshua. *The Demon of the Continent: Indians and the Shaping of American Literature*. Philadelphia: University of Pennsylvania Press, 2000.

Bergland, Renée L. *The National Uncanny: Indian Ghosts and American Subjects*. Hanover: University Press of New England, 2000.

Bhabha, Homi K. *The Location of Culture*. New York: Routledge, 1994.

Bosmajian, Hamida. "Robert Frost's 'The Gift Outright': Wish and Reality in History and Poetry." *American Quarterly* 22 (1970): 95-105.

Brower, Reuben A. *The Poetry of Robert Frost: Constellations of Intention*. New York: Oxford University Press, 1963.

Bush, Harold K., Jr. *American Declarations: Rebellion and Repentance in American Cultural History*. Urbana: University of Illinois Press, 1999.

Butler, Judith. "Further Reflections on Conversations of Our Time." *Diacritics* 27.1 (1997): 13-15.

Cady, Edwin H., and Louis J. Budd, eds. *On Frost: The Best from America Literature*. Durham: Duke University Press, 1991.

Carruth, Hayden. "The New England Tradition." *Regional Perspectives: An Examination of America's Literary Heritage*. Ed. John Gordon Burke. Chicago: American Library Association, 1973.

Cheyfitz, Eric. *The Poetics of Imperialism: Translation and Colonization from* The Tempest *to* Tarzan. Expanded ed. Philadelphia: University of Pennsylvania Press, 1997.

Cook, Reginald L. "Frost's Asides on His Poetry." *On Frost: The Best from American Literature*. Ed. Edwin H. Cady and Louis J. Budd. Durham: Duke University Press, 1991.

Cox, Sidney. *A Swinger of Birches: A Portrait of Robert Frost*. Washington Square: New York University Press, 1957.

Cramer, Jeffrey S. *Robert Frost among His Poems: A Literary Companion to the Poet's Own Biographical Contexts and Associations*. Jefferson, N.C.: McFarland, 1996.

Faggen, Robert. *Robert Frost and the Challenge of Darwinism*. Ann Arbor: University of Michigan Press, 1997.

Francis, Lesley Lee. "Frost and the Majesty of Stones upon Stones." *Journal of Modern Literature* 9 (1981/82): 3-26.

Frost, Robert. *The Poetry of Robert Frost*. Ed. Edward Connery Lathem. New York: Holt, Rinehart and Winston, 1969.

_____. *Robert Frost: Collected Poems, Prose, & Plays*. Ed. Richard Poirier and Mark Richardson. New York: Library of America, 1995.

_____. *Selected Letters of Robert Frost*. Ed. Lawrance Thompson. New York: Holt, Rinehart and Winston, 1964.

Huhndorf, Shari M. *Going Native: Indians in the American Cultural Imagination*. Ithaca, N.Y.: Cornell University Press, 2001.

Kennedy, John Fitzgerald. "Poetry and Power." *Atlantic Monthly* Feb. 1964: 53-54.

Kilcup, Karen L. *Robert Frost and Feminine Literary Tradition*. Ann Arbor: University of Michigan Press, 1998.

Lawrence, D. H. *Studies in Classic American Literature*. New York: Penguin, 1964.

Maddox, Lucy. *Removals: Nineteenth-Century American Literature and the Politics of Indian Affairs*. New York: Oxford University Press, 1991.

Meyers, Jeffrey. *Robert Frost: A Biography*. Boston: Houghton Mifflin, 1996.

Poirier, Richard. *Robert Frost: The Work of Knowing*. New York: Oxford University Press, 1977.

Renan, Ernest. "What Is a Nation?" *Nation and Narration*. Ed. by Homi Bhabha. New York: Routledge, 1990.

Richardson, Mark. *The Ordeal of Robert Frost: The Poet and His Poetics*. Urbana: University of Illinois Press, 1997.

Robbins, J. Albert. "America and the Poet: Whitman, Hart Crane and Frost." *American Poetry*. Stratford-upon-Avon Studies 7. Ed. Irvin Ehrenpreis. New York: St. Martin's Press, 1965.

Rotella, Guy. "Economies of Frost: 'Synonymous with Kept.'" *The Cambridge Companion to Robert Frost*. Ed. Robert Faggen. New York: Cambridge University Press, 2001.

Scheckel, Susan. *The Insistence of the Indian: Race and Nationalism in Nineteenth-Century American Culture*. Princeton: Princeton University Press, 1998.

Spencer, Benjamin T. *Patterns of Nationality: Twentieth-Century Literary Versions of America*. New York: Burt Franklin, 1981.

Walker, Cheryl. *Indian Nation: Native American Literature and Nineteenth-Century Nationalisms*. Durham: Duke University Press, 1997.

Williams, William Carlos. *The Collected Poems of William Carlos Williams*. Volume I (1909-1939). Ed. A. Walton Litz and Christopher MacGowan. New York: New Directions, 1986.

Robert Frost

Denis Donoghue

Robert Frost discovered at an early age that he had an engaging personality. The discovery was unfortunate and might easily have been disastrous. No one, least of all a poet, can afford to admire himself beyond the point of reasonable discrimination. Here is excess:

> Thine emulous fond flowers are dead, too,
> And the daft sun-assaulter, he
> That frighted thee so oft, is fled or dead:
> Save only me
> (Nor is it sad to thee!)
> Save only me
> There is none left to mourn thee in the fields.[1]

The object is supposed to be a butterfly, but the real focus of attention is directed elsewhere, to its handsome observer. The poet is too pleasurably aware that he is an attractive youth and that the flowers of language, those assonances and rhymes, will ask nothing better than to serve his beauty. The butterfly will collaborate, as Grantchester collaborated with Rupert Brooke. But the young poet knows too much, and it is the wrong kind of knowingness, the deadly half-truth that he is worthy to adorn any landscape, fit to give it savor, just by being in it. So the world is his backdrop. He has but to pose in an engaging scene and his distinction will be revealed. It is all done with mirrors. Here is one of many:

> And if by noon I have too much of these,
> I have but to turn on my arm, and lo,
> The sun-burned hillside sets my face aglow,
> My breathing shakes the bluet like a breeze,
> I smell the earth, I smell the bruised plant,
> I look into the crater of the ant.

We know little or nothing about Frost's escape from the exorbitant self—how it was achieved, what propelled that movement of feeling by which the self was persuaded to give up its privilege. But there it is, in *North of Boston, Mountain Interval, New Hampshire*, and *West-Running Brook*—pervadingly, if not always. Frost would never draw a veil over the self, nor would he ever commit himself so deeply to the "otherness" of the object as to put himself into a lower case. He would have nothing to do with objective correlatives or escapes from personality. "Dying to give something life," as Sir Claude Mulhammer puts it in *The Confidential Clerk*, was not in Frost's line. He would always insert a quirk of phrase, a telling rhythm, a knack of attitude, to remind us that we are listening to Robert Frost, not some other fellow. And when he had given modesty its way for several poems, he would regret this laxity and strut about in the robes of a sage. This was his worldly version of that sensitive plant who exhibited himself in *A Boy's Will*. And then he would never lay aside that insidious charm.

But there it is—at its best, a rich personality. Aristotle knew that he who owns such a personality and the ways of revealing it is more than halfway toward communicative success. The critic discussed it in his *Rhetoric* as a method of winning, not by force of reason but by giving the impression of a solid character, true gold. In Frost's case, or that of his persona in the poems, the speaker is rural, though not rustic. He knows sorrow but is reticent about its deeds ("My November Guest"). He can hold his tongue. He has a flair for the behavior of things and for the weird configurations in which, darkly, they can appear ("The Road Not Taken," "Mending Wall"). He knows the code ("Trespass"), just as Faulkner's pious hunters know theirs. He is aware that there are finalities besides the grave ("The Oft-Repeated Dream"). More, or trying again, he knows that one of his hardest tasks will be to adjudicate between rival claims and to settle at last—gently and often inarticulately—for the greatest:

The woods are lovely, dark and deep.
But I have promises to keep,
And miles to go before I sleep,
And miles to go before I sleep.

So he moves on. He knows that human relationships have their own rituals and that the good neighbor will allow for them, thereby celebrating them:

Baptiste knew how to make a short job long
For love of it, and yet not waste time either.

He knows that these rituals are often a matter of decent limits, of letting well enough alone, and he says of John Smith the explorer:

It became an explorer of the deep
Not to explore too deep in others' business.

This man has a stake in the country; he knows its values. He is gentle as long as he can be, as long as no one trespasses upon his property. After that, there will be trouble. And in any event he asks no quarter.

When Frost is secure in his ways, when he does not feel that he has to throw his weight about, he can often invite the world into his autobiography without asking it to do his work. Here is a case in point, one of the love poems:

As I went down the hill along the wall
There was a gate I had leaned at for the view
And had just turned from when I first saw you
As you came up the hill. We met. But all
We did that day was mingle great and small
Footprints in summer dust as if we drew
The figure of our being less than two

But more than one as yet. Your parasol
Pointed the decimal off with one deep thrust.
And all the time we talked you seemed to see
Something down there to smile at in the dust.
(Oh, it was without prejudice to me!)
Afterward I went past what you had passed
Before we met and you what I had passed.

It might have been a soft poem, self-indulgent with butterflies, but Frost tests the feeling as a force behind the words or under the words. He holds it back or holds it under with the sturdy geometrical conceit, making it earn its place, making it emerge, if it is good enough, from the rapt attention to details other than itself. And we err if we think the feeling is neither out far nor in deep. The fact that this is not a typical Frost poem merely tells us that our notion of a typical Frost poem may be too narrow. Frost asserts himself only in the parenthesis "(Oh, it was without prejudice to me!)" as if he were half afraid of losing his copyright. But he need not have worried.

We think we have this poet right when we have placed him beside other poets—beside Emerson, for instance, where we set him with some assurance because he did it himself. Or we place him between Clare and Wordsworth—Wordsworth for general affiliation, Clare for his confidence in the direct word whether it be the *mot juste* or not. And if we place him, as J. J. Hogan suggests, beside George Herbert, we are not far astray, though Herbert's country parson has a more severe role than the speaker in "The Black Cottage" and—when all is said—a finer intelligence. What Herbert and Frost share is a sense of "the way things are," though they adjusted themselves to that sense quite differently. In Herbert that sense was endowed by Christian belief with a "theoretic form," to which the poet was profoundly loyal even when his eyes and his fancies played truant. If Frost's poems have a "theoretic form," it is elusive, though I will suggest one later and argue for its presence in the poems as an allegiance, whether we approve it or not. One possibility may be set aside. The form cannot be severely of the mind, and is much more likely to be temperamental, even a crotchet of feeling. When we think of the *Cantos* we think of many things in Ezra Pound that we would willingly let die, but the indispensable things include the great hymns to the human intelligence, the emergence of form from chaos, the hymns to light and crystal:

> that the body of light come forth
> from the body of fire
> And that your eyes come to the surface
> from the deep wherein they were sunken,
> Reina—for 300 years,
> and now sunken
> That your eyes come forth from their caves
> & light then
> as the holly-leaf
>
> (*Canto* 91)

This is a note we never hear in Frost—the exaltation, the thrill in the sight of intelligence, mind, lucidity. Frost makes a rather strident gesture in "Sand Dunes," as if someone had challenged him and he wanted to produce his membership card, but it is not convincing. Indeed, reading the *Collected Poems* and the later collection *In the Clearing*, one is struck by Frost's frugality in the expense of mind, how little he concedes to it. He is happy enough that the mind should be there, but he takes care never to extend it or put it under strain. He will allow it to speculate, to toss up a few possibilities in the air, but always on the understanding that it doesn't really matter, it's only a game. This is one of the things we least admire in Frost, and sometimes we resent it. There are many things in Eliot's poems that we would be happy to lose—his contempt for ordinary people, his reluctance to accept the fact that he is human, his distaste for men like Hardy and Lawrence because they are not Dante—but the one concession we must make is that Eliot has spent a lifetime trying to get things straight and concentrating all his mental powers to that end. With Frost we have the feeling that he used only enough of his mind to fix himself in an attractive pose. And we find this aspect of him tedious. The systematic repudiation of systematic thought cannot help us, at the last, especially if it involves—as it often does in Frost—an undue willingness *not* to understand one's experience. This is nothing like Keats's "negative capability"; it is much nearer to complacency. Often what proclaims itself as detachment or disengagement is merely intellectual slackness:

> I love to toy with the Platonic notion
> That wisdom need not be of Athens Attic,
> But well may be Laconic, even Boeotian.
> At least I will not have it systematic.

He toys too much.

But there it is. Frost communicates through one resource. He has it, and he expects his reader to have it—a sense of "the way things are." He counts on nothing more than humane axioms, self-evident truths incapable of proof:

> The witch that came (the withered hag)
> To wash the steps with pail and rag,
> Was once the beauty Abishag,
>
> The picture pride of Hollywood.
> Too many fall from great and good
> For you to doubt the likelihood.
>
> Die early and avoid the fate.
> Or if predestined to die late,
> Make up your mind to die in state.

Make the whole stock exchange your own!
If need be occupy a throne,
Where nobody can call *you* crone.

Some have relied on what they knew;
Others on being simply true.
What worked for them might work for you.

No memory of having starred
Atones for later disregard,
Or keeps the end from being hard.

Better to go down dignified
With boughten friendship at your side
Than none at all. Provide, Provide!

There are poems by Frost that are all manner, all voice, and these are dispensable. And there are poems like "The Most of It" and "An Old Man's Winter Night" that Frost hands over to the facts of the case, committing all the feeling to the facts and giving the famous voice only enough leeway to be audible. These are the great poems, I would argue. And then there are several poems in which the relation between fact and voice is just, however precarious. The present poem, "Provide, Provide," is one of these. What gives the poem its power is its sense of "the way things are." Eliot would give its values short shrift, implying that the difference between the several conditions described is in any event negligible, the difference between boughten friendship and the other kind trivial. In "Little Gidding" the gifts reserved for age are:

First, the cold friction of expiring sense
Without enchantment, offering no promise
But bitter tastelessness of shadow fruit
As body and soul begin to fall asunder.

Second, the conscious impotence of rage
   At human folly, and the laceration
   Of laughter at what ceases to amuse.
And last, the rending pain of re-enactment
   Of all that you have done, and been; the shame
   Of motives late revealed, and the awareness
Of things ill done and done to others' harm
   Which once you took for exercise of virtue.
   Then fools' approval stings, and honor stains.

There is no way of mediating between these voices. Frost will say that shadow fruit is better than no fruit, fools' approval better than none. Eliot will say that all such distinctions are, in any event, beside the spiritual point. If judgments are based on the jury system, Frost will win. If the verdict is given by a rigorous and independent judge who is strong on ultimate values and the ascetic way to them, Eliot will be endorsed. But meanwhile we can say this: Frost is weak on ultimates, but he knows that most of life is lived in "the element of antagonisms," and this is the source of the poem's pain. The last dry "Provide, Provide" is almost a parody of the Biblical apocalyptic voice, but Frost knows the difference between the two voices and would not deride the first. This is the poem's saving grace.

Frost will appeal, then, only to those truths or half-truths that we know by being human and extant. Hence there is his trust in numinous anecdote, the story that begins as an incident and flowers into a fable without losing the resilience of contingency, illustrated in poems like "The Death of the Hired Man," "The Ax-Helve," "Paul's Wife," "An Old Man's Winter Night," and the terrible "Out, Out." These poems find common ground between Jew, Gentile, American, European, Tory, Communist, Warren the Hired Man and any tycoon you care to name, provided that each of these imagined readers has retained his feeling for "the way things are," his feeling for human axioms, in the press of rival commitments. Take a classic case in point:

Some say the world will end in fire,
Some say in ice.
From what I've tasted of desire
I hold with those who favor fire.
But if it had to perish twice,
I think I know enough of hate
To say that for destruction ice
Is also great
And would suffice.

The problem of communication is clearly in abeyance for the life of this poem. What is rendered is a response to common experience, a psychological event brought to a degree of generalization without sacrificing its momentum. We can all share it, admiring in the syntax the speaker's control over the facts, his humility, knowing that the humility is nine-tenths of the control. There must be many readers who wonder why all poems can't communicate so easily. And they can point to many other poems—this one, for instance, in Yeats:

Others because you did not keep
That deep-sworn vow have been friends of mine;
Yet always when I look death in the face,
When I clamber to the heights of sleep,
Or when I grow excited with wine,
Suddenly I meet your face.

These poems are what they are, with finality. They move into central areas of experience, say what they have to say, and make no further demands. And there are hundreds of poems complete in this way—Wordsworth's "Complaint of a Forsaken Indian Woman," Synge's "Riders to the Sea," for example. I am reminded of Wallace Stevens, who said in an uncharacteristic moment in the *Adagia* that "Literature is the better part of life. To this it seems inevitably necessary to add, provided life is the better part of literature." Life is indeed the better part of these poems by Frost and Yeats, and this is why they enter the lives of their readers so unerringly. But they do not solve all our problems, and there are many areas of life that they do not touch and that we still retain, mostly to our distress.

When Yeats faced this problem he tried to undercut those contentious areas—mind, ideology, dogma, argument—and to effect human contact through those motives that are prior to all radical contention: the axioms of the body, our sense of the heroic, or even the Great Memory. Or again he would try to burn all contentions away with the great symbolic brand or flame that he invokes in several poems. Frost has his own strategy. He addresses us through our basic "drives"—nutritive, sexual, self-protective—through our sense of isolation, of idiosyncrasy. Thus he will present, as a parable of inner emptiness, a landscape at night and the snow obliterating the "quiddity" of things:

> And lonely as it is that loneliness
> Will be more lonely ere it will be less—
> A blanker whiteness of benighted snow
> With no expression, nothing to express.
>
> They cannot scare me with their empty spaces
> Between stars—on stars where no human race is.
> I have it in me so much nearer home
> To scare myself with my own desert places.

Responding to this poem, we warm to the speaker's tact, the high courtesy that leaves so much unspecified. The poet refrains from minute disclosures, because fine breeding and the circumstances of the case suggest that he should, not because he covets the murky splendors of ambiguity; he will be literal when the time comes. Meanwhile the poem reaches us because we have our own desert places. We share an incorrigible experience, contributing a little of the meaning from our own drought. This is how the poem works. But it would not work at all except for the speaker's tact. In Frost's poems a man has this "tact of words" if he can say:

> He fell at Gettysburg or Fredericksburg,
> I ought to know—it makes a difference which:
> Fredericksburg wasn't Gettysburg, of course . . .

Or if he can say this, he has it:

> They meet him in the general store at night,
> Preoccupied with formidable mail,
> Riffling a printed letter as he talks.
> They seem afraid. He wouldn't have it so:
> Though a great scholar, he's a democrat,
> If not at heart, at least on principle.

The tact goes with understatement and the preservation of decent limits, and it reveals itself most urbanely in the middle range of experience. Hence Frost's cultivation of the mean or tempered style, which affects ease of discourse:

> Spades take up leaves
> No better than spoons,
> And bags full of leaves
> Are light as balloons.
>
> I make a great noise
> Of rustling all day
> Like rabbit and deer
> Running away.

But the mountains I raise
Elude my embrace,
Flowing over my arms,
And into my face.

I may load and unload
Again and again
Till I fill the whole shed,
And what have I then?

Next to nothing for weight
And since they grew duller
From contact with earth,
Next to nothing for color.

Next to nothing for use.
But a crop is a crop,
And who's to say where
The harvest shall stop?

This poem is a liberal education, it justifies itself as easily as the crop. Wallace Stevens once agreed with someone who argued that in a poem the "something said" is important, but "only in so far as the saying of that particular something in a special way is a revelation of reality." And he added on his own behalf, "the reality so imposed need not be a great reality."[2] I suppose he meant that it need not be a momentous reality, or that smaller realities will do for most poems; life and death need not hang on the word of every poem. The reality imposed in Frost's poem is large enough for the claims he makes. There is nothing glib, nothing portentous, in his assertion, for these notes are alien to the true Horatian "ease" that will not harden into the mold of formula. The decorum the poem serves is that of polite discourse, the statement— neither "low" nor "grand"—that knows its own range and is content.

Frost's poems rarely make new meanings; mostly they remind us of ancient meanings and place them in settings that, perhaps for the first time, do them justice.

To propose Frost as a master of the "middle" style is at once to praise him, to point to his particular strength, and to mark his limitations. For it is useless to think of him as a poet in command of all the poetic resources. For one thing, he lacks the range of Eliot, from the remorseless acid of "The Fire Sermon"—a masterpiece of the "low" style—

> Unreal City
> Under the brown fog of a winter noon
> Mr. Eugenides, the Smyrna merchant
> Unshaven, with a pocket full of currants
> C.i.f. London: documents at sight,
> Asked me in demotic French
> To luncheon at the Cannon Street Hotel
> Followed by a weekend at the Metropole—

to the choruses from "The Rock," or "Burnt Norton"—a poem that would have pleased Longinus—

> The Word in the desert
> Is most attacked by voices of temptation,
> The crying shadow in the funeral dance,
> The loud lament of the disconsolate chimera.

And Frost lacks that art of elevation by which a major poet may sometimes, in a moment of grace, move into charged meditation. There is Yeats:

> Some moralist or mythological poet
> Compares the solitary soul to a swan;
> I am satisfied with that,

Satisfied if a troubled mirror show it,
Before that brief gleam of its life be gone,
An image of its state;
The wings half spread for flight,
The breast thrust out in pride
Whether to play, or to ride
Those winds that clamour of approaching night.

And there is Stevens:

Was the sun concoct for angels or for men?
Sad men made angels of the sun, and of
The moon they made their own attendant ghosts,
Which led them back to angels, after death.

Let this be clear that we are men of sun
And men of day and never of pointed night,
Men that repeat antiquest sounds of air
In an accord of repetitions. Yet,
If we repeat, it is because the wind
Encircling us, speaks always with our speech.

Frost never commands this kind of meditation. His own kind is a slack affair, hardly more than whimsical patter, especially in the longer poems. When he chooses to "raise" his style, it is usually to claim a "public" and representative emotion:

The land was ours before we were the land's.
She was our land more than a hundred years
Before we were her people. She was ours
In Massachusetts, in Virginia,
But we were England's, still colonials.

This kind of thing would do well enough as a slogan, perhaps even as a pseudo-Emersonian essay, but not as a poem. I have no objection to the sentiments, and would vote for them if it were a question of voting and if I had a vote. But one of the functions of the imagination is to drive us harder than we are driven in the market place, to hold out against such simplicity, because the imagination is nothing if not critical. Indeed, sooner than let us sink into the loud clichés so dear to our hearts, the imagination will go to the very edge of subversion. In the present poem Frost has thrown aside his most engaging mask and picked up one that does him less than justice. The real Frost is like Antaeus, the giant whose strength depends upon contact with his mother, Earth; when Hercules lifts him off the ground, Antaeus is lost. The earth, which, as Frost tells us, is the right place for love, is also the right place for Frost's strength. When he abandons it and sings falsetto, he is betrayed by his familiars—slogan, pamphlet, evasion, whimsy.

Frost knows this, on the whole. He knows that his most reliable source of strength is the actual, the rock bottom, the bare human fact. Hence his piety toward everything elemental. We call it piety, he calls it love:

> I'd like to get away from earth awhile
> And then come back to it and begin over.
> May no fate wilfully misunderstand me
> And half grant what I wish and snatch me away
> Not to return. Earth's the right place for love:
> I don't know where it's likely to go better.

When Frost commits himself to the actual, his tone is nearly always beautifully poised, not with the poise of virtuosity—the trapeze artist's, William Empson's style—in-the-teeth-of-a-despair—but the steadier poise of humility and trust. This is the sign of his civility. But when this commitment breaks down or falls away in fear or weariness, he becomes strident, complacent, oracular. And sometimes, even in poems that otherwise are magnificent, he slips into self-pity:

> I have been one acquainted with the night.
> I have walked out in rain—and back in rain.
> I have outwalked the furthest city light.
>
> I have looked down the saddest city lane.
> I have passed by the watchman on his beat
> And dropt my eyes, unwilling to explain.
>
> I have stood still and stopped the sound of feet
> When far away an interrupted cry
> Came over houses from another street,
>
> But not to call me back or say goodbye;
> And further still at an unearthly height,
> One luminary clock against the sky
>
> Proclaimed the time was neither wrong nor right.
> I have been one acquainted with the night.

It is one of Frost's most impressive poems. Indeed, all that can be said against it is quickly said. The moral of the story is that the time is neither wrong nor right. We can't play Hamlet and curse the time for being out of joint, as Robinson did, for instance, in several poems that we have looked at. And yet Frost does, in a sense. He presents himself as the "man against the sky," the sensitive man keeping his own counsel in the black city. This is a song of experience, but unlike Blake's, it is a little ingrown. The city lane, the watchman, the rain, and the anonymous cry can hardly avoid becoming theatrical props to cosset the isolation and the tenacity of the silent hero. When Blake wanders through a blackened London, what he sees and hears is offered as evidence of misery—not, in the first instance at least, his. In fact, he detaches himself from the evidence so that it will stand there in its own right. Frost rarely manages to do this in his first-person poems; the events are invariably reflected back upon the nature of the man who was sensitive enough to notice them. This may help to explain why Frost's greatest poems are objective narratives—poems like "A Servant to Servants," "The Fear," and "Out, Out."

What is remarkable in the first of these poems is Frost's power to turn an anecdote of tiredness into a fable of radical dissociation, a dissociation felt by the speaker only locally, in literal terms, and resisted by her in the same terms:

> It seems to me
> I can't express my feelings any more
> Than I can raise my voice or want to lift
> My hand (oh, I can lift it when I have to).

And the deadpan speech goes on until suddenly the servant says:

> I have my fancies: it runs in the family.
> My father's brother wasn't right . . .

This is the flowering of what was darkly implicit from the beginning. And it is achieved without forcing the facts to deny themselves in the service of the tragic tone. Reading the poem makes one wonder if there are any facts from the dark side of life that it doesn't encompass or imply. And we think that it is closer to Hawthorne, Melville, and Faulkner than to anything else in modern American poetry.

"The Fear" is, of course, an early figuring of the drama that is to be played again in "The Hill Wife." In the early poem the black presences that inhabit the world of man and wife are given spectral "body," as in a surrealist film. If these presences turn out, in the later poem, to be a tramp who walks away leaving behind him the image of a dank smile,

and a dark pine scraping on the bedroom window, we are not therefore
mistaken—even when the husband becomes himself a black presence,
in "The Impulse" and "Home Burial." These presences are not specified in "Out, Out," but we have to assume their existence in order to
make the fable endurable. They are discernible in the sweet scent of the
sawdust, in the buzz saw that, snarling, leaped out at the boy's hand,
and certainly in the stern, blameless practicality with which the on-
lookers, "since they/ Were not the one dead," turned to their affairs:

> The buzz saw snarled and rattled in the yard
> And made dust and dropped stove-length sticks of wood,
> Sweet-scented stuff when the breeze drew across it.
> And from there those that lifted eyes could count
> Five mountain ranges one behind the other
> Under the sunset far into Vermont.
> And the saw snarled and rattled, snarled and rattled,
> As it ran light, or had to bear a load.
> And nothing happened: day was all but done.
> Call it a day, I wish they might have said
> To please the boy by giving him the half hour
> That a boy counts so much when saved from work.
> His sister stood beside them in her apron
> To tell them "Supper." At the word, the saw,
> As if to prove saws knew what supper meant,
> Leaped out at the boy's hand, or seemed to leap—
> He must have given the hand. However it was,
> Neither refused the meeting. But the hand!
> The boy's first outcry was a rueful laugh,
> As he swung toward them holding up the hand
> Half in appeal, but half as if to keep
> The life from spilling. Then the boy saw all—
> Since he was old enough to know, big boy
> Doing a man's work, though a child at heart—

He saw all spoiled. "Don't let him cut my hand off—
The doctor, when he comes. Don't let him, sister!"
So. But the hand was gone already.
The doctor put him in the dark of ether.
He lay and puffed his lips out with his breath.
And then—the watcher at his pulse took fright.
No one believed. They listened at his heart.
Little—less—nothing—and that ended it.
No more to build on there. And they, since they
Were not the one dead, turned to their affairs.

Thinking of this poem, we recall what Frost said on several occasions, that poetry is what is lost in translation. But the present poem contradicts that aphorism, or at least modifies it so that it applies to some poems but not to others. I should prefer to argue, at the other extreme, that poetry is what survives translation. Goethe said that the important thing is what remains of a poet when he is translated into prose. This is a harsh test, and there is no present reason to enforce it, except to say that Frost's greatest poems could be separated from the rest by this means. And the present poem would survive the test. Charles Tomlinson says in one of his poems that "fact has its proper plenitude," and this is in line with our present argument. The plenitude of "Out, Out" is not, at least in the first instance, a verbal or linguistic plenitude; it is the plenitude of fact, of event, of plot, of what happened. And to this Frost adds the proper plenitude of modest words, which—when they have something to point at—point and take themselves off.

* * *

A question arises from Frost's poems in the present context: What are the possibilities for a poetry based upon little more than a shared sense of "the way things are"? Is this enough? Will it serve in place of those other "certainties" that are, for many readers, insecure?

Frost would seem to answer yes. Yeats relied on nervous improvisations, the record of exemplary lives, the pull of mind and body, or even religious patterns rented for the occasion of the poem. Eliot relied on Christian assumptions, some well in the light of day, others half-buried in the common language itself. Frost committed himself to the common ground he *knew* existed between himself and his putative reader. He knew, in several poems, that if he were to tell a moving story in a few common words, we would respond feelingly. And that, if not everything, was something. Hence he spent a lifetime finding out how much he could say on those terms. He is the poet most devoted to bare human gesture.

But this does not answer the question. Think of Frost and then of a poet like Traherne. Traherne "solves" the problems of his world, in many poems, by removing them to a higher ground on which only the pure can breathe. He annoys us when the removal arrangements are glib and automatic, especially when we feel that it cost him no real heartache to translate himself out of the human world. (Eliot often annoys us in this way too.) Frost is different. He doesn't solve the difficult problems, rather he evades them, mainly by living on the frontier, where a certain few problems arise so insistently that others may be ignored.

We will try again. The question before us is pretty close to Kenneth Burke's concerns in *Permanence and Change*, where he considers communication in its broadest sense as the sharing of sympathies and purposes. I. A. Richards would seem to answer our question, joylessly, by saying that once our attitudes and impulses are driven back upon their biological justification, those that are strong enough to survive are too crude to satisfy a finely developed sensibility. Such a sensibility, Richards warns us, cannot live by warmth, food, drink, and sex alone. But wait. Frost has shown in his poems that even if we are driven to rock bottom, to the biological imperative, enough remains to ensure the survival of human feeling, if not its constant operation. And that again is something. Warmth, food, fighting, drink, and sex are interim simplifications, local releases from the painful pursuit of "wholeness." Frost's poems acknowledge this, but without moving above rock bottom they also find interim peace in a bird twittering, "Let what will be, be," in flowers lodged but not dead, in women spinning their own cocoon of smoke. As to Burke, what he envisaged in *Permanence and Change* was not the preservation of a former homogeneity—he had Eliot's cultural program in his sights—but the establishment of a new one through the powers of fusion provided by a fresh unity of purpose.

Burke's writing at this point in *Permanence and Change* is unusually optative and hortatory. He speaks of cooperation to replace competition, yearning for a world devoted to ingratiation and persuasion. And he almost identifies style, piety, and decorum. It is a beautiful vision, almost a conceptual translation of *The Tempest*, and by its favored words it persuades toward its own end—words like *congregational*, *fusive*, *cooperative*, *participant*, *communicative*, *civic*. These are fine, resonant words, and the vision behind them glows with custom and good will. But—and here is our point—is the myth any more comprehensive than Frost's, the limitations of which we have seen? These myths differ in at least one crucial respect, which we will examine. But they are together in this, that they propose to build from the ground up, the ground being man as symbol-using animal. This is fine as far as it goes, but it doesn't go very far. And when is the fresh unity of purpose to emerge? And whose purpose will it be? And how will we prevent such a purpose from being a highly controversial linkage, just like the theological one?

Examining further the theological linkage, we find that Frost pretends to evade it, though in fact he rejects it out of hand. And although he was a gentleman, he would not have minded breaking other people's idols provided he could avoid being caught. Being caught, of course, would mean a fight on his hands that he could hardly hope to win by the famous charm, a matey wink, or a grin that said, "Take it easy, pal, I'm just a simple country boy." In Burke there is neither simple evasion nor simple rejection; there is, instead, translation. I have sometimes thought that what he offers in *Permanence and Change* is a method of "taking the harm out" of the Christian religion as an imperative by clinging to a secular version of it as an optative. In this respect his program is the reverse of Eliot's. Eliot, notably in his plays, uses the secular imprints of Christianity to push his audiences to the end of the line, into Christian worship itself. When he talks about the unconscious effect of poetry, this is really what he means and what he hopes for. Being a Christian, I should want the harm left in the Christian religion, and I should feel that Burke's program, however stylishly grounded upon the poetic metaphor, is feasible only if we all agree not to recall the divisive topics that he would translate out of dogmatic existence. And few of us could make or keep that promise. What life would be like in a Burkean condition of "pure" ingratiation I do not know. Most poems are the better for a good deal of impurity. And my own life seems to need a great deal of argumentative impurity to make it feel substantial. With that, we are back again in the gritty world of specific belief, specific commitment. Perhaps, then, Frost's poems provide at once the enactment of Burke's program and its critique. Reading Frost gives no scope for the trickwork of polemic. The best of his poems have a way of making the reader over in their own image, and this is their persuasive power. But they leave many of our stirrings unanswered.

There is one important element in Frost's poems that I have not discussed, but it is necessary to mention it at this stage, especially in the light of our speculations on *Permanence and Change*. I mentioned that Burke's vision of an ideal community would replace competition by cooperation. But of course there is no equivalent of this in Frost's poems. And this makes a difference. Burke would change the world by the sweetness of cooperation; Frost would leave the world pretty much as it is, only taking care to make himself strong enough to withstand it. And there are other differences. It often seems that everything in Frost's poems is to be explained as a nudging of temperament. Certainly the poems give an impression, through all their differences, of an identifiable temperament at work, answerable to no one. And this tends to make us conclude that there was no structure of conviction or idea in his society, in his background, from which the temperament emerged or to which it stands in any close relation. But this is wrong. If we look for such a structure in the America of Frost's youth, we find it—I shall argue—in the ideas of the Social Darwinists, especially in men like Herbert Spencer and William Graham Sumner and other voices that clamored in America from the 1870's up to the end of the century.

To support this it is necessary to bring the leading tenets of the Social Darwinists together, at least in rough paraphrase,[3] and to show their presence in a number of Frost's poems. The basic idea is that the natural world is a competitive situation in which the best competitors will win. Hence it follows that those who win are the best, and therefore the fittest to survive. Herbert Spencer believed that the pressure of subsistence upon population is bound to have a good effect on the human race. In any event, the whole effort of nature is to get rid of the weak, the unfit. "If they are sufficiently complete to live, they *do* live, and it is well they should live. If they are not sufficiently complete to live, they die, and it is best they should die." Hence the only feasible ethical standard is the right of every man to do as he pleases, subject only to the condition that he does not infringe upon the equal rights of others. (This is why good fences make good neighbors.) There is also the idea of the conservation of energy, or—as Spencer preferred to call it—the persistence of force. "Everywhere in the universe man observes the incessant re-distribution of matter and motion, rhythmically apportioned between evolution and dissolution. Evolution is the progressive integration of matter, accompanied by dissipation of motion; dissolution is the disorganization of matter accompanied by the absorption of motion." Hence Spencer inferred that anything that is homogeneous is inherently unstable, since the different effects of persistent force upon its various parts must cause differences to arise in their future development. Thus the homogeneous will inevitably develop into the heterogeneous. (Frost's version of this, in a poem of *In the Clearing*, is:

> A nation has to take its natural course
> Of Progress round and round in circles
> From King to Mob to King to Mob to King
> Until the eddy of it eddies out.[4]

And this belief also throws light upon his presentation of the family unit, in many poems, as a pretty desolate structure.) And, finally, the Darwinian view is that all changes in types of survival and kinds of fitness are considered without relation to ultimate values; there is no relevant value beyond survival itself. There is, of course, a milder version of this to which we would all subscribe: "the desire of the body is to continue, the deepest need of the mind is for order,"[5] and where there is a quarrel, the body claims priority. But the Social Darwinists went much further than this.

If we look at a few of Frost's poems in this setting, the relation between his temperament and the ideas of Social Darwinism seems very close. There is the famous instance, "Two Tramps in Mud Time." The narrator is splitting wood when two tramps come by, and one of them drops behind, hoping to get the job for pay:

> Nothing on either side was said.
> They knew they had but to stay their stay
> And all their logic would fill my head:
> As that I had no right to play
> With what was another man's work for gain.
> My right might be love but theirs was need.
> And where the two exist in twain
> Theirs was the better right—agreed.

These arguments are strong, but the tramps don't get the job:

> But yield who will to their separation,
> My object in living is to unite
> My avocation and my vocation
> As my two eyes make one in sight.
> Only where love and need are one,
> And the work is play for mortal stakes,
> Is the deed ever really done
> For Heaven and the future's sakes.

So need is not reason enough. The narrator has need and love on his side, hence he survives and nature blesses him as the best man. The tramps are unfit to survive because they have only their need, and the Darwinist law is that they should not survive. And if people think that they should survive and should be helped to survive, there is another poem, "A Roadside Stand," that says of another kind of poor:

> It is in the news that all these pitiful kin
> Are to be bought out and mercifully gathered in
> To live in villages next to the theater and store
> Where they won't have to think for themselves any more;
> While greedy good-doers, beneficent beasts of prey,
> Swarm over their lives enforcing benefits
> That are calculated to soothe them out of their wits,
> And by teaching them how to sleep the sleep all day,
> Destroy their sleeping at night the ancient way.

This is the dogma of Herbert Spencer set to a tune characteristic of Robert Frost. And there are many poems that would document the case if it were necessary.

The shoddy part of all this, of course, is that one can only talk about the survival of the fittest if one has already survived. And the complacent acceptance of this fact induces a nasty tone in these poems that no amount of rural minstrelsy will evade. Complacency about war, for in-

---

stance, proliferates through such poems as "The Flood," "On Looking Up by Chance at the Constellations," "A Serious Step Lightly Taken," "It Bids Pretty Fair," and this one, "Bursting Rapture":

> I went to the physician to complain,
> The time had been when anyone could turn
> To farming for a simple way to earn;
> But now 'twas there as elsewhere, any gain
> Was made by getting science on the brain;
> There was so much more every day to learn,
> The discipline of farming was so stern,
> It seemed as if I couldn't stand the strain.
> But the physician's answer was "There, there,
> What you complain of all the nations share.
> Their effort is a mounting ecstasy
> That when it gets too exquisite to bear
> Will find relief in one burst. You shall see.
> That's what a certain bomb was sent to be."

And then there is complacency about evil, as in the poem "Quandary," and complacency about waste, which is called "the good of waste," in "Pod of the Milkweed." In "New Hampshire" Frost says:

> We get what little misery we can
> Out of not having cause for misery.
> It makes the guild of novel writers sick
> To be expected to be Dostoievskis
> On nothing worse than too much luck and comfort.

As if this disposed of William Faulkner. In "Our Hold on the Planet" Frost argues from the fact that world population is increasing and therefore "surviving," that things can't be too bad:

We may doubt the just proportion of good to ill.
There is much in nature against us. But we forget:
Take nature altogether since time began,
Including human nature, in peace and war,
And it must be a little more in favor of man,
Say a fraction of one per cent at the very least,
Or our number living wouldn't be steadily more,
Our hold on the planet wouldn't have so increased.

In the little poem "Pertinax" he says:

> Let chaos storm!
> Let cloud shapes swarm!
> I wait for form.

He says it, of course, because he is a survivor, and he can afford to wait. And there is a poem with the fantastic title "Evil Tendencies Cancel," to which the only response is "No, by God, they don't!":

> Will the blight end the chestnut?
> The farmers rather guess not.
> It keeps smoldering at the roots
> And sending up new shoots
> Till another parasite
> Shall come to end the blight.

We either gloss this over or accept the challenge it implies. If the chestnut is man, and the blight is evil, and the smoldering is pain and suffering, then what is this anticipated parasite that will end the evil blight? In what sense does one evil cancel out another? And even in such a transaction how can man gain? How can his suffering be reduced?

There is only one answer: Make sure that *you* are the one who survives; keep one step ahead of all the games. This is the moral of several poems—"A Drumlin Woodchuck," "In Time of Cloudburst," "A Leaf Treader," and many others. And the tone in which you do this is suggested by the poem "Bravado":

Have I not walked without an upward look
Of caution under stars that very well
Might not have missed me when they shot and fell?
It was a risk I had to take—and took.

This means, in effect, "*I* ignored God and *I* survived." And another version, which might well be the slogan of a reactionary politics today rather than an adornment of the New Frontier by its poet laureate, is "One Step Backward Taken":

Not only sands and gravels
Were once more on their travels,
But gulping muddy gallons
Great boulders off their balance
Bumped heads together dully
And started down the gully.
Whole capes caked off in slices.
I felt my standpoint shaken
In the universal crisis.
But with one step backward taken
I saved myself from going.
A world torn loose went by me.
Then the rain stopped and the blowing
And the sun came out to dry me.

If we bring most of this together, it seems to converge on those poems in which Frost defines his essential vision of man. And one poem seems particularly relevant, "The Figure in the Doorway." From a train traveling through mountains the narrator sees a man standing at his cabin door. He is utterly alone, no wife, no family, utterly self-reliant, far away from other people, societies, institutions:

> The miles and miles he lived from anywhere
> Were evidently something he could bear.
> He stood unshaken, and if grim and gaunt,
> It was not necessarily from want.
> He had the oaks for heating and for light.
> He had a hen, he had a pig in sight.
> He had a well, he had the rain to catch.
> He had a ten-by-twenty garden patch.
> Nor did he lack for common entertainment.
> That I assume was what our passing train meant.
> He could look at us in our diner eating,
> And if so moved uncurl a hand in greeting.

Social Darwinism petered out toward the end of the century; when the war came in 1914 its glibness and cruelty seemed repellent. (But it has emerged again in the 1960's.) In Frost it persisted through the wars, it persisted after Hiroshima, mainly because it was a matter of temperament rather than argument. And because it didn't have a label, it couldn't be inspected too closely. But it was there.

It follows that Frost's greatest poems are those in which he holds himself so firmly to the facts, devotes himself so lavishly to them, that they are, for the time being, everything there is. Even a meager list, which leaves out as many as it puts in, has to include these: the servant in "A Servant to Servants" saying "I shan't catch up in this world, anyway"; the pressure of the ladder in "After Apple-Picking"; the voice that says "Nothing" in "The Fear"; the sound like beating on a box in "An Old Man's Winter Night"; the smile that "never came of being gay" in "The Hill Wife"; the great buck pushing through the water in "The Most of It"; the horror on the girl's tongue in "The Subverted

Flower." And to acknowledge that the best poems are sometimes the famous poems, here is "After Apple-Picking"—or rather, the end of it:

> For I have had too much
> Of apple-picking: I am overtired
> Of the great harvest I myself desired.
> There were ten thousand thousand fruit to touch,
> Cherish in hand, lift down, and not let fall.
> For all
> That struck the earth,
> No matter if not bruised or spiked with stubble,
> Went surely to the cider-apple heap
> As of no worth.
> One can see what will trouble
> This sleep of mine, whatever sleep it is.
> Were he not gone,
> The woodchuck could say whether it's like his
> Long sleep, as I describe its coming on,
> Or just some human sleep.

The noble, curial tone is supported by Frost's fidelity to the facts of the case. Indeed, when he is at his best—as here—it is characteristic of him to let the feeling ride upon the precision with which the facts are given. In this poem he is concerned with the quality of his tiredness, the nature of his sleep, but these will come—in the poem—as they come in fact, after he has done his job. First the job, the apples that are gathered, then those that fell, and the cider-apple heap; and only then the giving in, the tiredness, the sleep. There is as much daring in the structure of this poem as there is in the quirkiest details. (And, incidentally, what other poet would start a poem with the line, "Back out of all this now too much for us"?) This is where Frost really survives.

Notes

1. Robert Frost, *Complete Poems* (New York: Henry Holt. 1949), p. 41.
2. Wallace Stevens, *The Necessary Angel* (New York: Knopf, 1951), p. 99.
3. What follows in these paragraphs is taken from Richard Hofstadter, *Social Darwinism in American Thought* (rev. ed.; Boston: Beacon Press, 1955), esp. pp. 36-37, 39, 41, 198.
4. Frost, *In the Clearing* (New York: Holt, Rinehart and Winston, 1962), p. 80.
5. John Peale Bishop, *Collected Essays* (New York: Scribners, 1948), p. 32.

RESOURCES

1874	Robert Frost is born in San Francisco, California, to William Prescott Frost and Isabelle Moodie Frost.
1876	Frost's parents briefly separate and Frost's sister, Jeanie, is born while Isabelle visits her in-laws in Lawrence, Massachusetts. She returns to William in San Francisco with her two children in the fall.
1885	Frost's father dies and his mother moves the family to Lawrence. Over the next few years they live in Salem, New Hampshire, where Isabelle teaches school, and Ocean Park, Maine, where Isabelle works as a chambermaid, before moving back to Lawrence in 1890.
1892	Frost graduates from Lawrence High School and is co-valedictorian with Elinor White. During the summer, the two secretly become engaged. In the fall Elinor leaves for St. Lawrence University in Canton, New York. Frost attends Dartmouth College, but leaves before finishing his first term and spends the next few years working odd jobs.
1894	Frost's first published poem, "My Butterfly: An Elegy," appears in the *Independent*, a New York magazine.
1895	Frost starts a private school with his mother. He marries Elinor White.
1896	Frost's son Elliot is born.
1897-1899	Frost studies at Harvard College.
1899	Frost leaves Harvard without finishing his degree and moves his family to a rented farm in Methuen, Massachusetts. His daughter Lesley is born.
1900	Elliot dies of cholera in July. In the fall, the family moves to a farm in Derry, New Hampshire, that was purchased by Frost's grandfather. Frost's mother dies in November. For the next twelve years, Frost divides his time among farming, teaching, and writing poetry, occasionally publishing in small journals and newspapers.

1901	Frost's grandfather dies, leaving Frost with the Derry farm and a sizable annuity.
1902	Frost's son Carol is born.
1903	Frost's daughter Irma is born.
1905	Frost's daughter Marjorie is born.
1906	Frost begins teaching English at Pinkerton Academy. "The Tuft of Flowers" and "The Trial by Existence" are published.
1907	Frost's daughter Elinor Bettina dies shortly after her birth.
1911	Frost leaves Pinkerton Academy to teach at the New Hampshire Normal School.
1912	Frost sells the Derry farm and moves his family to Beaconsfield, England.
1913	*A Boy's Will* is published in England by David Nutt. Frost begins meeting other prominent poets of the period, such as Ezra Pound and William Butler Yeats.
1914	Frost moves to Gloucestershire with his family in April; *North of Boston* appears in May.
1915	Frost returns to the United States with his family. The American editions of *A Boy's Will* and *North of Boston* are published and widely acclaimed.
1916	Frost buys a farm and settles his family in Franconia, New Hampshire. *Mountain Interval* is published. Frost is inducted into the National Institute of Arts and Letters.
1917	Frost takes a teaching position at Amherst College; he holds the position, with a few interruptions, until 1938.
1920	Frost leaves Amherst temporarily and, after an incident in Portland, Maine, commits his sister, Jeanie, to a mental institution.

1921-1923	Frost teaches at the University of Michigan as poet-in-residence and then returns to Amherst.
1923	*New Hampshire* is published and wins the Pulitzer Prize the following year.
1925-1926	Frost teaches at the University of Michigan as fellow in letters, then returns to Amherst.
1928	*West-Running Brook* is published.
1929	Frost's one-act play *A Way Out* is published. He moves with Elinor to Gully Farm in Bennington, Vermont. Jeanie dies.
1930	*Collected Poems* is published and wins the Pulitzer Prize the following year. Frost is inducted into the American Academy of Arts and Letters.
1934	Frost's daughter Marjorie dies as the result of puerperal fever after childbirth.
1936	*A Further Range* is published and wins the Pulitzer Prize the following year. Frost is named Charles Eliot Norton Professor of Poetry at Harvard University.
1938	Elinor dies. Frost leaves Amherst College permanently.
1939	The National Institute of Arts and Letters awards Frost the Gold Medal for Poetry. Harvard University names Frost the Ralph Waldo Emerson Fellow in Poetry, a post he holds until 1942.
1940	Frost's son Carol commits suicide.
1942	*A Witness Tree* is published and wins the Pulitzer Prize the following year.
1945	*A Masque of Reason* is published.
1947	*Steeple Bush* and *A Masque of Mercy* are published.
1949	*Complete Poems* is published.

1950	The U.S. Congress passes a resolution to extend "felicitations" to Frost on his seventy-fifth birthday.
1954	Frost travels to Brazil on behalf of the U.S. State Department for the World Congress of Writers.
1957	Frost travels to Britain on behalf of the U.S. State Department; he receives honorary doctorates from Oxford and Cambridge universities and is received by the National University of Ireland.
1958	The Library of Congress names Frost Consultant in Poetry.
1961	Frost recites "The Gift Outright" at the inauguration of President John F. Kennedy. He travels to Israel and Greece.
1962	*In the Clearing* is published. President Kennedy presents Frost with the Congressional Gold Medal. Frost travels to the Soviet Union at Kennedy's request to meet Russian writers and Premier Nikita Khrushchev.
1963	Frost dies on January 29 in a Boston hospital, following an operation.

Works by Robert Frost

Poetry

A Boy's Will, 1913
North of Boston, 1914
Mountain Interval, 1916
New Hampshire: A Poem with Notes and Grace Notes, 1923
Selected Poems, 1923
West-Running Brook, 1928
Collected Poems, 1930
A Further Range, 1936
Collected Poems, 1939
A Witness Tree, 1942
A Masque of Reason, 1945
A Masque of Mercy, 1947
Steeple Bush, 1947
Complete Poems, 1949
How Not to Be King, 1951
In the Clearing, 1962
The Poetry of Robert Frost, 1969

Drama

A Way Out, 1929

Nonfiction

The Letters of Robert Frost to Louis Untermeyer, 1963
The Record of a Friendship, 1963
Selected Letters of Robert Frost, 1964
Selected Prose, 1966
The Notebooks of Robert Frost, 2006
The Collected Prose of Robert Frost, 2007

Bibliography

Angyal, Andrew J. "From Swedenborg to William James: The Shaping of Robert Frost's Religious Beliefs." *Robert Frost Review* (Fall 1994): 69-81.

Auden, W. H. "Robert Frost." *The Dyer's Hand and Other Essays*. New York: Random House, 1962. 337-53.

Bacon, Helen. "For Girls: From 'Birches' to 'Wild Grapes.'" *Yale Review* 67 (1977): 13-29.

Bagby, George F. *Frost and the Book of Nature*. Knoxville: University of Tennessee Press, 1993.

Barry, Elaine. *Robert Frost*. New York: Frederick Ungar, 1973.

Berger, Harry, Jr. "Poetry and Revision: Interpreting Robert Frost." *Criticism* 10 (1968): 1-22.

Bloom, Harold, ed. *Robert Frost*. New York: Chelsea House, 2003.

Bogan, Louise. *A Poet's Alphabet*. New York: McGraw-Hill, 1970.

Borroff, Marie. *Language and the Poet: Verbal Artistry in Frost, Stevens, and Moore*. Chicago: University of Chicago Press, 1979.

Brodsky, Joseph. "On Grief and Reason." *The New Yorker* September 26, 1994: 70-75.

Bromwich, David. *A Choice of Inheritance: Self and Community from Edmund Burke to Robert Frost*. Cambridge, MA: Harvard University Press, 1989.

Brower, Reuben A. *The Poetry of Robert Frost: Constellations of Intention*. New York: Oxford University Press, 1963.

Buxton, Rachel. *Robert Frost and Northern Irish Poetry*. New York: Oxford University Press, 2004.

Cook, Reginald L. *The Dimensions of Robert Frost*. New York: Rinehart, 1958.

_____. *Robert Frost: A Living Voice*. Amherst: University of Massachusetts Press, 1974.

Cowley, Malcolm. "Robert Frost: A Dissenting Opinion." *A Many-Windowed House: Collected Essays on American Writers and American Writing*. Carbondale: Southern Illinois University Press, 1970. 201-12.

Cox, Earl J., and Jonathan N. Barron, eds. *Roads Not Taken: Rereading Robert Frost*. Columbia: University of Missouri Press, 2004.

Cox, James M., ed. *Robert Frost: A Collection of Critical Essays*. Englewood Cliffs, NJ: Prentice-Hall, 1962.

Cox, Sidney. *A Swinger of Birches: A Portrait of Robert Frost*. New York: New York University Press, 1960.

D'Avanzo, Mario L. *A Cloud of Other Poets: Robert Frost and the Romantics*. Lanham, MD: University Press of America, 1991.

Dawes, James R. "Masculinity and Transgression in Robert Frost." *American Literature* 65 (June 1993): 297-312.

Dickey, James. "Robert Frost." *Babel to Byzantium: Poets and Poetry Now*. New York: Farrar, Straus and Giroux, 1968. 200-209.

Donoghue, Denis. "Robert Frost." *Connoisseurs of Chaos*. New York: Macmillan, 1984.

Doreski, William. "Robert Frost's 'The Census-Taker' and the Problem of the Wilderness." *Twentieth-Century Literature* 34, no. 1 (Spring 1988): 30-39.

Dowell, Peter W. "Counter-images and Their Function in the Poetry of Robert Frost." *Tennessee Studies in Literature* 14 (1969): 15-30.

Faggen, Robert, ed. *The Cambridge Companion to Robert Frost*. New York: Cambridge University Press, 2001.

_____. *Robert Frost and the Challenge of Darwin*. Ann Arbor: University of Michigan Press, 1997.

Frattali, Steven. *Person, Place, and World: A Late-Modern Reading of Robert Frost*. Victoria, BC: English Literary Studies, University of Victoria, 2002.

Frost, Robert. *Interviews with Robert Frost*. Ed. Edward Connery Lathem. New York: Holt, Rinehart and Winston, 1966.

Gerber, Philip L. *Robert Frost*. New York: Twayne, 1966.

Hadas, Rachel. *Form, Cycle, Infinity: Landscape Imagery in the Poetry of Robert Frost*. Lewisburg, PA: Bucknell University Press, 1985.

Harris, Kathryn Gibbs, ed. *Robert Frost: Studies of the Poetry*. Boston: G. K. Hall, 1979.

Hass, Robert Bernard. *Going by Contraries: Robert Frost's Conflict with Science*. Charlottesville: University Press of Virginia, 2002.

Haynes, Donald T. "The Narrative Unity of *A Boy's Will*." *PMLA* 137 (1972): 452-64.

Heaney, Seamus. "Above the Brim." *Homage to Robert Frost*. Joseph Brodsky, Seamus Heaney, and Derek Walcott. New York: Farrar, Straus and Giroux, 1996. 61-88.

Hoffman, Tyler B. *Robert Frost and the Politics of Poetry*. Hanover, N.H.: University Press of New England, 2001.

Howe, Irving. "Robert Frost: A Momentary Stay." *A World More Attractive: A View of Modern Literature and Politics*. New York: Horizon Press, 1963. 144-57.

Ingebretsen, S. J., ed. *Robert Frost's "Star in a Stone Boat": A Grammar of Belief*. San Francisco: Catholic Scholars Press, 1994.

Jarrell, Randall. "The Other Frost" and "To the Laodiceans." *Poetry and the Age*. New York: Alfred A. Knopf, 1953. 28-36, 37-69.

Kearns, Katherine. *Robert Frost and a Poetics of Appetite*. New York: Cambridge University Press, 1994.

Kemp, John C. *Robert Frost and New England: The Poet as Regionalist*. Princeton, NJ: Princeton University Press, 1979.

Kennedy, John F. "Poetry and Power." *Atlantic Monthly* February 1964: 53-54.

Kilcup, Karen L. *Robert Frost and Feminine Literary Tradition*. Ann Arbor: University of Michigan Press, 1998.

Lea, Sidney. "From Sublime to Rigamarole: Relations of Frost to Wordsworth." *Studies in Romanticism* 19 (1980): 83-108.

Lentricchia, Frank. *Modernist Quartet*. New York: Cambridge University Press, 1994.

_____. *Robert Frost: Modern Poetics and the Landscapes of Self*. Durham, NC: Duke University Press, 1975.

Lynen, John F. *The Pastoral Art of Robert Frost*. New Haven, CT: Yale University Press, 1960.

McGavran, Dorothy. "The Building Community: Houses and Other Structures in the Poetry of Robert Frost." *Robert Frost Review* (Fall 1994): 1-12.

Marcus, Mordecai. *The Poems of Robert Frost: An Explication*. Boston: G. K. Hall, 1991.

Marks, Herbert. "The Counter-intelligence of Robert Frost." *Yale Review* 71 (1982): 554-78.

Maxon, H. A. *On the Sonnets of Robert Frost*. Jefferson, NC: McFarland, 1997.

Meyers, Jeffrey. *Robert Frost: A Biography*. Boston: Houghton Mifflin, 1996.

Michaels, Walter Benn. "Getting Physical." *Raritan* 2, no. 2 (Fall 1982): 103-13.

Monteiro, George. "Frost's Hired Hand." *College Literature* 14 (1987): 128-35.

_____. *Robert Frost and the New England Renaissance*. Lexington: University Press of Kentucky, 1988.

Munson, Gorham. *Robert Frost: A Study in Sensibility and Good Sense*. Port Washington, NY: Kennikat Press, 1927.

Newdick, Robert. *Newdick's Season of Frost: An Interrupted Biography of Robert Frost*. Ed. William A. Sutton. Albany: State University of New York Press, 1976.

Nitchie, George W. *Human Values in the Poetry of Robert Frost: A Study of Poetic Convictions*. Durham, NC: Duke University Press, 1960.

Norwood, Kyle. "The Work of Not Knowing: Robert Frost and the Abject." *Southwest Review* 78 (1993): 57-75.

Oster, Judith. *Toward Robert Frost: The Reader and the Poet*. Athens: University of Georgia Press, 1991.

Pack, Robert. *Belief and Uncertainty in the Poetry of Robert Frost*. Lebanon, NH: University Press of New England, 2003.

_____. "Frost's Enigmatical Reserve: The Poet as Teacher and Preacher." *Affirming Limits: Essays on Mortality, Choice and Poetic Form*. Amherst: University of Massachusetts Press, 1985. 174-88.

Parini, Jay. *Robert Frost: A Life*. New York: Henry Holt, 1999.

Pearce, Roy Harvey. *The Continuity of American Poetry*. Princeton, NJ: Princeton University Press, 1961.

Perrine, Laurence. "Provide, Provide." *Robert Frost Review* (Fall 1992): 33-39.

Poirier, Richard. "Frost, Winnicott, Burke." *Raritan* 2, no. 2 (Fall 1982): 114-27.

_____. *Robert Frost: The Work of Knowing*. New York: Oxford University Press, 1977.

Poole, Robert. "Robert Frost, William Carlos Williams, and Wallace Stevens: Reality and Poetic Vitality." *CLA Journal* 26 (1992): 12-23.

Pritchard, William H. *Frost: A Literary Life Reconsidered*. New York: Oxford University Press, 1984.

Richardson, Mark. *The Ordeal of Robert Frost: The Poet and His Poetics*. Urbana: University of Illinois Press, 1997.

_____. "Robert Frost and the Motives of Poetry." *Essays in Literature* 20, no. 2 (Fall 1993): 273-91.

Ridland, John. "Fourteen Ways of Looking at a Bad Man." *Southwest Review* 71, no. 2 (Spring 1986): 222-42.

Sabin, Margery. "The Fate of the Frost Speaker." *Raritan* 2, no. 2 (Fall 1982): 128-39.

Sears, John F. "The Subversive Performer in Frost's 'Snow' and 'Out, Out—.'" *The Motive for Metaphor*. Ed. Francis Blessington. Boston: Northeastern University Press, 1983.

Sheehy, Donald G. "(Re)figuring Love: Robert Frost in Crisis." *New England Quarterly* 63 (June 1990): 179-231.

Stanlis, Peter. *Robert Frost: The Poet as Philosopher*. Wilmington, DE: Intercollegiate Studies Institute, 2007.

Tharpe, Jac, ed. *Frost: Centennial Essays*. Jackson: University Press of Mississippi, 1974.

Thompson, Lawrance. *Fire and Ice: The Art and Thought of Robert Frost*. New York: Holt, Rinehart and Winston, 1942.

_____. *Robert Frost: The Early Years, 1874-1915*. London: Cape, 1967

_____. *Robert Frost: The Years of Triumph, 1915-1938*. New York: Holt, 1970.

Thompson, Lawrance, and R. H. Winnick. *Robert Frost: The Later Years, 1938-1963*. New York: Holt, Rinehart and Winston, 1976.

Timmerman, John H. *Robert Frost: The Ethics of Ambiguity*. Lewisburg, PA: Bucknell University Press, 2002.

Trilling, Lionel. "A Speech on Robert Frost: A Cultural Episode." *Partisan Review* 26 (Summer 1959): 445-52.

Tuten, Nancy Lewis, and John Zubizarreta, eds. *The Robert Frost Encyclopedia*. Santa Barbara, CA: Greenwood Press, 2000.

Van Doren, Mark. "The Permanence of Robert Frost." *The Private Reader: Selected Articles and Reviews*. New York: Henry Holt, 1942. 87-96.

Wagner, Linda W., ed. *Robert Frost: The Critical Reception*. New York: Burt Franklin, 1977.

Walcott, Derek. "The Road Taken." *Homage to Robert Frost*. Joseph Brodsky, Seamus Heaney, and Derek Walcott. New York: Farrar, Straus and Giroux, 1996.

Warren, Robert Penn. "The Themes of Robert Frost." *Selected Essays*. New York: Random House, 1958. 118-36.

Winters, Yvor. "Robert Frost: Or, The Spiritual Drifter as Poet." *The Function of Criticism*. Denver: Alan Swallow, 1957. 157-88.

CRITICAL
INSIGHTS

About the Editor

Morris Dickstein is Distinguished Professor of English at the Graduate Center of the City University of New York and senior fellow of the Center for the Humanities, which he founded in 1993 and directed for seven years. His books include *Keats and His Poetry* (1971), *Gates of Eden: American Culture in the Sixties* (1977, 1997), and *Double Agent: The Critic and Society* (1992). He also edited *The Revival of Pragmatism* (1998). His most recent books are *Leopards in the Temple: The Transformation of American Fiction, 1945-1970* (2002), *A Mirror in the Roadway: Literature and the Real World* (2005), and *Dancing in the Dark: A Cultural History of the Great Depression* (2009). His essays and reviews have appeared in *The New York Times Book Review*, *Partisan Review*, *The American Scholar*, *Raritan*, *The Nation*, *Literary Imagination*, *Slate*, *Dissent*, *The Washington Post*, the *Chronicle of Higher Education*, *Bookforum*, and the *Times Literary Supplement* (London). He has served as film critic of the *Bennington Review* and *Partisan Review* and was an adviser for a documentary film about four leading New York intellectuals, Joseph Dorman's *Arguing the World*. He was a founder and board member (1983-89) of the National Book Critics Circle and Vice-Chair of the New York Council for the Humanities from 1997 to 2001. He was a contributing editor of *Partisan Review* from 1972 to 2003 and served as president of the Association of Literary Scholars and Critics in 2006-07.

About *The Paris Review*

The Paris Review is America's preeminent literary quarterly, dedicated to discovering and publishing the best new voices in fiction, nonfiction, and poetry. The magazine was founded in Paris in 1953 by the young American writers Peter Matthiessen and Doc Humes, and edited there and in New York for its first fifty years by George Plimpton. Over the decades, the *Review* has introduced readers to the earliest writings of Jack Kerouac, Philip Roth, T. C. Boyle, V. S. Naipaul, Ha Jin, Jay McInerney, and Mona Simpson, and published numerous now classic works, including Roth's *Goodbye, Columbus*, Donald Barthelme's *Alice*, Jim Carroll's *Basketball Diaries*, and selections from Samuel Beckett's *Molloy* (his first publication in English). The first chapter of Jeffrey Eugenides's *The Virgin Suicides* appeared in the *Review*'s pages, as well as stories by Edward P. Jones, Rick Moody, David Foster Wallace, Denis Johnson, Jim Shepard, Jim Crace, Lorrie Moore, Jeanette Winterson, and Ann Patchett.

The Paris Review's renowned Writers at Work series of interviews, whose early installments include legendary conversations with E. M. Forster, William Faulkner, and Ernest Hemingway, is one of the landmarks of world literature. The interviews received a George Polk Award and were nominated for a Pulitzer Prize. Among the more than three hundred interviewees are Robert Frost, Marianne Moore, W. H. Auden, Elizabeth Bishop, Susan Sontag, and Toni Morrison. Recent issues feature conversations with Salman Rushdie, Joan Didion, Stephen King, Norman Mailer, Kazuo Ishiguro, and Umberto Eco. (A complete list of the interviews is available at www.theparisreview.org.) In November 2008, Picador will publish the third of a four-volume series of anthologies of *Paris Review* interviews. The first two volumes have received acclaim. *The New York Times* called the Writers at Work series "the most remarkable and extensive interviewing project we possess."

The Paris Review is edited by Philip Gourevitch, who was named to the post in 2005, following the death of George Plimpton two years earlier. Under Gourevitch's leadership, the magazine's international distribution has expanded, paid subscriptions have risen 150 percent, and newsstand distribution has doubled. A new editorial team has published fiction by Andre Aciman, Damon Galgut, Mohsin Hamid, Gish Jen, Richard Price, Said Sayrafiezadeh, and Alistair Morgan. Poetry editors Charles Simic, Meghan O'Rourke, and Dan Chiasson have selected works by Billy Collins, Jesse Ball, Mary Jo Bang, Sharon Olds, and Mary Karr. Writing published in the magazine has been anthologized in *Best American Short Stories* (2006, 2007, and 2008), *Best American Poetry*, *Best Creative Non-Fiction*, the Pushcart Prize anthology, and *O. Henry Prize Stories*.

The magazine presents two annual awards. The Hadada Award for lifelong contribution to literature has recently been given to William Styron, Joan Didion, Norman Mailer, and Peter Matthiessen in 2008. The Plimpton Prize for Fiction, given to a new voice in fiction brought to national attention in the pages of *The Paris Review*, was presented in 2007 to Benjamin Percy and to Jesse Ball in 2008.

The Paris Review won the 2007 National Magazine Award in photojournalism, and the *Los Angeles Times* recently called *The Paris Review* "an American treasure with true international reach."

Since 1999 *The Paris Review* has been published by The Paris Review Foundation, Inc., a not-for-profit 501(c)(3) organization.

The Paris Review is available in digital form to libraries worldwide in selected academic databases exclusively from EBSCO Publishing. Libraries can contact EBSCO at 1-800-653-2726 for details. For more information on *The Paris Review* or to subscribe, please visit: www.theparisreview.org.

Contributors

Morris Dickstein is Distinguished Professor of English at the Graduate Center of the City University of New York. He is a widely published reviewer and critic, perhaps best known for his book on the 1960s, *Gates of Eden* (1977, 1997). His most recent books are *Leopards in the Temple: The Transformation of American Fiction, 1945-1970* (2002), *A Mirror in the Roadway: Literature and the Real World* (2005), and *Dancing in the Dark: A Cultural History of the Great Depression* (2009). In 2006-07 he served as president of the Association of Literary Scholars and Critics.

James Norman O'Neill is retired and is living in Fort Myers, Florida. He previously taught English at Bryant University in Smithfield, Rhode Island. He has published on the English Victorian poet Alfred Tennyson and has written several articles for Salem Press.

Elizabeth Gumport is an M.F.A. candidate in fiction at The Johns Hopkins University. Her writing has appeared in *n+1*, *Canteen*, and *Slate*.

Matthew J. Bolton is Professor of English at Loyola School in New York City, where he also serves as the Dean of Students. He received his doctor of philosophy degree in English from the Graduate Center of the City University of New York in 2005. His dissertation at the university was titled "Transcending the Self in Robert Browning and T. S. Eliot." Prior to attaining his Ph.D., Bolton also earned a master of philosophy degree in English (2004) and a master of science degree in English education (2001). His undergraduate work was done at the State University of New York at Binghamton, where he studied English literature.

Janyce Marson is a doctoral student at New York University. She is writing a dissertation on the rhetoric of the mechanical in William Wordsworth, Samuel Taylor Coleridge, and Mary Shelley.

Jamey Hecht earned his Ph.D. at Brandeis University in 1994 with a dissertation on English and American literature. He is the author of an undergraduate guide, *Plato's Symposium: Eros and the Human Predicament* (1999); a translation, *Sophocles' Three Theban Plays* (2004); and a collection of poems, *Limousine, Midnight Blue: Fifty Frames from the Zapruder Film* (2009). His poetry, criticism, and journalism have appeared in some thirty-five publications, including *Black Warrior Review*, *ELH*, *Free Inquiry*, and *Tikkun*. He enjoys acting in Shakespearean plays with the Porters of Hellsgate. He maintains a website at www.jameyhecht.com and a blog, Poetry, Politics, Collapse, at http://poetrypoliticscollapse.blogspot.com.

Anastasia Vahaviolos Valassis is a Ph.D. student at the Graduate Center, City University of New York. Her primary interests are in the nineteenth-century British novel, narrative theory, and autobiography. She currently teaches composition and introductory literature courses at the Borough of Manhattan Community College. She delights in Robert Frost's poetics both as a scholar and as a teacher.

David Sanders is Professor of English at St. John Fisher College. His work has appeared in *The Robert Frost Encyclopedia* (2001), *Frost: Centennial Essays* (1976), *South Carolina Review*, and *Journal of Modern Literature*.

Tyler B. Hoffman is Associate Professor of English at Rutgers University, Camden. He is the Associate Editor of *The Robert Frost Review*, a member of the Executive Committee of the Robert Frost Society, and the author of *Robert Frost and the Politics of Poetry* (2001). He has also published work on Emily Dickinson, Elizabeth Bishop, Gary Snyder, Vachel Lindsay, and Thom Gunn.

Roger Gilbert is Professor of English at Cornell University. He has published widely on such twentieth-century poets as Robert Frost, A. R. Ammons, Allen Grossman, Wallace Stevens, Elizabeth Bishop, Adrienne Rich, and William Carlos Williams. He is the author of *Walks in the World: Representations of Experience in Modern American Poetry* (1991) and coeditor of *Consider the Radiance: Essays on the Poetry of A. R. Ammons* (2005).

Judith Oster is Associate Professor of English at Case Western Reserve University. She is the author of *Crossing Cultures: Creating Identity in Chinese and Jewish American Literature* (2003), *Toward Robert Frost: The Reader and the Poet* (1991), and *From Reading to Writing: A Rhetoric and Reader* (1984).

Frank Lentricchia is Katherine Everett Gilbert Professor of Literature and Theatre Studies at Duke University. A novelist and author of more than ten scholarly works on subjects ranging from W. B. Yeats, Wallace Stevens, Michel Foucault, William James, and Don DeLillo to literary theory, he has published two books on Robert Frost: *Robert Frost: A Bibliography, 1913-1974* (1976) and *Robert Frost: Modern Poetics and the Landscapes of Self* (1975).

Robert Bernard Hass is Assistant Professor of English at Edinboro University of Pennsylvania. His publications include *Going by Contraries: Robert Frost's Conflict with Science* (2002).

Shira Wolosky is Professor of English and American Literature at the Hebrew University of Jerusalem. A former Associate Professor of English at Yale University, she received a Guggenheim Fellowship in 2001 and was Drue Heinz Visiting Professor at Oxford University in 2008. Her publications include *Defending Identity* (2008), *The Art of Poetry* (2001), *Language Mysticism: The Negative Way of Language in Eliot, Beckett, and Celan* (1995), and *Emily Dickinson: A Voice of War* (1984).

Jeff Westover is Assistant Professor of English at Boise State University. His publications include *The Colonial Moment: Discoveries and Settlements in Modern American Poetry* (2004).

Denis Donoghue is Henry James Professor in English and American Letters at New York University. He is a fellow with the British Academy, the American Academy of Arts and Sciences, and the American Council of Learned Societies and a contributor to the *Times Literary Supplement*. His publications include *The American Classics: A Personal Essay* (2005), *Speaking Beauty* (2003), *Words Alone: The Poet T. S. Eliot* (2000), *Walter Pater: Lover of Strange Souls* (1995), *The Practice of Reading* (1988), *Connoisseurs of Chaos* (1984), and *Ferocious Alphabets* (1981).

Acknowledgments

"Robert Frost" by James Norman O'Neill. From *Cyclopedia of World Authors, Fourth Revised Edition*. Copyright © 2004 by Salem Press, Inc. Reprinted with permission of Salem Press.

"The *Paris Review* Perspective" by Elizabeth Gumport. Copyright © 2010 by Elizabeth Gumport. Special appreciation goes to Christopher Cox and Nathaniel Rich, editors for *The Paris Review.*

"Frost's *North of Boston*, Its Language, Its People, and Its Poet" by David Sanders. From *Journal of Modern Literature* 27, nos. 1/2 (2003): 70-78. Copyright © 2004 by Indiana University Press. Reprinted by permission of Indiana University Press.

"Robert Frost and the Politics of Labor" by Tyler B. Hoffman. From *Modern Language Studies* 29, no. 2 (Fall 1999): 110-135. Copyright © 1999 by Susquehanna University Press. Reprinted by permission of Susquehanna University Press.

"Robert Frost: The Walk as Parable" by Roger Gilbert. From *Walks in the World: Representation and Experience in Modern American Poetry*, pp. 49-74. Copyright © 1991 by Princeton University Press. Reprinted by permission of Princeton University Press.

"Nature and Poetry" by Judith Oster. From *Toward Robert Frost: The Reader and the Poet*, pp. 137-174. Copyright © 1991 by The University of Georgia Press. Reprinted by permission of The University of Georgia Press.

"The Resentments of Robert Frost" by Frank Lentricchia. From *American Literature* 62, no. 2 (June 1990): 175-200. Copyright © 1990 by Duke University Press. All rights reserved. Used by permission of the publisher.

"We Are Sick with Space" by Robert Bernard Hass. From *Going by Contraries: Robert Frost's Conflict with Science*, pp. 89-124. Copyright © 2002 by The University Press of Virginia. Reprinted by permission of The University Press of Virginia.

"The Need of Being Versed: Robert Frost and the Limits of Rhetoric" by Shira Wolosky. From *Essays in Literature* 18, no. 1 (1991): 76-92. Copyright © 1991 by Western Illinois University Press. Reprinted by permission of Western Illinois University Press.

"National Forgetting and Remembering in the Poetry of Robert Frost" by Jeff Westover. From *Texas Studies in Literature and Language* 46, no. 2 (Summer 2004): 213-244. Copyright © 2004 by the University of Texas Press. Reprinted by permission of the University of Texas Press.

"Robert Frost" by Denis Donoghue. From *Connoisseurs of Chaos*, pp. 160-189. Copyright © 1984 by Columbia University Press. Reprinted by permission of Columbia University Press.

Sound of sense, 10, 16, 45, 80, 100, 108, 356
"Spring Pools" (Frost), 6, 78, 181, 212
Stars, 149, 165, 178, 200, 207, 219, 256, 266, 289, 294, 399
Stevens, Wallace, 8, 66, 200, 240, 267, 380, 385
"Stopping by Woods on a Snowy Evening" (Frost), 18, 37, 46, 54, 190, 197, 217, 222
"Storm Fear" (Frost), 7, 179, 195, 216
Synecdoche, 29, 50, 161, 296, 320

Terza rima, 30
"There Are Roughly Zones" (Frost), 52
Thomas, Dylan, 66
Thompson, Lawrance, 45, 59, 81, 109, 113, 126, 192, 217, 220, 223, 256, 279
Thoreau, Henry David, 57, 143, 219
"Time Out" (Frost), 49
"Tintern Abbey" (Wordsworth), 9, 51, 115, 177
"To the Thawing Wind" (Frost), 79, 211
"Tree at My Window" (Frost), 19, 87, 187
Trees, 6, 19, 51, 78, 87, 115, 151, 171, 181, 185, 189, 194, 202, 218, 222, 282
Trilling, Lionel, 7, 77, 366
"Tuft of Flowers, The" (Frost), 68, 88
"Two Tramps in Mud Time" (Frost), 141, 395

Untermeyer, Louis, 41, 122, 134, 226, 231

Van Doren, Mark, 44
"Vanishing Red, The" (Frost), 333, 337, 343, 350

Walden (Thoreau), x, 57, 144, 174, 220
Wallace, Patricia, 328
Walsh, John Evangelist, 98, 108
Ward, Susan Hayes, 57, 129, 335
Warren, Robert Penn, 69, 191, 220, 237, 322
Waste Land, The (Eliot), 24
Water imagery, 6, 51, 71, 78, 121, 175, 181, 207, 211, 217, 221, 346
West-Running Brook (Frost), 27, 33, 119, 140, 217
Whitman, Walt, 61, 76, 89, 143, 265, 299
Wilson, Douglas, 109
Wilson, James S., 44
Wind imagery, 8, 18, 79, 179, 185, 195, 218, 308
Windows, 19, 58, 87, 159, 186, 206, 310
Winters, Yvor, 63, 139
"Wood-Pile, The" (Frost), 5, 67, 89, 106, 149, 157, 174
Woodring, Carl, 47
Wordsworth, William, 4, 9, 46, 51, 82, 88, 99, 115, 246, 375

Yeats, William Butler, 249, 380, 384, 391